3D Graphics File Formats

A Programmer's Reference

Keith Rule

Addison-Wesley Developers Press

Reading, Massachusetts • Menlo Park, California • New York
Don Mills, Ontario • Harlow, England • Amsterdam
Bonn • Sydney • Singapore • Tokyo • Madrid • San Juan
Paris • Seoul • Milan • Mexico City • Taipei

Library of Congress Cataloging-in-Publication Data

Rule, Keith.
3D graphics file formats : a programmer's reference / Keith Rule.
p. cm.
Includes index.
ISBN 0–201–48835–3
1. Computer graphics. 2. File organization (Computer science)
3. Three-dimensional display systems. I. Title.
T385.R86 1996
006.6—dc20 96–26609
CIP

A-W Developers Press is a division of Addison-Wesley Publishing Company, Inc.

Sponsoring Editor: Mary Treseler
Project Manager: Sarah Weaver
Production Coordinator: Erin Sweeney
Cover illustration: Andy Lackow
Cover design: Robert Dietz, Dietz Design Co.
Set in 11 point Times by A & B Typesetters, Inc.

1 2 3 4 5 6 7 8 9 -MA- 0099989796
First printing, September 1996

To my wife Eileen,
whose support made this book possible.

Acknowledgments

I want to acknowledge several people for their help with this book.

Eric Haines gave many hours of his time reviewing the book. He also allowed me to use elements from his SPD software in the *Crossroads* class library.

Hakan "Zap" Andersson gave his able assistance with the DXF file format. His real-world experience with DXF and his willingness to share his knowledge with others has made him a great resource on the Internet.

Chris Young allowed me to use his original POVRay grammar as the basis for the POVRay chapter. Chris has been the tireless coordinator of the POVRay project.

Contents

Preface

What to Expect from This Book

This book describes eight 3D file formats as well as how to write a reader/writer for each. The included CD-ROM contains all of the source code described in each chapter. You may use this source code royalty free if you agree to the licensing agreement that accompanies it. This software is the *Crossroads* class library, which allows the supported file formats to be read into an internal representation. It also allows an internal representation to be displayed by using OpenGL or to be written as another 3D file.

However, this book is not intended as the definitive reference for the 3D file formats described herein. To do full justice to many of them, each would need as many pages as used for this entire book. In fact, many do have entire books devoted to them. Note also that schedule constraints required me to omit discussion of several topics, including surface normals, tessellation, and bitmapped materials.

This book also describes a useful subset of each format that is interchangeable between other formats. These common constructs are primarily 3D geometry and materials. Some additional constructs, such as lights and cameras, may also be interchanged between formats that support them.

The formats are presented in an immediately useful manner. The software included on the CD-ROM was developed for Windows 95 and Windows NT using Visual C++ 4.0. It can be added to an existing PC program either by linking in the precompiled libraries or by using the OCX controls included on the CD-ROM. I chose the PC platform because I have limited resources to devote to the topic of the book and because I have a PC and am familiar with the tools and techniques required to write the software on the CD-ROM. Hence, this book does not offer a well-balanced discussion of all available 3D file formats. Also, I have not ported the source code to other compilers or platforms. I expect porting to be straightforward, but I can make no promises about this.

This book refers to Visual C++, Visual Basic, and the GNU tools Bison and Flex. However, it is not intended to be a tutorial for any of these. Nor does it describe the subtleties of using these tools.

Audience

This book is primarily targeted to sophisticated programmers who want to add 3D import and export capabilities to their programs. For this reason, the readers and writers for each format are provided as portable C++ source code, which should be relatively straightforward to integrate with existing applications on a variety of platforms.

The software on the CD-ROM also can be used by the casual programmer using any program that can accept OCX custom controls, such as Visual Basic, Visual C++, and Delphi. For example, someone who wanted to develop a program to create an application that displays 3D files could use Visual Basic and the OCX control provided.

The CD-ROM also includes a 3D file conversion utility. This program is useful to any 3D artist who wants to view 3D files, convert from one supported 3D file format to another, or convert to a format that isn't supported by the 3D software application you use regularly.

Contacting the Author

If you would like to contact me, feel free to check out the Web page at http://www.europa.com/~keithr. There you'll find information about this book and updates to the source code. Or you can comment on the book directly to me via email at keithr@europa.com.

Chapter 1

Introduction

In recent years, interest in producing 3D art has increased dramatically, the result in part of rapid advancements in computer technology and in software. The capabilities and computing power required to create 3D computer graphical images has moved from the realm of the 100K dollar computer to that of the personal computer. Today Pentium PCs and Power Macintoshes can create many of the same computer graphical effects found in television and movies.

In addition, just a few years ago the software necessary for creating 3D models, 3D animation, and highly accurate 3D renderings was the nearly exclusive domain of the professional artist. It was typically custom-created, proprietary, and expensive. Today, you can buy it off the shelf at your local software store or get it free off the Internet. Packages range from those like AutoDesk's 3D Studio, which costs several thousands of dollars, to POVRay, a very capable, copyrighted freeware raytracer.

File Babel

The increasing interest in 3D products has gone hand in hand with the development of a new generation of 3D file formats. Currently, 3D software packages are available for the Macintosh, PC, Amiga, SGI workstations, and other platforms. Each has a unique set of features and capabilities for addressing a particular audience. And, perhaps not surprising, each has a unique 3D file format.

As a result, a 3D package could be expected to support tens (if not hundreds) of file formats. However, supporting every format is impossible. In addition, exchanging data between software packages is difficult, sometimes even impossible. Often the best format to use for interchanging data depends on the type of 3D application, and even then, the process may not be easy. For example, if you were exchanging data between 3D CAD programs, you might use either the AutoDesk DXF file format, the IGES file format, or the ACIS *SAT* file format. (These are CAD file formats that include some 3D constructs.) Exchanging data between 3D modeling programs may require even more thought. For example, if you were exchanging data between different computer platforms, such as from an SGI workstation to a PC, you would probably choose a different format than if you were moving between programs on the same platform.

Clearly, an industry-standard 3D file interchange format is highly desirable, for both the user and developer of 3D software packages. As yet, no such format exists. There are, however, several de facto standards.

De Facto Standards

In the absence of an industry-standard 3D file interchange format, several de facto 3D file standards have appeared for the Macintosh, PC, Amiga, and UNIX platforms.

Probably the most popular for the PC are from AutoDesk, a pioneer in the PC 3D software market. Its formats include *DXF*, for exchanging CAD data from AutoCAD to other CAD programs, and *3DS*, a file format from its own 3D Studio package.

One of the most popular and open de facto standards is the Virtual Reality Modeling Language (VRML). VRML is a multiplatform file format originally designed to allow descriptions of virtual worlds on the World Wide Web ("Web"). Its V1.0 was adopted in late 1994; its first browser appeared in mid-1995. However, VRML appears to be a great way not only to create interesting Web pages but also to interchange 3D objects and scenes. New VRML scenes and models appear every day on the Internet. Vendors are adding the ability to read and write VRML to their existing programs. As a result of VRML's popularity, new 3D applications will likely have to read and write this format.

Despite these efforts at creating a universal file interchange format, no clear winner has emerged. So developers of software that needs to be able to import or export 3D information in a way that is useful for many potential users still must pick from dozens of existing formats. This is where this book comes in. In this book, I describe several popular formats. I also include on the CD-ROM that accompanies the book the source code for reading and writing each of these formats.

The 3D File Formats Described in This Book

The following formats are discussed in the book and are supported by the *Crossroads* 3D class library (see Table 1.1).

Table 1.1. Formats discussed in the book

Format Name	Application	Type of Format	Platform	Description
3DS	3D Studio	Binary	PC	Judging from the number of Usenet newsgroups and available 3D models, 3D Studio is one of the more popular professional modeling and animation packages.
COB	TrueSpace	Binary/ASCII	PC	TrueSpace is an easy-to-use 3D modeler/animation package.
DXF	AutoCAD	ASCII	PC	This is a popular CAD format for low-to-mid-range 3D CAD applications.
NFF-WTK	World Toolkit	ASCII	PC	This is a format from a popular VR toolkit on the PC.
OBJ	Wavefront	ASCII	UNIX, PC	This format must be supported if interchanging data with UNIX workstations is required. It is well documented by Wavefront.
POV	POVRay	ASCII	Multiplatform	This is a freeware, copyrighted raytracer. It is very popular because of its price and rich set of capabilities.
RAW	Open Standard	ASCII	Multiplatform	This format is used primarily by freeware and shareware tools available on the Internet. It is useful to support because of its simplicity.
VRML	Open Standard	ASCII	Multiplatform	VRML (Virtual Reality Modeling Language) is the fastest-growing support for any 3D file format in existence.

Chapter 2

Overview of the Crossroads Class Library

The 3D file format translators defined in this book are built using a common class library called *Crossroads*. Instances of this library represent 3D scenes and objects and are called the *internal representation*. This internal representation is the foundation for all of the software described in this book.

The *Crossroads* design has been strongly influenced by the organization of the VRML 3D file format; many of the language constructs of VRML have corresponding class definitions in the library.

The *Crossroads* library can be used in various ways. For example, you can add support for reading and writing 3D files by using only two functions from the library. You can display a 3D object by initializing the OpenGL library and then executing only a single member function call. And you'll find that adding new file format readers and writers is straightforward. In addition, the library can easily be incorporated into Microsoft Foundation Classes (MFC) as part of an MFC *CDocument* derived class (see this chapter and Chapter 12).

I am assuming you have some knowledge of the C++ classes and functions used to construct the internal representation. You don't need to fully understand the *Crossroads* library in order to use the software described here, but knowing the basic model and the organization of the classes will help you grasp the implementation of each file format reader described in the following chapters.

In this chapter, I give an overview of the classes and their usage. Several methods are shown for using the *Crossroads* library. The highest functional level usage requires you to understand one or two function calls; the lowest level requires that you understand 41 classes and type definitions. An in-depth discussion of each class is in Chapter 14. However, for the most part you'll need only a cursory understanding of the library.

The Model for the Crossroads Class Library

The library's internal organization uses the Virtual Reality Modeling Language (VRML) file format as the model for the library. VRML is a textual language that describes 3D scenes. Two key goals are achieved by using VRML. First, the model is compatible with the OpenGL graphics library. Second, the semantic distance between the class library and the underlying data that it represents is kept as small as possible.

VRML is derived from Open Inventor. Open Inventor is a file format developed by Silicon Graphics that was designed to be built on top of the OpenGL graphics library. This close relationship of the underlying model was inherited by VRML from Open Inventor. Since the class library design is based on VRML, its representation is very close to one of the file formats that will be supported. Consider this VRML scene description:

```
Separator {
    Translation {
          translation 3 0 0
    }
    Sphere {
          radius 2
    }
}
```

The following C++ code fragment creates the equivalent representation by creating the instances of class from the *Crossroads* library that corresponds to the VRML scene description:

```
// Create instances of objects used to define
// the internal representation.
GSeparator* separator = new GSeparator;
GTranslation* translation = new GTranslation;
GSphere* sphere = new Sphere;

// Add the correct "field" value to each instance
translation->Translation(SFVec3f(3.0, 0.0, 0.0));
sphere->Radius(2.0);

// Add the instances to the separator
separator->AddChild(translation);
separator->AddChild(sphere);
```

Notice that there is a one-to-one correspondence between the class instances and the VRML definition. This is intentional. Each VRML language element has a corresponding class definition. Each class defines member functions that set and retrieve the fields associated with that VRML construct. Consider the following VRML definition of a Cone:

```
# The definition of the Cone node
Cone {
      # Field Definitions
      fields [
            SFBitMask parts,
            SFFloat bottomRadius,
            SFFloat height
      ]

# Default Field Values
      parts             ALL
      bottomRadius      1
      height            2
}
```

This construct has the corresponding class definition of *GCone* with the following definition:

```
class GCone : public GNode {
public:
    // Constructor
    GCone();

    // Define members to access fields
    void        Parts(SFLong);
    SFLong      Parts(void);
    void        BottomRadius(SFFloat)
    SFFloat     BottomRadius(void);
    void        Height(SFFloat);
    SFFloat     Height(void);

    // Draw and emit construct (these functions
    // are common to all G-classes).
    void          DrawOpenGL(GState&);
    void          WriteWRL(FILE*, int = 0);
    void          Write(GState&, GWrite&);

    // Creates a new instance identical to this one.
    GNode*        Copy(void);
};
```

It is possible just by looking at the definition of each VRML construct to deduce the corresponding class library definition. The class name is constructed by prepending the VRML construct's name with the letter G. Each field defined in the VRML construct is represented by a pair of member functions that allow the corresponding field value to be set and retrieved.

Composition of the Crossroads Class Library

The *Crossroads* class library consists of a base class plus 24 classes derived from that class (see Figure 2.1).

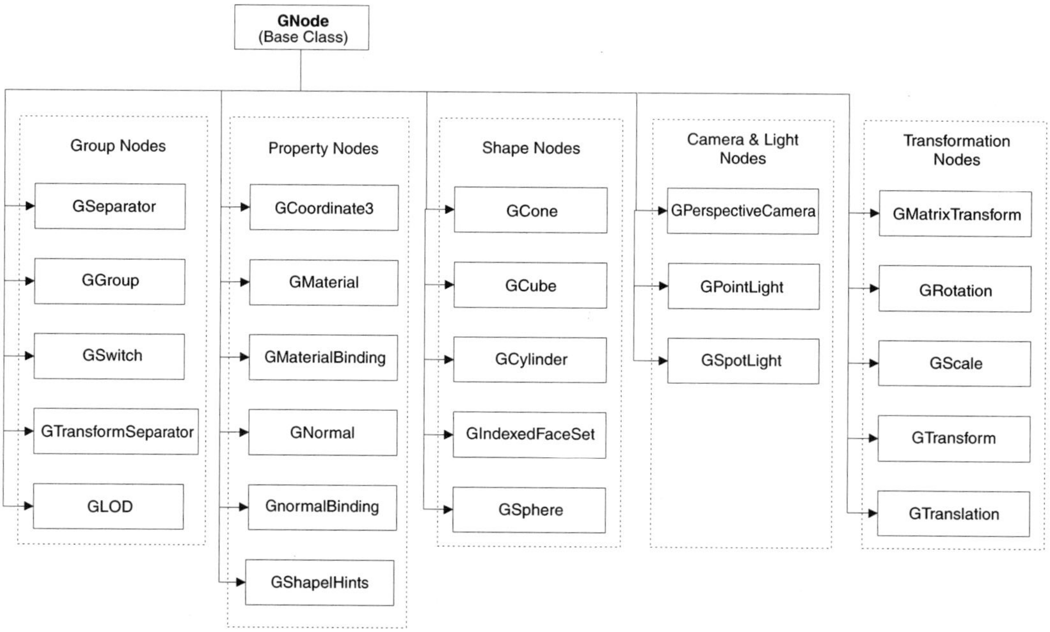

Figure 2.1. Composition of the library.

Each of the 24 classes corresponds to a VRML language entity. Not all of the language constructs in VRML are supported. However, those that are cover much of the VRML language.

Twelve other classes are used to define primitive types that correspond to the basic types built into the VRML language definition. Also there are four helper classes, which don't correspond to any VRML language constructs but which are used simply to expedite several common tasks. The library's 24 classes are discussed next.

Class GCone

The *GCone* class is used to create an instance of a Cone. It has the following member functions, which correspond to the equivalent fields in the VRML *Cone* command:

```
SFLong     Parts(void);       // Get parts field
void       Parts(SFLong);     // Set parts field
SFFloat    BottomRadius(void);      // Get bottomRadius field
void       BottomRadius(SFFloat);   // Set bottomRadius field
SFFloat    Height(void);      // Get height field
void       Height(SFFloat);   // Set height field
```

Class GCoordinate3

The *GCoordinate3* class is used to hold one or more 3D vertices. These vertices may be used by subsequent instances in the *Crossroads* internal representation. This class has the following member functions, which correspond to the equivalent fields in the VRML *Coordinate3* command:

```
void        Point(MFVec3f*);    // Set point field
MFVec3f*    Point(void);        // Get point field
```

Class GCube

The *GCube* class is used to represent an instance of a Cube. It has the following member functions, which correspond to the equivalent fields in the VRML *Cube* command:

```
SFFloat    Width(void);         // Set width field
void       Width(SFFloat);      // Get width field
SFFloat    Height(void);        // Get height field
void       Height(SFFloat);     // Set height field
SFFloat    Depth(void);         // Get depth field
void       Depth(SFFloat);      // Set depth field
```

Class GCylinder

The *GCylinder* class is used to represent an instance of a Cylinder. It has the following member functions, which correspond to the equivalent fields in the VRML *Cylinder* command:

```
SFLong      Parts(void);          // Get parts field
void        Parts(SFLong);        // Set parts field
SFFloat     Radius(void);         // Get radius field
void        Radius(SFFloat);      // Set radius field
SFFloat     Height(void);         // Get height field
void        Height(SFFloat);      // Set height field
```

Class GIndexedFaceSet

Instances of the *GIndexedFaceSet* class contain the faces for one or more polygons contained in the face set. Also represented in this instance may be the material definition for each face, the normal indexes for the faces, and the texture coordinate. This class has the following member functions, which correspond to the equivalent fields in the VRML *IndexedFaceSet* command:

```
void        CoordIndex(MFLong*);        // Set coordIndex field
MFLong*     CoordIndex(void);           // Get coordIndex field
void        MaterialIndex(MFLong*);     // Set materialIndex field
MFLong*     MaterialIndex(void);        // Get materialIndex field
void        NormalIndex(MFLong*);       // Set normalIndex field
MFLong*     NormalIndex(void);          // Get normalIndex field
void        TextureCoordIndex(MFLong*);
MFLong*     TextureCoordIndex(void);
```

Class GLOD

The *GLOD* class is used to represent an instance of a level-of-detail node. It has the following member functions, which correspond to the equivalent fields in the VRML *LOD* command:

```
MFFloat* Range(void);         // Get range field
void Range(MFFloat*);         // Set range field
SFVec3f Center(void);         // Get center field
void Center(SFVec3f);         // Set center field
```

Class GMaterial

The *GMaterial* class is used to represent the materials used in subsequent nodes. It has the following member functions, which correspond to the equivalent fields in the VRML *Material* command.

```
void        AmbientColor(MFVec3f*); // Set ambientColor field
MFVec3f*    AmbientColor(void);     // Get ambientColor field
void        DiffuseColor(MFVec3f*); // Set diffuseColor field
MFVec3f*    DiffuseColor(void);     // Get diffuseColor field
```

```
void        SpecularColor(MFVec3f*);// Set specularColor field
MFVec3f*    SpecularColor(void);    // Get specularColor field
void        EmissiveColor(MFVec3f*);// Set emissiveColor field
MFVec3f*    EmissiveColor(void);    // Get emissiveColor field
void        Shininess(MFFloat*);    // Set shininess field
MFFloat*    Shininess(void);        // Get shininess field
void        Transparency(MFFloat*); // Set transparency field
MFFloat*    Transparency(void);     // Get transparency field
```

Class GMaterialBinding

An instance of the *GMaterialBinding* class is used to specify how material is bound to subsequent shape items. This class has the following member functions, which correspond to the equivalent fields in the VRML *MaterialBinding* command:

```
void       Value(SFLong);      // Set value field
SFLong     Value(void);        // Get value field
```

Class GMatrixTransform

The *GMatrixTransform* class is used to define a 4 × 4 transformation matrix that is applied to subsequent items. It has the following member functions, which correspond to the equivalent fields in the VRML *MatrixTransform* command:

```
void       Matrix(SFMatrix&);        // Set matrix field
SFMatrix   Matrix(void);             // Get matrix field
```

Class GNode

The *GNode* class is the base class from which all classes that have equivalent VRML commands are derived. It defines a hierarchical list of *GNode* elements that is used to define the current 3D scene.

This list has a *child* component and a *next* component. The child component defines items that are part of the current construct. Only grouping nodes like the *GSeparator* class or the *GGroup* class have children. A node may also have a next component. In addition, the *GNode* base class maintains the object hierarchy by providing member functions to name a node, write a node, and copy a node. Also, several functions are intended to be overridden to provide the user information about the actions the class library is currently performing.

This class defines the following member functions that are common to the *Crossroads* class library:

```
// Get Next item.
GNode*          Next(void);

// Append item to the last node at this level.
GNode*          AddNext(GNode*);

// Get the Child item.
GNode*          Child(void);

// Append the item to the last node at the child level.
GNode*          AddChild(GNode*);

// Set & Get Name of the object
void            SetName(char*);
char*           GetName(void);

// Deep copy
virtual GNode*  Copy(void);

// Delete contents of instance w/o deleting instance.
virtual void    Clear(void);

// Writes OpenGL representation of current scene.
virtual void    DrawOpenGL(GState&);

// Writes current data structure as a WRL file
virtual void    WriteWRL(FILE*, int = 0);

// Traverses the scene with the specified GWrite instance.
virtual void    Write(GState&, GWrite&);

// Used to pass along information to the user.
virtual void    StatusMessage( char* fmt, ... );
virtual void    ErrorMessage( char* fmt, ... );
virtual void    WarningMessage( char* fmt, ... );

// Used to turn on and off busy indicator
virtual void    StartBusy(void);
virtual void    EndBusy(void);
```

Class GNormal

The *GNormal* class defines the normals vectors that may be used in subsequent items. This class has the following member functions, which correspond to the equivalent fields in the VRML *Normal* command:

```
void       Vector(MFVec3f*); // Set vector field
MFVec3f*   Vector(void);     // Get vector field
```

Class GNormalBinding

An instance of the *GNormalBinding* class is used to define how normals will be applied to subsequent items. It has the following member functions, which correspond to the equivalent fields in the VRML *NormalBinding* command:

```
SFLong      Value(void);         // Get value field
void        Value(SFLong);       // Set value field
```

Class GPerspectiveCamera

An instance of the *GPerspectiveCamera* class represents a perspective camera. This class has the following member functions, which correspond to the equivalent fields in the VRML *PerspectiveCamera* command.

```
void        Position(SFVec3f&);       // Set position field
SFVec3f     Position(void);           // Get position field
void        Orientation(SFRotation&); // Set orientation field
SFRotation  Orientation(void);        // Get orientation field
void        FocalDistance(SFFloat);   // Set focalDistance field
SFFloat     FocalDistance(void);      // Get focalDistance field
void        HeightAngle(SFFloat);     // Set heightAngle field
SFFloat     HeightAngle(void)         // Get heightAngle field
```

Class GPointLight

An instance of the *GPointLight* class represents a point light in the current scene. This class has the following member functions, which correspond to the equivalent fields in the VRML *PointLight* command:

```
SFLong     On(void);                 // Get on field
void       On(SFLong);               // Set on field
SFFloat    Intensity(void);          // Get intensity field
void       Intensity(SFFloat);       // Set intensity field
SFVec3f    Color(void);              // Get color field
void       Color(SFVec3f);           // Set color field
SFVec3f    Location(void);           // Get location field
voidLocation(SFVec3f);               // Set location field
```

Class GRotation

The *GRotation* class defines a rotation to be applied to subsequent items. It has the following member functions, which correspond to the equivalent fields in the VRML *Rotation* command:

```
void        Rotation(SFRotation);    // Set rotation field
SFRotation  Rotation(void);          // Get rotation field
```

Class GScale

The *GScale* class defines a scale to be applied to subsequent items. This class has the following member functions, which correspond to the equivalent fields in the VRML *Scale* command:

```
void      ScaleFactor(SFVec3f);    // Set scaleFactor field
SFVec3f   ScaleFactor(void);       // Get scaleFactor field
```

Class GSeparator

An instance of the *GSeparator* class is used to isolate the child nodes from the rest of the scene.

Class GShapeHints

The *GShapeHints* class defines an item that specifies attributes of the faces of the subsequent *GIndexedFaceSet* nodes. It has the following member functions, which correspond to the equivalent fields in the VRML *ShapeHints* command:

```
void      VertexOrdering(SFLong); // Set vertexOrdering
SFLong    VertexOrdering(void);   // Get vertexOrdering
void      ShapeType(SFLong);      // Set shapeType field
SFLong    ShapeType(void);        // Get shapeType field
void      FaceType(SFLong);       // Set faceType field
SFLong    FaceType(void);         // Get faceType field
void      CreaseAngle(SFFloat);   // Set creaseAngle field
SFFloat   CreaseAngle(void);      // Get creaseAngle field
```

Class GSphere

The *GSphere* class is used to create an instance of a Sphere. It has the following member functions, which correspond to the equivalent fields in the VRML *Sphere* command:

```
SFFloat   Radius(void);      // Get radius field
void      Radius(SFFloat);   // Set radius field
```

Class GSpotLight

An instance of the *GSpotLight* class represents a spotlight. This class has the following member functions, which correspond to the equivalent fields in the VRML *Spotlight* command:

```
void        On(SFLong);               // Set on field
SFLong      On(void);                 // Get on field
void        Intensity(SFFloat);       // Set intensity field
SFFloat     Intensity(void);          // Get intensity field
void        Color(SFVec3f);           // Set color field
SFVec3f     Color(void);              // Get color field
void        Location(SFVec3f);        // Set location field
SFVec3f     Location(void);           // Get location field
void        Direction(SFVec3f);       // Set direction field
SFVec3f     Direction(void);          // Get direction field
void        DropOffRate(SFFloat);     // Set dropOffRate field
SFFloat     DrapOffRate(void);        // Get dropOffRate field
void        CutOffAngle(SFFloat);     // Set cutOffAngle field
SFFloat     CutOffAngle(void);        // Get cutOffAngle field
```

Class GSwitch

An instance of the *GSwitch* class is used to allow one of several scene items to be chosen at traversal time. This class has the following member functions, which correspond to the equivalent fields in the VRML *Switch* command:

```
void        Switch(SFLong);           // Set switch field
SFLong      Switch(void);             // Get switch field
```

Class GTransform

The *GTransform* class is used to combine several common transformations into a single construct. It has the following member functions, which correspond to the equivalent fields in the VRML *Transform* command:

```
void         Translation(SFVec3f);     // Set translation field
SFVec3f      Translation(void);        // Get translation field
void         Rotation(SFRotation);     // Set rotation field
SFRotation   Rotation(void);           // Get rotation field
void         ScaleFactor(SFVec3f);     // Set scaleFactor field
SFVec3f      ScaleFactor(void);        // Get scaleFactor field
void         ScaleOrientation(SFRotation);
SFRotation   ScaleOrientation(void); // Get scaleOrientation
void         Center(SFVec3f);          // Set center field
SFVec3f      Center(void);             // Get center field
```

Class GTransformSeparator

An instance of the *GTransformSeparator* class is used to isolate a transformation to the child items.

Class GTranslation

The *GTranslation* class defines a rotation to be applied to subsequent items. It has the following member functions, which correspond to the equivalent fields in the VRML *Translation* command:

```
void      Translation(SFVec3f);    // Set translation field
SFVec3f   Translation(void);       // Get translation field
```

Helper Classes, Definitions, and Functions

Several classes, definitions, and functions that make up the *Crossroads* class library do not directly represent elements of a 3D scene (see Figure 2.2). They are used to hold primitive data types or to perform common tasks.

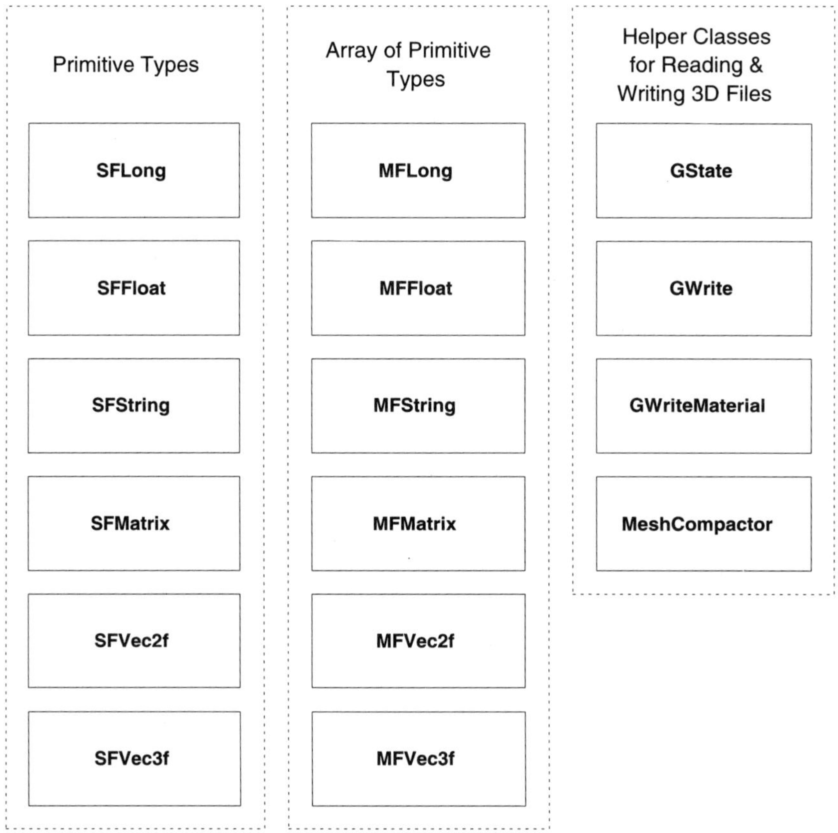

Figure 2.2. The *Crossroads* class library helpers.

Typedef SFLong

The type definition *SFLong* is used to represent a 32-bit signed integer and is defined as

```
typedef long            SFLong;
```

Typedef SFFloat

The type definition *SFFloat* is used to represent a 64-bit floating point number and is defined as

```
typedef double          SFFloat;
```

Class SFString

The *SFString* class is used to represent a null-terminated string. It has the following member functions and friend functions.

Member Functions

```
SFString(char* = ""); // Constructor
SFString(const SFString&); // Copy Constructor

// Assignment Operators
SFString& operator=(const SFString&);
SFString& operator=(const char*);
SFString& operator+=(const SFString&)
SFString& SFString::operator+=(const char*);

// Index operator
char& SFString::operator[](int);
char SFString::operator[](int) const;

// Cast to char* operator
operator SFString::char*();
```

Friend Functions

```
// Duplicate some "string.h" functions
int strlen(const SFString&);
char *strcat(SFString&, const char*);
char *strcat(char*, const SFString&);
char *strcat(SFString&, const SFString&);
char *strcpy(SFString&, const char*);
char *strcpy(char*, const SFString&);
char *strcpy(SFString&, const SFString&);
```

```
int strcmp(const SFString&, const char*);
int strcmp(const char*, const SFString&);
int strcmp(const SFString&, const SFString&);

// Use operator '+' as a concatenate operator
SFString operator+(const SFString&, const SFString&);
SFString operator+(const SFString& , const char*);
SFString operator+(const char*, const SFString&);

// Use operator '==' for equality check
int operator==(const SFString&, const char*);
int operator==(const char*, const SFString&);

// Use operator '!=' for inequality check
int operator!=(const SFString&, const SFString&);
int operator!=(const SFString&, const char*);
int operator!=(const char*, const SFString&);
```

Class SFMatrix

The *SFMatrix* class is used to represent a 4 × 4 transformation matrix. It has the following member functions and friend functions.

Member Functions

```
SFMatrix(void);                         // Constructor
SFMatrix(const SFMatrix&);              // Copy constructor
SFMatrix& operator=(const SFMatrix&);   // Assignment

SFFloat* operator[](int);               // Return a Row
SFMatrix operator+(const SFMatrix&);    // Add
SFMatrix operator-(const SFMatrix&);    // Subtract
SFMatrix operator*(const SFMatrix&);    // Multiply
int operator==(const SFMatrix&);        // Test equality
int operator!=(const SFMatrix&);        // Test inequality
```

Friend Functions

```
// Multiply
SFMatrix operator*(const SFMatrix&, const SFFloat);
SFMatrix operator*(const SFFloat, const SFMatrix&);
SFVec3f operator*(const SFMatrix&, const SFVec3f&);

// Return identity matrix
SFMatrix Identity(void);

// Return zero matrix.
SFMatrix Zero(void);
```

```
// Return matrix equivalent to specified translation.
SFMatrix Translate(const SFFloat, const SFFloat,
           const SFFloat);
SFMatrix Translate(const SFVec3f&);

// Return matrix equivalent to specified scale.
SFMatrix Scale(const SFFloat, const SFFloat, const SFFloat);
SFMatrix Scale(const SFVec3f&);

// Return matrix equivalent to specified rotation.
SFMatrix RotateX(const SFFloat);
SFMatrix RotateY(const SFFloat);
SFMatrix RotateZ(const SFFloat);
SFMatrix Rotate(const SFFloat, const SFFloat,
                const SFFloat, const SFFloat);
SFMatrix Rotate(const SFFloat, const SFFloat,
                const SFFloat);
SFMatrix Rotate(const SFRotation&);
```

Class SFVec2f

The *SFVec2f* class is used to represent a 2D vector. It has the following member functions.

Member Functions

```
SFVec2f(SFFloat = 0.0, SFFloat = 0.0);  // Constructor
SFVec2f(const SFVec2f&);                // Copy constructor
SFFloat X(void) const;                  // Access x value
SFFloat Y(void) const;                  // Access y value

// Assignment operators
SFVec2f& operator+=(const SFVec2f&);
SFVec2f& operator-=(const SFVec2f&);
SFVec2f& operator*=(const SFVec2f&);
SFVec2f& operator*=(const SFFloat&);
SFVec2f& operator/=(const SFFloat&);

// Comparison operators
int operator==(const SFVec2f&) const;
int operator!=(const SFVec2f&) const;
```

Class SFVec3f

The *SFVec3f* class is used to represent a 3D vector. It has the following member functions and friend functions.

Member Functions

```
// Constructor
SFVec3f(SFFloat = 0.0, SFFloat = 0.0, SFFloat = 0.0);
SFVec3f(const SFVec3f&);

// Retrieve X, Y, or Z values
SFFloat& X(void);
SFFloat& Y(void);
SFFloat& Z(void);
SFFloat X(void) const;
SFFloat Y(void) const;
SFFloat Z(void) const;

// Set X, Y, or Z values
void X(SFFloat);
void Y(SFFloat);
void Z(SFFloat);

// Retrieve Red (X), Green (Y), or Blue (Z) values
SFFloat& Red(void);
SFFloat& Green(void);
SFFloat& Blue(void);
SFFloat Red(void) const;
SFFloat Green(void) const;
SFFloat Blue(void) const;

// Set Red (X), Green (Y), Blue (Z) values
void Red(SFFloat);
void Green(SFFloat);
void Blue(SFFloat);

// Assignment operators
SFVec3f& operator+=(const SFVec3f&);
SFVec3f& operator-=(const SFVec3f&);
SFVec3f& operator*=(const SFVec3f&);
SFVec3f& operator*=(const SFFloat&);
SFVec3f& operator/=(const SFFloat&);

// Comparison Operators
int operator==(const SFVec3f&) const;
int operator!=(const SFVec3f&) const;
```

Friend Functions

```
// Return a Normalized vector.
SFVec3f Normalize(const SFVec3f&);

// Return the magnitude of a vector.
SFFloat Magnitude(const SFVec3f&);
```

```
// Compute the dot product of two vectors.
SFFloat Dot(const SFVec3f&, const SFVec3f&);

// Compute the cross product of two vectors.
SFVec3f Cross(const SFVec3f&, const SFVec3f&);

// Math operators
SFVec3f operator+(const SFVec3f&, const SFVec3f&);
SFVec3f operator-(const SFVec3f&, const SFVec3f&);
SFVec3f operator*(const SFVec3f&, const SFVec3f&);
SFVec3f operator*(const SFFloat, const SFVec3f&);
SFVec3f operator*(const SFVec3f&, const SFFloat);
SFVec3f operator*(const SFMatrix&, const SFVec3f&);
SFVec3f operator/(const SFVec3f&, const SFVec3f&);
SFVec3f operator/(const SFVec3f&, const SFFloat);
```

Class MFArray<T&>

The *MFArray<T&>* template class is the basis for all of the *MF** classes defined for the *Crossroads* class library. It defines a dynamically sizable array class. This class has the following member functions.

Member Functions

```
// Constructors
MFArray(void);
MFArray(const T);
MFArray(const MFArray&);

// Destructor
~MFArray(void);

// Reset the array.
void Clear(void);

// Assignment operator
MFArray& operator=(const MFArray&);

// Returns number of elements.
long Elements(void);

// Enlarges the storage
void Resize(long);

// Return an element of the array.
T& operator[](long);
T operator[](long) const;

// Append the argument to the array.
long Add(const T);
```

```
// Replace the specified index with the T value.
long Replace(const long, const T);
```

Class MFLong

The *MFLong* class is an array of *SFLong* values. It is created using the *MArray<T&>* template and with the following definition:

```
typedef MFArray<SFLong> MFLong;
```

Class MFFloat

The *MFFloat* class is an array of *SFFLoat* values. It is created using the *MArray<T&>* template and with the following definition:

```
typedef MFArray<SFFloat> MFFloat;
```

Class MFString

The *MFString* class is an array of *SFString* values. It is created using the *MArray<T&>* template and with the following definition:

```
typedef MFArray<SFString> MFString;
```

Class MFMatrix

The *MFMatrix* class is an array of *SFMatrix* values. It is created using the *MArray<T&>* template and with the following definition:

```
typedef MFArray<SFMatrix> MFMatrix.
```

Class MFVec2f

The *MFVec2f* class is an array of *SFVec2f* values. It is created using the *MArray<T&>* template and with the following definition:

```
typedef MFArray<SFVec2f> MFVec2f;
```

Class MFVec3f

The *MFVec3f* class is an array of *SFVec3f* values. It is created using the *MArray<T&>* template and with the following definition:

```
typedef MFArray<SFVec3f> MFVec3f;
```

Class GState

The *GState* class is used to hold the current state of the traversal of the internal representation. It is used when converting and drawing scenes.

Class GWrite

The *GWrite* class is the base class for most file format writers.

Class GWriteMaterial

The *GWriteMaterial* class is used to represent a single material. This class is used to simplify the usage of the *GMaterial* class. It has the following member functions and friend functions.

Member Functions

```
// Constructor
GWriteMaterial(
          SFVec3f = SFVec3f(0.2, 0.2, 0.2),
          SFVec3f = SFVec3f(0.8, 0.8, 0.8),
          SFVec3f = SFVec3f(0.0, 0.0, 0.0),
          SFVec3f = SFVec3f(0.0, 0.0, 0.0),
          SFFloat = 0.2,
          SFFloat = 0.0);

// Set the Material Properties
void AmbientColor(const SFVec3f&);
void DiffuseColor(const SFVec3f&);
void SpecularColor(const SFVec3f&);
void EmissiveColor(const SFVec3f&);
void Shininess(const SFFloat);
void Transparency(const SFFloat);

// Get the Material Properties
SFVec3f AmbientColor(void) const
SFVec3f DiffuseColor(void) const;
SFVec3f SpecularColor(void) const
SFVec3f EmissiveColor(void) const;
SFFloat Shininess(void) const;
SFFloat Transparency(void) const;
```

Friend Functions

```
// Comparison Operators
int operator==(const GWriteMaterial&,
       const GWriteMaterial&);
```

```
int operator!=(const GWriteMaterial& ,
        const GWriteMaterial&);

// Reduce material to a single color.
SFVec3f Color(void);

// Create a material from a single color
void Color(double, double, double);

// Convert material to an ambient coefficient.
SFFloat AmbientCoefficient(void);

// Convert material to a specular coefficient.
SFFloat SpecularCoefficient(void);

// Convert material to hilight coefficient.
SFFloat HilightCoefficient(void);
```

Class MeshCompactor

The *MeshCompactor* class is used to store polygon groups and convert them into a *Crossroads* representation. This class is easy to use and is a more natural representation for many file formats than is the *Crossroads* representation. It has the following member functions.

Member Functions

```
// Constructor
MeshCompactor(MFVec3f* = NULL, MFLong* = NULL);

// Destructor
~MeshCompactor(void);

// Delete contents
void Reset(MFVec3f* = NULL, MFLong* = NULL);

// Start a polygon
void BeginPolygon(GWriteMaterial* = NULL);

// End a polygon
void EndPolygon(void);

// Set name of current group
void Name(char*);

// Add vertex to polygon
void AddVertex(SFVec3f);
```

```
// Return global coordinates
MFVec3f* Coordinates(void);

// Return face array for the specified group
MFLong* Faces(long = 0);

// Return the material for the mesh.
GMaterial* Material(void);

// Return a material index array for the group.
MFLong* MaterialIndex(long = 0);

// Return the number of groups.
long Groups(void);

// Return TRUE if mesh is empty.
int IsEmpty(void);

// Convert the mesh into a GNode representation.
void AddTo(GNode*);
```

Examples: Using the Crossroads Class Library

At the simplest level, the *Crossroads* class library can be completely accessed via only two functions: `XRoad_Reader()` and `XRoad_Writer()`. These are the only functions needed to read and write every 3D file format supported by the *Crossroads* library.

Adding the Crossroads Library to MFC

Using the *Crossroads* library and source code doesn't require using Microsoft's *MFC* class library. However, providing access to the *Crossroads* library from a MFC *CDocument* derived class is very easy.

The *MFC* library uses a Document/View model, whereby data is typically represented by a class derived from the *CDocument* class and that data is written to a window or printed using a *CView* class.

Adding *Crossroads* support requires that the application's Document class inherit from both the *CDocument* class and the *GSeparator* class. In addition to deriving from *GSeparator*, it is a good idea to add support for the *GNode* member functions `StatusMessage()`, `ErrorMessage()`, `StartBusy()`, and `EndBusy()`. Doing this will allow status information and error messages to be forwarded to the user. The following C++ code is an example of a minimal set of changes required to support the *Crossroads* library in *MFC*.

```
class CXRoadAppDoc : public CDocument, public GSeparator
{
    .
    .
    .
    void StatusMessage( char* fmt, ... );
    void ErrorMessage( char* fmt, ... );
    void StartBusy( void )  {BeginWaitCursor();}
    void EndBusy(void)      {EndWaitCursor();}
    .
    .
    .
};

// Write a Status message to the status bar
void CXRoadAppDoc::
StatusMessage( char* fmt, ... )
{
    if (AfxGetApp() != NULL &&
        AfxGetApp()->m_pMainWnd != NULL) {
          char  buffer[256];
        CStatusBar*   pStatus = (CStatusBar*) AfxGetApp()-
>m_pMainWnd->GetDescendantWindow(AFX_IDW_STATUS_BAR);
          va_list     argptr;

          va_start(argptr, fmt);
          vsprintf( buffer, fmt, argptr );
          va_end(argptr);

          if (pStatus != NULL) {
                pStatus->SetPaneText(0, buffer);
                pStatus->UpdateWindow();
          }
   }
   return;
}

// Write an Error Message to a Message Box
void CXRoadAppDoc::
ErrorMessage( char* fmt, ... )
{
    va_list     argptr;
    char        buffer[256];

    va_start(argptr, fmt);
    vsprintf( buffer, fmt, argptr );
    va_end(argptr);
```

```
    MessageBox(NULL, buffer, "Error Message", MB_OK |
        MB_ICONEXCLAMATION);
}
```

Reading and Writing 3D Files

Reading and writing 3D files requires the use of only these three functions:

```
int XRoad_Reader(GNode* root, const char* filename,
                 const char* povray_path);
int XRoad_Writer(GNode* root, const char* filename);
void XRoad_CFileDialog_String(char*);
```

`XRoad_Reader()` reads the named file into the *GNode* instance passed in the first argument. The last argument of this function is optional; it defines the search path for the POVRay include files

`XRoad_Writer()` writes the current 3D internal representation passed in the first argument to the file name passed in the second argument. The file format is chosen by the suffix of the specified file.

`XRoad_CFileDialog_String()` returns a file filter string that defines all formats supported by the current version of the *Crossroads* library.

Reading 3D File Formats

The process of reading a 3D file from an application built using the *MFC* library is straightforward. First, the file filter string is read into the local variable `buffer`. Next, a file dialog is created and the filter is passed to it. Then the dialog is invoked so that the users can select the file to be read. If the user selects OK, the current scene is cleared and the specified file is read. If the read fails, an error message is issued using the `void GNODE::ErrorMessage(char*, ...)` member function. If the file is read successfully, then the views are updated. Notice that the document class responds as a *GNode* derived class. This allows *GNode* member functions to be invoked directly and instances of the document to be used as a *GNode* instance.

```
void CXRoadAppDoc::OnFileOpen()
{
    char  buffer[512];

    // Get 3D Format Filter String
    XRoad_CFileDialog_String(buffer);

    // Create the Read file dialog
    CFileDialogfileDlg( TRUE, NULL, NULL,
```

```
        OFN_HIDEREADONLY | OFN_PATHMUSTEXIST, buffer);
    // Open the file selected
    if (fileDlg.DoModal() == IDOK) {
        // Delete the current scene
        Clear();

        // Read the File
        if (XRoad_Reader((GNode*) this,
            lpszPathName, povray_path)) {
            UpdateAllViews(NULL);
        }
    }
}
```

Writing 3D Files

The process of writing a 3D file from an application built using the *MFC* library is similar to that of reading a file. First, the file filter string is read into the local variable `buffer`. Next, a file dialog is created and the filter is passed to it. Then the dialog is invoked so that the user can select the file to be written. If the user clicks OK, the specified file is written. Notice that since the document class is derived from *GSeparator*, it can be used as a *GNode* class.

```
void CXRoadAppDoc::OnFileSaveAs()
{
    char buffer[512];

    // Get 3D Format Filter String
    XRoad_CFileDialog_String(buffer);

    // Create the Write file dialog
    CFileDialogfileDlg( FALSE, NULL, NULL,
        OFN_HIDEREADONLY | OFN_OVERWRITEPROMPT, buffer);
    // Handle the user response
    if (fileDlg.DoModal() == IDOK) {
        // Write the file.
        XRoad_Writer((GNode*) this, lpszPathName));
    }
}
```

Thus only a few changes are needed for an *MFC* application to read and write all of the 3D file formats support by the *Crossroads* library.

Displaying 3D Files

The *Crossroads* library has been written to use the OpenGL 3D graphics library, which is available on many computer platforms, including Windows 95 and Window NT.

A more in-depth example of how a 3D scene is displayed is provided in Chapters 12. In a nutshell, to display a 3D scene you need only define an OpenGL windows device context, specify an OpenGL viewpoint, issue the OpenGL commands that describe the scene, and then render the image to the device context.

I won't go into detail about setting up OpenGL. However, issuing the OpenGL commands that describe the scene is handled by a single *GNode* member function, `DrawOpenGL()`. This function traverses the scene and makes the appropriate OpenGL calls that correspond to the graphics elements in the scene. The following *MFC* code shows how a scene is drawn:

```
void CXRoadAppView::OnDraw(CDC* pDC)
{

    CXRoadAppDoc*       pDoc = GetDocument();
    GState              state;

    // Setup OpenGL
          .
          .
          .
    // Draw the scene
    pDoc->DrawOpenGL(state);

    // Flush the OpenGL scene
           .
           .
           .
}
```

Converting a 3D Representation into Polygons

Let's say your application has read in a scene and now you want your application to do something with it. You could write code to traverse the scene yourself. However, with the help of the *GWrite* class, you can, with a single function call, traverse the scene and convert it to polygons.

To convert a scene into polygons, you need to create your own class derived from the *GWrite* class. A *GWrite* derived class can specify that it supports only polygons. This tells *GWrite* that it may use only polygons. After the scene is traversed, all objects are tessellated into polygons using the

`Polygon()` member function for each polygon encountered. The following code shows the definition for such a class:

```
class GWriteCvt : public GWrite {
private:
    MyClass*    m_cls;
public:
    GWriteCvt(MyClass* cls) : GWrite(), m_cls(cls) {;}
    short       PolygonSupported(void)  {return TRUE;}
    void  Polygon(GState&, long, MFVec3f*,
        MFVec3f* = NULL, GWriteMaterial* = NULL);
};
```

`Polygon()` has five arguments:

1. The current state of the OpenGL stack
2. The number of faces in the polygon
3. The array of vertices for the polygon
4. The normal array for the polygon
5. The material for the polygon

```
void Polygon(GState& state,
        long faceNum, MFVec3f* poly, MFVec3f* n = NULL,
        GWriteMaterial* m = NULL)
```

All that you need to do is intercept the polygons and do whatever your application requires to them. For example, the following function adds the polygons to an instance of the *MyClass* class defined in the *GWriteCvt* instance:

```
void GWriteCvt::Polygon(GState& state,

        long faceNum, MFVec3f* poly,
        MFVec3f* n,GWriteMaterial* m)  {

        m_cls.BeginPolygon();
        for (int i=0; i < faceNum; i++)  {
          m_cls.Vertex((*poly)[I]);
        }
        m_cls.EndPolygon();
}
```

To convert the scene into polygons, you need only create an instance of the *GWriteCvt* class and an instance of the *GState* class. Then call the `Write()` member function, which will then traverse the entire scene and call the member functions `MyClass::BeginPolygon()`, `MyClass::Vertex()`, and

`MyClass::EndPolygon()` for every polygon and vertex encountered in the scene.

```
void MyClass::ConvertPolygons(CXRoadAppDoc* pDoc)  {
    GWriteCvt*  write = new GWriteCvt(this);
    GState      state;

    pDoc->Write(state, *write);

    delete write;
}
```

Converting Polygons into a 3D Scene

An internal scene can be easily created from a polygon mesh without your having to construct the *Crossroads* internal representation directly. Instead you use a helper class named *MeshCompactor* to create the representation in a way that in many instances may be simpler to use.

The *MeshCompactor* instance will create a vertex list and a series of groups of polygon faces from the polygons that are added to it. A polygon definition begins when the `MeshCompactor::BeginPolygon()` member function is invoked. Vertices are added to the polygon via the `MeshCompactor::AddVertex(SFVec3f)` member function. The polygon is closed with the `MeshCompactor::EndPolygon()` member function. The group that the polygons are being added to is specified by the `MeshCompactor::Name(char*)`.

The following example shows how this class can be used to convert a series of polygons into a *Crossroads* internal representation without your having to build the underlying components directly:

```
MeshCompactor    mesh;
GSeparator       separator;

// Create a group name Face1 composed of a
// single triangle added to it.
mesh.Name("Face1");
mesh.BeginPolygon();
mesh.AddVertex(SFVec3f(0.0, 1.0, 0.0));
mesh.AddVertex(SFVec3f(0.0, 1.0, 1.0));
mesh.AddVertex(SFVec3f(0.0, 0.0, 1.0));
mesh.EndPolgon();

// Create a group name Face2 composed of
// a single triangle.
mesh.Name("Face2");
```

```
mesh.BeginPolygon();
mesh.AddVertex(SFVec3f(0.0, 0.0, 1.0));
mesh.AddVertex(SFVec3f(1.0, 0.0, 1.0));
mesh.AddVertex(SFVec3f(1.0, 0.0, 0.0));
mesh.EndPolgon();

// Convert the groups into an equivalent
// Crossroads internal representation. The
// Representation will be held as a child to
// the separator instance.
mesh.AddTo(&separator);
    .
    .
    .
```

Chapter 3

VRML

The Virtual Reality Modeling Language (VRML) is a textual language that describes 3D scenes. It differs from programming languages like C++ or BASIC in that instead of describing how the computer should act through a series of language specific commands, it describes how a 3D scene should look.

Languages like C++ and BASIC describe in extreme detail the explicit operations that the computer must perform to complete a task. Languages like VRML don't describe how something is done; they describe what something is. For example, to draw a 3D sphere on the screen in C++ would take many lines, even many *pages*, of code, depending on the graphics capability of your computer and the development software available. In VRML, a 3D sphere is drawn simply by

```
Sphere  {
    radius 5
}
```

VRML files are intended to be displayed using VRML browsers. These browsers are 3D applications that allow the Web user to move through the 3D world defined by the VRML language. Users may not only move through a scene, but also interact with it by selecting some objects, which then "teleport" the user to another location anywhere on the Web via hyperlinks. This means that VRML applications are currently intended to be both simple 3D scene viewers and simple 3D Web browsers.

VRML differs from many other 3D file formats in that with it, you can define a limited amount of interactive behavior explicitly through language constructs. For example, you can place a 3D model of a door in a scene and specify that when this door is selected by the user, the VRML browser is to load a new VRML file. This new VRML file could be located anywhere on the Web.

For our purposes, I ignore the constructs used to define interactive behavior in VRML. This is because this book deals with converting VRML files to and from other file formats, not with writing a VRML browser. I also ignore the constructs that display ASCII text in VRML, 3D lines, and 3D points.

Development of VRML

VRML is a very recent attempt to define an open, multiplatform, virtual reality language for the Web. The concept of VRML was put forward at the first annual World Wide Web Conference held in spring, 1994. There a virtual reality discussion group was formed that agreed on the need for a common 3D scene description language. The term Virtual Reality Modeling Language was coined, based on the notion that VRML was a 3D file format analogous to HTML for Web publishing.

A search for existing 3D file formats was started. Several candidates were considered. After much discussion of these, the group reached a consensus. The Open Inventor File Format defined by Silicon Graphics was selected to be the basis for VRML.

It is important to note that VRML wasn't defined specifically for the Web. It started out as Open Inventor, which is intended to be extensible and expressive. However, VRML is not Open Inventor. VRML is actually a small subset of Open Inventor, with extensions to make it capable of interacting with the Web.

Many of VRML's goals differ from those of Open Inventor. It is not clear that VRML and Open Inventor will ever converge into a single language, although VRML likely will continue to benefit from its Open Inventor heritage by borrowing syntax and semantics from Open Inventor for new graphical constructs.

The key people involved in the creation of VRML were Gavin Bell, Brian Behlendorf, Tony Parisi, Chris Marrin, and Jan Hardenbergh. These folks deserve our thanks.

As of this writing, VRML exists as a version 1.1 definition. However, it likely will evolve quickly as new features are added. Already there is interest in tightening up the current definition and adding the ability to include a sound to a VRML scene. Eventually graphical objects will be able to include a definition of behavior, such as its interaction with the "physics" of the defined world. Users soon will be able to define a world that is as rich and as interactive as that defined in games like *Doom*. But for now, VRML can be used only to define primarily static worlds. These worlds may be explored, but they offer little interaction with the user.

Overview of the VRML File Format

VRML is a textual file format. It is composed of *graphical nodes* arranged in a hierarchical structure. Graphical nodes are used to define more than just graphical constructs. They also embody the notion of *state*.

Changes in state affect the way graphical constructs are rendered later in the VRML file. For example, a translation or rotation node affects the rendered location of subsequent graphical constructs. Material nodes affect the appearance of graphical constructs defined later in the scene.

Each node in a VRML file has one or more of the following properties:

- *Type*. Several types of nodes are currently defined, including nodes that define properties of graphics primitives, that define transformations of graphics primitives, and that define cameras and lights. There are also nodes that allow other nodes to be grouped together.
- *Fields*. *Fields* are the parameters used to customize specific characteristics of nodes. A node can be made unique with the use of fields. For example, a Cone can have a unique radius for its base and a unique value for its height.
- *Name*. Naming a node is optional. However, a node's having a name allows its definition to be reused throughout a VRML file. The *DEF* command is used to define a node with a name. These definitions can be reused with the *USE* command.
- *Children*. A special class of nodes allows children (or subnodes) to be defined. This is how node hierarchy is defined.

The syntax for a VRML file is very simple and straightforward. It is defined using this very short BNF grammar:

```
// <name>   is a non-terminal
// ::=      is an assignment
// ...|...  means either this construct OR that construct
// [...]    means the bracketed construct is optional
// {...}    means the bracketed construct is repeated one
//          or more times.
// '...'    is a literal string definition.

<Start>           ::=    <VRML_ID> [ Node ]
                  ;
```

```
<VRML_ID>         ::=   '#VRML V1.0 ascii'
                  |     '#VRML V1.1 utf8'
                  ;

<Node>            ::=   [ 'DEF' <ObjectName> ]
                        <ObjectType> '{'
                              [ <FieldDef> ]
                              [ <FieldUsage> ]
                              [ <SubNodes> ]
                        '}'
                  |     'USE' <ObjectName>
                  ;

<ObjectType>      ::=   'AsciiText' | ... | 'WWWInline'
                  ;

<FieldDef>        ::=   'fields' '[' {<Type> <FieldName>} ']'
                  ;

<Type>            ::=   'SFLong' | 'SFFloat' | ... 'MFFloat'
                  ;

<FieldUsage>      ::=   { <FieldName> <Value> }
                  ;

<SubNodes>        ::=   {Node}
                  ;

<FieldName>       ::=   ('a'...'z' | 'A'...'Z')
                        [{'a'...'z' | 'A'...'Z' | '0'...'9' |
                              '_' | '+' }]
                  ;
```

For example, here is a simple example of a VRML file that defines a green Cone and a red Sphere illuminated by a point light defined at the camera location:

```
#VRML V1.0 ascii
Separator {
    # Define camera looking at <0, 0, 0>
    PerspectiveCamera {
          position 0 0 15
    }
```

```
    # Define a light at the camera position
    PointLight {
          location 0 0 15
    }

    # Define a Red Sphere centered (3, 0, 0)
    Separator {
          Material {
                ambientColor 0.1 0.0 0.0
                diffuseColor 0.7 0.0 0.0
          }
          Translation {
                translation 3 0 0
          }
          Sphere {
                radius 2
          }
    }

    # Define a Green Cone centered at (-3, 0, 0)
    Separator {
          Material {
                ambientColor 0.0 0.1 0.0
                diffuseColor 0.0 0.7 0.0
          }
          Translation {
                 translation -3 0 0
          }
          Cone {
                bottomRadius 2
                height 3
          }
    }
}
```

When this VRML file is rendered as a graphical scene, the image looks like Figure 3.1.

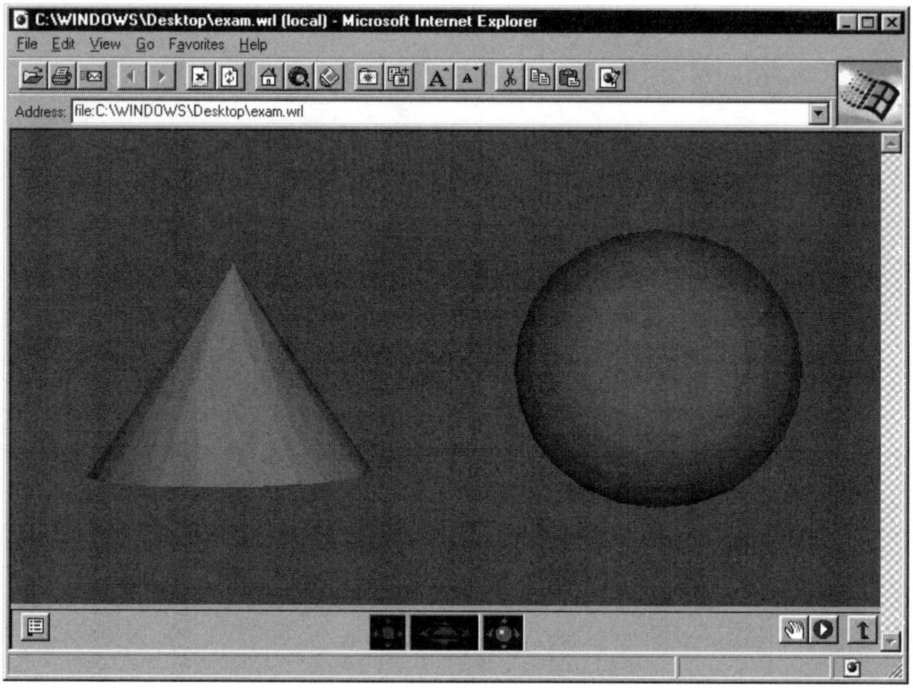

Figure 3.1. VRML file example of a Cone and Sphere.

Syntax of a VRML File

The first line of a VRML file is the literal string '#VRML V1.0 ascii' or the literal string '#VRML V1.1 utf8', depending on the version of VRML supported. This header is required for all VRML files.

Comments begin with the character # and end at the next newline. However, although the first line of a VRML file looks like a comment, it actually is a special language construct that identifies the file type as a VRML file. It is important that all VRML parsers look for this special construct and that all VRML emitters write out this special construct.

Comments, spaces, tabs, newlines, and other whitespace defined outside a double-quoted string are ignored by the VRML parser except for denoting a separation between syntactic entities.

The rest of the VRML file after the required header is a single node. This node may be a single graphical node or a group node such as a *Separator*.

Field Types

There are two kinds of field types:

1. Single-value, denoted with the prefix SF.
2. Multiple-value, denoted with the prefix MF, that are usually enclosed in square brackets. Each value in a multiple-value field is separated by a comma. The last element in the array may optionally be followed by a comma.

Table 3.1 defines all of the types defined for fields.

Table 3.1. VRML built-in types

Name	Definition	Example
MFColor	A multiple field that defines a color array. A series of one or more *SFColor* values are enclosed by square brackets and separated by commas.	`Material {ambientColor [0.1 0.1 0.1, 0.8 0.8 0.8]}`
MFFloat	A multiple field that defines an array of *SFFloat* values. Each value is separated by a comma. The entire series is enclosed in square brackets.	`Material {shininess [0.1, 0.2, 0.8]}`
MFLong	Defines an array of *SFLong* values. Each value is separated by a comma. The series of values is enclosed by square brackets.	`IndexedFaceSet {coordIndex [0, 1, 2 -1, 1, 3, 5, 4, -1]}`
MFString	A multiple field that defines an array of *SFString* values. Each value is separated by a comma. The entire series is enclosed by square brackets.	`AsciiText {string ["String1", "String2", "String3"]}`
MFVec2f	A multiple field type that defines an array of *SFVec2f* values. Each value is separated by a comma and the entire series is enclosed by square brackets.	`TextureCoordinate2 {point [0 0, 0.25, 0.5]}`
MFVec3f	A multiple field that defines an array of *SFVec3f* values. Each value is separated by a comma. The entire series is enclosed in square brackets.	`Coordinate3 {points [0 0 0, 0.1 0.1 0.1, 0.2 0.2 0.2]}`

(continued)

Table 3.1. VRML built-in types *(continued)*

Name	Definition	Example
SFBitMask	Contains a mask of bit flags. It can be thought of as an *SFLong* value with the ability to evaluate one or more 'or'ed values.	`Cylinder {parts TOP | SIDES}`
SFBool	Contains a single boolean value. A boolean value can be assigned the value 0, which represents false, or 1, which represents true, TRUE, or FALSE.	`PointLight {on TRUE}`
SFColor	Contains a set of three *SFFloat* values that represent the red, green, and blue components of an RGB color definition.	`PointLight {color 1 0 0} # a red light`
SFEnum	A field that may be assigned only predefined, named values.	`MaterialBinding {value OVERALL}`
SFFloat	A single-precision floating-point value. It corresponds to the 'float' type in the C/C++ language. *SFFloat* values are written using standard scientific notation.	`PerspectiveCamera {heightAngle 0.74}`
SFImage	Grayscale or color raster pictures that are defined using a series of integer values. The first two integer values define the width and height of the image. The third value defines the number of bytes per pixel. The last value defines the value for each pixel. For images with the third value of 1, each pixel defines a grayscale value that ranges from 0x00 to 0xff. The value 0x00 means no intensity, and the value 0xff means full intensity. For images with the third value of 3, each pixel is represented by three 1-byte RGB values. Again, 0x00 means no intensity and 0xff means full intensity for each of the RGB colors. For example, the color red is represented by 0xff0000.	`2 2 3 0xff0000 0x00ff00 0x0000ff 0x000000`

Table 3.1. VRML built-in types *(continued)*

Name	Definition	Example
SFLong	Defined as a 32-bit integer value. An *SFLong* value can be represented as a decimal, octal, or hexadecimal value.	`Switch {whichChild -1}`
SFMatrix	Defines a 4-x-4 transformation matrix. It is written as 16 *SFFloat* values separated by whitespace. The values are written in row order, where the first four values are row one, the second four values are row two, and so on.	`MatrixTransform {matrix 1 0 0 0 0 1 0 0 0 0 10 0 0 0 1}`
SFRotation	Defines the transformation around an axis. The first three *SFFloat* values define the axis of rotation. The fourth value defines the rotation angle in radians.	`Rotation {rotation 0 1 0 3.14159}`
SFString	A sequence of ASCII characters enclosed within double quotes. Double quotes are optional if the string contains no whitespace. Also, a string may include a newline if the string is enclosed within double quotes. The double-quote character may be included in a string if it is preceded by a backslash.	`AsciiText {"Hello world"}`
SFVec2f	A 2D vector defined as two *SFFloat* values separated by whitespace.	`Texture2Transform {translation 1 1}`
SFVec3f	A 3D vector defined as three *SFFloat* values separated by whitespace.	`PerspectiveCamera {position 6 1.7 4}`

Node Definitions

VRML has defined six types of nodes:

1. Shape
2. Camera and light
3. Property
4. Transformation
5. Grouping
6. WWW

Property nodes and transformation nodes directly affect the subsequent state seen while a browser is traversing a VRML file. Grouping nodes affect the scope of the subsequent state definitions. I discuss state later in this chapter.

Shape Nodes

Shape nodes define visible objects. At least one shape node should be defined in each VRML scene; otherwise, nothing can be rendered by a VRML browser. Following are the shape nodes.

The AsciiText Node

The *AsciiText* node defines strings of text to be displayed. The first string starts at the origin; all subsequent strings advance along the *y*-axis by –(size*spacing). A justification value of `LEFT` places the first character in the string at X=0. A justification value of `CENTER` places the center of each string at X=0. A justification value of `RIGHT` places the right edge of the last character at X= 0. The width field defines the suggested width constraint for a string. A value of 0 indicates that the natural width should be used.

The other nodes that may influence this node's appearance are *FontStyle*, *Material*, *MaterialBinding*, *MatrixTransformation*, *Rotation*, *Scale*, *Transform*, *Translation*, *Texture2*, *Texture2Transform*, and *TextureCoordinate2*.

The definition of the *AsciiText* node follows:

```
# The definition of the AsciiText node
AsciiText {
    # Field Definitions
    fields [
        MFString        string,
        SFFloat         spacing,
        SFEnum          justification,
        MFFloat         width
    ]

    # Default Field Values
    string              ""
    spacing               1
    justification         LEFT
    width                 0
}
```

The Cone Node

The *Cone* node defines a Cone centered at the origin. The default height is 2. It causes the Cone to extend on the *y*-axis from –1 (the base) to +1 (the top). The field variable *height* allows the height of the Cone to be modified. The default radius for the base is 2, which causes the base to extend along the *x*- and *z*-axes from –1 to +1. The field variable *bottomRadius* modifies the radius of the base. Each Cone is made of two parts: the sides and the bottom. The variable *parts* selects which of the parts of the Cone are visible. Its legal values are SIDES, BOTTOM, and ALL.

Material bindings of PER_PART or PER_PART_INDEX cause the material to be mapped first to the sides and then to the bottom of the cone. Any other material binding causes the first material to be mapped to the entire cone.

The other nodes that may influence this node's appearance are *Material*, *MaterialBinding*, *MatrixTransformation*, *Rotation*, *Scale*, *Transform*, *Translation*, *Texture2*, *Texture2Transform*, and *TextureCoordinate2*.

The definition of the *Cone* node follows:

```
# The definition of the Cone node
Cone {
      # Field Definitions
      fields [
            SFBitMask parts,          # SIDES, BOTTOM, ALL
            SFFloat bottomRadius,
            SFFloat height
      ]

      # Default Field Values
      parts             ALL
      bottomRadius      1
      height            2
}
```

The Cube Node

The *Cube* node defines a Cuboid that is centered at the origin. The Cuboid extends along the *x*-axis from –width/2 to width/2, along the *y*-axis from –height/2 to height/2, and along the *z*-axis from –depth/2 to depth/2.

If the material binding is set to PER_PART, PER_PART_INDEXED, PER_FACE, or PER_FACE_INDEXED, the material will be bound to the faces of the Cuboid in the following order: front, back, left, right, top, bottom.

The other nodes that may influence this node's appearance are *Material*, *MaterialBinding*, *MatrixTransformation*, *Rotation*, *Scale*, *Transform*, *Translation*, *Texture2*, *Texture2Transform*, and *TextureCoordinate2*.

The definition of the *Cube* node follows:

```
# The definition of the Cube node
Cube {
    # Field Definitions
    fields [
        SFFloat width,
        SFFloat height,
        SFFloat depth
    ]

    # Default Field Values
    width           2
    height          2
    depth           2
}
```

The Cylinder Node

The *Cylinder* node defines a Cylinder that is centered at the origin. The Cylinder extends along the *y*-axis from –height/2 to height/2. The radius field causes the Cylinder to extend along the *x*- and *z*-axes from –radius to radius. The Cylinder is composed of three parts: sides, top, and bottom.

A material binding of `PER_PART` or `PER_PART_INDEXED` causes the material to be bound in the following order: sides, top, bottom. Any other material binding maps the first texture to the entire Cylinder.

The other nodes that may influence this node's appearance are *Material*, *MaterialBinding*, *MatrixTransformation*, *Rotation*, *Scale*, *Transform*, *Translation*, *Texture2*, *Texture2Transform*, and *TextureCoordinate2*.

The definition of the *Cylinder* node follows:

```
# The definition of the Cylinder node
Cylinder {
    # Field Definitions
    fields [
          SFBitMask    parts,     #SIDES, TOP, BOTTOM, ALL
          SFFloat      radius,
          SFFloat height
    ]

    #Default Field Values
    parts            ALL
    radius           1
    height           2
}
```

The IndexedFaceSet Node

The *IndexedFaceSet* node defines a 3D object by forming one or more Polygons from the vertices defined by the previous *Coordinate3* node. Each Polygon is defined by four or more integer values that are placed in the *coordIndex* multiple-value field. The index of each vertex in the previously encountered *Coordinate3* node is specified by the integer value defined by each element in the *coordIndex* field. The index values range from 0 to the number of elements in the previous *Coordinate3* node. Each Polygon is terminated with the integer value –1.

The normal and material bindings `PER_PART` and `PER_FACE` map the first normal or material to the first face, the second with the second face, and so on. The `PER_VERTEX` maps the normal or material to each vertex. The `PER_PART_INDEXED` and `PER_FACE_INDEXED` map the first normal or material corresponding to the first entry in the *normalIndex* or *materialIndex* field, the second face to the second entry, and so on. The `DEFAULT` material binding maps to `OVERALL`, and the `DEFAULT` normal maps to `PER_VERTEX_INDEXED`.

The other nodes that may influence this node's appearance are *Material*, *MaterialBinding*, *Normal*, *NormalBinding*, *MatrixTransformation*, *Rotation*, *Scale*, *Transform*, *Translation*, *Texture2*, *Texture2Transform*, and *TextureCoordinate2*.

The definition of the *IndexedFaceSet* node follows:

```
# The definition of the IndexedFaceSet node
IndexedFaceSet {
    # Field Definitions
    fields [
        MFLong          coordIndex,
        MFLong          materialIndex,
        MFLong          normalIndex,
        MFLong          textureCoordIndex
    ]

    # Default Field Values
    coordIndex        0
    materialIndex     -1
    normalIndex       -1
    textureCoordIndex -1
}
```

The IndexedLineSet Node

The *IndexedLineSet* node defines a 3D Polyline by forming one or more line segments from the vertices defined by the previously encountered *Coordi-*

nate3 node. Each Polyline is defined by three or more integer values that are placed in the *coordIndex* multiple-value field. The index of each vertex in the previously encountered *Coordinate3* node is specified by the integer value defined by each element in the *coordIndex* field. The index values range from 0 to the number of elements in the previous *Coordinate3* node. Each Polyline is terminated with the integer value –1.

The `PER_PART` binding maps a normal or material to each line segment. The `PER_FACE` binding maps a normal or material to each Polyline. The `PER_VERTEX` binding maps each normal or material to each vertex. The `PER_PART_INDEXED`, `PER_FACE_INDEXED`, and `PER_VERTEX_INDEXED` work as described above; however, the actual indexes used are referenced from the corresponding *normalIndex* or *materialIndex* multiple-value field. The `DEFAULT` binding for normals correspond to `PER_VERTEX_INDEXED`, and the `DEFAULT` binding for material corresponds to `OVERALL`.

The other nodes that may influence this node's appearance are *Material*, *MaterialBinding*, *Normal*, *NormalBinding*, *MatrixTransformation*, *Rotation*, *Scale*, *Transform*, and *Translation*.

The definition of the *IndexedLineSet* node follows:

```
# The definition of the IndexedLineSet node
IndexedLineSet {
    # Field Definitions
    fields [
        MFLong          coordIndex,
        MFLong          materialIndex,
        MFLong          normalIndex,
        MFLong          textureCoordIndex
    ]

    # Default Field Values
    coordIndex        0
    materialIndex     -1
    normalIndex       -1
    textureCoordIndex -1
}
```

The PointSet Node

The *PointSet* node defines a set of points from the points specified by the previously encountered *Coordinate3* node. The field value *startIndex* defines the first index of the point set, and the field value *numPoints* defines the number of points to use. When *numPoints* is –1, all of the remaining points are used.

The bindings `PER_PART`, `PER_FACE`, and `PER_VERTEX` map one normal or material to each point. The `DEFAULT` binding for normals is equivalent to PER_VERTEX, and the DEFAULT binding for materials is equivalent to OVERALL.

The other nodes that may influence this node's appearance are *Material*, *MaterialBinding*, *Normal*, *NormalBinding*, *MatrixTransformation*, *Rotation*, *Scale*, *Transform*, and *Translation*.

The definition of the *PointSet* node follows:

```
# The definition of the PointSet node
PointSet {
    # Field Definitions
    fields [
        SFLong          startIndex,
        SFLong          numPoints
    ]

    # Default Field Values
    startIndex  0
    numPoints   -1
}
```

The Sphere Node

The *Sphere* node defines a Sphere centered on the origin. By default, the Sphere has a radius of 1. A Sphere doesn't have faces. It defines its own surface normals, so all materials are mapped to the entire Sphere.

The definition of the *Sphere* node follows:

```
# The definition of the Sphere node
Sphere {
    # Field Definitions
    fields [
        MFLong radius
    ]

    # Default Field Values
    radius              1
}
```

Camera and Light Nodes

Camera and light nodes affect the way a scene is rendered. A camera defines the viewpoint from which the scene is rendered. A light defines the illumination that a scene provides. By default, most VRML browsers will implicitly add a camera and lights to a scene if they don't already exist. To achieve maximum control of a scene's appearance, you should define these nodes in the scene. Following are the camera and light nodes.

The OrthographicCamera Node

The *OrthographicCamera* node does not cause objects to get smaller as they get farther away from the viewpoint. By default, an orthographic camera is located at (0, 0, 1) and looks down the negative *z*-axis. The field variables *position* and *orientation* can be used to modify the camera placement.

The other nodes that may influence this node are *MatrixTransformation*, *Rotation*, *Scale*, *Transform*, and *Translation*.

The definition of the *OrthographicCamera* node follows:

```
# The definition of the OrthographicCamera node
OrthographicCamera {
    # Field Definitions
    fields [
        SFVec3f         position,
        SFRotation      orientation,
        SFFloat         focalDistance,
        SFFloat         height
    ]

    # Default Field Values
    position            0 0 1
    orientation         0 0 1 0
    focalDistance       5
    height              2
}
```

The PerspectiveCamera Node

The *PerspectiveCamera* node causes objects to get smaller as they get farther away from the viewpoint. By default, a perspective camera is located at (0, 0, 1) and looks down the negative *z*-axis. The field variables *position* and *orientation* can be used to modify the camera placement.

The other nodes that may influence this node are *MatrixTransformation*, *Rotation*, *Scale*, *Transform*, and *Translation*.

The definition of the *PerspectiveCamera* node follows:

```
# The definition of the PerspectiveCamera node
PerspectiveCamera {
    # Field Definitions
    fields [
        SFVec3f         position,
        SFRotation      orientation,
        SFFloat         focalDistance,
```

```
        SFFloat         heightAngle
    ]

    # Default Field Values
    position            0 0 1
    orientation         0 0 1 0
    focalDistance       5
    height              0.785398
}
```

The DirectionalLight Node

The *DirectionalLight* node defines a directional light source. This light source illuminates along rays parallel to the defined direction vector. By default, the direction vector is the negative *z*-axis. The light can be turned on or off depending on the value in the *on* field; the default is TRUE. The light can be modified to emit any color via changing the *color* field variable; the default is white.

The *intensity* field variable allows you to control the light's intensity. The intensity is like a scalar multiply of the intensity by the color; the resulting value is the color emitted. Hence an intensity of 0 is equivalent to turning the light off. When a light is placed in a *Separator*, only the nodes in the *Separator* are illuminated by that light. No objects outside the *Separator* are affected.

The other nodes that may influence this node are *MatrixTransformation*, *Rotation*, *Scale*, *Transform*, and *Translation*.

The definition of the *DirectionalLight* node follows:

```
# The definition of the DirectionalLight node
DirectionalLight {
    # Field Definitions
    fields [
        SFBool          on,
        SFFloat         intensity,
        SFColor         color,
        SFVec3f         direction
    ]

    # Default Field Values
    on                  TRUE
    intensity           1
    color               1 1 1
    direction           0 0 -1
}
```

The PointLight Node

The *PointLight* node defines a light source that is located at a specific position and radiates light in all directions. The light can be on or off, depending on the value in the *on* field; the default is `TRUE`. The light can be modified to emit any color via changing the *color* field variable; the default is white.

The *intensity* field allows you to control the light's intensity. The intensity is a scalar multiply of the intensity by the color value of the light; the resulting value is the color emitted. Hence an intensity of 0 is equivalent to turning the light off. When a light is placed in a *Separator*, only the nodes in the *Separator* are illuminated. No objects outside the *Separator* are affected.

The other nodes that may influence this node are *MatrixTransformation*, *Rotation*, *Scale*, *Transform*, and *Translation*.

The definition of the *PointLight* node follows:

```
#The definition of the PointLight node
PointLight {
    # Field Definitions
    fields {
        SFBool          on,
        SFFloat         intensity,
        SFColor         color,
        SFVec3f         location
    ]

    # Default Field Values
    on                  TRUE
    intensity           1
    color               1 1 1
    location            0 0 1
}
```

The SpotLight Node

The *SpotLight* node defines a light source that illuminates from a specified position in a cone along a particular direction. The intensity of the light drops off exponentially toward the edge of the cone. The rate of drop off is controlled by the *dropOffRate* and *cutOffAngle* field values. The direction of the light is controlled by the *direction* field variable. The light can be on or off, depending on the value in the *on* field; the default is `TRUE`. The light can be modified to emit any color by changing the *color* field variable; the default is white.

The *intensity* field variable allows you to control the light's intensity. The intensity is like a scalar multiply of the intensity by the color; the resulting value is the color emitted. Hence an intensity of 0 is equivalent to turning the light off. When a light is placed in a *Separator*, only the nodes in the *Separator* are illuminated. No objects outside the *Separator* are affected.

The other nodes that may influence this node are *MatrixTransformation*, *Rotation*, *Scale*, *Transform*, and *Translation*.

The definition of the *SpotLight* node follows:

```
# The definition of the SpotLight node
Spotlight {
    # Field Definitions
    fields [
        SFBool          on,
        SFFloat         intensity,
        SFColor         color,
        SFVec3f         location,
        SFVec3f         direction,
        SFFloat         dropOffRate,
        SFFloat         cutOffAngle
    ]

    # Default Field Values
    on                  TRUE
    intensity           1
    color               1 1 1
    location            0 0 1
    direction           0 0 -1
    dropOffRate         0
    cutOffAngle         0.785398
}
```

Property Nodes

Property nodes aren't rendered into visible objects. However, their definitions may affect the way subsequent nodes are interpreted. All of them affect the current traversal state of the VRML file.

Following are the property nodes.

The Coordinate3 Node

The *Coordinate3* node defines a set of 3D vertices that can be used by subsequent *IndexedFaceSet*, *IndexedLineSet*, or *PointSet* nodes. This node replaces the current coordinates in the current traversal state. It is directly affected by subsequent *Coordinate3* nodes. The values of the vertices seen when referenced by subsequent *IndexedFaceSet*, *IndexedLineSet*, or *PointSet* nodes are affected by the transformation matrix that is current for those nodes.

The definition of the *Coordinate3* node follows:

```
# The definition of the Coordinate3 node
Coordinate3 {
    # Field Definitions
    fields [
        MFVec3f point
    ]

    # Default Field Values
    point 0 0 0
}
```

The FontStyle Node

The *FontStyle* node defines the font style to be used for subsequent *AsciiText* nodes. It overwrites the current values found at this point in the traversal state of the VRML file. The *size* field specifies the height of the font in object space units. The actual fonts used are determined by the browser used. Only subsequent *FontStyle* nodes can change the state of these values.

The definition of the *FontStyle* node follows:

```
# The definition of the FontStyle node
FontStyle {
    # Field Definitions
    fields [
        SSFloat       size,
        SFEnum        family, #SERIF, SANS, TYPEWRITER
        SFBitMask     style   #NONE, BOLD, ITALIC
    ]

    # Default Field Values
    size              10
    family            SERIF
    style             NONE
}
```

The Material Node

The *Material* node specifies the current surface material values to be used by subsequent shapes. The interpretations of these values are affected by *MaterialBinding* nodes; different shape nodes interpret the *Material* and *MaterialBinding* nodes differently.

Five color components affect the appearance of an object: ambient, diffuse, specular, emissive, and transparency. *Ambient* color defines the background color of an object. The ambient color is visible regardless of whether the object is directly illuminated. *Diffuse* color is affected by the angle of the light illuminating the object. The more direct the light, the more the diffuse color affects the color of the object. *Specular* color is actually the combination of specular color and shininess; these color components produce highlights on the object. The color is brightest along the angle of reflection. Specular color controls the color of the highlights, and shininess affects the size and brightness of the highlights. *Emissive* color specifies the amount of color the object appears to be emitting. Emissive color is seldom used. *Transparency* specifies how transparent the object is. A value of 0 means it is completely opaque; a value of 1 means it is completely clear.

The definition of the *Material* node follows:

```
# The definition of the Material node
Material {
    # Field Definitions
    fields [
        MFColor       ambientColor,
        MFColor       diffuseColor,
        MFColor       specularColor,
        MFColor       emissiveColor,
        MFFloat       shininess,
        MFFloat       transparency
    ]

    # Default Field Values
    ambientColor      0.2 0.2 0.2
    diffuseColor      0.8 0.8 0.8
    specularColor     0 0 0
    emissiveColor     0 0 0
    shininess         0.2
    transparency      0
}
```

The MaterialBinding Node

The *MaterialBinding* node specifies how the currently defined material is mapped to shape nodes. Each shape may interpret each binding differently. When multiple materials are bound to an object, the material value will be cycled if the number of indexes available in the material is less than those provided by the shape node. The material used is `current_index % Max(Len(ambientColor), …, Len(transparency))`. **Note:** The use of color cycling is strongly discouraged and will be unavailable in future versions of VRML.

The definition of the *MaterialBinding* node follows:

```
# The definition of the MaterialBinding node
MaterialBinding {
    # Field Definitions
    fields [
        SFEnum value   #DEFAULT, OVERALL, PER_PART
                       #PER_PART_INDEXED, PER_FACE
                       #PER_FACE_INDEXED, PER_VERTEX,
                       #PER_VERTEXT_INDEXED
    ]

    # Default Field Values
    value       DEFAULT
}
```

The Normal Node

The *Normal* node defines 3D surface normals that may be used by subsequent *IndexedFaceSet*, *IndexedLineSet*, and *PointSet* nodes. This node is not visible during rendering. It is affected only by subsequent *Normal* nodes. It is important to remember that the surface normals used by the shape nodes will be affected by the current transformation matrix defined for that shape node. Implementers should note that normals aren't transformed correctly by simply multiplying them by the current transformation matrix.

The definition of the *Normal* node follows:

```
# The definition of the Normal node
Normal {
    # Field Definitions
    fields [
        MFVec3f vector
    ]

    # Default Field Values
    vector      0 0 1
}
```

The NormalBinding Node

The *NormalBinding* node specifies how the currently defined surface normal vectors are mapped to shape nodes. Each shape may interpret each binding differently.

The definition of the *NormalBinding* node follows:

```
# The definition of the NormalBinding node
NormalBinding {
    # Field Definitions
    fields [
        SFEnum value  #DEFAULT, OVERALL, PER_PART
                      #PER_PART_INDEXED, PER_FACE,
                      #PER_FACE_INDEXED, PER_VERTEX,
                      #PER_VERTEX_INDEXED
    ]
    # Default Field Values
    value   DEFAULT
}
```

The Texture2 Node

The *Texture2* node defines the texture map to be applied to subsequent shapes. The *filename* field variable specifies the URL of the file to be used as the texture map. All browsers should support JPEG. Support for PNG is recommended, while support for GIF is not recommended due to licensing restrictions.

A texture can also be defined using the *image* field variable. Either the *filename* field variable or the *image* field variable is to be defined, but not both. The only way to guarantee that a VRML file, which uses a texture map, will work across multiple browsers is to use the *image* field variable. As more browsers support JPEG files, creating VRML files that work across several browsers will be much easier.

The definition of the *Texture2* node follows:

```
# The definition of the Texture2 node
Texture2 {
    # Field Definitions
    fields [
        SFString      filename,
        SFImage       image,
        SFEnum        wrapS, #REPEAT, CLAMP
        SFEnum        wrapT  #REPEAT, CLAMP
    ]

    # Default Field Values
    filename          ""
    image             0 0 0
    wrapS             REPEAT
    wrapT             REPEAT
}
```

The Texture2Transform Node

The *Texture2Transform* node defines a 2D transformation to be applied to a texture map. This node affects how texture maps are applied to surfaces of subsequent shapes. The transformation is applied from the center point in the following order: scale, rotation, translation. This node allows a user to customize the placement of a texture map on an object.

The definition of the *Texture2Transform* node follows:

```
# The definition of the Texture2Transform node
Texture2Transform {
    # Field Definitions
    fields [
        SFVec2f       translation,
        SFFloat       rotation,
        SFVec2f       scaleFactor,
        SFVec2f       center
    ]

    # Default Field Values
    translation       0 0
    rotation          0
    scaleFactor       1 1
    center            0 0
}
```

The TextureCoordinate2 Node

The *TextureCoordinate2* node defines a set of 3D coordinates that are used to place texture maps at specific locations on subsequent *IndexedFaceSet*, *IndexedLineSet*, or *PointSet* nodes. The texture coordinates range between 0 and 1 across the texture. The horizontal coordinate is defined, followed by the vertical coordinate.

The definition of the *TextureCoordinate2* node follows:

```
# The definition of the TextureCoordinate2 node
TextureCoordinate2 {
    # Field Definitions
    fields [
        MFVec2f       point
    ]

    # Default Field Values
    point             0 0
}
```

The ShapeHints Node

The *ShapeHints* node defines the vertex order and the shape and whether the polygons are convex for subsequent *IndexedFaceSet* nodes. This information is useful for VRML browsers in that it may help optimize rendering and may help the browser to automatically generate correct normals for the shape defined by the *IndexedFaceSet* node.

The definition of the *ShapeHints* node follows:

```
# The definition of the ShapeHints node
ShapeHints {
    # Field Definitions
    fields [
        SFEnum        vertexOrdering,     #UNKNOWN_ORDERING
                                          #CLOCKWISE
                                          #COUNTERCLOCKWISE

        SFEnum        shapeType,          #UNKNOWN_SHAPE_TYPE
                                          #SOLID

        SFEnum        faceType,           #UNKNOWN_FACE_TYPE
                                          #CONVEX

        SFFloat       creaseAngle
    ]

    # Default Field Values
    vertexOrdering    COUNTERCLOCKWISE
    shapeType         SOLID
    faceType          CONVEX
    creaseAngle       0.5
}
```

Transformation Nodes

Transformation nodes directly affect the current transformation matrix held when traversing the VRML file. Unlike the property nodes, which overwrite the previous state for a specified value, transformation nodes multiply the current transformation matrix by the transformation matrix that corresponds to the current node. The result is the new current transformation matrix.

Following are the transformation nodes.

The MatrixTransform Node

The *MatrixTransform* node defines a 3D transformation matrix. The default value is the identity matrix.

The definition of the *MatrixTransform* node follows:

```
# The definition of the MatrixTransform node
MatrixTransform {
    # Field Definitions
    fields [
        SFMatrix      matrix
    ]

    # Default Field Values
    matrix              1 0 0 0
                        0 1 0 0
                        0 0 1 0
                        0 0 0 1
}
```

The Rotation Node

The *Rotation* node defines a 3D rotation around a specified axis. The first three values for the rotation specify the rotation axis. The last value is the rotation angle in radians.

The definition of the *Rotation* node follows:

```
# The definition of the Rotation node
Rotation {
    # Field Definitions
    fields [
        SFRotation    rotation
    ]

    # Default Field Values
    rotation            0 0 1 0
}
```

The Scale Node

The *Scale* node defines a 3D scale factor. The first value specifies the scaling in the *x*-direction. The second value specifies the scaling in the *y*-direction. The last value specifies the scaling in the *z*-direction. A value of (1, 1, 1) results in no change to subsequent objects.

The definition of the *Scale* node follows:

```
# The definition of the Scale node
Scale {
    # Field Definitions
    fields [
        SFVec3f       scaleFactor
    ]
```

```
    # Default Field Values
    scaleFactor         1 1 1
}
```

The Transform Node

The *Transform* node is intended to reduce the several transformations that may be required to correctly position and scale an object into one node. The transformations are performed in the following order:

1. A translation operation is performed using the value of the *translation* field.
2. A translation operation is performed using the value of the *center* field.
3. A rotation operation is performed using the value of the *rotation* field.
4. A rotation operation is performed using the value of the *scaleOrientation* field.
5. A scale operation is performed using the value of the *scaleFactor* field.
6. A rotation operation is performed using –*scaleOrientation* value.
7. A translation operation is performed using –*translation* value.

The definition of the *Transform* node follows:

```
# The definition of the Transform node
Transform {
    # Field Definitions
    fields [
        SFVec3f         translation,
        SFRotation      rotation,
        SFVec3f         scaleFactor,
        SFRotation      scaleOrientation,
        SFVec3f         center
    ]

    # Default Field Values
    translation         0 0 0
    rotation            0 0 1 0
    scaleFactor         1 1 1
    scaleOrientation    0 0 1 0
    center              0 0 0
}
```

The Translation Node

The *Translation* node defines a translation vector. Its definition follows:

```
# The definition of the Translation node
Translation {
    # Field Definitions
    fields [
        SFVec3f translation
    ]

    # Default Field Values
    translation        0 0 0
}
```

Grouping Nodes

Grouping nodes serve two purposes. First, they are a convenient way of organizing VRML files for better readability. Second, they are a means of controlling the scoping of property and transformation nodes.

The Group Node

The *Group* node is a container for other nodes. It does not affect the scoping or state. Subsequent changes to the traversal state will remain visible outside of the *Group* node definition. **Note:** Using this node is discouraged. The node will be unavailable in a future definition of VRML.

The definition of the *Group* node follows:

```
# The definition of the Group node
Group {
    # A group may contain 0 or more node definitions
}
```

The Separator Node

The *Separator* node pushes the traversal state before traversing its children. The traversal state is popped after the children are traversed. This allows nodes that change the traversal state to be isolated from the rest of the scene. *Separator* nodes may perform render culling, thereby allowing the node to ignore during traversal children that will not be rendered. Render culling is specified by the *renderCulling* field variable and may be set to `ON`, `OFF`, or `AUTO` (the default).

The definition of the *Separator* node follows:

```
# The definition of the Separator node
Separator {
    # Field Definitions
    fields [
```

```
        SFEnum   renderCulling      #ON, OFF, AUTO
    ]

    # Default Field Values
    renderCulling     AUTO

    #A Separator may contain 0 or more node definitions
}
```

The Switch Node

The *Switch* node specifies which child will be traversed. In version 1.0, this node does not affect the scoping or the state. Subsequent change to the traversal state remains visible outside of the Group node definition. In version 1.1 and greater, this node will push and pop the state like a *Separator* node does.

The field variable *whichChild* selects the child or children that will be traversed. A value of –1 specifies that none of the children are to be traversed and –3 means all are to be. A value of 0 or greater specifies the child to be evaluated, where 0 means the first child is evaluated, 1 means the second child is evaluated, and so on.

The definition of the *Switch* node follows:

```
# The definition of the Switch node
Switch {
    # Field Definitions
    fields [
        SFLong  whichChild
    ]

    # Default Field Values
    whichChild -1

    # A Switch may contain 0 or more node definitions
}
```

The TransformSeparator Node

The *TransformSeparator* node pushes the current transformation matrix before traversing its children. The transformation matrix is popped after the children are traversed. This allows nodes that change the current transformation matrix to be isolated from the rest of the scene. **Note:** Using this node is discouraged. The node will be removed in a future definition of VRML.

The definition of the *TransformSeparator* node follows:

```
# The definition of the TransformSeparator node
TransformSeparator {
    # A TransformSeparator may contain 0 or
    # more node definitions
}
```

WWW Nodes

WWW (World Wide Web) nodes allow VRML to interact with the Web. Currently only two nodes of this type are defined in VRML:

1. The *WWWInline* node, which loads a VRML file from anywhere on the Web
2. The *WWWAnchor* node, which allows the user to select a VRML object that then "teleports" the user to a new VRML file located anywhere on the Web

The WWWInline Node

The *WWWInline* node is the equivalent of the #include in C/C++. It does an inline load using the URL specified by the name field variable. The time at which the data associated with a URL is loaded is undefined, thereby allowing browsers to implement an optimized loading mechanism.

The field variables *bboxSize* and *bboxCenter* allow the size and center of the *WWWInline* node to be determined without doing an inline load. The *bboxSize* variable gives an approximate size for the object, and the *bboxCenter* provides an approximate location. The result of specifying a non-VRML file in the URL is undefined.

The definition of the *WWInline* node follows:

```
# The definition of the WWWInline node
WWWInline {
    # Field Definitions
    fields [
        SFString        name,
        SFVec3f         bboxSize,
        SFVec3f         bboxCenter
    ]

    # Default Field Values
    name                ""
    bboxSize            0 0 0
    bboxCenter          0 0 0
}
```

The WWWAnchor Node

The *WWWAnchor* node behaves like a *Separator* node. It pushes the traversal state before traversing its children and then pops the state after the children have been traversed. This node allows a user of a VRML browser to select a child. How this selection is accomplished is up to the browser.

When a child is selected, the URL defined by the *name* field variable is loaded. If *name* is the null string, then no action occurs. The *description* field variable contains a string that might be more user friendly than the full URL. Use of this string is left up to the browser. The *map* field variable specifies whether the 3D coordinates of the object selected will be transmitted along with the URL using the syntax `"?x,y,z"`. The value `NONE` means the coordinates aren't passed; the value `POINT` means they are.

The definition of the *WWWAnchor* node follows:

```
# The definition of the WWWAnchor node
WWWAnchor {
    # Field Definitions
    fields [
        SFString        name,
        SFString        description,
        SFEnum          map            #NONE, POINT
    ]

    # Default Field Values
    name                ""
    description         ""
    map                 NONE

    # A WWWAnchor may contain 0 or more node definitions
}
```

State in a VRML File

The concept that the traversal of a VRML file maintains state may seem foreign at first. But it is a powerful concept that actually makes complex hierarchies easier to understand and the underlying software more straightforward to implement. It can be easily demonstrated with a small intuitive example.

Consider a simple VRML file that defines a Sphere and translates it from the origin to a new position. This is done via the following VRML language fragment:

```
Translation {
    translation 3 0 0}
```

```
}
Sphere {
    radius 2
}
```

This example may appear a bit odd at first because the translation is defined before the Sphere is. Think of it this way: There is always a transform matrix held in the current state. A translation node that is encountered is converted to an equivalent transform matrix, which is multiplied by the current transform matrix. The result is placed in the current transform matrix. Each new shape node encountered is then multiplied by the current transform matrix. In this case, if the initial transform matrix were the identity matrix, which is the default value, then the Sphere would be translated from the origin to the location (3, 0, 0).

The concept of state in a VRML file is equivalent to the concept of stacks in an Reverse Polish Notation (RPN) calculator. As with an RPN calculator, certain commands set the current state. Other commands allow the state to be pushed and popped. The following VRML nodes set the current state:

- *Coordinate3*
- *FontStyle*
- *Material*
- *MaterialBinding*
- *Normal*
- *NormalBinding*
- *Texture2*
- *Texture2Transform*
- *TextureCoordinate2*
- *ShapeHints*

Nodes that can save the current state are always grouping nodes. They allow the state to be modified for some local shape nodes without affecting the entire file.

The state is saved in some grouping nodes by pushing the current state on entry and popping the current state when leaving the group. This is very similar to how an RPN calculator saves a value by pushing it onto the stack and popping values off the stack after they are used. With an RPN calculator, however, the state is simply a numeric value. In VRML, the state embodies all of the information that can be used by subsequent nodes. Following are the nodes that push and pop the current traversal state of a VRML file:

- *Separator.* Pushes the current state on entry and pops the current state on exit.

- *TransformSeparator*. Pushes only the current transform matrix on entry and pops the current transform matrix on exit. It affects no other state.
- *WWWAnchor*. Pushes the current state on entry and pops the current state on exit.

A VRML file that pushes and pops the state can be easily demonstrated with this small intuitive example, a simple VRML file that defines a red Sphere and a green Cone:

```
Separator {
    # Define the surface color Red
    Material {
          ambientColor 0.1 0.0 0.0
          diffuseColor 0.7 0.0 0.0
    }
    Translation {
          translation 3 0 0
    }
    Sphere {
          radius 2
    }
}
Separator {
    # Define the surface color Green
    Material {
          ambientColor 0.0 0.1 0.0
          diffuseColor 0.0 0.7 0.0
    }
    Translation {
          translation -3 0 0
    }
    Cone {
          bottomRadius 2
          height 3
    }
}
```

Here, the material and translation definitions in each *Separator* node affect only nodes within the *Separator*. This is because the *Separator* node pushes the current state on entry and pops the current state on exit. Saving the state in this manner allows the material nodes and the translation nodes to be applied only to the subsequent shape nodes within the *Separator* node and not influence any other nodes outside the *Separator* node.

Implementing a VRML Reader

The VRML reader described in this chapter differs slightly in architecture from that of the readers described in subsequent chapters. Typically a reader has two tasks: First, read the data from the file, and second, convert that data into the internal representation for the program. How difficult it is to convert into the internal representation depends on how much the model embodied by the file format differs from the model embodied by the internal representation. For most of the formats in this book, this difference adds additional steps to the conversion process. However, for VRML the model embodied in the internal representation is the same as the model of the file format.

The design of the classes used for describing the internal data representation were created with VRML in mind. This is mainly because VRML is "hot." And VRML is hot because the Internet is hot. VRML is a 3D file format that most vendors of 3D applications will likely have to support. Making the core representation of the code map one-to-one with VRML makes it much easier for the code to track with the fast-moving VRML standard. A lesser but still important reason for a VRML-like core representation is that mapping a VRML-style internal representation to OpenGL function calls is very easy. Hence displaying the internal representation as a wireframe or solid model is straightforward and porting it is simple.

Currently there is a class library that reads VRML files. Called QvLib, it is freely available on the Web. Its implementation is very different from the class library implementation described here. QvLib is a C++ class library intended to represent only VRML; its VRML reader is embedded directly in the class library. In contrast, the internal representation used here separates the reader from the class library representation. Doing this has several advantages. The reader described in this section is written using the parser generation tools Bison and Flex. These tools allow complicated new language features to be added in a more straightforward manner. For example, suppose a future version of VRML added algebraic expressions. Adding this feature to QvLib would be very difficult, while adding it to this code would be simple.

VRML Reader Design

The VRML reader implemented in this chapter is made of three parts:

1. A Flex lexical analyzer
2. A Bison parser
3. Symbol tables

The Flex lexical analyzer reads the file and converts keywords, numbers, and symbols into tokens. The Bison parser interprets each of these tokens and determines whether the token is either an appropriate part of the VRML grammar or a syntax error.

There are four symbol tables in the VRML parser, one each for looking up (a) VRML keywords, (b) predefined numeric symbols (the define table), (c) named instances of language constructs (the uses table), and (d) one that contains the information about each VRML language construct (the node table). Figure 3.2 illustrates the relationship between these constructs. Some of the information in the symbol tables, such as named nodes, is created at runtime. Most symbol tables are used by both the lexical analyzer and the parser. The lexical analyzer uses them to look up keywords and tokens. The parser may add new tokens to some of the symbol tables as new VRML components are defined.

```
Title: D:\CDROM\book\chapter3\krch03_2.eps
Creator:  ImageMark Software Labs
CreationDate:  () ()
```

Figure 3.2. Parser organization.

The grammar for the VRML file format was described earlier in this chapter. Even though the VRML language is fairly large, the grammar for it is actually quite small. This is because the VRML language was designed to be extensible. Many VRML features thought of as built-in can actually be implemented as if they were defined using the extensibility of the VRML language. Doing this separates the bulk of the language features from the base VRML grammar.

Implementing the VRML Lexical Analyzer

The VRML lexical analyzer has to recognize only these constructs: a VRML comment, whitespace, newlines, decimal integers, octal integers, hexadecimal integers, real numbers, quoted strings, predefined keywords, symbols, and identifiers. This number of lexical constructs is small for a language with the capabilities of VRML. Such efficiency says a lot about the abilities of the architects of the Open Inventor language and the VRML language.

Each regular expression has a C/C++ production function that is executed when it is recognized. Table 3.2 describes each regular expression in the lexical analyzer and the corresponding C/C++ action that is taken.

Table 3.2. Regular expressions in the lexical analyzer and the corresponding C/C++ actions

	Expression	Corresponding C/C++ Action
VRML Identification	`"#VRML V1.0 ascii" | "#VRML V1.1 utf8"`	Matches the legitimate VRML file headers. All VRML files begin with one of these literal strings.
Recognizing Comments	`"#" [^\n\r]*`	Matches an occurrence of the # symbol and matches all the subsequent characters up to the next newline. This production is empty because comments are ignored.
Recognizing Whitespace	`[ \t]+`	Matches either a space or a tab. These characters are ignored. Their primary function, from a lexical analysis point of view, is to provide a separation between tokens. Of course, from a language usability point of view, whitespace allows the language to be organized in a more human-readable fashion.
Recognizing Newlines	`"\n" | "\r\n" | "\n\r" | "\r"`	Matches newlines. It may seem strange for a PC program to recognize so many forms of newlines. However, it is important to remember that VRML is a multiplatform language. Many computer platforms have different line-end indicators. We need to be able to read VRML files without having to alter them for the platform to which they have been moved. This expression covers any case that is likely to occur. These characters are ignored and function as whitespace.
Recognizing Integers	`-?[0-9][0-9]*` `0[1-7][0-7]*` `0x[0-9a-fA-F]+`	VRML files can have these representations of an integer value: decimal, octal, and hexadecimal. These regular expressions recognize the different numeric bases and convert them into an integer value, which is returned with an `INTEGERVAL_TOK`.
Recognizing Floating-Point Values	`-?[0-9]*\.?[0-9]*([eE][-+]?[0-9]+)?`	Recognizes floating-point values. This production converts the ASCII floating-point representation into an *SFFloat*, which is returned to the parser with an `DOUBLEVAL_TOK` token.

Table 3.2. Regular expressions in the lexical analyzer and the corresponding C/C++ actions *(continued)*

	Expression	Corresponding C/C++ Action
Recognizing Strings	`\"(\\.|[^\"])*\"`	Recognizes a double-quoted string. The code associated with this regular expression converts the escaped characters into their equivalent values. The resultant string is returned with the `STRINGVAL_TOK` token.
Recognizing Keywords, Symbols, and Identifiers	`[a-zA-Z0-9_+]+`	Recognizes character strings. This production handles the symbol table lookup for the lexical analyzer. The string found is compared with the keywords and symbols. If it matches either, the value and token associated with that keyword or symbol is returned. Otherwise, the string is returned with the `ID_TOK` token.

Initializing the Lexical Analyzer

Often GNU Flex and GNU Bison are used in programs that parse a file to completion and then the program terminates. However, this lexical analyzer needs to work in an interactive environment where the parser may be envoked many times. To allow the parser to be called repeatedly a function `void yyinit(FILE*)` called prior to the calling of the parser. This is because, first, the keyword symbol table must be initialized properly before it is used and, second, the lexical analyzer must be reset to function properly in subsequent invocations.

Flex Source for the VRML Lexical Analyzer

The following source code is the file wrl_lex.l. It is processed by Flex, which converts it into a C language file:

```
%{
#include <ctype.h>
#include <string.h>
#include <stdlib.h>
#include <stddef.h>
#include <io.h>
#include "symtbl.h"
#include "wrl.h"
```

```
/*
 * Define struct that holds the keyword
 * symbol table. Using a keyword table such
 * as this is usually the simplest way to
 * handle keywords in a lex/flex based lexical
 * analyzer.
 */
typedef struct KEYWORD {
    char*              name;
    int                        value;
    struct KEYWORD*    next;
} KEYWORD;

/*
 * This array of symbols contains the key words found
 * in the wrl file. A yyhash table is created out of these
 * values and checked each time an identifier is found.
 * The result of doing this is a smaller and faster lexer.
 */
static KEYWORD  yysymbols[] = {
    "DEF",             DEF_TOK,           (KEYWORD *) NULL,
    "fields",          FIELDS_TOK,        (KEYWORD *) NULL,
    "USE",             USE_TOK,           (KEYWORD *) NULL,
    "SFBitMask",       SFBITMASK_TOK,     (KEYWORD *) NULL,
    "SFBool",          SFBOOL_TOK,        (KEYWORD *) NULL,
    "SFColor",         SFCOLOR_TOK,       (KEYWORD *) NULL,
    "SFColor",         SFCOLOR_TOK,       (KEYWORD *) NULL,
    "SFEnum",          SFENUM_TOK,        (KEYWORD *) NULL,
    "SFFloat",         SFFLOAT_TOK,       (KEYWORD *) NULL,
    "SFImage",         SFIMAGE_TOK,       (KEYWORD *) NULL,
    "SFLong",          SFLONG_TOK,        (KEYWORD *) NULL,
    "SFMatrix",        SFMATRIX_TOK,      (KEYWORD *) NULL,
    "SFRotation",      SFROTATION_TOK,    (KEYWORD *) NULL,
    "SFString",        SFSTRING_TOK,      (KEYWORD *) NULL,
    "SFVec2f",         SFVEC2F_TOK,       (KEYWORD *) NULL,
    "SFVec3f",         SFVEC3F_TOK,       (KEYWORD *) NULL,
    "MFColor",         MFCOLOR_TOK,       (KEYWORD *) NULL,
    "MFLong",          MFLONG_TOK,        (KEYWORD *) NULL,
    "MFVec2f",         MFVEC2F_TOK,       (KEYWORD *) NULL,
    "MFVec3f",         MFVEC3F_TOK,       (KEYWORD *) NULL,
    "MFString",        MFSTRING_TOK,      (KEYWORD *) NULL,
};

/* Calculates the number of keywords */
#define NUMOFKEYWORDS(sizeof(yysymbols)/sizeof(KEYWORD))

/* Calculates a reasonable hash table size */
#define LEX_HASHSIZE(NUMOFKEYWORDS+NUMOFKEYWORDS/4)
```

```
/* Hash table for keywords */
KEYWORD*        yyhashTbl[LEX_HASHSIZE] = {NULL};

/* number of lines read */
long            yylineno = 1;

/* Forward for Keyword lookup function */
static KEYWORD*yylookUp(char*);
%

%%

"#VRML V1.0 ascii" |
"#VRML V1.1 utf8"    {return VRMLHEADER_TOK;}

"#"[^\n\r]*          {/* ignore comments */;}
[ \t]+               {/* ignore whitespace */;}
"\n"|"\r\n"|"\n\r"|"\r"
    {
        yylineno++;
        if (toplevel != NULL) {
            /*
             * Calculate the
             * percentage of the file
             * that has been read at
             * the end of each line.
             */
            toplevel->StatusMessage(
                "Read %6.1f%% complete",
                ((double)ftell(yyin))/
                    ((double) fileSize)*
                            100.0);
        }
    }

-?[0-9][0-9]*
    {
        long  value;
        sscanf(yytext, "%ld", &value);
        yylval.sflong = value;
        return INTEGERVAL_TOK;
    }

0[1-7][0-7]*
    {
        long  value;
        sscanf(yytext, "%lo", &value);
        yylval.sflong = value;
```

```
            return INTEGERVAL_TOK;
    }

0x[0-9a-fA-F]+
    {
            long  value;
            scanf(yytext, "0x%lx", &value);
            yylval.sflong = value;
            return INTEGERVAL_TOK;
    }

-?[0-9]*\.?[0-9]*([eE][-+]?[0-9]+)?
    {
            double      value;
            scanf(yytext, "%lf", &value);
            yylval.sffloat = value;
            return DOUBLEVAL_TOK;
    }

[a-zA-Z0-9_+]+
          {
            KEYWORD*            np;
            NodeBodyDecl*       nbp;
            FieldDecl*          fdp;
            Define*             dfp;

            /* Lookup keyword */
            if ((np=yylookUp((char *) yytext)) != NULL) {
                  return np->value;
            }

            /* Lookup a defined value */
            if ((dfp = LookupDefine(yytext)) != NULL) {
                  switch (dfp->Type()) {
                  case SFLONG_TOK:
                        yylval.sflong = (SFLong) (*dfp);
                        return INTEGERVAL_TOK;
                  case SFFLOAT_TOK:
                        yylval.sffloat = (SFFloat) (*dfp);
                        return DOUBLEVAL_TOK;
                  case SFSTRING_TOK:
                        yylval.sfstring = (SFString) (*dfp);
                        return STRINGVAL_TOK;
                  }
            }

            /* Lookup a node name */
            if((nbp = LookupNode(yytext)) != NULL) {
```

```
        yylval.nodesym = nbp;
        if (yylval.nodesym->AllowChildren()) {
            return NODEWITHCHILDSYM_TOK;
        }
        return NODESYM_TOK;
}

/* Lookup a field name */
if ((fdp = LookupField(yytext)) != NULL) {
        yylval.fieldsym = fdp;
        switch (yylval.fieldsym->type) {
        case SFBITMASK_TOK:
            return SFBITMASK_FIELDSYM_TOK;
        case SFBOOL_TOK:
            return SFBOOL_FIELDSYM_TOK;
        case SFCOLOR_TOK:
            return SFCOLOR_FIELDSYM_TOK;
        case SFENUM_TOK:
            return SFENUM_FIELDSYM_TOK;
        case SFFLOAT_TOK:
            return SFFLOAT_FIELDSYM_TOK;
        case SFIMAGE_TOK:
            return SFIMAGE_FIELDSYM_TOK;
        case SFLONG_TOK:
            return SFLONG_FIELDSYM_TOK;
        case SFSTRING_TOK:
            return SFSTRING_FIELDSYM_TOK;
        case SFVEC2F_TOK:
            return SFVEC2F_FIELDSYM_TOK;
        case SFVEC3F_TOK:
            return SFVEC3F_FIELDSYM_TOK;
        case SFROTATION_TOK:
            return SFROTATION_FIELDSYM_TOK;
        case SFMATRIX_TOK:
            return SFMATRIX_FIELDSYM_TOK;
        case MFCOLOR_TOK:
            return MFCOLOR_FIELDSYM_TOK;
        case MFLONG_TOK:
            return MFLONG_FIELDSYM_TOK;
        case MFVEC2F_TOK:
            return MFVEC2F_FIELDSYM_TOK;
        case MFVEC3F_TOK:
            return MFVEC3F_FIELDSYM_TOK;
        case MFSTRING_TOK:
            return MFSTRING_FIELDSYM_TOK;
        case MFFLOAT_TOK:
            return MFFLOAT_FIELDSYM_TOK;
        }
}
```

```
                /*
                 * Didn't find string in a symbol table
                 * so must be a new ID.
                 */
                yylval.sfstring = new char[strlen(yytext)+1];
                strcpy(yylval.sfstring, yytext);

                return ID_TOK;
        }

\"(\\.|[^\"])*\"
        {
                int i, j;
                int length = strlen((char *) yytext)-2;
                yylval.sfstring = new char[length+1];
                strncpy(yylval.sfstring, (char *) &yytext[1],
                        length);
                yylval.sfstring[length] = '\0';

                /* Handle escape characters in the string */
                for (i = 0; i < length; i++) {
                        if (yylval.sfstring[i] == '\\') {
                                switch (yylval.sfstring[i+1]) {
                                case 'n':
                                        yylval.sfstring[i] = '\n';
                                        for (j=i+1; j < length; j++) {
                                                yylval.sfstring[j] =
                                                        yylval.sfstring[j+1]
                                                ;
                                        }
                                        break;
                                case 'r':
                                        yylval.sfstring[i] = '\r';
                                        for (j=i+1; j < length; j++) {
                                                yylval.sfstring[j] =
                                                        yylval.sfstring[j+1]
                                                ;
                                        }
                                        break;
                                case 't':
                                        yylval.sfstring[i] = '\t';
                                        for (j=i+1; j < length; j++) {
                                                yylval.sfstring[j] =
                                                        yylval.sfstring[j+1]
                                                ;
                                        }
                                        break;
                                default:
```

```
                                for (j=i; j < length; j++) {
                                      yylval.sfstring[j] =
                                            yylval.sfstring[j+1]
                                      ;
                                }
                                break;
                          }
                    }
              }
              return STRINGVAL_TOK;
        }

.       {
              return yytext[0];
        }

%%

/* Calculate the hash value for a string */
static int
yyhash(char *s)
{
    int yyhashval;

    for (yyhashval=0; *s != '\0';) {
          yyhashval += *s++;
    }
    return (yyhashval % LEX_HASHSIZE);
}

/* Lookup string in keyword hash table */
static KEYWORD*
yylookUp(char *s)
{
    KEYWORD *np;

    for (np=yyhashTbl[yyhash(s)]; np != (KEYWORD *) NULL;
          np = np->next) {
          if (strcmp(s, np->name) == 0) {
                return np;
          }
    }
    return (KEYWORD *) NULL;
}

/* Initialize the hash table */
void
yyinitHash()
```

```
{
    int i, yyhashval;

    for (i=0; i < LEX_HASHSIZE; i++) {
          yyhashTbl[i] = NULL;
    }

    for (i=0; i < NUMOFKEYWORDS; i++) {
          yysymbols[i].next = NULL;
          yyhashval = yyhash(yysymbols[i].name);
          yysymbols[i].next = yyhashTbl[yyhashval];
          yyhashTbl[yyhashval] = &yysymbols[i];
    }
}

/*
 * Initialize the lexical analyzer. Notice that
 * calling the lexical analyzer a second time causes
 * a different behavior. Calling yyrestart() on subsequent
 * invocations reinitializes the internal state of the
 * lexical analyzer.
 */
void
yyinit(FILE* fp)
{
    static int firstflag = TRUE;
    yyinitHash();
    if (!firstflag) {
          yyrestart(yyin=fp);
    } else {
          yyin = fp;
          firstflag = FALSE;
    }
    ylineno = 1;
}
```

Implementing the VRML Parser

This VRML parser has been implemented using Bison. To generate a parser, Bison takes in a file using the Bison language syntax that describes the grammar of the language to be parsed. The GNU Bison language is a combination of BNF language productions and C/C++ code. After Bison has read the grammar description, it emits two files: a C/C++ source file and a C/C++ header file. These files are then compiled using a C/C++ compiler along with the lexical analyzer and any other required files to create an executable parser.

The Bison Grammar File Organization

A Bison grammar description file has the following structure:

```
%{
    /* includes, type, and global variable declarations */
%}

%union {
    /*
     * The type and symbolic name of values that can be
     * passed from the lexical analyzer or Bison
     * productions.
     */
}

%token      /*
             * Defines tokens that are returned from
             * the lexical analyzer and the tokens' return
             * type.
             */

%type       /*
             * Defines the BNF production names and the
             * data types returned by the production.
             */

%%

/* BNF style productions */

%%

/* Additional C/C++ code */
```

Representing the Key VRML Data Types

The key to understanding the Bison grammar is understanding the types the grammar uses in the `%union` declaration. These types represent the core features of the VRML parser. The `%union` definition in the VRML file is as follows:

```
%union {
    SFString        sfstring;
    SFFloat         sffloat;
    SFLong          sflong;
    SFVec2f*        sfvec2f;
    SFVec3f*        sfvec3f;
```

```
    SFRotation*        sfrotation;
    SFMatrix*          sfmatrix;
    MFString*          mfstring;
    MFFloat*           mffloat;
    MFLong*            mflong;
    MFVec2f*           mfvec2f;
    MFVec3f*           mfvec3f;
    GNode*             node;
    NodeBodyDecl*      nodesym;
    FieldDecl*         fieldsym;
}
```

The first three types in the union are *sfstring*, *sffloat*, and *sflong*. These are the basic data types that are returned by the lexical analyzer. If you look closely at the implementation of the integer, real, and string portions of the parser, you should see a C/C++ line in the regular expression production that looks like `'yylval.sflong = value;'`. This C/C++ statement assigns the value found by the lexical analyzer to the value for the token being returned. This is how Flex communicates values to Bison.

The types *sfvec2f*, *sfvec3f*, *sfrotation*, *sfmatrix*, *mfstring*, *mffloat*, *mflong*, *mfvec3f*, and *mfvec2f* are composite types constructed by the parser. A composite type is made up of *sfstring*, *sffloat*, or *sflong* types. An example of how a composite type is defined is demonstrated in the *SFVec3f* production:

```
SFVec3f:          SFFloat SFFloat SFFloat
                  {$$ = new SFVec3f($1, $2, $3);}
    ;
```

The production is used in the Bison grammar description wherever the next value should be interpreted as an *SFVec3f* type. This production reads the next three floating-point values and constructs a new *SFVec3f* type, which is returned.

The last three type definitions in the `%union` declaration are responsible for much of the magic in the Bison parser:

- *node*. Holds an instance of a VRML language construct.
- *nodesym*. Contains the symbol information about a VRML language construct, such as how to create a *node* instance of the construct or the number of fields and the type of fields in the *node*.
- *fieldsym*. Contains the symbolic information for each field in a *node* instance.

Node Instances

Recall from Chapter 2 that for the internal representation, each VRML language construct is mapped directly to a C++ class. The representation's base class is *GNode*. All VRML language-based classes are derived from this class. Examples of some derived classes are *GSeparator*, *GCoordinate3*, and *GIndexedFaceSet*. So a *node* value is an instance of any VRML-equivalent language construct that has an C++ class definition in the internal representation.

Nodesym Instances

Nodesym values are the instances of the symbol table representation for each VRML language construct supported by the parser. Instances to these elements are returned by the lexical analyzer when keywords such as *Separator*, *Coordinate3*, and *GIndexedFaceSet* are encountered at runtime. Each *nodesym* instance has a generic interface to create a new *GNode* instance for the language construct. It also has a generic interface to identify field variables of the VRML language construct.

FieldDecl Instances

A *fieldDecl* value is also returned by the lexical analyzer. The symbol table lookup in the analyzer also checks the field symbols defined for the current VRML language construct. If a match is found, then an instance to a *fielddecl* is returned. This allows the field values assigned to a VRML language construct to be identified and handled appropriately at runtime.

Making Sense of the Bison VRML Grammar

The grammar in the Bison VRML parser is really quite small. However, if you were to look at the Bison source code, you might not get that impression. In this section, I discuss each production and the semantics associated with it.

Consider the following two productions:

```
start:          VRMLHeader Nodes
    ;

Nodes:          /* empty */
    |           Nodes Node
    ;
```

These define the body of a VRML file. They state that a VRML file must first define a VRML header literal string that is followed by zero or more *Node* definitions. The C/C++ actions for the production *Nodes* simply concatenate the node instances together. The C/C++ action for `start` simply places the top-level node instance in the variable *root*.

The next production defines what a *Node* looks like:

```
Node:          NodeBody
    |          DEF_TOK ID_TOK NodeBody
    |          USE_TOK ID_TOK
    ;
```

A *Node* is either a '*NodeBody*,' a '`DEF` *`name`* *NodeBody*', or a '`USE` *`name`*' construct. The C/C++ action for the '*NodeBody*' is to pass the associated node instance through. The C/C++ action for '`DEF` *`name`* *NodeBody*' is to add the node instance to the uses symbol table and then to pass through the instance variable for *NodeBody*. The C/C++ action for the '`USE` *`name`*' construct is to look up the name in the uses symbol table, duplicate the node instance associated with the symbol table entry, and then pass the duplicated node instance through the production.

The following productions come next:

```
NodeBody:      ID_TOK '{' FieldSpecs FieldUsage Nodes '}'
    |          NODESYM_TOK '{' FieldSpecs FieldUsage '}'
    |          NODEWITHCHILDSYM_TOK
               '{' FieldSpecs FieldUsage Nodes '}'
    ;
```

The *NodeBody* production defines the general organization of each VRML language construct. The first construct is "`ID_TOK '{' FieldSpecs FieldUsage Nodes '}'`." It allows unrecognized language constructs to be defined. The inclusion of the *NodeBody* production is one reason VRML is so extensible.

The next production is "`NODESYM_TOK '{' FieldSpecs FieldUsage '}'`." This production recognizes VRML language constructs that have no child fields. For example, VRML language constructs such as Cone, Cylinder, or Sphere are examples of constructs with no children. The C/C++ action for this part of the production results in the creation of a node instance for this language construct and initializes the fields associated with this production to their default values. A `NODESYM_TOK` is returned by the lexical analyzers.

The final part of this production is "`NODEWITHCHILDSYM_TOK '{' FieldSpecs FieldUsage Nodes '}'`." It recognizes VRML language constructs that have children. An example of a language construct with a child is a Separator or Group construct. The C/C++ action for this part of the production is similar to the NODESYM_TOK action. The only substantial difference is that children are allowed.

The next several productions deal with fields within a VRML language construct:

```
FieldSpecs:       /* empty */
    |             FIELDS_TOK '[' FieldDefs ']'
    ;

FieldDefs:        FiedDef
    |             FieldDefs ',' FieldDef
    ;

FieldDef:         type ID_TOK
    |             type Fieldtype

FieldType:        SFBITMASK_FIELDSYM_TOK
    |             SFBOOL_FIELDSYM_TOK
                        .
                        .
                        .
    |             MFFLOAT_FIELDSYM_TOK
    ;

type:             SFBITMASK_TOK
    |             SFBOOL_TOK
                        .
                        .
                        .
    |             MFFLOAT_TOK
    ;
```

The FieldSpecs production allows new field variables to be defined. This is useful when creating new language constructs or extending the behavior of old constructs.

Next comes the FieldDecl production, which recognizes and evaluates fields within the current language construct:

```
FieldDecl:        SFBITMASK_FIELDSYM_TOK BitMaskExpr
    |             SFBOOL_FIELDSYM_TOK SFBool
                        .
                        .
                        .
    |             SFIMAGE_FIELDSYM_TOK SFImage
    ;
```

```
BitMaskExpr:      '(' BitMaskExpr ')'
    |             BitMaskExpr '|' BitMaskExpr
    |             SFLong
    ;
```

Notice that the C/C++ action for all of the productions within `FieldDecl` are identical. This is because all *GNode* instances have the `SetField()` member function. This function recognizes the field names that are acceptable to the *GNode* instance and sets the corresponding internal value.

The remaining productions define the data types that are recognized by the VRML language:

```
SFBool:           SFLong
    ;

SFEnum:           SFLong
    ;

SFLong:           INTEGERVAL_TOK
    ;

SFString:         STRINGVAL_TOK
    ;

SFColor:          SFVec3f
    ;

SFFloat:          DOUBLEVAL_TOK
    ;

              .
              .
              .

MFLong:           SFLong
    |             '[' MFLongList OptComma ']'
    ;

MFLongList:       SFLong
    |             MFLongList ',' SFLong
    ;

              .
              .
              .
```

Bison Source for the VRML Parser

The GNU Bison VRML parser follows. This file contains both the grammar productions and the C/C++ actions.

```
%{

#include <stdio.h>
#include <stdlib.h>
#include <string.h>
#include <ctype.h>
#include <stdarg.h>
#include "symtbl.h"
#include "wrl.h"

extern long     yylineno;
GNode*          root = NULL;
GNode*          coord3 = NULL;

%}

%union {
    SFString            sfstring;
    SFFloat             sffloat;
    SFLong              sflong;
    SFVec2f*            sfvec2f;
    SFVec3f*            sfvec3f;
    SFRotation*         sfrotation;
    SFMatrix*           sfmatrix;
    SFString*           mfstring;
    MFFloat*            mffloat;
    MFLong*             mflong;
    MFVec2f*            mfvec2f;
    MFVec3f*            mfvec3f;
    GNode*              node;
    NodeBodyDecl*       nodesym;
    FieldDecl*          fieldsym;
}

%token                  VRMLHEADER_TOK
%token    <sffloat>     DOUBLEVAL_TOK
%token    <sfstring>    ID_TOK STRINGVAL_TOK
%token    <sflong>      INTEGERVAL_TOK
%token                  DEF_TOK USE_TOK
%token                  FIELDS_TOK
%token                  SFBITMASK_TOK SFBOOL_TOK SFCOLOR_TOK
%token                  SFENUM_TOK SFFLOAT_TOK SFIMAGE_TOK
%token                  SFLONG_TOK SFMATRIX_TOK SFROTATION_TOK
```

```
%token                  SFSTRING_TOK SFVEC2F_TOK SFVEC3F_TOK
%token                  MFCOLOR_TOK MFLONG_TOK MFVEC2F_TOK
%token                  MFVEC3F_TOK
%token                  MFSTRING_TOK MFFLOAT_TOK
%token     <fieldsym>   SFBITMASK_FIELDSYM_TOK
%token     <fieldsym>   SFBOOL_FIELDSYM_TOK
%token     <fieldsym>   SFCOLOR_FIELDSYM_TOK
%token     <fieldsym>   SFENUM_FIELDSYM_TOK
%token     <fieldsym>   SFFLOAT_FIELDSYM_TOK
%token     <fieldsym>   SFIMAGE_FIELDSYM_TOK
%token     <fieldsym>   SFLONG_FIELDSYM_TOK
%token     <fieldsym>   SFMATRIX_FIELDSYM_TOK
%token     <fieldsym>   SFROTATION_FIELDSYM_TOK
%token     <fieldsym>   SFSTRING_FIELDSYM_TOK
%token     <fieldsym>   SFVEC2F_FIELDSYM_TOK
%token     <fieldsym>   SFVEC3F_FIELDSYM_TOK
%token     <fieldsym>   MFCOLOR_FIELDSYM_TOK
%token     <fieldsym>   MFLONG_FIELDSYM_TOK
%token     <fieldsym>   MFVEC2F_FIELDSYM_TOK
%token     <fieldsym>   MFVEC3F_FIELDSYM_TOK
%token     <fieldsym>   MFSTRING_FIELDSYM_TOK
%token     <fieldsym>   MFFLOAT_FIELDSYM_TOK
%token     <nodesym>    NODESYM_TOK NODEWITHCHILDSYM_TOK

%type      <sflong>     type
%type      <fieldsym>   FieldType
%type      <node>       NodeBody Node Nodes
%type      <sfvec2f>    SFVec2f
%type      <sfvec3f>    SFVec3f SFColor
%type      <sflong>     SFBool SFEnum SFLong BitMaskExpr
%type      <sffloat>    SFFloat
%type      <sfstring>   SFString
%type      <sfrotation>SFRotation
%type      <sfmatrix>   SFMatrix
%type      <mflong>     MFLong MFLongList
%type      <mfstring>   MFString MFStringList
%type      <mffloat>    MFFloat MFFloatList
%type      <mfvec2f>    MFVec2f MFVec2fList
%type      <mfvec3f>    MFVec3f MFVec3fList MFColor

%left      '|'

%%

start:     VRMLHEADER_TOK Nodes
           {
                 root = $2;
           }
```

```
    ;

Nodes:    /* empty */{$$ = NULL;}
    |     Nodes Node
          {
                if ($1 != NULL) {
                      if ($2 != NULL) {
                            $1->AppendAtLast($2);
                      }
                      $$ = $1;
                } else if ($2 != NULL) {
                      $$ = $2;
                } else {
                      $$ = NULL;
                }
          }
    ;

Node:     NodeBody            {$$ = $1;}
    |     DEF_TOK ID_TOK NodeBody
          {
                Uses* up = (Uses*) uses_table.Lookup($2);
                if (up == NULL) {
                      uses_table.Add(new Uses($2, $3));
                } else {
                      up->node($3);
                }
                $$ = $3;
                if ($3 != NULL) {
                      $3->SetName($2);
                }
          }
    |     USE_TOK     ID_TOK
          {
                GNode*      np =
                      ((Uses*)
                      uses_table.Lookup($2))->node();
                if (np != NULL) {
                      $$ = np->Copy();
                } else {
                      $$ = NULL;
                }
          }
    ;

NodeBody: ID_TOK
          {
```

```
            PushNodeDecl(AddNode($1));
        }
        '{' FieldSpecs FieldUsage Nodes '}'
        {
            PopNodeDecl();
            $$ = NULL;
        }
    |   NODESYM_TOK
        {
            NodeBodyDecl*     nbp = $1;
            short fieldcnt = nbp->Elements();
            NodeCreateFunc    func;

            PushNodeDecl($1);
            func = $1->NodeFunc();
            if (func != NULL) {
                GNode*      np = (*func)();
                if (np != NULL) {
                    np->Parent(CurrentNode());
                }
                PushNode(np);
                /* add default values to the node */
                for (int i=0; i < fieldcnt; i++) {
                    FieldDecl*fp = (*nbp)[i];
                    if (fp != NULL && np != NULL) {
                        switch (fp->type) {
                        case SFLONG_TOK:
                            np->SetField(
                                fp->name,
                                fp->u.sflong);
                            break;
                        case SFFLOAT_TOK:
                            np->SetField(
                                fp->name,
                                fp->u.sffloat
                                );
                            break;
                        case SFSTRING_TOK:
                            np->SetField(
                                fp->name,
                                fp->u.sfstring
                                );
                            break;
                        case SFVEC3F_TOK:
                            np->SetField(
                                fp->name,
                                fp->u.sfvec3f
                                );
```

```
                                        break;
                                case SFVEC2F_TOK:
                                        np->SetField(
                                                fp->name,
                                                fp->u.sfvec2f
                                                );
                                        break;
                                case SFMATRIX_TOK:
                                        np->SetField(
                                                fp->name,
                                                fp->u.sfmatrix
                                                );
                                        break;
                                case MFLONG_TOK:
                                        np->SetField(
                                                fp->name,
                                                fp->u.mflong);
                                        break;
                                case MFFLOAT_TOK:
                                        np->SetField(
                                                fp->name,
                                                fp->u.mffloat
                                                );
                                        break;
                                case MFVEC2F_TOK:
                                        np->SetField(
                                                fp->name,
                                                fp->u.mfvec2f
                                                );
                                        break;
                                case MFVEC3F_TOK:
                                        np->SetField(
                                                fp->name,
                                                fp->u.mfvec3f
                                                );
                                        break;
                                }
                        }
                }
        } else {
                PushNode(NULL);
        }
}
'{' FieldSpecs FieldUsage '}'
{
        PopNodeDecl();
        $$ = CurrentNode();
        PopNode();
```

```
        }
|       NODEWITHCHILDSYM_TOK
        {
              NodeBodyDecl*      nbp = $1;
              short fieldcnt = nbp->Elements();
              NodeCreateFunc     func;
              PushNodeDecl($1);
              func = $1->NodeFunc();
              coord3 = NULL;
              if (func != NULL) {
                    GNode*       np = (*func)();
                    if (np != NULL) {
                          np->Parent(CurrentNode());
                    }
                    PushNode(np);
                    /* add default values to the node */
                    for (int i=0; i < fieldcnt; i++) {
                          FieldDecl*fp = (*nbp)[i];
                          if (fp != NULL && np != NULL) {
                                switch (fp->type) {
                                case SFLONG_TOK:
                                      np->SetField(
                                            fp->name,
                                            fp->u.sflong
                                            );
                                      break;
                                case SFFLOAT_TOK:
                                      np->SetField(
                                            fp->name,
                                            fp->u.sffloat
                                            );
                                      break;
                                case SFSTRING_TOK:
                                      np->SetField(
                                            fp->name,
                                            fp->u.sfstring
                                            );
                                      break;
                                case SFVEC3F_TOK:
                                      np->SetField(
                                            fp->name,
                                            fp->u.sfvec3f
                                            );
                                      break;
                                case SFVEC2F_TOK:
                                      np->SetField(
                                            fp->name,
                                            fp->u.sfvec2f
```

```
                                        );
                                break;
                        case SFMATRIX_TOK:
                                np->SetField(
                                        fp->name,
                                        fp->u.sfmatrix
                                        );
                                break;
                        case MFLONG_TOK:
                                np->SetField(
                                        fp->name,
                                        fp->u.mflong
                                        );
                                break;
                        case MFFLOAT_TOK:
                                np->SetField(
                                        fp->name,
                                        fp->u.mffloat
                                        );
                                break;
                        case MFVEC2F_TOK:
                                np->SetField(
                                        fp->name,
                                        fp->u.mfvec2f
                                        );
                                break;
                        case MFVEC3F_TOK:
                                np->SetField(
                                        fp->name,
                                        fp->u.mfvec3f
                                        );
                                break;
                        }
                }
        }
    } else {
        PushNode(NULL);
    }
}
'{' FieldSpecs FieldUsage Nodes '}'
{
    GNode*      np = CurrentNode();

    if (np != NULL) {
        if ($6 != NULL) {
            np->AddChild($6);
            $6->Parent(np);
        }
```

```
                }

                PopNodeDecl();
                $$ = CurrentNode();
                PopNode();
          }
    ;

FieldSpecs:     /* empty */
    |           FIELDS_TOK '[' FieldDefs ']'
    ;

FieldDefs:      FieldDef
    |           FieldDefs ',' FieldDed
    ;

FieldDef: type ID_TOK
          {
                NodeBodyDecl* np = CurrentNodeDecl();

                if (np != NULL) {
                      FieldDecl* fp = np->LookupField($2);
                      if (fp == NULL) {
                            np->AddField($2, $1);
                      }
                }
          }
    |     type FieldType
          {
                $2->type = $1;
          }
    ;

FieldType: SFBITMASK_FIELDSYM_TOK
    |     SFBOOL_FIELDSYM_TOK
    |     SFCOLOR_FIELDSYM_TOK
    |     SFENUM_FIELDSYM_TOK
    |     SFFLOAT_FIELDSYM_TOK
    |     SFIMAGE_FIELDSYM_TOK
    |     SFLONG_FIELDSYM_TOK
    |     SFMATRIX_FIELDSYM_TOK
    |     SFROTATION_FIELDSYM_TOK
    |     SFSTRING_FIELDSYM_TOK
    |     SFVEC2F_FIELDSYM_TOK
    |     SFVEC3F_FIELDSYM_TOK
    |     MFCOLOR_FIELDSYM_TOK
    |     MFLONG_FIELDSYM_TOK
    |     MFVEC2F_FIELDSYM_TOK
```

```
    |       MFVEC3F_FIELDSYM_TOK
    |       MFSTRING_FIELDSYM_TOK
    |       MFFLOAT_FIELDSYM_TOK
    ;

type:       SFBITMASK_TOK       {$$=SFBITMASK_TOK;}
    |       SFBOOL_TOK          {$$=SFBOOL_TOK;}
    |       SFCOLOR_TOK         {$$=SFCOLOR_TOK;}
    |       SFENUM_TOK          {$$=SFENUM_TOK;}
    |       SFFLOAT_TOK         {$$=SFFLOAT_TOK;}
    |       SFIMAGE_TOK         {$$=SFIMAGE_TOK;}
    |       SFLONG_TOK          {$$=SFLONG_TOK;}
    |       SFMATRIX_TOK        {$$=SFMATRIX_TOK;}
    |       SFROTATION_TOK      {$$=SFROTATION_TOK;}
    |       SFSTRING_TOK        {$$=SFSTRING_TOK;}
    |       SFVEC2F_TOK         {$$=SFVEC2F_TOK;}
    |       SFVEC3F_TOK         {$$=SFVEC3F_TOK;}
    |       MFCOLOR_TOK         {$$=MFCOLOR_TOK;}
    |       MFLONG_TOK          {$$=MFLONG_TOK;}
    |       MFVEC2F_TOK         {$$=MFVEC2F_TOK;}
    |       MFVEC3F_TOK         {$$=MFVEC3F_TOK;}
    |       MFSTRING_TOK        {$$=MFSTRING_TOK;}
    |       MFFLOAT_TOK         {$$=MFFLOAT_TOK;}
    ;

FieldUsage:         /* empty */
    |               FieldDecls
    ;

FieldDecls:         FieldDecl
    |               FieldDecls FieldDecl
    ;

FieldDecl: SFBITMASK_FIELDSYM_TOK BitMaskExpr
            {
                    GNode*      np = CurrentNode();
                    if (np != NULL) {
                          np->SetField($1->name, $2);
                    }
            }
    |       SFBOOL_FIELDSYM_TOK SFBool
            {
                    GNode*      np = CurrentNode();
                    if (np != NULL) {
                          np->SetField($1->name, $2);
                    }
            }
    |       SFCOLOR_FIELDSYM_TOK SFColor
```

```
        {
                GNode*       np = CurrentNode();
                if (np != NULL) {
                        np->SetField($1->name, $2);
                }
        }
|       SFENUM_FIELDSYM_TOK SFEnum
        {
                GNode*       np = CurrentNode();
                if (np != NULL) {
                        np->SetField($1->name, $2);
                }
        }
|       SFFLOAT_FIELDSYM_TOK SFFloat
        {
                GNode*       np = CurrentNode();
                if (np != NULL) {
                        np->SetField($1->name, $2);
                }
        }
|       SFLONG_FIELDSYM_TOK SFLong
        {
                GNode*       np = CurrentNode();
                if (np != NULL) {
                        np->SetField($1->name, $2);
                }
        }
|       SFSTRING_FIELDSYM_TOK SFString
        {
                GNode*       np = CurrentNode();
                if (np != NULL) {
                        np->SetField($1->name, $2);
                }
        }
|       SFVEC2F_FIELDSYM_TOK SFVec2f
        {
                GNode*       np = CurrentNode();
                if (np != NULL) {
                        np->SetField($1->name, $2);
                }
        }
|       SFVEC3F_FIELDSYM_TOK SFVec3f
        {
                GNode*       np = CurrentNode();
                if (np != NULL) {
                        np->SetField($1->name, $2);
                }
        }
```

```
|       MFCOLOR_FIELDSYM_TOK MFColor
        {
                GNode*      np = CurrentNode();
                if (np != NULL) {
                        np->SetField($1->name, $2);
                }
        }
|       MFLONG_FIELDSYM_TOK MFLong
        {
                GNode*      np = CurrentNode();
                if (np != NULL) {
                        np->SetField($1->name, $2);
                }
        }
|       MFVEC2F_FIELDSYM_TOK MFVec2f
        {
                GNode*      np = CurrentNode();
                if (np != NULL) {
                        np->SetField($1->name, $2);
                }
        }
|       MFVEC3F_FIELDSYM_TOK MFVec3f
        {
                GNode*      np = CurrentNode();
                if (np != NULL) {
                        np->SetField($1->name, $2);
                }
        }
|       MFFLOAT_FIELDSYM_TOK MFFloat
        {
                GNode*      np = CurrentNode();
                if (np != NULL) {
                         np->SetField($1->name, $2);
                }
        }
|       MFSTRING_FIELDSYM_TOK MFString
        {
                GNode*      np = CurrentNode();
                if (np != NULL) {
                        np->SetField($1->name, $2);
                }
        }
|       SFMATRIX_FIELDSYM_TOK SFMatrix
        {
                GNode*      np = CurrentNode();
                if (np != NULL) {
                        np->SetField($1->name, $2);
                }
```

```
        }
    |   SFROTATION_FIELDSYM_TOK SFRotation
        {
            GNode*      np = CurrentNode();
            if (np != NULL) {
                np->SetField($1->name, $2);
            }
        }
    |   SFIMAGE_FIELDSYM_TOK SFImage
    ;

/* Does expression evaluation while parsing */
BitMaskExpr:    '(' BitMaskExpr ')'
                {$$ = $2;}
    |           BitMaskExpr '|' BitMaskExpr
                {$$ = $1 | $3;}
    |           SFLong
                {$$ = $1;}
    ;

/* Variable Type definitions */

SFBool:         SFLong
                {$$=$1;}
    ;

SFEnum:         SFLong
                {$$=$1;}
    ;

SFLong:         INTEGERVAL_TOK
                {$$=$1;}
    ;

SFString:       STRINGVAL_TOK
                {$$=$1;}
    ;

SFColor:        SFVec3f
                {$$=$1;}
    ;

SFFloat:        DOUBLEVAL_TOK
                {$$ = $1;}
    |           INTEGERVAL_TOK
                {$$ = (SFFloat) $1;}
    ;
```

```
SFImage:            INTEGERVAL_TOK INTEGERVAL_TOK I
                    NTEGERVAL_TOK ImageMap
        ;

ImageMap:           /* empty */
        |           ImageDef
        ;

ImageDef:           INTEGERVAL_TOK
        |           ImageDef INTEGERVAL_TOK
        ;

SFMatrix:           SFFloat SFFloat SFFloat SFFloat
                    SFFloat SFFloat SFFloat SFFloat
                    SFFloat SFFloat SFFloat SFFloat
                    SFFloat SFFloat SFFloat SFFloat
                    {
                          $$ = new SFMatrix;
                          /* Row 1 */
                          (*$$)[0][0] = $1; (*$$)[0][1] = $2;
                          (*$$)[0][2] = $3; (*$$)[0][3] = $4;

                          /* Row 2 */
                          (*$$)[1][0] = $5; (*$$)[1][1] = $6;
                          (*$$)[1][2] = $7; (*$$)[1][3] = $8;

                          /* Row 3 */
                          (*$$)[2][0] = $9; (*$$)[2][1] = $10;
                          (*$$)[2][2] = $11;(*$$)[2][3] = $12;

                         /* Row 4 */
                         (*$$)[3][0] = $13; (*$$)[3][1] = $14;
                         (*$$)[3][2] = $15; (*$$)[3][3] = $16;
                    }
        ;

SFRotation:         SFFloat SFFloat SFFloat SFFloat
                    {
                          $$ = new SFRotation($1, $2, $3, $4);
                    }
        ;

MFLong:             SFLong
                    {$$ = new MFLong; $$->Add($1);}
        |           '[' MFLongList OptComma ']'
                     {$$=$2;}
        ;
```

```
MFLongList:         SFLong
                    {$$ = new MFLong; $$->Add($1);}
      |             MFLongList ',' SFLong
                    {$$ = $1; $1->Add($3);}
      ;

MFString:           SFString
                    {$$ = new MFString; $$->Add($1);}
      |             '[' MFStringList OptComma ']'
                    {$$ = $2;}
      ;

MFStringList:       SFString
                    {$$ = new MFString; $$->Add($1);}
      |             MFStringList ',' SFString
                    {$$ = $1; $1->Add($3);}
      ;

SFVec2f:            SFFloat SFFloat
                    {$$ = new SFVec2f($1, $2);}
      ;

SFVec3f:            SFFloat SFFloat SFFloat
                    {$$ = new SFVec3f($1, $2, $3);
      ;

MFColor:            MFVec3f
                    {$$ = $1;}
      ;

MFVec2f:            SFVec2f
                    {$$ = new MFVec2f; $$->Add(*$1);}
      |             '[' MFVec2fList OptComma ']'
                    {$$ = $2;}
      ;

MFVec2fList:        SFVec2f
                    {$$ = new MFVec2f; $$->Add(*$1);}
      |             MFVec2fList ',' SFVec2f
                    {$$ = $1; $$->Add(*$3);}
      ;

MFVec3f:            SFVec3f
                    {$$ = new MFVec3f; $$->Add(*$1);}
      |             '[' MFVec3fList OptComma ']'
                    {$$ = $2;}
      ;
```

```
MFVec3fList:        SFVec3f
                    {$$ = new MFVec3f; $$->Add(*$1);}
     |              MFVec3fList ',' SFVec3f
                    {$$ = $1; $$->Add(*$3);}

     ;

MFFloat:            SFFloat
                    {$$ = new MFFloat; $$->Add($1);}
     |              '[' MFFloatList OptComma ']'
                    {$$ = $2;}

     ;

MFFloatList:        SFFloat
                    {$$ = new MFFloat; $$->Add($1);}
     |              MFFloatList ',' SFFloat
                    {$$ = $1; $$->Add($3);}

     ;

OptComma:           /* empty */
     |              ','
     ;

%%

void
yyerror( char* fmt, ... )
{
    charbuffer[1024];
    va_list     argptr;
    va_start( argptr, fmt );
    vsprintf( buffer, fmt, argptr );
    va_end(argptr);

    toplevel->ErrorMessage("%s, line %d.\n",
        buffer, yylineno);
}
```

Additional Sources for the VRML Parser

The first two functions discussed in this section create the define symbol table and the node symbol table: `AddDefine()` and `AddDefautlNodeBodies()`. The last function, `AddDefaultNodeBodies(void)`, puts all the pieces together into the single user function `wrl_reader()`, which reads the specified VRML file.

Filling in the Define Symbol Table

The define symbol table associates keywords that may be used in assignment expressions for fields with their underlying values. To add a new symbol to this table, you need only pass the name of the symbol as the first argument to `AddDefine()` and the associated *SFLong* as the second value to `AddDefine()`.

```
void
AddDefaultDefines(void)
{
    AddDefine("LEFT", G_LEFT);
    AddDefine("RIGHT", G_RIGHT);
    AddDefine("CENTER", G_CENTER);
    AddDefine("SIDES", G_SIDES);
    AddDefine("BOTTOM", G_BOTTOM);
    AddDefine("ALL", G_ALL);
    AddDefine("TOP", G_TOP);
    AddDefine("TRUE", G_TRUE);
    AddDefine("FALSE", G_FALSE);
    AddDefine("SERIF", G_SERIF);
    AddDefine("SANS", G_SANS);
    AddDefine("TYPEWRITER", G_TYPEWRITER);
    AddDefine("NONE", G_NONE);
    AddDefine("BOLD", G_BOLD);
    AddDefine("ITALIC", G_ITALIC);
    AddDefine("DEFAULT", G_DEFAULT);
    AddDefine("OVERALL", G_OVERALL);
    AddDefine("PER_PART", G_PER_PART);
    AddDefine("PER_PART_INDEXED", G_PER_PART_INDEXED);
    AddDefine("PER_FACE", G_PER_FACE);
    AddDefine("PER_FACE_INDEXED", G_PER_FACE_INDEXED);
    AddDefine("PER_VERTEX", G_PER_VERTEX);
    AddDefine("PER_VERTEX_INDEXED", G_PER_VERTEX_INDEXED);
    AddDefine("ON", G_ON);
    AddDefine("OFF", G_OFF);
    AddDefine("AUTO", G_AUTO);
    AddDefine("UNKNOWN_ORDERING", G_UNKNOWN_ORDERING);
    AddDefine("CLOCKWISE", G_CLOCKWISE);
    AddDefine("COUNTERCLOCKWISE", G_COUNTERCLOCKWISE);
    AddDefine("UNKNOWN_SHAPE_TYPE", G_UNKNOWN_SHAPE_TYPE);
    AddDefine("SOLID", G_SOLID);
    AddDefine("UNKNOWN_FACE_TYPE", G_UNKNOWN_FACE_TYPE);
    AddDefine("CONVEX", G_CONVEX);
    AddDefine("REPEAT", G_REPEAT);
    AddDefine("CLAMP", G_CLAMP);
    AddDefine("POINT", G_POINT);
}
```

Filling in the Node Symbol Table

The `AddDefaultNodeBodies()` function creates the node symbol table that recognizes built-in VRML language construct. The syntax for defining a new language construct is:

```
PushNodeDecl(AddNode(symName, childFlag, constructorFunc);
AddField(fieldName, fieldToken, defaultValue);
          .
          .
          .
PopNodeDecl();
```

The *symName* value is the name of the language construct. The *childFlag* value is the boolean value `TRUE` or `FALSE`, where `TRUE` indicates that the language construct has children (like a Separator or Group construct) and `FALSE` indicates that the construct has no children (like a Sphere or Cone construct). The argument *constructorFunc* is a constructor function that is a C wrapper around the C++ constructor for the corresponding class in the internal representation. This allows the creation of the correct class instance to be handled generically. However, if you need to define a language construct but don't wish to support it, simply pass the value `NULL` to the *constructorFunc* argument.

The function `PushNodeDecl()` indicates that the subsequent `AddField()` functions apply to the symbol passed in as an argument. The `PopNodeDecl()` function takes the symbol out of scope for subsequent calls. All `PushNodeDecl()` functions must have a corresponding `PopNodeDecl()` function.

The `AddField()` function adds new fields to the current symbol. The *fieldName* argument specifies the name of this field. The *fieldToken* argument specifies the value that the lexical analyzer should return if this field symbol is encountered. And the *defaultValue* argument specifies the default value for this field.

```
void
AddDefaultNodeBodies(void)
{

    /* Nodes with children */
     PushNodeDecl(AddNode("Separator", TRUE,
          GSeparatorCreate));
     AddField("renderCulling", SFENUM_TOK, (SFLong) G_AUTO);
     PopNodeDecl();
```

```
PushNodeDecl(AddNode("Group", TRUE, GGroupCreate));
PopNodeDecl();

PushNodeDecl(AddNode("LOD", TRUE, GLODCreate));
AddField("range", MFFLOAT_TOK, new MFFloat);
AddField("center", SFVEC3F_TOK,
      new SFVec3f(0.0, 0.0, 0.0));
PopNodeDecl();

PushNodeDecl(AddNode("Switch", TRUE, GSwitchCreate));
AddField("whichChild", SFLONG_TOK, (SFLong) -1);
PopNodeDecl();

PushNodeDecl(AddNode("TransformSeparator", TRUE,
    GTransformSeparatorCreate));
PopNodeDecl();

PushNodeDecl(AddNode("WWWAnchor", TRUE,
      GWWWAnchorCreate));
AddField("name", SFSTRING_TOK, "");
AddField("description", SFSTRING_TOK, "");
AddField("map", SFENUM_TOK, (SFLong) G_NONE);
PopNodeDecl();

/* Nodes without children */
PushNodeDecl(AddNode("AsciiText", FALSE, NULL));
AddField("string", MFSTRING_TOK,
      (MFString*) new MFString(""));
AddField("spacing", SFFLOAT_TOK, (SFFloat) 1.0);
AddField("justification", SFENUM_TOK, (SFLong) G_LEFT);
AddField("width", MFFLOAT_TOK,
      (MFFloat*) new MFFloat(0.0));
PopNodeDecl();

PushNodeDecl(AddNode("Cone", FALSE, GConeCreate));
AddField("parts", SFBITMASK_TOK, (SFLong) G_ALL);
AddField("bottomRadius", SFFLOAT_TOK, (SFFloat) 1.0);
AddField("height", SFFLOAT_TOK, (SFFloat) 2.0);
PopNodeDecl();

PushNodeDecl(AddNode("Coordinate3", FALSE,
      GCoordinate3Create));
AddField("point", MFVEC3F_TOK,
      new MFVec3f(SFVec3f(0.0, 0.0, 0.0)));
PopNodeDecl();

PushNodeDecl(AddNode("Cube", FALSE, GCubeCreate));
AddField("width", SFFLOAT_TOK, (SFFloat) 2.0);
```

```
AddField("height", SFFLOAT_TOK, (SFFloat) 2.0);
AddField("depth", SFFLOAT_TOK, (SFFloat) 2.0);
PopNodeDecl();

PushNodeDecl(AddNode("Cylinder", FALSE,
    GCylinderCreate));
AddField("parts", SFBITMASK_TOK, (SFLong) G_ALL);
AddField("radius", SFFLOAT_TOK, (SFFloat) 1.0);
AddField("height", SFFLOAT_TOK, (SFFloat) 2.0);
PopNodeDecl();

PushNodeDecl(AddNode("DirectionalLight", FALSE, NULL));
AddField("on", SFBOOL_TOK, (SFLong) G_ON);
AddField("intensity", SFFLOAT_TOK, (SFFloat) 1.0);
AddField("color", SFCOLOR_TOK,
      new SFVec3f(1.0, 1.0, 1.0));
AddField("direction", SFVEC3F_TOK,
      new SFVec3f(0.0, 0.0, -1.0));
PopNodeDecl();

PushNodeDecl(AddNode("FontStyle", FALSE, NULL));
AddField("size", SFFLOAT_TOK, (SFFloat) 10.0);
AddField("family", SFENUM_TOK, (SFLong) G_SERIF);
AddField("style", SFBITMASK_TOK, (SFLong) G_NONE);
PopNodeDecl();

PushNodeDecl(AddNode("IndexedFaceSet", FALSE,
    GIndexedFaceSetCreate));
AddField("coordIndex", MFLONG_TOK, (SFLong) 0);
AddField("materialIndex", MFLONG_TOK, (SFLong) -1);
AddField("normalIndex", MFLONG_TOK, (SFLong) -1);
AddField("textureCoordIndex", MFLONG_TOK, (SFLong) -1);
PopNodeDecl();

PushNodeDecl(AddNode("IndexedLineSet", FALSE, NULL));
AddField("coordIndex", MFLONG_TOK, (SFLong) 0);
AddField("materialIndex", MFLONG_TOK, (SFLong) -1);
AddField("normalIndex", MFLONG_TOK, (SFLong) -1);
AddField("textureCoordIndex", MFLONG_TOK, (SFLong) -1);
PopNodeDecl();

PushNodeDecl(AddNode("Info", FALSE, DefaultCreate));
AddField("string", SFSTRING_TOK, "<Undefined info>");
PopNodeDecl();

PushNodeDecl(AddNode("Material", FALSE,
    GMaterialCreate));
AddField("ambientColor", MFCOLOR_TOK,
```

```
    new MFVec3f(SFVec3f(0.2, 0.2, 0.2)));
AddField("diffuseColor", MFCOLOR_TOK,
    new MFVec3f(SFVec3f(0.8, 0.8, 0.8)));
AddField("specularColor", MFCOLOR_TOK,
    new MFVec3f(SFVec3f(0.0, 0.0, 0.0)));
AddField("emissiveColor", MFCOLOR_TOK,
    new MFVec3f(SFVec3f(0.0, 0.0, 0.0)));
AddField("shininess", MFFLOAT_TOK, new MFFloat(0.2));
AddField("transparency", MFFLOAT_TOK, new MFFloat(0.0));
PopNodeDecl();

PushNodeDecl(AddNode("MaterialBinding", FALSE,
    GMaterialBindingCreate));
AddField("value", SFENUM_TOK, (SFLong) G_DEFAULT);
PopNodeDecl();

PushNodeDecl(AddNode("MatrixTransform", FALSE,
      GMatrixTransformCreate));
AddField("matrix", SFMATRIX_TOK,
      new SFMatrix(Identity()));
PopNodeDecl();

PushNodeDecl(AddNode("Normal", FALSE, GNormalCreate));
AddField("vector", MFVEC3F_TOK,
    new MFVec3f(SFVec3f(0.0, 0.0, 0.1)));
PopNodeDecl();

PushNodeDecl(AddNode("NormalBinding", FALSE,
    GNormalBindingCreate));
AddField("value", SFENUM_TOK, (SFLong) G_DEFAULT);
PopNodeDecl();

PushNodeDecl(AddNode("OrthographicCamera", FALSE,
      NULL));
AddField("position", SFVEC3F_TOK,
      new SFVec3f(0.0, 0.0, 0.1));
AddField("orientation", SFROTATION_TOK,
      new SFRotation(0.0, 0.0, 1.0, 0.0));
AddField("focalDistance", SFFLOAT_TOK, (SFFloat) 5.0);
AddField("height", SFFLOAT_TOK, (SFFloat) 2.0);
AddField("nearDistance", SFFLOAT_TOK, (SFFloat) 0.0);
AddField("farDistance", SFFLOAT_TOK, (SFFloat) 100.0);
PopNodeDecl();

PushNodeDecl(AddNode("PerspectiveCamera", FALSE,
      GPerspectiveCameraCreate));
AddField("position", SFVEC3F_TOK,
      new SFVec3f(0.0, 0.0, 0.1));
```

```
AddField("orientation", SFROTATION_TOK,
      new SFRotation(0.0, 0.0, 1.0, 0.0));
AddField("focalDistance", SFFLOAT_TOK, (SFFloat) 5.0);
AddField("heightAngle", SFFLOAT_TOK, (
      SFFloat) 0.785398);
AddField("nearDistance", SFFLOAT_TOK, (SFFloat) 0.0);
AddField("farDistance", SFFLOAT_TOK, (SFFloat) 100.0);
PopNodeDecl();

PushNodeDecl(AddNode("PointLight", FALSE,
      GPointLightCreate));
AddField("on", SFBOOL_TOK, (SFLong) G_ON);
AddField("intensity", SFFLOAT_TOK, (SFFloat) 1.0);
AddField("color", SFCOLOR_TOK,
      new SFVec3f(1.0, 1.0, 1.0));
AddField("location", SFVEC3F_TOK,
      new SFVec3f(0.0, 0.0, 1.0));
PopNodeDecl();

PushNodeDecl(AddNode("PointSet", FALSE, NULL));
AddField("startIndex", SFLONG_TOK, (SFLong) 0);
AddField("numPoints", SFLONG_TOK, (SFLong) -1);
PopNodeDecl();

PushNodeDecl(AddNode("Rotation", FALSE,
      GRotationCreate));
AddField("rotation", SFROTATION_TOK,
      new SFRotation(0.0, 0.0, 1.0, 0.0));
PopNodeDecl();

PushNodeDecl(AddNode("Scale", FALSE, GScaleCreate));
AddField("scaleFactor", SFVEC3F_TOK,
      new SFVec3f(1.0, 1.0, 1.0));
PopNodeDecl();

PushNodeDecl(AddNode("ShapeHints", FALSE, NULL));
AddField("vertexOrdering", SFENUM_TOK,
    (SFLong) G_UNKNOWN_ORDERING);
AddField("shapeType", SFENUM_TOK,
    (SFLong) G_UNKNOWN_ORDERING);
AddField("faceType", SFENUM_TOK, (
    SFLong) G_CONVEX);
AddField("creaseAngle", SFFLOAT_TOK,
    (SFFloat) 0.5);
PopNodeDecl();

PushNodeDecl(AddNode("Sphere", FALSE, GSphereCreate));
AddField("radius", SFFLOAT_TOK, (SFFloat) 1.0);
```

```
PopNodeDecl();

PushNodeDecl(AddNode("SpotLight", FALSE,
    GSpotLightCreate));
AddField("on", SFBOOL_TOK, (SFLong) G_ON);
AddField("intensity", SFFLOAT_TOK, (SFFloat) 1.0);
AddField("color", SFVEC3F_TOK,
    new SFVec3f(1.0, 1.0, 1.0));
AddField("location", SFVEC3F_TOK,
    new SFVec3f(0.0, 0.0, 1.0));
AddField("direction", SFVEC3F_TOK,
    new SFVec3f(0.0, 0.0, -1.0));
AddField("dropOffRate", SFFLOAT_TOK,
    (SFFloat) 0.0);
AddField("cutOffAngle", SFFLOAT_TOK,
    (SFFloat) 0.785398);
PopNodeDecl();

PushNodeDecl(AddNode("Texture2", FALSE, NULL));
AddField("filename", SFSTRING_TOK, "");
AddField("image", SFIMAGE_TOK);
AddField("wrapS", SFENUM_TOK, (SFLong) G_REPEAT);
AddField("wrapT", SFENUM_TOK, (SFLong) G_REPEAT);
PopNodeDecl();

PushNodeDecl(AddNode("Texture2Transform", FALSE, NULL));
AddField("translation", SFVEC2F_TOK,
    new SFVec3f(0.0, 0.0, 0.0));
AddField("rotation", SFFLOAT_TOK, (SFFloat) 0.0);
AddField("scaleFactor", SFVEC2F_TOK,
    new SFVec2f(1.0, 1.0));
AddField("center", SFVEC2F_TOK,
    new SFVec2f(0.0, 0.0));
PopNodeDecl();

PushNodeDecl(AddNode("TextureCoordinate2", FALSE,
    GTextureCoordinate2Create));
AddField("point", MFVEC2F_TOK,
    new MFVec2f(SFVec2f(0.0, 0.0)));
PopNodeDecl();

PushNodeDecl(AddNode("Transform", FALSE,
    GTransformCreate));
AddField("translation", SFVEC3F_TOK,
    new SFVec3f(0.0, 0.0, 0.0));
AddField("rotation", SFROTATION_TOK,
    new SFRotation(0.0, 0.0, 1.0, 0.0));
AddField("scaleFactor", SFVEC3F_TOK,
```

```
            new SFVec3f(1.0, 1.0, 1.0));
        AddField("scaleOrientation", SFROTATION_TOK,
            new SFRotation(0.0, 0.0, 1.0, 0.0));
        AddField("center", SFVEC3F_TOK,
            new SFVec3f(0.0, 0.0, 0.0));
        PopNodeDecl();

        PushNodeDecl(AddNode("Translation", FALSE,
            GTranslationCreate));
        AddField("translation", SFVEC3F_TOK,
            new SFVec3f(0.0, 0.0, 0.0));
        PopNodeDecl();

        PushNodeDecl(AddNode("WWWInline", FALSE, NULL));
        AddField("name", SFSTRING_TOK, "");
        AddField("bboxSize", SFVEC3F_TOK,
            new SFVec3f(0.0, 0.0, 0.0));
        AddField("bboxCenter", SFVEC3F_TOK,
            new SFVec3f(0.0, 0.0, 0.0));
        PopNodeDecl();

}
```

The wrl_reader() Function

The `wrl_reader()` function reads the specified VRML file and places it into the *GNode* that is passed in. This function opens the named file, gets the file's length, initializes the lexical analyzer and symbol tables, and then reads the VRML file. The file read is re-represented as a *GNode* instance hierarchy and then attached as a child to the *GNode* passed to the `wrl_reader()` function.

```
void
wrl_reader(GNode* top, const char* filename)
{
    FILE*fp = fopen(filename, "r");

    toplevel = top;

    if (fp != NULL) {
          /* Get Length of File for status message */
          fseek(fp, 0L, SEEK_END);
          fileSize = ftell(fp);
          rewind(fp);

          /* initialize */
          root = NULL;
          yyinit(fp);
```

```
            AddDefaultDefines();
            AddDefaultNodeBodies();

            /* read file */
            yyparse();

            /* put the file into top */
            top->AddChild(root);

            /* clean up */
            node_table.Clear();
            define_table.Clear();
            uses_table.Clear();
            fclose(fp);
            return;
        }
        return;
    }
```

Implementing the VRML Writer

As with the VRML reader, the VRML writer uses a different architecture than that used to implement the other 3D file format readers discussed in this book. This is because the VRML writer is very easy to implement as a built-in function to the classes derived from *GNode*.

Since *GNode* derived classes represent VRML language constructs directly, implementing a writer can be handled by iterating through the *GNode* instance hierarchy when calling the `WriteWRL()` member function.

The *GNode* class defines `WriteWRL()` as

```
virtual void WriteWRL(FILE*, int = 0);
```

The first argument to this function is a `FILE` pointer to the open VRML file. The second argument is the indention level. An example usage of `WriteWRL()` to write a VRML file follows:

```
FILE* fp = fopen(lpszPathName, "w");
if (fp != NULL) {
      StartBusy();
      topLevel->WriteWRL(fp, 0);
      fclose(fp);
      EndBusy();
      SetPathName( lpszPathName );
      return TRUE;
}
```

The variable *topLevel* is the top of the *GNode* instance hierarchy. This variable is usually a *GSeparator*, though it could be any *GNode* derived class that can have a child entry. Typically the initial call to `WriteWRL()` passes an indention level of 0. This means the VRML language construct at the *topLevel*, when written, has no indention. Each level of child typically increases the indention level by 1.

Rather than including `WriteWRL()` here for every *GNode* derived class in the *Crossroads* library, I describe two representative functions. It should be easy to recreate `WriteWRL()` for any *GNode* derived class by using the VRML language definition given earlier in this chapter and the description of the *Crossroads* library given in Chapter 2.

The two representative member functions are `GSeparator::WriteWRL()` and `GSphere::WriteWRL()`. `GSeparator::WriteWRL()` implements the VRML writing function for a VRML language construct Separator and is a good illustration of a class that has children. `GSphere::WriteWRL()` implements the VRML language construct Sphere. It is useful in showing an implementation of a class that has field variables but no children.

Implementation of GSeparator::WriteWRL()

Each *GNode* derived class that supports children implements a very similar `WriteWRL()` member function. `WriteWRL()` indents the current VRML construct represented by the *GNode* derived class appropriately as a function of the `WriteWRL()` iteration depth. If the current construct has a name, it is written using the VRML *DEF* syntax. The type of the construct is then written, followed by any fields that have unique (nondefault) values. After the fields have been written, the children of this construct are emitted. They are emitted in order by iterating through the *m_child* list for the *GNode* instance. Each child is written using the syntax:

```
np->WriteWRL(fp, indent+1);
```

This syntax ensures that each child of this construct will be written at a higher indentation level, thereby making the VRML file easier to read. Finally, after all the children have been emitted, the closing brace is emitted.

The following source shows the implementation for the *GSeparator* class, which is derived from the *GNode* class:

```
void GSeparator::
WriteWRL(FILE* fp, int indent) {
    GNode*      np = m_child;
```

```
    // Write Indention
    Indent(fp, indent);

    // Print name for node, if one exists
    if (GetName() != NULL) {
          fprintf(fp, "DEF %s ", GetName());
    }

    // Print the construct type and opening brace
    fprintf(fp, "Separator {\n");

    // Write each child element
    for ( ;np != NULL; np = np->Next()) {
          np->WriteWRL(fp, indent+1);
    }

    // Write indention and closing brace
    Indent(fp, indent);
    fprintf(fp, "}\n");
}
```

Implementation of GSphere::WriteWRL()

Each *GNode* derived class implements a very similar `WriteWRL()` member function. `WriteWRL()` indents the current VRML construct represented by the *GNode* derived class appropriately as a function of the `WriteWRL()` iteration depth. If the current construct has a name, it is written using the VRML *DEF* syntax. The type of the construct is then written, followed by any fields that have unique (nondefault) values. After the fields have been written, the closing brace is emitted.

The following source shows the implementation for the *GSphere* class, which is derived from the *GNode* class:

```
void GSphere::
WriteWRL(FILE* fp, int indent)
{
    // Write Indention
    Indent(fp, indent);

    // Write name for node, if one exists
    if (GetName() != NULL) {
          fprintf(fp, "DEF %s ", GetName());
    }
```

```
    // Print the construct type and opening brace
    fprintf(fp, "Sphere {\n");

    // Write indention for the field value
    Indent(fp, indent+1);

    // Write the field name and value
    fprintf(fp, "radius %f\n", m_radius);

    // Write indention and closing brace
    Indent(fp, indent);
    fprintf(fp, "}\n");
}
```

References

Bell, Gavin, Anthony Parisi, and Mark Pesce. *The Virtual Reality Modeling Language Version 1.0 Specification.* 1995. http://vrml.wired.com/vrml.tech/vrml10-3.html.

Pesce, Mark. *VRML Browsing & Building Cyberspace.* 1995. Indianapolis, Ind.: New Riders Publishing Company.

Roehl, Bernie. *VRML 1.1 Changes.* Sept 8, 1995. http://sunee.uwaterloo.ca/~broehl/vrml/approved.html.

Chapter 4

RAW File Format

The RAW file format is commonly used for shareware and freeware 3D utilities. Its advantages include simplicity and portability. Its disadvantages include its being a very minimal format and the fact that there are few commercial 3D applications that read or write it.

RAW stands for "raw triangles." The format is simply a list of triangle vertices; it writes out triangles as simply as possible. Each triangle may optionally define normals for each vertice and may optionally define a material name. The triangles may be grouped together under a common name.

Development of RAW

Steve Anger is the author of several tools that can read and write RAW files. He has been involved with the RAW format since its appearance in the graphic community. He was kind enough to provide this history of the RAW format:

"The earliest use I've seen of the RAW format was in Mike Schoenborn's program Sandpaper, which read in RAW triangle data in the format `x1 y1 z1 x2 y2 z2 x3 y3 z3` and wrote unbounded DBK smooth triangle files. The input format was totally free-form and ignored all blanks and carriage returns.

"My program was written before I ran into Sandpaper. It was originally called TXT2DBK and read triangle data in the format `x1 y1 z1 x2 y2 z2 x3 y3 z3 <CR>`. TXT2DBK was originally an experiment in bounding. The smoothing was added later.

"Later I wrote a utility that converted Atari 3D2 files to TXT (RAW) format. I needed support for multiple objects and texture names, so that was added to the TXT format. After I found Sandpaper, I decided to rewrite

TXT2DBK to make it compatible with Sandpaper (free-form input) and eventually renamed it to RAW2POV.

"There are probably earlier uses of the format. In its basic form, the format is rather obvious, so it's likely been reinvented a dozen times or more."

Syntax of RAW

The syntax of a RAW file is very simple. A RAW file defines a series of triangles, one per line, which define a 3D object.

The triangles can be defined as a series of groups or as one large nameless group. Each triangle definition includes the three vertices required to define a triangle. Also, an optional material name may be included as well as an optional normal definition for each of the three vertices.

Following is a simple BNF that defines the grammar for a RAW file. This BNF assumes newlines and whitespace have been removed. However, it is important to remember that the triangle definition *must* remain on a single line.

```
// <name>     a non-terminal.
// ::=        an assignment.
// ...|...    either this construct or that construct
// [...]      the bracketed construct is optional
// {...}      the bracketed construct is repeated one
//            or more times.
// '...'      a literal string definition.

<Start>      ::=    {Group | Triangle}
             |
             ;

<Group>      ::=    <Name> {Triangle}
             ;

<Triangle>   ::=    <Vertex> <Vertex> <Vertex>
                    [<Normal> <Normal> <Normal>]
                    [<Material>]
             ;

<Vertex>     ::=    <Float> <Float> <Float>
             ;

<Normal>     ::=    <Vertex>
             ;
<Material>   ::=    <String>
             ;
```

```
<Name>          ::=     <String>
                ;

<Float>         ::=     ['-'] {'0'..'9'} [ '.' {'0'..'9'}]
                        ['e' ['-'] {'0'..'9'}]
                ;

<String>        :=      ('a'..'z' | 'A'..'Z')
                        {'a'..'z' | 'A'..'Z' | '0'..'9' | '_'}
                |       '"' {' ' | 'a'..'z' | 'A'..'Z' |
                        '0'..'9' | '_'} '"'
                ;
```

Following is a short example of a RAW file. It defines a single group named Dolph01 that contains four triangles.

```
Dolph01
1.6 7.34 0.0 0.8 6.62 0.0 0.9 6.6 0.17
0.9 6.6 0.17 1.77 7.3 0.13 1.6 7.3 0.0
2.29 7.67 0.0 1.6 7.34 0.0 1.7 7.3 0.13
1.76 7.31 0.13 2.35 7.6 0.07 2.28 7.67 0.0
```

Implementing a RAW Reader

The RAW reader function has the following syntax:

```
void raw_reader(GNode* root, char* filename);
```

The first argument must contain a pointer to a *GNode* class that can have children, most likely a *GSeparator* class. The second argument contains the full path name to the file that is read.

The RAW reader uses the *MeshCompactor* class to convert the triangle read by the RAW reader into the internal 3D object representation. The algorithm used is very simple. For each line read, the first nonwhitespace character is checked to see if it starts a numeric value. If it does, then a triangle is read. If it doesn't, then it is assumed to be a group name. After all the lines have been read, the resultant object is converted to the internal representation and placed in the *root* argument.

Each triangle is converted into a polygon using the *MeshCompactor* instance *mesh*. The function `MeshCompactor::BeginPolygon()` is called to define the beginning of each new triangle. The function `MeshCompactor::AddVertex(SFVec3f)` is used to add each vertex to the polygon. At least three vertices must be defined for each polygon definition. The function `MeshCompactor::EndPolygon()` is called to close the current polygon definition.

A group is defined by calling the `MeshCompactor::Name(char*)` member function. This function defines the specified group as the current group for subsequent polygon definitions.

The function `MeshCompactor::AddTo(GNode*)` converts the polygon mesh held by the current *MeshCompactor* instance into the internal representation.

```
void
raw_reader(GNode* root, char* filename)
{
  FILE*                    fp;
  MeshCompactor            mesh;
  long                     lineno = 0;

  if ((fp = fopen(filename, "r")) != NULL) {
     char  buffer[LLEN+1];
     long  fileSize;

     // Get Length of file for status message
     fseek(fp, 0L, SEEK_END);
     fileSize = ftell(fp);
     rewind(fp);

     // Read each line
     for (fgets(buffer, LLEN, fp) ; !feof(fp);
              fgets(buffer, LLEN, fp), lineno++) {
        float    x1, y1, z1;
        float    x2, y2, z2;
        float    x3, y3, z3;
        int         fieldsRead;
        char     name[256];

        // Report the status every 100 lines.
        if (lineno % 100 == 0) {
           root->StatusMessage("Reading %3.1f%% Complete",
                    ((float) ftell(fp))/((float)
                          fileSize)*100.0f);
        }

        // Remove the whitespace
        for (int i = 0; isspace(buffer[i]; i++)
           ;

        // Read the Triangle (if the first character starts
        // with a numeric value).
```

```
        if (isdigit(buffer[i]) || buffer[i] == '-') {
           fieldsRead = sscanf( buffer,
                        "%g %g %g %g %g %g %g %g %g",
                        &x1, &y1, &z1, &x2, &y2, &z2,
                        &x3, &y3, &z3);

           if (fieldsRead != 9) continue;

           mesh.BeginPolygon();
           mesh.AddVertex(SFVec3f(x1, y1, z1));
           mesh.AddVertex(SFVec3f(x2, y2, z2));
           mesh.AddVertex(SFVec3f(x3, y3, z3));
           mesh.EndPolygon();

        } else {
           // If the first value isn't a number then it
           // must be a string for the group name.
           if (buffer[i] == '\"') {
              i++;
              for (int j = 0; buffer[i] != '\"' &&
                     buffer[i]; i++, j++) {
                 name[j] = buffer[i];
              }
              name[j] = '\0';
           } else {
              for (int j = 0; !isspace(buffer[i]) &&
                     buffer[i]; i++, j++) {
                 name[j] = buffer[i];
              }
              name[j] = '\0';
           }

           // Define the group name.
           mesh.Name(name);
        }
     }

     // Add the finished object to our root object.
     mesh.AddTo(root);

     // Write the final status message.
     root->StatusMessage("Reading %3.1f%% Complete",
           ((float) ftell(fp))/((float) fileSize)*100.0f);

     fclose(fp);
  }
  return;
}
```

Implementing a RAW Writer

Writing a RAW file is almost as easy as reading one. A *GWrite* derived class named *GWriteRaw* is declared. This new class is used to define the implementation of the RAW reader. The *GWriteRaw* class is passed to the top-level *GNode* class in the scene representation by using the member function `GNode::Write(GState&, GWrite&)`. This function iterates through the scene. When supported constructs are encountered, it calls the appropriate member functions in the *GWriteRAW* instance.

The GWriteRAW Class Definition

For the RAW format, the only supported construct is the polygon. This is noted by the *GWriteRAW* class by returning `TRUE` from the `GWriteRAW::PolygonSupported(void)` member function. The *GWriteRAW* instance will be informed of all shapes encountered during the scene traversal. These shapes will be tessellated to Polygons if necessary. During traversal, the member function `GWriteRAW::StartPolygons(GState&, char*)` is called every time a new group of Polygons is encountered. The member function `GWriteRAW::Polygon(GState&, long, MFVec3f, MFVec3f*, GWriteMaterial*)` is called for each Polygon encountered.

The member variable *m_name* is used to check whether the name passed to `StartPolygons()` differs from the previous group name. Checking this ensures the group name is written to the file only once.

```
class GWriteRAW : public GWrite {
private:
   char  m_name[256];

public:
   GWriteRAW(void)  : GWrite() {strcpy(m_name, "");}
   short PolygonSupported(void)  {return TRUE;}
   void  StartPolygons(GState&, char*);
   void  Polygon(GState&, long, MFVec3f*,
            MFVec3f* = NULL, GWriteMaterial* = NULL);
};
```

StartPolygons(GState&, char*)

The `StartPolygons(GState&, char)` member function is called every time a new group of Polygons is encountered during the scene traversal. Now is an ideal time to write the group name for a set of Polygons. The only issue is that the same group name may occur several times in a scene. Rather than writing the group name for adjacent groups with the same name, this function saves the previous group name and checks to see that the names are different before writing a new group name to the RAW file.

```
void GWriteRAW::
StartPolygons(GState& state, char* name)
{
  // This function is called each time a group of
  // polygons is prepared for calling the Polygon()
  // function. We only write the group name if it
  // hasn't been previously written.
  if (state.HeirName() != NULL &&
           strcmp(m_name, state.HeirName()) != 0) {
        strcpy(m_name, state.HeirName());
        fprintf(m_fp, "%s\n", state.HeirName());
  }
}
```

void Polygon(GState&, long, MFVec3f, MFVec3f*, GWriteMaterial*)*

This member function performs the real meat of the conversion process. It writes the Polygon defined in the third argument as a set of triangles. The Polygon is assumed to be convex. This function tessellates a Polygon into adjacent triangles.

```
void GWriteRAW::
Polygon(GState& state, long faceNum, MFVec3f* v,
           MFVec3f* n, GWriteMaterial* m)
{
  if (m_fp != NULL && v->Elements() >= 3) {
     SFVec3ftriangle[3];
     triangle[0] = (*v)[0];

     // A very simple polygon tessellator.
     for (int i = 2; i < v->Elements(); i++) {
        triangle[1] = (*v)[i-1];
        triangle[2] = (*v)[i];

        // Write the triangle
        fprintf(m_fp, "%g %g %g %g %g %g %g %g %g\n",
              triangle[0].X(),
              triangle[0].Y(),
              triangle[0].Z(),
              triangle[1].X(),
              triangle[1].Y(),
              triangle[1].Z(),
```

```
                    triangle[2].X(),
                    triangle[2].Y(),
                    triangle[2].Z());
        }
    }
}
```

Chapter 5

Wavefront OBJ File Format

In this chapter, I describe the Wavefront OBJ file format. This is an ASCII format that defines geometric and other properties for objects in Wavefront's Advanced Visualizer.

The OBJ file format allows the definition of polygon-based objects, as well as of free-form curves and surfaces. For our purposes, I discuss only the parts of the OBJ file format that describe polygon-based objects.

Syntax of the OBJ File Format

The OBJ file format has a fairly free-form organization. The following BNF defines a typical organization for an OBJ file. This file has many other language statements in addition to those defined here. All language statements can be resolved in the first few characters. If a statement is encountered that isn't recognized, the statement should be ignored.

```
// <name>      a non-terminal.
// ::=         an assignment.
// ...|...     either this construct or that construct
// [...]       the bracketed construct is optional
// {...}       the bracketed construct is repeated one
//             or more times.
// '...'       a literal string definition.
// <CR>        newline character.

<Start>        ::=   {<Vertices> <Groups>}
               ;

<Vertices>     ::=   {<Vertex>}
               ;
```

```
<Vertex>        ::=   'v' <Float> <Float> <Float> <CR>
                |     'vn' <Float> <Float> <Float> <CR>
                |     <CR>
                ;
<Groups>        ::=   {[<Group>] <Faces>}
                ;

<Group>         ::=   'g' {<String>} <CR>
                ;

<Faces>         ::=   {<Face>}
                ;

<Face>          ::=   'f' {<VertexIndex>
                              ['/' [<TextureIndex>]
                              ['/' <NormalIndex>]]} <CR>
                |     <CR>
                ;

<VertexIndex>   ::=   <Integer>
                ;

<TextureIndex>  ::=   <Integer>
                ;

<NormalIndex>   ::=   <Integer>
                ;

<Integer>       ::=   {'0'..'9'}
                ;

<Float>         ::=   ['-'] {'0'..'9'} [ '.' {'0'..'9'}]
                      ['e' ['-'] {'0'..'9'}]
                ;

<String>        ::=   ('a'..'z' | 'A'..'Z')
                      {'a'..'z' | 'A'..'Z' | '0'..'9' | '_'}
                ;
```

The v x y z Construct

The `v x y z` construct is called the vertex statement. This statement defines the *x*-, *y*-, and *z*-coordinates for a face vertex. Polygons are constructed out of three or more vertices. Each vertex is referenced by its index, where the index of the first vertex definition is 1, of the second is 2, and so on. Following is an example of using vertices to create a box:

```
# Define a box
v -0.00000  0.50000  0.70711
v -0.00000 -0.50000  0.70711
v  0.70711 -0.50000  0.00000
v  0.70711  0.50000  0.00000
v -0.70711  0.50000 -0.00000
v -0.70711 -0.50000 -0.00000
v  0.00000 -0.50000 -0.70711
v  0.00000  0.50000 -0.70711

f 1 2 3 4
f 8 7 6 5
f 4 3 7 8
f 5 1 4 8
f 5 6 2 1
f 2 6 7 3
```

The vn i j k Construct

The `vn i j k` construct defines the vertex normal statement. Vertex normals are used to smooth a Polygon surface. A vertex normal statement begins with the characters `vn` and is followed by three floating-point values that define the normal vector. Following is an example of the usage of vertex normals in conjunction with vertices and face definitions:

```
# Defines a Dome Shape
v 0.00000 0.00003 0.00000
v 0.00060 -0.00003 0.00000
v 0.00055 -0.00003 0.00023
v 0.00042 -0.00003 0.00042
v 0.00023 -0.00003 0.00055
v 0.00000 -0.00003 0.00060
v -0.00023 -0.00003 0.00055
v -0.00042 -0.00003 0.00042
v -0.00055 -0.00003 0.00023
v -0.00060 -0.00003 0.00000
v -0.00055 -0.00003 -0.00023
v -0.00042 -0.00003 -0.00042
v -0.00023 -0.00003 -0.00055
v 0.00000 -0.00003 -0.00060
v 0.00023 -0.00003 -0.00055
v 0.00042 -0.00003 -0.00042
v 0.00055 -0.00003 -0.00023
v 0.00117 -0.00020 0.00000
vn 0.00000 1.00000 0.00000
vn 0.07511 0.76318 0.00000
vn 0.06942 0.76339 0.02874
```

```
vn 0.05313 0.76359 0.05313
vn 0.02874 0.76339 0.06942
vn 0.00000 0.76318 0.07511
vn -0.02874 0.76339 0.06942
vn -0.05313 0.76359 0.05313
vn -0.06942 0.76339 0.02874
vn -0.07511 0.76318 0.00000
vn -0.06942 0.76339 -0.02874
vn -0.05313 0.76359 -0.05313
vn -0.02874 0.76339 -0.06942
vn 0.00000 0.76318 -0.07511
vn 0.02874 0.76339 -0.06942
vn 0.05313 0.76359 -0.05313
vn 0.06942 0.76339 -0.02874
vn 0.00000 0.00000 0.00000

f 1//1 2//2 3//3
f 1//1 3//3 4//4
f 1//1 4//4 5//5
f 1//1 5//5 6//6
f 1//1 6//6 7//7
f 1//1 7//7 8//8
f 1//1 8//8 9//9
f 1//1 9//9 10//10
f 1//1 10//10 11//11
f 1//1 11//11 12//12
f 1//1 12//12 13//13
f 1//1 13//13 14//14
f 1//1 14//14 15//15
f 1//1 15//15 16//16
f 1//1 16//16 17//17
f 1//1 17//17 2//2
```

The f v1/vt1/vn1 v2/vt2/vn2 ... Construct

The `f v1/vt1/vn1 v2/vt2/vn2 ...` construct defines a face statement. Face statements are used with the vertex statements to define a Polygon. A face is constructed from three or more vertex indexes. Each vertex indexset contains an index into the defined vertices. It also defines an optional texture vertex index and an optional vertex normal index. Each vertex index is separated with a forward slash character.

Faces without normals are defined using the following syntax:

```
v -0.00000  0.50000  0.70711
v -0.00000 -0.50000  0.7071
v  0.70711 -0.50000  0.00000
```

```
v  0.70711  0.50000  0.00000
v -0.70711  0.50000 -0.00000
v -0.70711 -0.50000 -0.00000
v  0.00000 -0.50000 -0.70711
v  0.00000  0.50000 -0.70711

f 4 3 7 8
```

This example defines a Polygon with four vertices. The face statement says that the first vertex in the Polygon is the fourth vertex defined by the vertex statements. This means that the first vertex is the value (0.70711, 0.5, 0.0). The second vertex in the Polygon is the third vertex defined by the vertex statements. So the second vertex is the value (0.70711, –0.5, 0.0). By the same process, the third and fourth vertices are (0.0 –0.5, –0.70711) and (0.0, 0.5, –0.70711).

Faces with normals defined use the following syntax:

```
v 0.00000 0.00003 0.00000
v 0.00060 -0.00003 0.00000
v 0.00055 -0.00003 0.00023
vn 0.00000 1.00000 0.00000
vn 0.07511 0.76318 0.00000
vn 0.06942 0.76339 0.02874
f 1//1 2//2 3//3
```

This example defines a Polygon with three vertices and three normals, where one normal is associated with each vertex. The Polygon defined in this example has the vertices (0.0, 0.0003, 0.0), (0.0006, –0.0003, 0.0), and (0.00055, –0.0003, 0.00023). The normals for the Polygon are (0.0, 1.0, 0.0), (0.07511, 0.76339, 0.0), and (0.06942, 0.76339, 0.02874).

The g string ... Construct

The `g string ...` construct defines a group statement. A group is a set of Polygons that form a single named subobject. The elements that follow a group statement are part of the group. A group may define multiple group names. When multiple names are defined in a single group statement, the subsequent face elements are included in all of the group names. In the implementation, all group names in a single group statement are concatenated into a group name.

The following example illustrates how group statements may be used in an OBJ file:

```
# Define a box
v -0.00000  0.50000  0.70711
v -0.00000 -0.50000  0.70711
v  0.70711 -0.50000  0.00000
v  0.70711  0.50000  0.00000
v -0.70711  0.50000 -0.00000
v -0.70711 -0.50000 -0.00000
v  0.00000 -0.50000 -0.70711
v  0.00000  0.50000 -0.70711

g box side1
f 1 2 3 4
g box side2
f 8 7 6 5
g box side3
f 4 3 7 8
g box side4
f 5 1 4 8
g box side5
f 5 6 2 1
g box side6
f 2 6 7 3
```

Comments

Comments are allowed in OBJ files. Comments begin with a # symbol and continue until the end of the line. Comments are ignored in the parsing process and have no semantic meaning. They are included as a convenience for the human reader of an OBJ file.

```
# Define the vertices for a box
v -0.00000  0.50000  0.70711
v -0.00000 -0.50000  0.70711
v  0.70711 -0.50000  0.00000
v  0.70711  0.50000  0.00000
v -0.70711  0.50000 -0.00000
v -0.70711 -0.50000 -0.00000
v  0.00000 -0.50000 -0.70711
v  0.00000  0.50000 -0.70711

# Define the boxes sides
f 1 2 3 4
f 8 7 6 5
f 4 3 7 8
f 5 1 4 8
f 5 6 2 1
f 2 6 7 3
```

Implementing an OBJ Reader

The job of the OBJ file format reader is to read the specified OBJ file and convert the recognized constructs into the internal representation. It does this by reading the recognized language, locally caching the necessary data, and then constructing the representation.

Since the internal representation is the C++ equivalent to a subset of VRML, it is necessary to convert the OBJ representation into a VRML style of representation.

Internal Representation of an OBJ File

The OBJ reader builds a VRML-style internal representation of the OBJ file that is read. Since the internal representation is the C++ equivalent of a subset of the VRML language, an OBJ file will be compared to its converted VRML file to show the relationship of the OBJ file and its internal representation.

Consider the following familiar OBJ file:

```
# Define a box
v -0.00000  0.50000  0.70711
v -0.00000 -0.50000  0.70711
v  0.70711 -0.50000  0.00000
v  0.70711  0.50000  0.00000
v -0.70711  0.50000 -0.00000
v -0.70711 -0.50000 -0.00000
v  0.00000 -0.50000 -0.70711
v  0.00000  0.50000 -0.70711

g box side1
f 1 2 3 4
g box side2
f 8 7 6 5
g box side3
f 4 3 7 8
g box side4
f 5 1 4 8
g box side5
f 5 6 2 1
g box side6
f 2 6 7 3
```

When this file is read by the OBJ reader and is immediately written, the following VRML file results. This file shows the organization that will be created for the internal representation of an OBJ file.

```
#VRML V1.0 ascii
Separator {
  NormalBinding {
    value DEFAULT
  }
  MaterialBinding {
    value OVERALL
  }
  Material {
    ambientColor 0.2 0.2 0.2
    diffuseColor 0.8 0.8 0.8
    specularColor 0.0 0.0 0.0
    emissiveColor 0.0 0.0 0.0
    shininess 0.2
    transparency 0.0
  }
  Coordinate3 {
    point [
      0.000000 0.500000 0.707110,
      0.000000 -0.500000 0.707110,
      0.707110 -0.500000 0.000000,
      0.707110 0.500000 0.000000,
      -0.707110 0.500000 0.000000,
      -0.707110 -0.500000 0.000000,
      0.000000 -0.500000 -0.707110,
      0.000000 0.500000 -0.707110]
  }
  DEF box_side1 Separator {
    IndexedFaceSet {coordIndex [0, 1, 2, 3, -1]}
  }
  DEF box_side2 Separator {
    IndexedFaceSet {coordIndex [7, 6, 5, 4, -1]}
  }
  DEF box_side3 Separator {
    IndexedFaceSet {coordIndex [3, 2, 6, 7, -1]}
  }
  DEF box_side4 Separator {
    IndexedFaceSet {coordIndex [4, 0, 3, 7, -1]}
  }
  DEF box_side5 Separator {
    IndexedFaceSet {coordIndex [4, 5, 1, 0, -1]}
  }
  DEF box_side6 Separator {
    IndexedFaceSet {coordIndex [1, 5, 6, 2, -1]}
  }
}
```

Notice the similarity between the OBJ file and the VRML file. The vertex values are defined first. The series of vertex statements from the OBJ file are converted into a *Coordinate3* statement. The subsequent groups and their adjoining face statements are converted into a named *Separator* in the VRML and an *IndexedFaceSet*. The only additional information in the VRML file is the *NormalBinding*, *MaterialBinding*, and default *Material* that has been added to the internal representation.

In the internal representation, the *Coordinate3*, *Separator*, *IndexedFaceSet*, *Normal*, *NormalBinding*, *Material*, and *MaterialBinding* constructs are all converted into the equivalent C++ class instances. The classes for these constructs are *GCoordinate3*, *GSeparator*, *GIndexedFaceSet*, *GNormal*, *GNormalBinding*, *GMaterial*, and *GMaterialBinding*.

A Tour of the Source Code

The Wavefront OBJ file reader is a function with the following declaration:

```
void obj_reader(GNode*, char*);
```

The first argument is a *GNode* instance that can support children. Usually this instance is either a *GSeparator* or a class derived from *GSeparator*. The second argument is the full path of the OBJ file to be opened.

The OBJ reader parses vertex and normal statements. The vertex values are added to the `coord_list`, which is an *MFVec3f* type. The normal values are added to the `normal_list`, which is an *MFVec3f* type.

Group information is held in several variables, each of which is an array. The array index refers to the group being referenced.

- `max_face_list` contains the number of groups that currently have storage assigned to them.
- `MaxFaceList` defines the maximum number of groups.
- `cur_face_list` defines the current group. It contains the index of the current group for which subsequent face statements are applied.
- `face_name` contains an array of names for the defined groups.
- `face_list` contains an array of face lists for the defined groups.
- `nface_list` contains an array of normal lists for the defined groups.

The name for the current group is `face_name[cur_face_list]`, which is either a pointer to a null-terminated string or the `NULL` pointer. It is legal for a group to have no name.

The face list for the current group is `face_list[cur_face_list]`. This face list is an *MFLong* type and contains an array of indexes into the `coord_list` variable. The vertex value in `coord_list` corresponds to the index of each vertex of each Polygon defined by the face list. Each Polygon is terminated with a value of –1.

The normals list for the face of the current group is `nface_list[cur_face_list]`. The vertex value in `normal_list` corresponds to the index of each vertex normal of the Polygons defined by the normal list. Each Polygon vertex normal list is terminated with a value of –1.

```
#include "obj.h"
#include <stdio.h>
#include <stdlib.h>
#include <ctype.h>

#define LLEN          (2048)
#define POLYSIZE      (256)
#define MaxFaceList   (2048)

void
obj_reader(GNode* root, char* filename)
{
   // Pointer to OBJ file
   FILE*                 fp;

   // Storage for Vertices and Normals
   MFVec3f*              coord_list = new MFVec3f;
   MFVec3f*              normal_list = new MFVec3f;

   // Storage for Groups
   char*                 face_name[MaxFaceList];
   MFLong*               face_list[MaxFaceList];
   MFLong*               nface_list[MaxFaceList];
   long                  max_face_list = 0;
   long                  cur_face_list = 0;

   // Status information
   long                  lineno = 0;
   long                  fileSize;

   // Initialize group information
   for (int i = 0; i < MaxFaceList; i++) {
      face_list[i] = NULL;
      nface_list[i] = NULL;
      face_name[i] = NULL;
   }

   // Create storage for a default group.
   face_list[max_face_list] = new MFLong;
   nface_list[max_face_list] = new MFLong;
```

```
// Open OBJ file
if ((fp = fopen(filename, "r")) != NULL) {
   // Storage for the line read
   char              buffer[LLEN+1];

   // Internal representation for materials,
   // material binding, and normal binding.
   GMaterial*        material = new GMaterial;
   GMaterialBinding* materialBinding =
                        new GMaterialBinding;
   GNormalBinding*   normalBinding =
                           new GNormalBinding;

   // Set the value
   material->DefaultColors();
   materialBinding->Value(G_OVERALL);

   // Add to root GNode*
   root->AddChild((GNode*) normalBinding);
   root->AddChild((GNode*) materialBinding);
   root->AddChild((GNode*) material);

   // Get Length of File
   fseek(fp, 0L, SEEK_END);
   fileSize = ftell(fp);
   rewind(fp);

   // Read and process each line
   for (fgets(buffer, LLEN-1, fp) ; !feof(fp);
               fgets(buffer, LLEN-1, fp)) {
      char     command[LLEN+1], s[LLEN+1];
      char*    cp;
      char*    sp;
      long     i;
        cp = command;
        sp = s;

      lineno++;

      // Write status information every 100 lines.
      if (lineno % 100 == 0) {
         root->StatusMessage("Reading %3.1f%% Complete",
                     ((float) ftell(fp))/
                        ((float) fileSize)*100.0f);
      }

      // Place the command into *cp.
      for (i=0;  i < LLEN && buffer[i] &&
```

```
         !isspace(buffer[i]); i++) {
   *cp++ = buffer[i];
}
*cp = '\0';

// Skip whitespace.
for (; i < LLEN && buffer[i] &&
            isspace(buffer[i]); i++)
   ;

// Place the rest of the command in *sp.
for (; i < LLEN && buffer[i] ; i++) {
   *sp++ = buffer[i];
}
*sp = '\0';

// Check for each recognized command type.
if (strncmp( command, "g", 1) == 0) {
   char  lbuf[LLEN+1];
   short exists = FALSE;

   // Found a group definition

   // convert argument into a usable string
   for (sp = lbuf, i=0; s[i]; i++) {
      if (s[i] == '\n' || s[i] == '\r') {
      } else if (isspace(s[i])) {
         *sp++ = '_';
         while (s[i+1] && isspace(s[i+1])) {
            i++;
         }
      } else if (isalnum(s[i])) {
         *sp++ = s[i];
      } else {
         *sp++ = '_';
      }
   }
   *sp = '\0';

   // In a new group. Check to see if name exists.
   for (i = 0; i <= max_face_list; i++) {
      if (face_name[i] != NULL &&
               strcmp(lbuf, face_name[i]) == 0) {
         cur_face_list = i;
         exists = TRUE;
         break;
      }
   }
```

```
    // If the group doesn't exist we need to
    // create a new group
    if (!exists) {
       short recycled = FALSE;

       // Look for space
       for (i = 0; i <= max_face_list; i++) {
          if (face_list[i]->Elements() == 0) {
             // Found an empty spot, let's
             // recycle it.
             cur_face_list = max_face_list;
             face_name[cur_face_list] =
                new char[strlen(lbuf)+1];
             strcpy(face_name[cur_face_list], lbuf);
             recycled = TRUE;
          }
       }

       // If we didn't find any recycle space then
       // we will create new group storage.
       if (!recycled) {
          // Create a new bin
          max_face_list++;
          cur_face_list = max_face_list;
          face_name[cur_face_list] =
                new char[strlen(lbuf)+1];
          strcpy(face_name[cur_face_list], lbuf);
          face_list[cur_face_list] = new MFLong;
          nface_list[cur_face_list] = new MFLong;
       }
    }
} else if (strncmp(command, "vn", 2) == 0) {
    float x, y, z;

    // Detected a vector normal command

    // Find next numeric value
    for( i=0; i < LLEN && s[i] && !isdigit(s[i]) &&
            s[i] != '-'; i++)
       ;

    // Parse numeric value
    if (i < LLEN && (isdigit(s[i]) ||
            s[i] == '-')) {
       x = (float) atof( &s[i] );
    } else {
       fclose(fp);
       root->ErrorMessage("Syntax error file '%s',
```

```
                line %ld", filename, lineno);
        return;
    }

    // Find next numeric value
    for (; i < LLEN && s[i] && !isspace(s[i]); i++)
        ;

    for(; i < LLEN && s[i] && !isdigit(s[i]) &&
            s[i] != '-'; i++)
        ;

    // Parse next numeric value
    if (i < LLEN && (isdigit(s[i]) || s[i] == '-')){
        y = (float) atof( &s[i] );
    } else {
        fclose(fp);
        root->ErrorMessage("Syntax error file '%s',
                line %ld", filename, lineno);
        return;
    }

    // Find next numeric value
    for (; i < LLEN && s[i] && !isspace(s[i]); i++)
        ;

    for(; i < LLEN && s[i] && !isdigit(s[i]) &&
            s[i] != '-'; i++)
        ;

    // Parse next numeric value
    if (i < LLEN && (isdigit(s[i]) || s[i] == '-')){
        z = (float) atof( &s[i] );
    } else {
        fclose(fp);
        root->ErrorMessage("Syntax error file '%s',
                line %ld", filename, lineno);
        return;
    }

    // Add normal to vertice list
    normal_list->Add(SFVec3f(x, y, z));
} else if (strncmp(command, "v", 1) == 0) {
    float x, y, z;

    // Found Vertex command

    // Find next numeric value
```

```
for( i=0; i < LLEN && s[i] && !isdigit(s[i]) &&
       s[i] != '-'; i++)
   ;

// Parse numeric value
if (i < LLEN && (isdigit(s[i]) || s[i] == '-')){
   x = (float) atof( &s[i] );
} else {
   fclose(fp);
   root->ErrorMessage("Syntax error file '%s',
            line %ld", filename, lineno);
   return;
}

// Find next numeric value
for (; i < LLEN && s[i] && !isspace(s[i]); i++)
   ;

for(; i < LLEN && s[i] && !isdigit(s[i]) &&
         s[i] != '-'; i++)
   ;

// Parse numeric value
if (i < LLEN && (isdigit(s[i]) || s[i] == '-')){
   y = (float) atof( &s[i] );
} else {
   fclose(fp);
   root->ErrorMessage("Syntax error file '%s',
            line %ld", filename, lineno);
   return;
}

// Find next numeric value
for (; i < LLEN && s[i] && !isspace(s[i]); i++)
   ;

for(; i < LLEN && s[i] && !isdigit(s[i]) &&
         s[i] != '-'; i++)
   ;

// Parse numeric value
if (i < LLEN && (isdigit(s[i]) || s[i] == '-')){
   z = (float) atof( &s[i] );
} else {
   fclose(fp);
   root->ErrorMessage("Syntax error file '%s',
            line %ld", filename, lineno);
   return;
```

```
                    }

                    // Add point to vertice list
                    coord_list->Add(SFVec3f(x, y, z));

                } else if (strncmp(command, "f", 2) == 0 ||
                    strncmp(command, "fo", 2) == 0) {
                    long        count = 0, i = 0;
                    long        elements = coord_list->Elements();
                    short       normFlag = FALSE;

                    // Found face command

                    // Read each vertex index value set
                    while (i < LLEN && s[i]) {

                        // Find next numeric value
                        for(; i < LLEN && s[i] &&
                                !isdigit(s[i]); i++)
                            ;

                        // Parse numeric value
                        if (i < LLEN && isdigit(s[i])) {
                            face_list[cur_face_list]->Add(atol(&s[i])-
                            1);
                        }

                        // Skip value just read
                        for (; i < LLEN && s[i] &&
                                    isdigit(s[i]); i++)
                                ;

                        if (s[i] == '/') {
                            i++;
                            // Skip texture index number
                            for (; i < LLEN && s[i] &&
                                    isdigit(s[i]); i++)
                                ;
                            if (s[i] == '/') {
                                i++; normFlag = TRUE;
                                // Get Normal index number
                                if (i < LLEN && isdigit(s[i])) {
                                    nface_list[cur_face_list]-
>Add(atol(&s[i])-1);

                                    // Skip texture index number
                                    for (; i < LLEN && s[i] &&
                                            isdigit(s[i]); i++)
```

```
                    ;
                }
            }
        }

        for (; i < LLEN && s[i] &&
                    !isspace(s[i]); i++)
                ;

        count++;
      }

      // Terminate polygon with a -1
      face_list[cur_face_list]->Add(-1);

      if (normFlag) {
         nface_list[cur_face_list]->Add(-1);
      }
   }
}

// Update Status for the last time.
root->StatusMessage("Reading %3.1f%% Complete",
            ((float) ftell(fp))/
            ((float) fileSize)*100.0f);

// Create our Coordinate3 and Normal constructs
GCoordinate3*  coord = new GCoordinate3;
GNormal*    normal = new GNormal;

// Add normal list to Normal construct
if (normal_list->Elements() > 0) {
   normal->Vector(normal_list);
   root->AddChild((GNode*) normal);
}

// Add vertex list to Coordinate3 construct.
coord->Point(coord_list);
root->AddChild((GNode*) coord);

// Loop through all the groups found
for (int i=0; i <= max_face_list; i++) {

   if (face_list[i]->Elements() == 0) {
      // Delete empty groups
      if (face_list[i] != NULL) {
         delete face_list[i];
         face_list[i] = NULL;
```

```
                }
                if (nface_list[i] != NULL) {
                   delete nface_list[i];
                   nface_list[i] = NULL;
                }
             } else {
                // Create a new named separator for the
                // group and fill it in with the face list and
                // normal list.
                GSeparator*       current = new GSeparator;
                GIndexedFaceSet*  face = new GIndexedFaceSet;

                if (face_name[i] != NULL) {
                   current->SetName(face_name[i]);
                }
                face->CoordIndex(face_list[i]);

                if (nface_list[i] != NULL &&
                         nface_list[i]->Elements() > 0) {
                   face->NormalIndex(nface_list[i]);
                } else if (nface_list[i] != NULL) {
                   delete nface_list[i];
                   nface_list[i] = NULL;
                }

                root->AddChild(current);
                current->AddChild((GNode*) face);
             }
          }

          fclose(fp);
          return;
       }

       root->ErrorMessage("Unable to open file '%s'", filename);

       return;
    }
```

Implementing an OBJ Writer

Writing an OBJ file is much easier than reading one. A *GWrite* derived class named *GWriteOBJ* is declared. This new class is used to define the implementation of the OBJ reader. The *GWriteOBJ* class is passed to the top-level *GNode* class in the scene representation using the member function `GNode::Write(GState&, GWrite&)`. This function iterates through the scene. When supported constructs are encountered, it calls the appropriate member functions in *GWriteOBJ*.

The GWriteOBJ Class Definition

For the OBJ format, the only supported construct is the polygon. This is noted by the *GWriteOBJ* class by returning `TRUE` from the `GWriteOBJ::PolygonSupported(void)` member function. The *GWriteOBJ* instance is informed of all shapes encountered during the scene traversal. These shapes will be tessellated to Polygons if necessary. During traversal, the member function `GWriteOBJ::Polygon(GState&, long, MFVec3f, MFVec3f*, GWriteMaterial*)` is called for each Polygon encountered. The member function `GWriteOBJ::Epilog(GNode*, GState&)` is called after all of the Polygons have been processed.

The member variable *m_name* is used to check whether the name passed to `Polygons()` differs from the previous group name. As a result, fewer calls are made to the `m_mesh.Name()` member function.

The member variable *m_mesh* is used to compact and hold all of the vertices and faces. These will be filled in by the `GWriteOBJ::StartPolygon()` and `GWriteOBJ::Polygon()` member functions. They will be retrieved and written after all of the Polygons have been read by the `GWriteOBJ::Epilog()` member function.

```
class GWriteOBJ : public GWrite {
private:
   char            m_name[256];
   MeshCompactor   m_mesh;

public:
   GWriteOBJ(void) : GWrite() {strcpy(m_name, "");}
   short     PolygonSupported(void)  {return TRUE;}

   void  Polygon(GState&, long, MFVec3f*, MFVec3f* = NULL,
                 GWriteMaterial* = NULL);
   void  Epilog(GNode*, GState&);
};
```

void Polygon(GState&, long, MFVec3f, MFVec3f*, GWriteMaterial*)*

This member function checks whether the current object name differs from the previous call to the member function. If it does, the `m_mesh.Name()` function is called to make the name change take effect. The calls to `m_mesh.BeginPolygon()`, `m_mesh.AddVertex()`, and `m_mesh.End-`

`Polygon()` add the polygon to the *m_mesh* member variable, thereby breaking the Polygon into its vertices and faces. Each face is added to the current group. The *m_mesh* information is stored in the `GWriteObj` instance until it is written in the `GWriteOBJ::Epilog()` member function.

```
void GWriteOBJ::
Polygon(GState& state, long faceNum, MFVec3f* v, MFVec3f* n,
GWriteMaterial* m)
{
   // Notice Name changes
   if (state.HeirName() != NULL &&
         strcmp(m_name, state.HeirName()) != 0) {
      m_mesh.Name(state.HeirName());
      strcpy(m_name, state.HeirName());
   }
   // Add polygon
   m_mesh.BeginPolygon();
   for (int i = 0; i < v->Elements(); i++) {
      m_mesh.AddVertex((*v)[i]);
   }
   m_mesh.EndPolygon();
}
```

void Epilog(GNode, GState&)*

The `void Epilog(GNode*, GState&)` member function writes the OBJ file. All Polygons saved in the *m_mesh* member variable by calls to the `GWriteOBJ::Polygon()` member function are split into their vertices and faces.

First, the vertices are written. They are retrieved using the `m_mesh.Coordinates()` member function, which returns an *MFVec3f** type that is placed in the variable *coords*. The vertices in this variable are looped through and written to the OBJ file.

The next step is to loop through each group and retrieve the faces associated with each. The number of groups is found by a call to the `m_mesh.Groups()` member function.. Each group retrieves its face list by a call to the `m_mesh.Faces(group)`. The group writes its name as a OBJ group statement. Then the face is looped through and each Polygon face is written into the OBJ file.

```
void GWriteOBJ::
Epilog(GNode*, GState&)
{
   MFVec3f*      coords = m_mesh.Coordinates();
```

```
    // Check to see if we have any coordinates
    if (coords != NULL && coords->Elements() > 0) {
       // Write all the vertices
       for (long i = 0; i < coords->Elements(); i++) {
          SFVec3f vertex = (*coords)[i];
          fprintf(m_fp, "v %g %g %g\n",
                vertex.X(), vertex.Y(), vertex.Z());
       }

       // Cycle through each of the groups
       for (long group = 0; group < m_mesh.Groups();
                group++) {
          MFLong*  faces = m_mesh.Faces(group);

          // Print the name of the group
          if (m_mesh.Name(group) != NULL) {
             fprintf(m_fp, "g %s\n", m_mesh.Name(group));
          } else {
             fprintf(m_fp, "g NoName\n");
          }

          // Print the face lists
          if (faces->Elements() > 0) {
             fprintf(m_fp, "f ");
             for (i = 0; i < faces->Elements(); i++) {
                SFLong  face = (*faces)[i];
                if (face < 0 && i < (faces->Elements()-1)) {
                   fprintf(m_fp, "\nf ");
                } else if (face >= 0) {
                   fprintf(m_fp, "%d ", face+1);
                }
             }
             fprintf(m_fp, "\n\n");
          }
       }
    }
}
```

Chapter 6

TrueSpace

Caligari TrueSpace is a recent entry into the PC 3D software market. It is a very popular application because of its power, ease of use, and relatively low price.

Many 3D applications are designed to have a unique user interface for each type of object created. For example, there might be a lathe interface or an extrusion interface to allow these features to be accessed. TrueSpace, however, has only one user interface paradigm. The user can perform all object manipulation without having to go into a special screen or to another application. This highly integrated user interface, along with several novel features, makes TrueSpace one of the easiest to learn of the 3D modeling tools available. While TrueSpace does not have the broad feature set of high-end PC tools like 3DS, for ease of learning and price, it's hard to beat.

TrueSpace has two file types. They have the suffixes COB and SCN. The underlying format for both is the same, with one exception. They differ in that a SCN usually contains more than one object definition plus some extra information such as lighting and camera positions, while a COB contains only one 3D object. The following discussion about the COB suffix describes both COB and SCN file formats.

The TrueSpace COB file format is unique among the formats discussed in this book in that a COB file can be represented as either ASCII or binary. Most COB files are saved as binary (although saving to binary requires an extra step). For this reason, this chapter implements only a binary file reader and writer. (However, the ASCII format is definitely worth investigating because it makes understanding the binary file format easier.)

COB is a binary file format. This format requires special consideration because extra design effort is required to make its source portable. This is because the integer formats of computer microprocessors may differ in byte ordering. The implementation in this chapter is designed to allow easy portability. However, it has not actually been ported. Porting issues are discussed in the implementation section later in the chapter.

The content of a COB file is very simple, in both organization and makeup. The file contains primarily Polygons, the basic shape primitive in a TrueSpace file. It also may contain lights, cameras, and grouping and texture information. Even though TrueSpace appears to support more exotic shape primitives, these are all converted into Polygons in COB files.

Special Considerations

Two issues influence the design of a TrueSpace reader and writer: binary file reading and Polygon tessellation. Understanding them is important if you are planning to write your own reader or writer from scratch.

Portability Issues for Binary Files

Binary file formats can be a fast, efficient, and flexible means of storing data to files. However, the same basic numeric data types are often stored differently on different types of computer systems. This different representation derives from how bytes in multibyte values are stored in different microprocessors. This byte representation comes in two flavors: little-endian and big-endian. The "endianness" of values has to do with the byte ordering of values. For example, Intel-based computers are little-endian machines, that is, they store the least significant byte first. In contrast, 680x0 CPUs and most RISC machines are big-endian machines—they store the most significant byte first. Table 6.1 shows the endian representation of selected data types.

Table 6.1. Endian representation of selected data types

Data Type	Size (in bytes)	Example Value	Big-Endian Representation	Little-Endian Representation
Byte	1	0x12	0x12	0x12
Short	2	0x1234	0x1234	0x3412
Long	4	0x12345678	0x12345678	0x78563412
Float	4	1.2e3	0x44960000	0x00009644
Double	8	1.2e3	0x4092c00000000	0x0000000000c09240

This means that binary files written on a PC probably cannot be correctly read on a Macintosh simply by recompiling the same C/C++ code and vice versa. However, with careful thought up front you can write C/C++ code that can be compiled with minimal alterations on computers with different "endianness."

To safely access these basic types, you are advised to encapsulate the binary read and write functions. For example, by defining `ReadLong(FILE*, long&)` and `WriteLong(FILE*, long&)` you can ensure that the actual byte ordering can be handed transparently to the upper-level layers of your program.

The `ReadLong(FILE*, long&)` and `WriteLong(FILE*, long&)` functions might be implemented as follows on a PC:

```
short ReadLong(FILE* fp, long& value)
{
    return (fread(&value, sizeof(value), 1, fp) == 1)
}

short WriteLong(FILE* fp, const long value)
{
    return (fwrite(&value, sizeof(value), 1, fp) == 1);
}
```

However, to read the same files on a Macintosh you would probably alter these functions as follows:

```
void Reverse(void* v, int size)
{
    unsigned char buffer[8];
    unsigned char *s = (unsigned char*) v;

    for (int i = 0; i < size; i++) {
        buffer[i] = v[size - i - 1];
    }
   for (i = 0; i < size; i++) {
     v[i] = buffer[i];
   }
}

short ReadLong(FILE* fp, long& value)
{
  short retval;
    retval = (fread(&value, sizeof(value), 1, fp) == 1);
    Reverse((void*) &value, sizeof(long));
    return retval;
}
```

```
short WriteLong(FILE* fp, const long value)
{
  Reverse((void*) &value, sizeof(long));
   return (fwrite(&value, sizeof(value), 1, fp) == 1);
}
```

Tessellating Polygons

TrueSpace allows you to create very complicated Polygons. For example, when character strings are typed in, extruded, and then saved as a 3D object each character face is saved as one very large Polygon.

These Polygons must be reduced in complexity via a process called tessellation. A detailed discussion of tessellation is beyond the scope of this book. However, there are several graphics books and papers that discuss it in detail. A good place to look for tessellation algorithms is the Graphic Gems book series by Academic Press or the technical proceedings from Siggraph.

Overview of the TrueSpace Format

TrueSpace files are organized in a very straightforward manner. The first entry in the file is a 32-byte header followed by zero or more binary chunks. These chunks are simply a generic way of defining sections in the file. The beginning of a chunk is defined by a 20-byte header.

Following is an example of a minimal reader for TrueSpace files:

```
#include <stdio.hh
#include <string.h>

const int   FALSE = 0;
const int   TRUE = 1;

// Encapsulate Binary Read Functions
int ReadByte(FILE* fp, char& value)
{return (fread(&value, sizeof(value), 1, fp) == 1);}

int ReadShort(FILE* fp, short& value)
{return (fread(&value, sizeof(value), 1, fp) == 1);}

int ReadLong(FILE* fp, long& value)
{return (fread(&value, sizeof(value), 1, fp) == 1);}

// Read chunk
int ReadChunk(FILE* fp, char* chunktype, short& major,
    short& minor, long& id, long& parent, long& size)
{
```

```
        if (!ReadByte(fp, chunktype[0])) return FALSE;
        if (!ReadByte(fp, chunktype[1])) return FALSE;
        if (!ReadByte(fp, chunktype[2])) return FALSE;
        if (!ReadByte(fp, chunktype[3])) return FALSE;
        chunktype[4] = '\0';

        if (!ReadShort(fp, major)) return FALSE;
        if (!ReadShort(fp, minor)) return FALSE;

        if (!ReadLong(fp, id)) return FALSE;
        if (!ReadLong(fp, parent)) return FALSE;
        if (!ReadLong(fp, size)) return FALSE;

        return TRUE;
}

// Read and verify header
int ReadHeader(FILE* fp, char* header)
{
    for (int i = 0; i < 32; i++) {
        if (!ReadByte(fp, header[i])) return FALSE;
    }

    // Return TRUE if file is a TrueSpace binary file.
    return (strncmp(header, "Caligari ", 9) == 0 &&
            header[15] == 'B');
}

int
main(int argc, char** argv)
{
    while (argc > 1) {
        char* filename = argv[1];
        FILE* fp = fopen(filename, "rb");

        // Storage for the header
        char  header[32];

        // Storage for the chunk
        char  chunktype[5];
        short major, minor;
        long  id, parent, size;

        if (fp != NULL) {
            if (ReadHeader(fp, header)) {
                // Read all of the chunks in the file
                while (ReadChunk(fp, chunktype, major,
                                 minor, id, parent, size))
```

```
                    {
                // Read contents of the chunk
                for (long i = 0; i < size; i++)
                        {
                    char  value;
                    if (!ReadByte(fp, value))
                              {
                        break;
                    }
                }
            }
        } else {
            fprintf(stderr,
                    "%s is not a binary COB file.\n",
                        filename);
        }

        fclose(fp);
    }

    argv++; argc--;
  }
}
```

This minimal reader shows some of the important issues to consider when reading binary COB files: how to encapsulate binary reads, how to open files for binary reading (the *rb* argument in `fopen`), and the basic organization of a COB file. The semantics of each chunk are defined in the next section.

Syntax of a COB File

The syntax of a COB file is very straightforward: the COB file header followed by a series of zero or more chunks. The COB file format derives its meaning from the definition and semantics of each chunk. This section defines each component of a COB file in detail.

The File Header

A COB file begins with a 32-byte file header that identifies it as a Caligari COB file. When reading a COB file, you are advised to verify that the file is indeed a binary COB file. You can do this by reading the entire header and then verifying that the first 9 bytes are 'Caligari' and the fifteenth is a 'B'. Table 6.2 shows the make-up of the chunk header.

Table 6.2. The file header

Data Type	Size	Starting Position	Description
Char	9	0	The literal string 'Caligari '. Note the trailing blank in the literal string.
Char	6	9	The version number of the COB file format. The version described in this chapter is 'V00.01'.
Char	1	15	Contains either an 'A', for an ASCII file, or a 'B', for a binary file. This chapter defines the binary format.
Char	2	16	Describes the byte order of the binary data in the file. The legal values are 'LH' for little endian, and 'HL' for big endian. This chapter describes only 'LH', which is Intel's format.
Char	13	18	Contains blanks.
Char	1	31	A new line (0xa).

The Chunk Header

Each section in a TrueSpace file is defined by a chunk header. The chunk begins with a 20-byte header. This header identifies the type of the chunk, its major and minor revision, its ID, and its parent ID. It also identifies the chunk's size, which denotes the number of bytes in the chunk following the 20-byte header. This organization allows unrecognized chunks to be read and ignored if needed simply by reading the chunk header and the subsequent data defined in the size field. Table 6.3 shows the breakdown of the chunk header.

Table 6.3. The chunk header

Data Type	Size	Starting Position	Description
Char	4	0	The chunk type.
Short	2	4	Denotes a major revision of the chunk type definition.
Short	2	6	Denotes a minor revision of the chunk type definition.
Long	4	8	A unique chunk identifier. This value uniquely identifies this chunk.

Table 6.3. The chunk header *(continued)*

Data Type	Size	Starting Position	Description
Long	4	12	The parent identifier. This field identifies the parent chunk of this chunk by the parent's unique identifier. This is how a hierarchy is defined.
Long	4	16	The size in bytes of the data in the chunk, exclusive of the chunk header.

Common Chunk Subelements

A chunk may contain zero or more common subelements: strings, names, a local axis, and/or a current position.

String

A string is an arbitrary-length field that contains an ASCII string. Table 6.4 shows its breakdown.

Table 6.4. String

Data Type	Size	Starting Position	Description
Short	2	0	The string length in bytes.
Char	Variable	2	The size of the string defined by the string length field.

Name

A name is simply a string with a *dupcount.* A dupcount is a count of the number of usages of a particular name within the COB file. Table 6.5 shows the breakdown of a name.

Table 6.5. Name

Data Type	Size	Starting Position	Description
Short	2	0	Contains the dupcount.
Short	2	2	The string length in bytes.
Char	Variable	4	The size of the string defined by the string length field.

Local Axes

Many chunks define their current location and orientation in a scene. The position is the *x*-, *y*-, and *z*-coordinates of the center of the object, followed by a direction for each of the *x*-, *y*-, and *z*-axes. Each *x*-, *y*-, and *z*-direction should be perpendicular to the others. Table 6.6 shows the breakdown of local axes.

Table 6.6. Local axes

Data Type	Size	Starting Position	Description
float*3	12	0	The *x*-, *y*-, and *z*-coordinates for the center of the object.
float*3	12	12	Defines the direction for the *x*-axis.
float*3	12	24	Defines the direction for the *y*-axis.
float*3	12	36	Defines the direction for the *z*-axis.

Current Position

Many chunks define their 3D geometry in local space. The current position subelement defines the matrix transform that converts local space into world space. The matrix transform is defined as the first three rows of a 4×4 matrix. The last row is assumed to always be [0, 0, 0, 1]. Table 6.7 shows the breakdown of a current position.

Table 6.7. Current position

Data Type	Size	Starting Position	Description
float*4	16	0	The first row of the transformation matrix.
float*4	16	16	The second row of the transformation matrix.
float*4	16	32	The third row of the transformation matrix.

End Chunk Header

The End chunk header denotes the end of the COB file. Always 20 bytes, this chunk must be the last chunk in a file. Table 6.8 shows the breakdown of an End chunk header.

Table 6.8. End chunk header

Chunk Type	Major Revision	Minor Revision
'End'	0	1

Group Chunk Header

A group chunk header is usually the parent of one or more subchunks. Each group chunk contains a chunk header, a name subelement, a local axes subelement, and a current position subelement. Table 6.9 shows the breakdown of a group chunk header.

Table 6.9. Group chunk header

Chunk Type	Major Revision	Minor Revision
'Grou'	0	1

Group Chunk Organization

The entire group chunk consists of the group chunk header, the group name, the local axes for all of the subcomponents in the group, and the current position. The size of this chunk is 120 bytes plus the length of the name string. Table 6.10 shows the breakdown of group chunk organization.

Table 6.10. Group chunk organization

Element	Size	Starting Position	Description
Group Chunk Header	20	0	Denotes the beginning of the group chunk.
Group Name	4 + string length	20	Defines the name of the group.
Local Axes	48	24 + name length	Defines the local axes for the subcomponents of the group.
Current Position	48	72 + name length	Defines the local coordinate-to-world transformation.

Polygon Chunk Header

A Polygon chunk header is the only shape component defined for a TrueSpace file. All other shapes defined in TrueSpace are converted into Polygons before they are written to a COB file. The length of this file is highly variable and depends on the number of vertices and faces in the Polygon. This chunk is often a child to a group and is usually a parent to one or more material chunks. Table 6.11 shows the breakdown of a Polygon chunk header.

Table 6.11. Polygon chunk header

Chunk Type	Major Revision	Minor Revision
'PolH'	0	2

Polygon Chunk Organization

The Polygon chunk is the most complicated of all of the chunks defined for the COB file format. This chunk consists of seven subelements: header, name, local axes, current position, local vertex list, UV vertex list, and face list. Table 6.12 describes these parts.

Table 6.12. Polygon chunk organization

Element	Size	Starting Position	Description
Polygon Chunk Header	20	0	Denotes the beginning of the polygon chunk.
Name	4 + string length	20	Defines the name of the polygon.
Local Axes	48	24 + name length	Defines the local axes for the subelements of the Polygon.
Current Position	48	72 + name length	Defines the local coordinate-to-world transformation.
Local Vertex List	Variable	120 + name length	Defines the vertices to be used when defining polygon faces. See the local vertex list description later in this section for more information.

Table 6.12. Polygon chunk organization *(continued)*

Element	Size	Starting Position	Description
UV Vertex List	Variable	Variable	Defines the list of UV texture positions. See the UV vertex list description later in this section for more information.
Face List	Variable	Variable	Defines the list of faces and holes that define each polygon face in the polygon definition. See the face list description later in this section for more information.

Local Vertex List

The local vertex list defines each vertex used to define the points for each line segment that encloses each Polygon face in the Polygon chunk. This subelement contains a vertex count followed by that number of 3D coordinates. Table 6.13 shows the breakdown of the local vertex list.

Table 6.13. Local vertex list

Data Type	Size	Starting Position	Description
Long	4	0	The number of vertices in the local vertex list. The legal values are greater than or equal to zero.
float*3*numVert	12*numVert	4	Contains the *x*-, *y*-, and *z*- coordinates for each vertex in the local vertex list.

UV Vertex List

The UV vertex list is a list of UV (texture) positions. These values are used to correctly position a bitmapped texture onto each face of the Polygon. Each UV vertex value consists of two floating-point values. Table 6.14 shows the breakdown of the UV list.

Table 6.14. UV Vertex list

Data Type	Size	Starting Position	Description
Long	4	0	The number of vertices in the UV vertex list. The legal values are greater than or equal to 0.
float*2*numVert	8*numVert	4	Contains the UV coordinates for each vertex in the UV vertex list.

Face List

The face list defines a list of faces and holes. A face subelement is denoted by setting bit 3 of the first byte to 0, and a hole is denoted by setting bit 3 of the first byte to 1. Faces and holes vary in length depending on the number of indexes defined for the face or hole. Table 6.15 shows the breakdown of the face list.

Table 6.15. Face list

Element	Size	Starting Position	Description
Long	4	0	The number of faces or holes in the face list.
(Faces or Holes)* number in the first field	Variable	4	The number of faces and/or holes definitions described in the first field.

Face Type

The face type defines a planar Polygon that describes a face for the Polygon chunk. The planar Polygon is specified using an index into the local vertex list and the UV vertex list to define the vertices used in the face. Table 6.16 shows the breakdown of a face type.

Table 6.16. Face type

Element	Size	Starting Position	Description
Byte	1	0	The flag byte. Bit 3 set to 0 denotes a face type.

Table 6.16. Face type *(continued)*

Element	Size	Starting Position	Description
Short	2	1	The number of vertices in the face.
Short	2	3	The material index for the face.
Long*2*numVertices	8*numVertices	5	The face vertices. The first long is the index into the local vertex list; the second long is the index into the UV vertex list.

Hole Type

A hole type specifies a hole in a face. Table 6.17 shows the breakdown of a hole type.

Table 6.17. Hole type

Element	Size	Starting Position	Description
Byte	1	0	The flag byte. Bit 3 set to 1 denotes a hole type.
Short	2	1	The number of vertices in the hole.
Long*2*vertices	8*vertices	3	A long index into the local vertex list followed by a long index into the UV vertex list.

Material Chunk

A material chunk is one of two types of texture chunks. (The second type is a procedural chunk, discussed in the next section.) A material chunk defines the basic color and other physical properties of an object. A material chunk can also have zero or more of the following optional definitions: the environment map, the texture map, and the bump map.

Material Chunk Header

Table 6.18 shows the composition of the material chunk header.

Table 6.18. Material chunk header

Chunk Type	Major Revision	Minor Revision
'Mat1'	0	5

Material Chunk Organization

A material specifies many physical properties of an object that influence the object's color, highlighting, transparency, and so forth. The material property has a fixed set of properties that are required for all material definitions and that may be followed by zero or more optional definitions. These optional definitions are the environment map, the texture map, and the bump map. The organization of a material chunk is:

```
Chunk Header
Material Data
Environment Map (optional)
Texture Map (optional)
Bump Map (optional)
```

Material chunks are subelements of the Polygon chunk ('PolH'). A Polygon chunk should use each material defined as a subelement at least once. A material may not be a parent; it must have a parent ID that exists and that ID may not be 0.

Material Data

The material data defines the surface properties of the object. This includes smoothing information and the color, and highlighting properties.

Table 6.19. Material data

Data Type	Size	Starting Position	Description
Short	2	0	The material number. This is the number the parent chunk uses to specify the mapping of a material to an object.
Byte	1	2	The shader type. The options are flat, 'f'; phong, 'p'; or metal, 'm.' Flat shading means that no shading is done. This allows objects to be

Table 6.19. Material data *(continued)*

Data Type	Size	Starting Position	Description
			rendered quickly. Phong shading is a good general-purpose shader type. Metal shading is good for metal and glass.
Byte	1	3	The *Facet* type. The values are faceted, 'f'; autofaceted, 'a'; and smooth, 's.' Faceted means the object is not smoothed. Autofaceted means the object is smoothed when the angle between two Polygons is less than the autofacet angle. Smoothed means all the Polygons in the object are smoothed.
Byte	1	4	The autofacet angle. This value is specified in degrees. It is used when the *Facet* type is set to autofacet to determine the angle at which two Polygons are smoothed.
Float*3	12	5	The RGB (red, green, blue) value of the material. The legal values for each color value are 0.0–1.0. The value 0.0 means zero intensity; the value 1.0 means full intensity for the color.
Float	4	17	The opacity of the material. The legal values are 0.0–1.0. The value 0.0 means transparent; the value 1.0 means opaque.
Float	4	21	The ambient coefficient. The legal values are 0.0–1.0.
Float	4	25	The specular coefficient. The legal values are 0.0–1.0.
Float	4	29	The hilight size coefficient. The legal values are 0.0–1.0.
Float	4	33	The index of refraction. A value of 1.0 means no refraction occurs.

Environment Map

An environment map is used to simulate reflection of the environment on a shiny object. An environment map construct contains the full path name to the environment map file.

An environment map file may have either the *.T1D or the *.E2D file suffix. The T1D file format is a color gradient used to simulate highlighting of an object. The E2D file format is a 2D image that simulates the environment for the object to which the material is attached. Table 6.20 lists the parts of an environment map.

Table 6.20. Environment map

Data Type	Size	Starting Position	Description
Byte	2	0	The identifier for the environment map. The value must be 'e:'.
Byte	1	2	The environment map flag. Bit 1 is the ENVR_USE flag and is always set. Bit 0 is the ENVR_CUBIC flag. When it is 1, the environment map is cubic; otherwise, the environment map is spherical.
String	2 + string length	3	The full path name to the environment file. It will have either a T1D or a E2D file suffix.

Texture Map

A Texture map maps a bitmap image onto an object. This map adds several new fields in addition to the fields found in the environment map: U offset (horizontal offset), V offset (vertical offset), U repetitions (number of repetitions horizontally), and V repetitions (number of repetitions vertically). Table 6.21 lists the parts of a texture map.

Table 6.21. Texture map

Data Type	Size	Starting Position	Description
Byte	2	0	The identifier for the texture map. The value must be 't:'.
Byte	1	2	The environment map flag. Bit 1 is the TXTR_USE flag and is always set. Bit 0 is the TXTR_OVERLAY flag. When it is 1, the texture map is allowed to be transparent.

(*continued*)

Table 6.21. Texture map *(continued)*

Data Type	Size	Starting Position	Description
String	2 + string length	3	The full path name to the texture file. The file type may be a Windows BMP file, a TXR file, a TARGA (TGA) file, a JPEG (JPG) file, or a Windows AVI file for an animated texture.
Float	4	5 + string length	The U offset (horizontal offset). The legal values are 0.0–1.0.
Float	4	9 + string length	The V offset (vertical offset). The legal values are 0.0–1.0.
Float	4	13 + string length	The U repetitions (horizontal repetitions). The legal values are 0.0–1.0.
Float	4	17 + string length	The V repetitions (vertical repetitions). The legal values are 0.0–1.0.

Bump Map

A bump map is a raster image in which the pixel intensity specifies the apparent height of a position on the object. The more intense the pixel value, the higher the apparent bump. Table 6.22 lists the parts of a bump map.

Table 6.22. Bump map

Data Type	Size	Starting Position	Description
Byte	2	0	The identifier for the texture map. The value must be 'b:'.
Byte	1	2	The texture map flag. Bit 1 is the BUMP_USE flag and is always set.
String	2 + string length	3	The full path name to the bump file. The file type may be a Windows BMP file, a TXR file, a TAB file, a TARGA (TGA) file, a JPEG (JPG) file, or a Windows AVI file for an animated bump map.
Float	4	5 + string length	The U offset (horizontal offset). The legal values are 0.0–1.0

Table 6.22. Bump map *(continued)*

Data Type	Size	Starting Position	Description
Float	4	9 + string length	The V offset (vertical offset). The legal values are 0.0–1.0.
Float	4	13 + string length	The U repetitions (horizontal repetitions). The legal values are 0.0–1.0.
Float	4	17 + string length	The V repetitions (vertical repetitions). The legal values are 0.0–1.0.
Float	4	21 + string length	The amplitude of the bump map. A value of 0.0 means no bumps are visible.

Procedural Chunk Header

A procedural chunk header is an alternative way of describing a texture. It allows three common algorithmic textures to be defined and parameterized: granite, marble, and wood. This chunk is very similar to the material chunk. However, instead of a texture map there is an optional granite, marble, or wood procedural definition. The organization of this chunk is:

```
Chunk Header
Material Data
Environment Map (optional)
One of Wood, Marble, or Granite (optional)
Bump Map (optional)
```

Procedural chunks are subelements of the Polygon chunk (‘PolH’). A Polygon chunk should use each material defined as a subelement at least once. A procedural chunk may not be a parent; it must have a parent ID that exists and that ID may not be 0. Table 6.23 shows the procedural chunk header.

Table 6.23. Procedural chunk header

Chunk Type	Major Revision	Minor Revision
‘PrTx’	0	1

Procedural Chunk Organization

The organization of a procedural chunk closely resembles that of the material chunk. The only significant difference is that a procedural chunk has either a granite, marble, or wood definition instead of a texture map.

Granite Definition

A granite texture has four color definitions. These colors are randomly distributed throughout the texture. Each definition has a value for the amount that is used to determine the amount of that color in the overall texture. The sharpness value specifies the amount of noise that is applied to the texture. Table 6.24 lists the parts of a granite definition.

Table 6.24. The granite texture definition

Data Type	Size	Starting Position	Description
Byte*2	2	0	The procedural texture identifier. The value for this field in a granite definition is 'g:'.
Byte	1	2	Reserved. Should be set to 0.
Float*4	16	3	The definition of color 1. The color definition order is red, green, blue, alpha. The primary colors may range from 0.0 to 1.0, where 0.0 is the least intensity and 1.0 is the maximum intensity. The alpha value is the opacity of the color. The range for alpha is 0.0 to 1.0, where 0.0 means transparent and 1.0 means opaque.
Float*4	16	19	The definition of color 2. The color definition order is red, green, blue, alpha. The primary colors may range from 0.0 to 1.0, where 0.0 is the least intensity and 1.0 is the maximum intensity. The alpha value is the opacity of the color. The range for alpha is 0.0 to 1.0, where 0.0 means transparent and 1.0 means opaque.
Float*4	16	35	The definition of color 3. The color definition order is red, green, blue, alpha. The primary colors may range from 0.0 to 1.0, where 0.0 is the least intensity and 1.0 is the maximum intensity. The alpha value is the opacity of the color. The range for alpha is 0.0 to 1.0, where 0.0 means transparent and 1.0 means opaque.

Table 6.24. The granite texture definition *(continued)*

Data Type	Size	Starting Position	Description
Float*4	16	51	The definition of color 4. The color definition order is red, green, blue, alpha. The primary colors may range from 0.0 to 1.0, where 0.0 is the least intensity and 1.0 is the maximum intensity. The alpha value is the opacity of the color. The range for alpha is 0.0 to 1.0, where 0.0 means transparent and 1.0 means opaque.
Float	4	67	The weight of color 1. The range for the value is 0.0–1.0. The larger the value, the more of the texture that will be rendered using this color.
Float	4	71	The weight of color 2. The legal values are 0.0–1.0. The larger the value, the more of the texture that will be rendered using this color.
Float	4	75	The weight of color 3. The legal values are 0.0–1.0. The larger the value, the more of the texture that will be rendered using this color.
Float	4	79	The weight of color 4. The legal values are 0.0–1.0. The larger the value, the more of the texture that will be rendered using this color.
Float	4	83	The sharpness field. It is used to specify the amount of noise that is applied to the turbulence function. The legal values are 0.0–1.0, where 0 means no noise is applied and 1 means the maximum amount of noise is applied.
Float	4	87	The X scale field. This scales the textures in the *x*-direction. The legal values are 0.0–10.0.
Float	4	91	The Y scale field. This scales the textures in the *y*-direction. The legal values are 0.0–10.0.
Float	4	95	The Z scale field. This scales the textures in the *z*-direction. The legal values are 0.0–10.0.
Short	2	99	The random seed. This value defines the seed value for the random number generated used by the turbulence function for this texture.

Marble Definition

A marble texture is a procedural texture with two colors. The predominate color is the stone color, and the lesser color running through the texture is the vein color. Table 6.25 lists the parts of the marble texture definition.

Table 6.25. The marble texture definition

Data Type	Size	Starting Position	Description
Byte*2	2	0	The procedural texture identifier. The value for this field in a marble definition is 'm:'.
Byte	1	2	Reserved. Should be set to 0.
Float*4	16	3	The definition of the stone color. The color definition order is red, green, blue, alpha. The primary colors may range from 0.0 to 1.0, where 0.0 means the least intensity and 1.0 is the maximum intensity. The alpha value is the opacity of the color. The range for alpha is 0.0 to 1.0, where 0.0 means transparent and 1.0 means opaque.
Float*4	16	19	The definition of the vein color. The color definition order is red, green, blue, alpha. The primary colors may range from 0.0 to 1.0, where 0.0 is the least intensity and 1.0 is the maximum intensity. The alpha value is the opacity of the color. The range for alpha is 0.0 to 1.0, where 0.0 means transparent and 1.0 means opaque.
Float	4	35	The sharpness field. It is used to specify the amount of noise that is applied to the turbulence function. The legal values are 0.0 to 1.0, where 0 means no noise is applied and 1 means that the maximum amount of noise is applied.
Float	4	39	The X scale field. This scales the textures in the *x*-direction. The legal values are 0.0–10.0.
Float	4	43	The Y scale field. This scales the textures in the *y*-direction. The legal values are 0.0–10.0.
Float	4	47	The Z scale field. This scales the textures in the *z*-direction. The legal values are 0.0–10.0.
Short	2	49	The vein turbulence. The legal values are 0–10, where 0 is no turbulence and 10 is maximum turbulence.

Table 6.25. The marble texture definition *(continued)*

Data Type	Size	Starting Position	Description
Short	2	51	The XYZ grain flag. A value of 1 in the bit corresponding with the *x*-, *y*-, or *z*-axis means that the vein flows along that axis. Bit 1 denotes the *x*-axis, bit 2 denotes the *y*-axis, and bit 3 denotes the *z*-axis. This field is really an enumeration, so only one bit should be set.
Short	2	53	The random number seed. The legal range of this value is 1–32767. This value defines the seed value for the random number used by the turbulence function for this texture.

Wood Definition

A wood texture is a procedural texture with two colors that resembles wood grain. This texture applies the specified colors in concentric cylinders and then applies a turbulence function to give a realistic wood look. Many parameters influence how the wood texture is created, including the wood colors, their ratios, the ring density, the ring width, and the ring shape variation. Table 6.26 lists the parts of the wood texture definition.

Table 6.26. The wood texture definition

Data Type	Size	Starting Position	Description
Byte*2	2	0	The procedural texture identifier. The value for this field in a marble definition is 'w:'.
Byte	1	2	Reserved. Should be set to 0.
Float*4	16	3	The spring wood color. The color definition order is red, green, blue, alpha. The primary colors may range from 0.0 to 1.0, where 0.0 is the least intensity and 1.0 is the maximum intensity. The alpha value is the opacity of the color. The range for alpha is 0.0–1.0, where 0.0 means transparent and 1.0 means opaque.
Float*4	16	19	The summer wood color. The color definition order is red, green, blue, alpha. The primary colors may range from 0.0 to 1.0, where 0.0 is the least

(continued)

Table 6.26. The wood texture definition *(continued)*

Data Type	Size	Starting Position	Description
			intensity and 1.0 is the maximum intensity. The alpha value is the opacity of the color. The range for alpha is 0.0–1.0, where 0.0 means transparent and 1.0 means opaque.
Float	4	35	The spring-to-summer color ratio. The legal range for this value is 0.0–1.0. Lower values allow the summer color to dominate, while higher values allow the spring color to dominate.
Float	4	39	The ring density. The legal values are 0.0–10.0. Lower values produce fewer rings, while higher values produce more rings.
Float	4	43	The ring width variation. The legal values are 0.0–1.0. A value of 0 indicates no variation between rings; a value of 1.0 indicates much variation between rings.
Float	4	47	The ring shape variation. The legal values are 0.0–1.0. This field specifies how much a ring will vary from a circular shape. A value of 0.0 indicates nearly circular; a value of 1.0 indicates a large amount of variation.
Float*3	12	51	The X, Y, Z center of the textures. These fields are not currently available for modification and must be set to (1.0, 1.0, 1.0).
Float*3	12	63	The X, Y, Z scale of the texture. The legal values are 0.0–10.0.
Short	2	75	The XYZ grain flag. A value of 1 in the bit corresponding with the *x*-, *y*-, or *z*-axis means the vein flows along that axis. Bit 1 denotes the *x*-axis, bit 2 denotes the *y*-axis, and bit 3 denotes the *z*-axis. This field is really an enumeration, so only one bit should be set.
Short	2	77	The random number seed. The legal values are 1–32767. This value defines the seed value for the random number used by the turbulence function for this texture.

Figure 1C: A Viewpoint cow model, displayed in the standalone executable application that was created using Visual C++ 4.0 and the *Crossroads* class library. The creation of this application is described in Chapter 12.

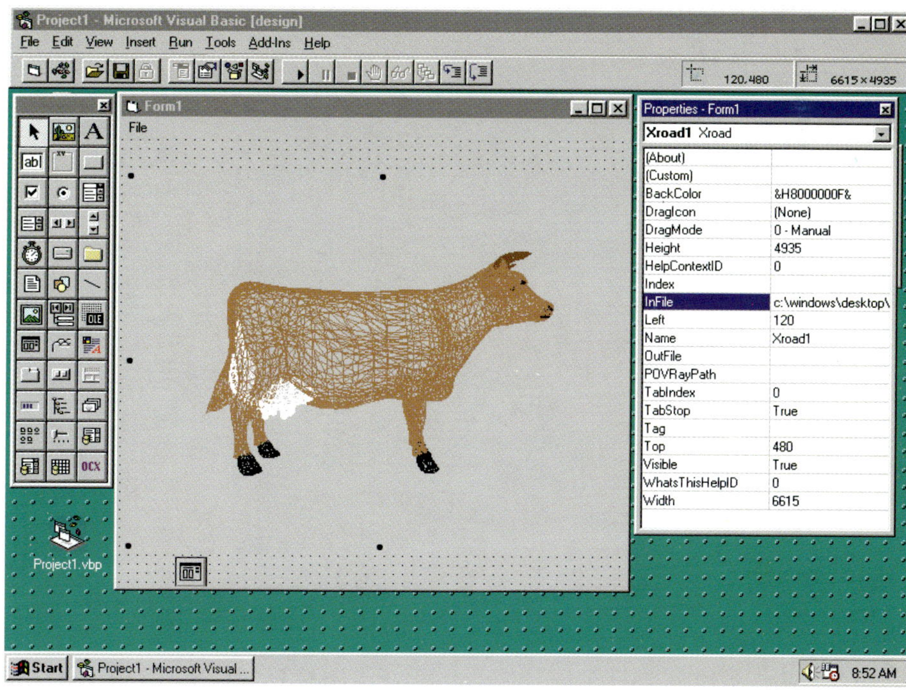

Figure 2C: A Visual Basic 4.0 project using the *Crossroads* OCX developed in Chapter 13. Notice that a 3D model can be read in at design time using the property sheet associated with the *Crossroads* OCX.

Figure 3C: This is the runtime version of the Visual Basic 4.0 project shown in Figure 2C. This program has about the same functionality as the standalone application shown in Figure 1C, but required only the *Crossroads* OCX and about 30 lines of Visual Basic code.

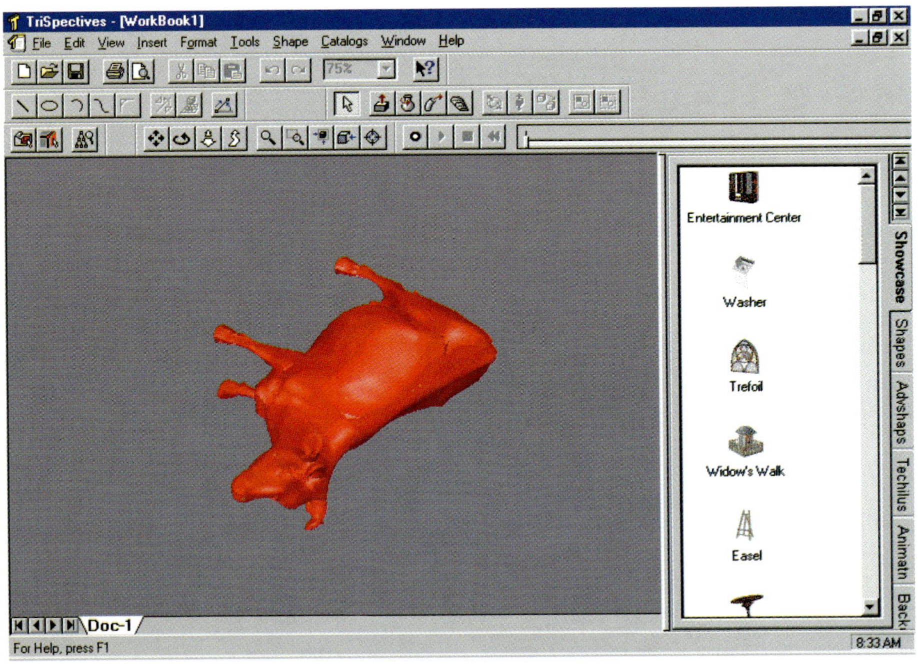

Figure 4C: Trispective is a 3D design program for Windows 95. A trial version of Trispective is included on the CD-ROM accompanying this book. The trial version comes with many 3D models and is able to save these models in formats supported by the *Crossroads* class library. This allows you to create multiple test models for your *Crossroads*-based applications.

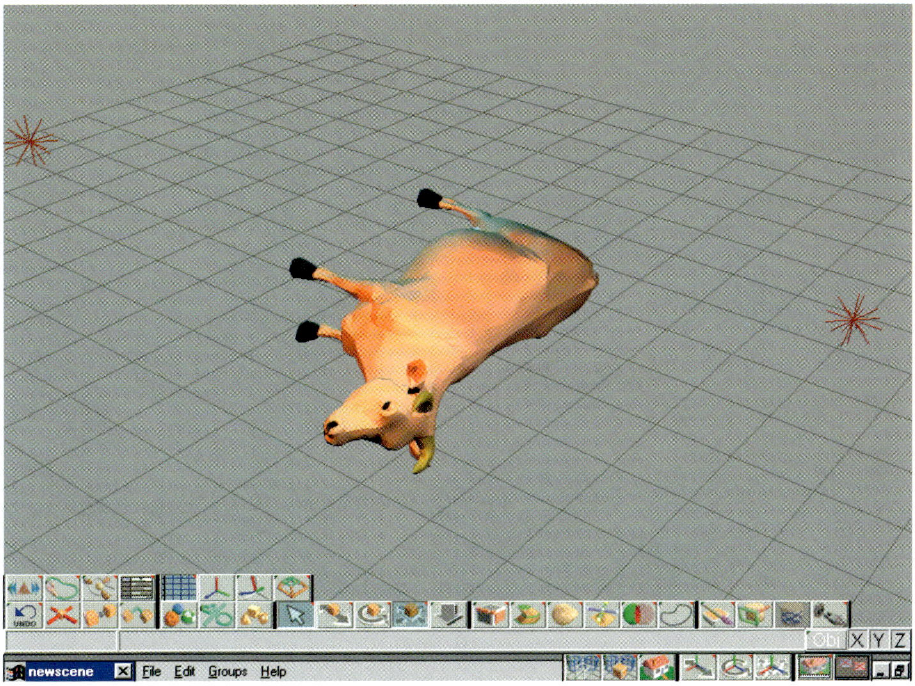

Figure 5C: TrueSpace is an easy-to-use 3D application. A trial version of TrueSpace is found on the accompanying CD-ROM. TrueSpace has been provided to help you verify your *Crossroads* TrueSpace model reader and writer.

Figure 6C: These models are provided by Viewpoint from the Avalon 3D model repository. Find additional free models at `http://www.viewpoint.com`.

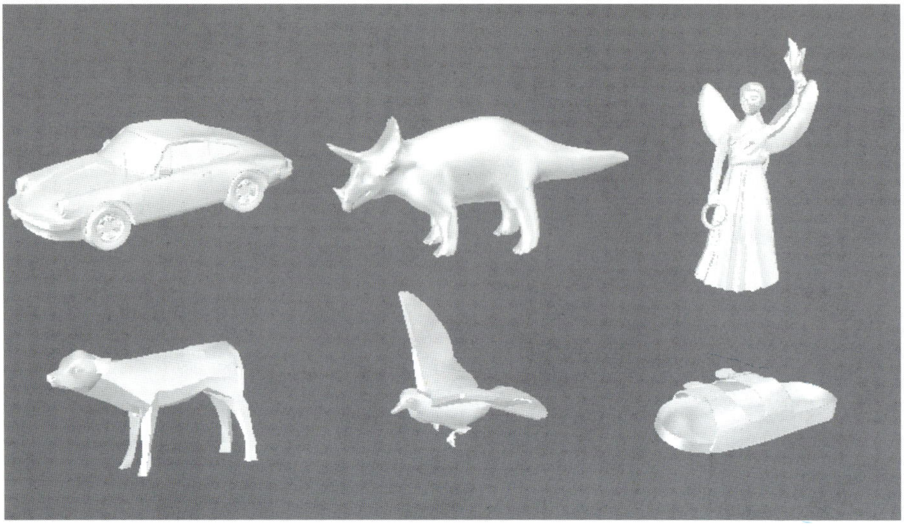

Figure 7C: Shown above are just a few of the many models provided by Viewpoint that are found on the accompanying CD-ROM.

Figure 8C: An anchor, weather vane, magnifying glass, microscope, Italianate structure, and piggy bank are a few of the many 3D models provided on the CD-ROM by 3D Eye.

Implementing a TrueSpace Reader

A TrueSpace file contains only a modest number of components to convert into the internal file format: groups, polygons, and materials. In this implementation, only basic materials are converted into the internal representation. The optional components of the 'Mat1' chunk and the 'PrTx' chunk, both of which include an environment map, bump map, and texture map, are ignored in this implementation.

Mapping TrueSpace Chunks to the Internal Representation

In this implementation, each 'Grou' chunk maps directly to a *GSeparator* class instance. Each child of 'Grou' is made a child of the corresponding *GSeparator* instance for the 'Grou'.

The 'PolH' chunk creates multiple components in the internal representation, including vertices, faces, and materials.

Reading a Chunk

A chunk is the fundamental component in a TrueSpace file. It denotes the beginning of a new component. Each chunk does the following:

- Identifies the chunk type with a four-character ASCII string. The meaning of many types of chunks was specified earlier in this chapter.
- Is identified with a specific revision, thereby enabling readers to verify that each chunk recognized matches the specific revision of the reader.
- Identifies the identifier for the specified chunk, and the specified chunk's parent.
- Specifies a size, thereby allowing unrecognized chunks to be ignored by simply reading the specified number of bytes. However, a size can be –1, which means the chunk doesn't know its length. When writing a TrueSpace file, you are advised to fill in the size value with the actual size of the chunk section rather than writing a –1.

The implementation of the chunk reader follows:

```
// Chunk Data
typedef struct {
   char  chunkType[4];
   short majorVersion;
   short minorVersion;
   long  chunkID;
   long  parentID;
   long  size;
```

```
} Chunk;

// Read a Chunk, return Chunk Data and read success
int ReadChunk(GNode* root, FILE* fp, Chunk& chunk)
{
   for (int i = 0; i < 4; i++) {
      if (!ReadByte(fp, chunk.chunkType[i]))
               return FALSE;
   }

   if (!ReadShort(fp, chunk.majorVersion)) return FALSE;
   if (!ReadShort(fp, chunk.minorVersion)) return FALSE;
   if (!ReadLong(fp, chunk.chunkID)) return FALSE;
   if (!ReadLong(fp, chunk.parentID)) return FALSE;
   if (!ReadLong(fp, chunk.size)) return FALSE;
   return TRUE;
}
```

Verifying the File Type

It is important to verify that a file type is actually the type expected. The following function `IsCobFile()` reads the TrueSpace file header and verifies that it is a binary COB or SCN file:

```
// Check File Type
int IsCobFile(GNode* root, FILE* fp
{
   char  buffer[32];

   for (int i = 0; i < 32; i++) {
      if (!ReadByte(fp, buffer[i])) {
         root->ErrorMessage("Premature EOF");
         return FALSE;
      }
   }
   if (strncmp(buffer, "Caligari", 8) == 0 &&
        buffer[15] == 'B') {
      return TRUE;
   }

   root->ErrorMessage("Selected file is not a binary
Caligari COB file");
   return FALSE;
}
```

Reading Basic Data Types

A TrueSpace file has several basic data types, including a string, a name, a local axis, and a current position. The following section defines functions to read each of these data types:

```
// Read a Cob string
int ReadString(GNode* root, FILE* fp, char* name)
{
   short length;

   if (!ReadShort(fp, length)) return FALSE;

   for (int i = 0; i < length; i++) {
      if (!ReadByte(fp, name[i])) return FALSE;
   }
   name[i] = '\0';
   return TRUE;
}

// Read a Cob name
int ReadName(GNode* root, FILE* fp, char* name)
{
   short dupcount;

   if (!ReadShort(fp, dupcount)) return FALSE;
   return ReadString(root, fp, name);
}

// Read a local axis matrix - it returns whether the
// read was successful and the center, x_axis, y_axis, and
// z_axis.
int ReadLocalAxis(GNode* root, FILE*fp, SFVec3f& center,
        SFVec3f& x_axis, SFVec3f& y_axis, SFVec3f& z_axis)
{
   float    c_x, c_y, c_z;
   float    x_x, x_y, x_z;
   float    y_x, y_y, y_z;
   float    z_x, z_y, z_z;

   if (!ReadFloat(fp, c_x)) return FALSE;
   if (!ReadFloat(fp, c_y)) return FALSE;
   if (!ReadFloat(fp, c_z)) return FALSE;
   center = SFVec3f(c_x, c_y, c_z);


   if (!ReadFloat(fp, x_x)) return FALSE;
   if (!ReadFloat(fp, x_y)) return FALSE;
```

```
    if (!ReadFloat(fp, x_z)) return FALSE;
    x_axis = SFVec3f(x_x, x_y, x_z);

    if (!ReadFloat(fp, y_x)) return FALSE;
    if (!ReadFloat(fp, y_y)) return FALSE;
    if (!ReadFloat(fp, y_z)) return FALSE;
    y_axis = SFVec3f(y_x, y_y, y_z);

    if (!ReadFloat(fp, z_x)) return FALSE;
    if (!ReadFloat(fp, z_y)) return FALSE;
    if (!ReadFloat(fp, z_z)) return FALSE;
    z_axis = SFVec3f(z_x, z_y, z_z);

    return TRUE;
}

// Read the current position matrix
int ReadCurrentPosition(GNode* root, FILE* fp, SFMatrix&
transform)
{
    for (int i = 0; i < 3; i++) {
        for (int j = 0; j < 4; j++) {
            float value;
            if (!ReadFloat(fp, value)) return FALSE;
            transform[j][i] = value;
        }
    }
    for (int j = 0; j < 4; j++) {
        transform[j][3] = (j != 3 ? 0.0 : 1.0);
    }

    return TRUE;
}
```

Reading a Group Chunk

Reading a group chunk is very straightforward. You simply read the group name, the local axis, and the current position. For the purposes here, you can ignore both the local axis and the current position.

Once you have the group name, you need only rename the current *GSeparator* to the name of the group. Then you register the identifier for the group with the corresponding separator. Last, you check whether this group has a parent and, if it does, add this group to the parent's child list.

The following code reads in the group chunk:

```
    if (strncmp(chunk.chunkType, "Grou", 4) == 0) {
       char      name[256];
       SFVec3f   center, x_axis, y_axis, z_axis;
       SFMatrix matrix;
       GSeparator* group = new GSeparator;
       GNode*    parent;

    if (!ReadName(root, fp, name)) goto error;
    if (!ReadLocalAxis(root, fp, center,
               x_axis, y_axis, z_axis)) goto error;
    if (!ReadCurrentPosition(root, fp, matrix)) goto error;

    // If we encountered a name, set the name of
    // the separator to it. Please note that 'NoName'
    // is often used as a null name in TrueSpace files.
    if (name[0] != '\0' && strcmp(name, "NoName") != 0) {
       group->SetName(name);
    }

    // Register the group id
    obj_dict.Add(chunk.chunkID, group);

    // Lookup the parent
    parent = obj_dict.Lookup(chunk.parentID);

    if (parent != NULL) {
       // Add to parent
       parent->AddChild(group);
    } else {
       // Add to base object
       root->AddChild(group);
    }
}
```

Reading a Polygon Chunk

Recall that the only shape object in the current TrueSpace file definition is a Polygon, so all shapes in a TrueSpace file are a collection of Polygons.

Reading a Polygon chunk is a bit more involved than reading a group chunk. As with a group chunk, you must read the Polygon name, the local axis, and the current position. In addition, there are several other types of constructs that must be read: the local vertex list, the UV vertex list, and the face list.

The vertex list is converted into a *GCoordinate3* instance. The UV vertex list is ignored because this code doesn't support environment maps, texture maps, or bump maps. The face list is converted into a *GIndexedFaceSet* instance.

As with the group chunk, you must rename the *GSeparator* to the name contained in the name construct and register the identifier for the group with the corresponding separator. In addition, if the current position construct is not the identity matrix, it must be converted to a matrix transform. This transform then must be inserted in the internal representation before the *GIndexedFaceSet*. This is because the vertices must be multiplied by this matrix to convert them to world coordinates.

The last step is to check whether this group has a parent and, if it does, add this group to the parent's child list.

The following code reads a polygon chunk:

```
if (strncmp(chunk.chunkType, "PolH", 4) == 0) {
   char          name[256];
   SFVec3f       center, x_axis, y_axis, z_axis;
   SFMatrix      matrix;
   GNode*        parent;

   GSeparator*     group = new GSeparator;
   GMatrixTransform* transform = new GMatrixTransform;
   GIndexedFaceSet*  poly = new GIndexedFaceSet;
   GCoordinate3*   coords = new GCoordinate3;

   MFVec3f*      vertex = new MFVec3f;
   MFVec2f*      uv_vertex = new MFVec2f;
   MFLong*       faces = new MFLong;
   MFLong*       uv_faces = new MFLong;
   MFLong*       m_indexs = new MFLong;

   if (!ReadName(root, fp, name)) goto error;
   if (!ReadLocalAxis(root, fp, center,
                    x_axis, y_axis, z_axis)) goto error;
   if (!ReadCurrentPosition(root, fp, matrix)) goto error;
   if (!ReadVertexList(root, fp, *vertex)) goto error;
   if (!ReadUVVertexList(root, fp, *uv_vertex))
        goto error;

     if (!ReadFaces(root, fp, *vertex,
                   *uv_vertex, *faces, *uv_faces,
                   *m_indexs)) goto error;

   // We don't support bitmap materials in this version.
   delete uv_vertex;
   delete uv_faces;

   // If we encountered a name, set the name of
   // the separator to it.
```

```
    if (name[0] != '\0' && strcmp(name, "NoName") != 0) {
        group->SetName(name);
    }

    // Add transform matrix, only if it will make
    // a difference
    if (matrix != Identity()) {
        transform->Transform(matrix);
        group->AddChild((GNode*)transform);
    }

    // Add the points to the current group
    coords->Point(vertex);
    group->AddChild((GNode*) coords);

    // Add the faces to the current group
    poly->CoordIndex(faces);
    group->AddChild((GNode*) poly);

    // Add materials
    if (m_indexs->Elements() > 0) {
        GMaterialBinding* binding = new GMaterialBinding;
        binding->Value(G_PER_FACE_INDEXED);
        group->InsertChild(binding);
        poly->MaterialIndex(m_indexs);
    } else {
        // No materials defined so delete the storage.
        delete m_indexs;
        m_indexs = NULL:
    }

    // Register the group id
    obj_dict.Add(chunk.chunkID, group);

    // Lookup the parent
    parent = obj_dict.Lookup(chunk.parentID);

    if (parent != NULL) {
        // Add to parent
        parent->AddChild(group);
    } else {
        // Add to base object
        root->AddChild(group);
    }
}
```

Three functions still must be defined so that the reader can fully read the polygon chunk: `ReadVertexList()`, `ReadUVVertexList()`, and `ReadFaces()`. `ReadVertexList()` reads a 3D vertex list, `ReadUVVertexList()` reads a 2D vertex list, and `ReadFaces()` reads the actual series of polygons that use the vertices.

The ReadVertexList() Function

A vertex list starts with a long value that is the number of vertices to be read. The following entries are an X, Y, Z tuple that represents each vertex:

```
// Read a vertex list
int ReadVertexList(GNode* root, FILE* fp, MFVec3f& vertex)
{
   long  count;
   float x, y, z;

   if (!ReadLong(fp, count)) return FALSE;
   for (long i = 0; i < count; i++) {
      if (!ReadFloat(fp, x)) return FALSE;
      if (!ReadFloat(fp, y)) return FALSE;
      if (!ReadFloat(fp, z)) return FALSE;

      vertex.Add(SFVec3f(x, y, z));
   }

   return TRUE;
}
```

The ReadUVVertexList() Function

A UV vertex is a list of 2D vertexes that specify the mapping of an environment map, texture map, or bump map onto a polygon. A vertex list starts with a long value that is the number of vertices to be read. The following entries are a U, V (horizontal and vertical) tuple that represents each vertex:

```
// Read the UV Vertex lists
int ReadUVVertexList(GNode* root, FILE* fp, MFVec2f&
uv_vertex)
{
   long  count;
   float u, v;

   if (!ReadLong(fp, count)) return FALSE;
   for (long i = 0; i < count; i++) {
      if (!ReadFloat(fp, u)) return FALSE;
```

```
      if (!ReadFloat(fp, v)) return FALSE;

      uv_vertex.Add(SFVec2f(u, v));
   }

   return TRUE;
}
```

The ReadFaces() Function

TrueSpace has two types of face components: holes and faces. For this reader, you can ignore holes. However, if you were to incorporate holes into a reader, you would apply the hole component that was applied to the previously defined face.

A face is a series of indexes into the vertex list and the UV vertex list. These indexes specify the polygon and the mapping of environment maps, texture maps, or bump maps onto the polygon.

This function reads a series of faces into the variables *faces* and *uv_faces*. The materials encountered are placed in the variable *material*.

```
// Read the face lists
int ReadFaces(GNode* root, FILE* fp, MFVec3f& vertex,
        MFVec2f& uvvertex, MFLong& faces,
        MFLong& uv_faces, MFLong& material)
{
   long          count;
   unsigned char flag;
   short         v_count;
   short         m_index;
   long          v_index, uv_index;

   // Read the number of faces into count
   if (!ReadLong(fp, count)) return FALSE;

   // Loop through the face count
   for (long i = 0; i < count; i++) {

      // Read the type for this face
      if (!ReadUByte(fp, flag)) return FALSE;

      // Read the number of vertex indexes.
      if (!ReadShort(fp, v_count)) return FALSE;
      if (flag & 0x08) {
         // Hole - read the indexes and ignore them
         for (long j = 0; j < v_count; j++) {
            if (!ReadLong(fp, v_index))
```

```
                              return FALSE;
            if (!ReadLong(fp, uv_index))
                              return FALSE;
         }
      } else {
         // Face - read the indexes
         long     m;
         MFLong   polyfaces;
         MFLong   polyuvfaces;

         // Read material index
         if (!ReadShort(fp, m_index)) return FALSE;

                m = m_index;
         material.Add(m);

         // Read the indexes
         for (long j = 0; j < v_count; j++) {
            if (!ReadLong(fp, v_index))
                              return FALSE;
            if (!ReadLong(fp, uv_index))
                              return FALSE;
            polyfaces.Add(v_index);
            polyuvfaces.Add(uv_index);
         }
      }
   }

   return TRUE;
}
```

Reading a Material Chunk

Material chunks give shapes their interesting color and texture. The current TrueSpace specification defines two types of material chunks: 'Mat1' and 'PrTx'. For this reader, you need to read only the 'Mat1' chunk.

A 'Mat1' chunk consists of fields that define the physical properties of a texture. There also may be several optional fields that may define the environment map, the texture map, or the bump map for the material.

```
// Read a material
int ReadMaterial(GNode* root, FILE* fp, short& mat_number,
                        GMaterial& material)
{
   char     shader_type, facet_type, autofacet_angle;
   float    red, green, blue;
   float    opacity, ambient, specular, hilight, ior;
```

```
char      ident[2];
MFVec3f* ambientColor = material.AmbientColor();
MFVec3f* diffuseColor = material.DiffuseColor();
MFVec3f* specularColor= material.SpecularColor();
MFVec3f* emissiveColor= material.EmissiveColor();
MFFloat* shininess = material.Shininess();
MFFloat* transparency = material.Transparency();

SFVec3f  my_ambient;
SFVec3f  my_diffuse;
SFVec3f  my_specular;
SFVec3f  my_emissive;
SFFloat  my_shininess;
SFFloat  my_transparency;

// Required values
if (!ReadShort(fp, mat_number)) return FALSE;
if (!ReadByte(fp, shader_type)) return FALSE;
if (!ReadByte(fp, facet_type)) return FALSE;
if (!ReadByte(fp, autofacet_angle)) return FALSE;
if (!ReadFloat(fp, red)) return FALSE;
if (!ReadFloat(fp, green)) return FALSE;
if (!ReadFloat(fp, blue)) return FALSE;
if (!ReadFloat(fp, opacity)) return FALSE;
if (!ReadFloat(fp, ambient)) return FALSE;
if (!ReadFloat(fp, specular)) return FALSE;
if (!ReadFloat(fp, hilight)) return FALSE;
if (!ReadFloat(fp, ior)) return FALSE;

if (ambient == (SFFloat) 0.0) {
   ambient = (SFFloat) 0.1;
}

// Map to ambient coefficient to ambient color
my_ambient = SFVec3f(red*ambient,
                      green*ambient, blue*ambient);

// Map color to diffuse color
my_diffuse = SFVec3f(red, green, blue);

// Map specular value to specular color
my_specular = SFVec3f(specular, specular, specular);

// There is no value that corresponds to emissive
my_emissive = SFVec3f(0.0, 0.0, 0.0);

// Map hilight to shininess
my_shininess = hilight;
```

```
// Map opacity to transparency
my_transparency = 1.0-opacity;

ambientColor->Replace(mat_number, my_ambient);
diffuseColor->Replace(mat_number, my_diffuse);
specularColor->Replace(mat_number, my_specular);
emissiveColor->Replace(mat_number, my_emissive);
transparency->Replace(mat_number, my_transparency);
shininess->Replace(mat_number, my_shininess);

// Now read optional fields
if (!ReadByte(fp, ident[0])) return FALSE;
if (!ReadByte(fp, ident[1])) return FALSE;

// Optional environment Map
if (strncmp(ident, "e:", 2) == 0) {
   char  flags;
   char  filename[256];
   if (!ReadByte(fp, flags))
         return FALSE;
   if (!ReadString(root, fp, filename))
         return FALSE;

   // Get next identifier
  if (!ReadByte(fp, ident[0])) return FALSE;
   if (!ReadByte(fp, ident[1])) return FALSE;
   }

// Optional Texture Map
if (strncmp(ident, "t:", 2) == 0) {
   char  flags, filename[256];
   float u_offset, v_offset, u_repeat, v_repeat;

   if (!ReadByte(fp, flags)) return FALSE;
   if (!ReadString(root, fp, filename))
         return FALSE;

   if (!ReadFloat(fp, u_offset)) return FALSE;
   if (!ReadFloat(fp, v_offset)) return FALSE;
   if (!ReadFloat(fp, u_repeat)) return FALSE;
   if (!ReadFloat(fp, v_repeat)) return FALSE;

   // Get next identifier
   if (!ReadByte(fp, ident[0])) return FALSE;
   if (!ReadByte(fp, ident[1])) return FALSE;
}

// Optional Bump map
```

```
    if (strncmp(ident, "b:", 2) == 0) {
        char  flags, filename[256];
        float u_offset, v_offset, u_repeat;
              float  v_repeat, amplitude;

        if (!ReadByte(fp, flags)) return FALSE;
        if (!ReadString(root, fp, filename)) return FALSE;

        if (!ReadFloat(fp, u_offset)) return FALSE;
        if (!ReadFloat(fp, v_offset)) return FALSE;
        if (!ReadFloat(fp, u_repeat)) return FALSE;
        if (!ReadFloat(fp, v_repeat)) return FALSE;
        if (!ReadFloat(fp, amplitude)) return FALSE;
    } else {

        // Put back the unused ident tokens
        ungetc(ident[1], fp);
        ungetc(ident[0], fp);
    }

    return TRUE;
}
```

The open_cob() Function

The previous few sections described the functions required to build a TrueSpace reader. However, the top-level reader still has not been defined. The reader verifies that the file is a TrueSpace file and then reads all of the chunks in the file.

The following code implements the top level of a TrueSpace reader:

```
void
cob_reader(GNode* root, char* filename)
{
    FILE*          fp;
    long           fileSize;
    Chunk          chunk;
    CobDict         obj_dict;
    GMaterialBinding* mbinding = new GMaterialBinding;

    mbinding->Value(G_OVERALL);
    root->AddChild((GNode*) mbinding);

    // Z is up in truespace, so let's rotate it so it
    // looks right in wrl.
    root->AddChild((GNode*) new GRotation(
          SFRotation(1.0, 0.0, 0.0, -1.570795)));
```

```
root->AddChild((GNode*) new GRotation(
      SFRotation(0.0, 0.0, 1.0, -1.570795)));

// Open the file - remember to use 'rb'
if ((fp = fopen(filename, "rb")) != NULL) {

   // Get Length of File
   fseek(fp, 0L, SEEK_END);
   fileSize = ftell(fp);
   rewind(fp);

   // Make sure it's a cob file
   if (!IsCobFile(root, fp)) {
      fclose(fp);
      return;
   }

   // Read all the chunks in the file
   while (ReadChunk(root, fp, chunk))
   {
      // Status message
      root->StatusMessage(
                   "Reading %3.1f%% Complete",
                   ((float) ftell(fp))/((float)
                         fileSize)*100.0f);

      // Check for supported groups
      if (strncmp(chunk.chunkType, "Grou", 4)==0)
            {
         char     name[256];
         SFVec3f  center, x_axis;
                    SFVec3fy_axis, z_axis;
         SFMatrix matrix;
         GSeparator* group = new GSeparator;
         GNode*   parent;

         if (!ReadName(root, fp, name))
                         goto error;
         if (!ReadLocalAxis(root, fp,
                         center, x_axis, y_axis,
                         z_axis))
                         goto error;

         if (!ReadCurrentPosition(root,
                         fp, matrix)) goto error;

         // If we encountered a name, set
         // the name of the separator to it.
```

```
    if (name[0] != '\0' &&
                strcmp(name, "NoName") != 0) {
        group->SetName(name);
    }

    // Register the group id
    obj_dict.Add(chunk.chunkID, group);

    // Lookup the parent
    parent = obj_dict.Lookup(
                        chunk.parentID);

    if (parent != NULL) {
        // Add to parent
        parent->AddChild(group);
    } else {
        // Add to base object
        root->AddChild(group);
    }
} else if (strncmp(chunk.chunkType,
                "PolH", 4) == 0) {
    char      name[256];
    SFVec3f   center, x_axis, y_axis;
                SFVed3fz_axis;
    SFMatrix matrix;
    GNode*    parent;

    GSeparator* group = new GSeparator;
    GMatrixTransform* transform =
                        new GMatrixTransform;
    GIndexedFaceSet*  poly =
                        new GIndexedFaceSet;
    GCoordinate3*coords =
                        new GCoordinate3;

    MFVec3f* vertex = new MFVec3f;
    MFVec2f* uv_vertex = new MFVec2f;
    MFLong*  faces = new MFLong;
    MFLong*  uv_faces = new MFLong;
    MFLong*  m_indexs = new MFLong;

    if (!ReadName(root, fp, name))
                goto error;
    if (!ReadLocalAxis(root, fp, center,
                x_axis, y_axis, z_axis))
                goto error;
    if (!ReadCurrentPosition(root, fp,
                matrix)) goto error;
```

```
if (!ReadVertexList(root, fp,
                  *vertex)) goto error;
if (!ReadUVVertexList(root, fp,
                  *uv_vertex)) goto error;
if (!ReadFaces(root, fp, *vertex,
                  *uv_vertex, *faces, *uv_faces,
                  *m_indexs)) goto error;

// We don't support bitmap
// materials in this version.
delete uv_vertex;
delete uv_faces;

// If we encountered a name, set
// the name of
// the separator to it.
if (name[0] != '\0' &&
                 strcmp(name, "NoName") != 0) {
   group->SetName(name);
}

// Add transform matrix, only if
// it will make a difference

if (matrix != Identity()) {
   transform->Transform(matrix);
   group->AddChild(
                        GNode*)transform);
}

// Add the points to the
// current group
coords->Point(vertex);
group->AddChild((GNode*) coords);

// Add the faces to the current group
poly->CoordIndex(faces);
group->AddChild((GNode*) poly);

// Optimize materials
if (m_indexs->Elements() > 0) {
   // Multiple materials found,
   // define them.
   GMaterialBinding* binding =
                       new GMaterialBinding;
   binding->Value(
                       G_PER_FACE_INDEXED);
   group->InsertChild(binding);
```

```
            poly->MaterialIndex(m_indexs);
        } else {
            // No materials defined
                        // so delete the storage.
            delete m_indexs;
            m_indexs = NULL;
        }

        // Register the group id
        obj_dict.Add(chunk.chunkID, group);

        // Lookup the parent
        parent = obj_dict.Lookup(
                            chunk.parentID);

        if (parent != NULL) {
            // Add to parent
            parent->AddChild(group);
        } else {
            // Add to base object
            root->AddChild(group);
        }
    } else if (strncmp(chunk.chunkType,
                    "Mat1", 4) == 0) {
        short    number;
        GMaterial*  material =
                        obj_dict.Material(
                                chunk.parentID);
        GNode*   parent = obj_dict.Lookup(
                                chunk.parentID);

        // If the material is not defined,
        // define it
        if (material == NULL) {
            material = new GMaterial;
            if (parent != NULL) {
                // Register the ID
                obj_dict.AddMaterial(
                                chunk.parentID,
                                material);

                // Add the material to
                // the parent
                parent->InsertChild(
                                 (GNode*) material);
            }
        }
```

```
            // Read the material
            if (!ReadMaterial(root, fp,
                            number, *material)) goto error;

            // If no parent, then ignore
            // the material
            if (parent == NULL) {
               delete material;
               material = NULL;
            }
         } else if (chunk.size >= 0) {
            char  byte;
            // Unknown chunk, so ignore it
            for (long i = 0; i < chunk.size; i++)
                        {
               if (!ReadByte(fp, byte))
                                 goto error;
            }
         }
      }

      fclose(fp);
      return;
error:
      root->ErrorMessage("Premature EOF");
      return;
   }
}
```

Implementing a TrueSpace Writer

Creating a TrueSpace file format writer means writing C++ code that can convert from the internal *Crossroads* representation into the TrueSpace file format. Luckily this process is fairly straightforward, with help from the *GWrite* class.

The `GNode::Write()` member function traverses the scene, and the appropriate member functions of a *GWrite* derived class are called for each recognized *GNode* instance encountered. This means implementers of a format writer don't have to understand all of the details of the internal representation. Instead, they need to address just the details that are important for their file formats. This enables the *GWrite* class to be overridden by the *GWriteCOB* class and the implementation of only the functionality that is necessary.

Following is the definition of the *GWriteCOB* class:

```
class GWriteCOB : public GWrite {
private:
   char         m_name[256];
   MeshCompactor  m_mesh;

public:
   // Constructor
   GWriteCOB(void) : GWrite() {strcpy(m_name, "");}

   // Tessellate all shapes into polygons
   short PolygonSupported(void)  {return TRUE;}

   // Output file is binary
   short FileMode(void) {return GWriteBinaryFile;}
   // Override the polygon entry
   void  Polygon(GState&, long, MFVec3f*,
                MFVec3f* = NULL, GWriteMaterial* = NULL);

    // Override the Epilog funcion. This function
    // is called prior to the corresponding FILE*
    // being closed.
   void  Epilog(GNode*, GState&);
};
```

Notice that only a few of the member functions available in the *GWrite* class need to be overridden. This is because only polygons are supported by this format. All other shapes are tessellated into equivalent polygons, thereby reducing the number of member functions that need to be handed to the `GWriteCOB::Polygon()` member function.

An example of how a TrueSpace file is written using the *GWriteCOB* class follows:

```
void C3DviewDoc::OnFileSaveCob()
{
   CFileDialog   fileDlg( FALSE, NULL, NULL,
                      OFN_HIDEREADONLY | OFN_OVERWRITEPROMPT,
         "TrueSpace (*.cob)|*.cob||");

   if (fileDlg.DoModal() == IDOK) {
      char  buffer[256];

      strcpy(buffer, fileDlg.GetPathName());

      FILE* fp = fopen(buffer, "wb");
      if (fp != NULL) {
         GWriteCOB   write;
         GState   state;
```

```
            // Display hourglass cursor
            StartBusy();

            // Open the output file
            write.Open(this, state, buffer);

            // Traverse the internal database, calling
            // the write class as appropriate.
            Write(state, write);

            // Close the write class, flushing any
            // remaining information.
            write.Close(this, state);

            // Restore previous cursor
            EndBusy();

            // Update current file name
            SetPathName( fileDlg.GetPathName() );
        }
    }
}
```

All that is required to complete the TrueSpace writer is to fill in the `GWriteCOB::Polygon()` and `GWriteCOB::Epilog()` member functions.

Implementing the GWriteCOB:: Polygon() Function

The `GWriteCOB::Polygon()` function uses the *MeshCompactor* class that is instantiated with the *GWriteCOB* class. The *MeshCompactor* instance converts a series of polygons into a group of polygons. The *MeshCompactor* compacts the polygon vertex lists into a single vertex list and corresponding face list by group name. The resultant representation is used by the `GWriteCOB::Epilog()` member function to actually write the TrueSpace file.

This organization may seem wasteful in that it results in multiple representations of the same scene being stored in memory at once. However, the representation that TrueSpace needs is probably quite different from the native representation that makes this conversion necessary.

Following is the implementation of the `GWriteCOB::Polygon()` member function.

```
void GWriteCOB:
Polygon(GState& state, long faceNum, MFVec3f* v,
        MFVec3f* n, GWriteMaterial* m)
{
    // Notice Name changes
    if (state.HeirName() != NULL &&
```

```
        strcmp(m_name, state.HeirName()) != 0) {
      m_mesh.Name(state.HeirName());
      strcpy(m_name, state.HeirName());
   }

   // Add polygon
   m_mesh.BeginPolygon(m);
   for (int i = 0; i < v->Elements(); i++) {
      m_mesh.AddVertex((*v)[i]);
   }
   m_mesh.EndPolygon();
}
```

Implementing the GWriteCOB:: Epilog( ) Function

The `GWriteCOB::Epilog()` function is the meat of TrueSpace writer. It converts the data stored in the *MeshCompactor* instance into a TrueSpace file.

This function writes the object in a top-level group named 'Object.' All of the named groups are saved as children to 'Object.' Each subgroup has a 'PolH' child that contains the vertices and faces for the group. The material to the group is saved as a 'Mat1' child to the 'PolH' chunk.

The first step is to scale the object. COB objects, when loaded into TrueSpace, aren't automatically resized to fit a scene. Hence, the object must be prescaled or it will not work well in a default TrueSpace scene. An object that has a maximum width, height, or depth of 12 seems to load into the TrueSpace scene well. Centering and unitizing the object and multiplying it by 6 will give it a maximum dimension of 12. After the object has been resized, the top-level group chunk is written. This chunk is followed by the subgroups that make up the pieces of the object.

Each subgroup must compute its range. The range is used to compute the center and axes to the object for the local axis portions of the group chunk. After the center and axes for the subgroup have been calculated, the subgroup chunk can be written. Then, the polygon chunk associated with the subgroup is written.

Writing a polygon chunk ('PolH') to a COB file is straightforward, except for two minor issues. First, the size of the polygon chunk must be written in the chunk header. However, you won't easily know the size of the written polygon until you've output it. Second, the *m_mesh* variable has stored the vertices as one single array. You need to break that array into the individual vertices for each polygon that is written.

You can defer writing the polygon chunk size. Do this by saving the location of the size value in the COB file. A bogus value is written initially. As the polygon elements are written, the size of the chunk is calculated. Once the polygon has been written, you can overwrite the previously saved (but incorrect) value with the correct value.

Getting the vertex list for the subgroup requires saving the subgroup in a local *MeshCompactor* instance. Doing this allows just the vertices that are used by the faces used in the subgroup to be saved. Once the *sub_mesh* variable has been filled in, writing out the polygons is simple.

The final step is to write the materials for the polygon chunk. This is accomplished by saving the index of the materials encountered while writing the polygons in the variable *mat_list*. The material indexes saved in the COB file are actually the index into *mat_list*. This allows the material indexes written to the COB file to be contiguous. TrueSpace will crash if the material indexes don't start at zero or if the indexes aren't contiguous.

```
// Called after all the polygons have been read.
void GWriteCOB::
Epilog(GNode* root, GState& state)
{
   MFVec3f*     coords = m_mesh.Coordinates();
   SFVec3f      objectCenter, center, min, max;
   SFFloat      scale = (SFFloat) 1.0;
   char*        name = "Object";
   SFMatrix     matrix;
   const long   topID         = 5000L;
   const long   subgroupID    = 100000L;
   const long   polyID        = 150000L;
   Chunk        chunk;

   root->StatusMessage("Computing Object Dimension");

   // Compute the range for the entire object
   min = (*coords)[0];
   max = (*coords)[0];
   for (long i = 1; i < coords->Elements(); i++) {
      SFVec3f  cur = (*coords)[i];
      min = Min(cur, min);
      max = Max(cur, max);
   }

   root->StatusMessage("Rescaling Object");

   // Compute a scale the will make the object fit
   // in the default TrueSpace view.
   scale = (1.0/Max(Max(max.X()-min.X(),
          max.Y()-min.Y()), max.Z()-min.Z()))*6.0;
```

```
   // Calculate the center of the object
   objectCenter = SFVec3f((max.X()-min.X())/
                       ((SFFloat) 2.0) + min.X(),
                    (max.Y()-min.Y())/((SFFloat) 2.0) +
                       min.Y(),
                    (max.Z()-min.Z())/((SFFloat) 2.0) +
                       min.Z());

   // Center and rescale the vertices of the object.
   if (coords != NULL && coords->Elements() > 0) {
      min = ((*coords)[0]-objectCenter)*scale;
      max = max;
      for (i = 0; i < coords->Elements(); i++) {
         SFVec3f cur = ((*coords)[i]-objectCenter)*scale;
         min = Min(cur, min);
         max = Max(cur, max);
         coords->Replace(i, cur);
      }
   }

   // Recompute the center of object
   objectCenter = SFVec3f((SFFloat) 0.0, (SFFloat) 0.0,
(SFFloat) 0.0);

   // Write Cob Header
   if (!WriteString(m_fp,
         "Caligari V00.01BLH              \012", 32))
      goto error;

   // Write Chunk
   strncpy(chunk.chunkType, "Grou", 4);
   chunk.majorVersion = 0;
   chunk.minorVersion = 1;
   chunk.chunkID = topID;
   chunk.parentID = 0;
   chunk.size = strlen(name)+100;
   if (!WriteChunk(root, m_fp, chunk)) goto error;

   // Write Name
   if (!WriteName(root, m_fp, name)) goto error;

   // Write Local Axis
   if (!WriteLocalAxis(root, m_fp, objectCenter,
            SFVec3f((SFFloat) 1.0, (SFFloat) 0.0,
               (SFFloat) 0.0),
            SFVec3f((SFFloat) 0.0, (SFFloat) 1.0,
               (SFFloat) 0.0),
```

```
            SFVec3f((SFFloat) 0.0, (SFFloat) 0.0,
               (SFFloat) 1.0))) goto error;

    // Current Position
    if (!WriteCurrentPosition(root, m_fp, Identity()))
          goto error;

    // Check to see if we have any coordinates
    if (coords != NULL && coords->Elements() > 0) {

       // Cycle through each of the groups
       for (long group = 0; group < m_mesh.Groups();
              group++)
          MFLong*  faces = m_mesh.Faces(group);
          MFLong   mat_list;
          char* name = (m_mesh.Name(group) == NULL ?
                          "NoName" : m_mesh.Name(group));
          SFLong   polySizeLoc = 0, polySize = 0;

          root->StatusMessage(
             "Computing range for group '%s'", name);

          // Compute Range of group
          if (faces->Elements() > 0) {
             min = (*coords)[(*faces)[0]];
             max = min;

             for (long i = 0; i < faces->Elements(); i++) {
                SFLong   face = (*faces)[i];
                if (face >= 0) {
                   SFVec3f value = (*coords)[face];
                   max = Max(max, value);
                   min = Min(min, value);
                }
             }
          }

          // Compute center of group
          center = SFVec3f((max.X()-min.X())/((SFFloat) 2.0)
                          + min.X(),
                      (max.Y()-min.Y())/((SFFloat) 2.0) +
                          min.Y(),
                      (max.Z()-min.Z())/((SFFloat) 2.0) +
                          min.Z());

          root->StatusMessage("Writing group '%s'", name);
```

```
// Output Group Chunk
strncpy(chunk.chunkType, "Grou", 4);
chunk.majorVersion = 0;
chunk.minorVersion = 1;
chunk.chunkID = (group+1)*subgroupID;
chunk.parentID = topID;
chunk.size = strlen(name)+100;
if (!WriteChunk(root, m_fp, chunk)) goto error;

// Write Name
if (!WriteName(root, m_fp, name)) goto error;

// Write Local Axis
if (!WriteLocalAxis(root, m_fp, center,
         SFVec3f((SFFloat) 1.0, (SFFloat) 0.0,
            (SFFloat) 0.0),
         SFVec3f((SFFloat) 0.0, (SFFloat) 1.0,
            (SFFloat) 0.0),
         SFVec3f((SFFloat) 0.0, (SFFloat) 0.0,
            (SFFloat) 1.0))) goto error;

// Current Position
if (!WriteCurrentPosition(root, m_fp, Identity()))
   goto error;

// Output Polygons for group
if (faces->Elements() > 0) {
   SFLong         vertexCnt = 0;
   SFLong         faceCnt = 0;

   // We need to compact the coordinates
   // into a single, local list for smoothing
   // to work in TrueSpace.
   MeshCompactor  sub_mesh;
   MFVec3f*    sub_coords = NULL;
   short       sub_polyOpen = TRUE;

   // Compact and count vertices and faces
   sub_mesh.BeginPolygon(
      &m_mesh.FaceIndex2Material(group, faceCnt));
   for (long i = 0; i < faces->Elements(); i++) {
      SFLong   face = (*faces)[i];
      if (face >= 0) {
         SFVec3f vertex = (*coords)[face];
         sub_mesh.AddVertex(vertex);
      } else {
         sub_mesh.EndPolygon();
         sub_polyOpen = FALSE;
```

```
        faceCnt++;
        if (i+1 < faces->Elements()) {
            sub_mesh.BeginPolygon(
                &m_mesh.FaceIndex2Material(group,
                    faceCnt));
            sub_polyOpen = TRUE;
        }
    }
}

if (sub_polyOpen) {
    sub_mesh.EndPolygon();
}

// Get coordinates and faces
sub_coords = sub_mesh.Coordinates();
faces = sub_mesh.Faces();
vertexCnt = sub_coords->Elements();

// Output Polygon Chunk

// Chunk Type
if (!WriteString(m_fp, "PolH", 4)) goto error;
// Major Rev
if (!WriteShort(m_fp, 0)) goto error;
// Minor Rev
if (!WriteShort(m_fp, 2))
    goto error;
// ID
if (!WriteLong(m_fp, (group+1)*polyID))
    goto error;
// Parent ID
if (!WriteLong(m_fp, (group+1)*subgroupID))
    goto error;

// Save the current position so that
// we can write the actual size later
// when we really know it.
polySizeLoc = ftell(m_fp);

// Write a BOGUS value as a place holder

if (!WriteLong(m_fp, -1)) goto error;

// Write Name
if (!WriteName(root, m_fp, name)) goto error;
polySize += 4 + strlen(name);
```

```
// Write Local Axis
if (!WriteLocalAxis(root, m_fp, center,
        SFVec3f((SFFloat) 1.0, (SFFloat) 0.0,
           (SFFloat) 0.0),
        SFVec3f((SFFloat) 0.0, (SFFloat) 1.0,
           (SFFloat) 0.0),
        SFVec3f((SFFloat) 0.0, (SFFloat) 0.0,
           (SFFloat) 1.0))) goto error;
polySize += 48;

// Current Position
if (!WriteCurrentPosition(root, m_fp,
      Identity())) goto error;
polySize += 48;

// Output vertex Count
if (!WriteLong(m_fp, sub_coords->Elements()))
      goto error;
polySize += 4;

// Output each vertex
for (i = 0; i < sub_coords->Elements(); i++) {
   SFVec3f vertex = (*sub_coords)[i];
   if (!WriteFloat(m_fp, (float) vertex.X()))
      goto error;
   if (!WriteFloat(m_fp, (float) vertex.Y()))
      goto error;
   if (!WriteFloat(m_fp, (float) vertex.Z()))
      goto error;
   polySize += 12;
}

// Output UV vertex List - we don't have to
// do much because we don't support bitmap
// textures.
if (!WriteLong(m_fp, 0)) goto error;
polySize += 4;

// Output face count
if (!WriteLong(m_fp, faceCnt)) goto error;
polySize += 4;


// Output Faces
mat_list.Clear(); vertexCnt = 0;
for (faceCnt = 0, i = 0; i < faces->Elements();)
{
   SFLong   vcnt = 0;
```

```
SFLong   mat =
            sub_mesh.FaceIndex2MaterialIndex(
                  group, faceCnt);
SFLong   next;

// Save the material indexs
long matindex = mat_list.Add(mat, TRUE);

// Find the end of this polygon
next = faces->NextOccurance(-1L, i);

// Calculate the number of vertices in this
// polygon
vcnt = next - i;

// Output that this is a face
if (!WriteByte(m_fp, 0)) goto error;
polySize += 1;

// Write the number of vertices
if (!WriteShort(m_fp, (short) vcnt))
   goto error;
polySize += 2;

// Save the material index
if (!WriteShort(m_fp, (short) matindex))
   goto error;
polySize += 2;

// Save the face indexes
for (; i < faces->Elements(); i++) {
   SFLong   face = (*faces)[i];
   if (face >= 0) {
      if (!WriteLong(m_fp, face)) goto error;
      polySize += 4;

      // Save UV face - we don't support this
      // so we just output a 0
      if (!WriteLong(m_fp, 0)) goto error;
      polySize += 4;

      // Update vertex count
      vertexCnt++;
   } else {
      // Found the end of a face - update
      // face count and increment the current
      // face position.
      i++; faceCnt++;
```

```
                    break;
                }
            }
        }

        // Save the current position
        SFLong   curPos = ftell(m_fp);

        // Backpatch the size of the PolH
        fseek(m_fp, polySizeLoc, SEEK_SET);
        if (!WriteLong(m_fp, polySize)) goto error;

        // Restore the current position
        fseek(m_fp, curPos, SEEK_SET);

        // Write materials
        root->StatusMessage(
           "Writing materials for group '%s'", name);
        for (i = 0; i < mat_list.Elements(); i++) {
           GWriteMaterial material =
                       sub_mesh.MaterialIndex2Material(
                          group, mat_list[i]);
           if (!WriteMaterial(root, m_fp, group, polyID,
                    i, material))
              goto error;
        }
      }
    }
  }

  // Output End Chunk
  strncpy(chunk.chunkType, "END ", 4);
  chunk.majorVersion = 1;
  chunk.minorVersion = 0;
  chunk.chunkID = 0;
  chunk.parentID = 0;
  chunk.size = 0;
  if (!WriteChunk(root, m_fp, chunk)) goto error;

  root->StatusMessage("Write Complete");
  return;
error:
  root->ErrorMessage("Write Failed");
  return;
}
```

Reference

Caligari TrueSpace2 File Format—Document Version 2.0. 1995. Mountain View, Calif.: Caligari Corporation. http://www.caligari.com/ftp/pub/trueSpace/info/format2.rtf.

Chapter 7

DXF AutoCAD R13

AutoCAD runs on DOS, Windows, Windows NT, and most UNIX platforms. One file format it supports is the Drawing Interchange Format (DXF). This format was developed by AutoDesk to allow CAD data to be interchanged between different applications. It is basically an ASCII version of the AutoCAD drawing database. For example, AutoDesk's popular 3D Studio program can read and write DXF, thus enabling AutoCAD drawings to be rendered and animated in that program.

Because of AutoCAD's popularity—more than one million units have been sold—DXF files have become a very common interchange format for CAD programs and 3D applications. On the PC, DXF is one of the few file formats supported in most 3D applications.

Since DXF is primarily an interchange format for CAD drawings, it contains both 2D and 3D components. Developers implementing DXF readers for 3D applications have a couple of choices to make when providing DXF support. They can choose to support 2D constructs by allowing them to be extruded as 3D objects, or they can choose to recognize only 3D constructs.

The DXF file format can be either binary or ASCII. The binary version is not very common, so I focus on the ASCII version in this chapter and discuss only the entities required to read the 3D constructs.

Note that when dealing with DXF files, you will find it much harder to write a good DXF reader than a good DXF writer. This is because writing 3D polygons is straightforward, if you use the 3DFACE entity or a polyface mesh. 3DFACE entities aren't particularly space efficient, but they do work and are usually all that most 3D applications need to emit to create a credible DXF writer. Polyface meshes are more efficient but require some additional work.

However, there are many other types of graphical and nongraphical constructs that come together to produce a DXF drawing. Discussing all of these elements adequately is a very large task and is beyond the scope of this chapter.

In this chapter, I address only a small subset of the DXF file format, the portions that represent 3D polygons and 3D polyface meshes. If you are interested in providing broader DXF support than is defined here, check out the AutoCAD manuals. They contain a wealth of information and are considered the definitive reference for DXF. For many 3D applications, the description provided here should be adequate for reading and writing DXF files.

Development of the DXF Format

The DXF format has been defined by AutoDesk as part of AutoCAD. Because of this, the DXF format is closely related to the internal construction of AutoCAD, and hence the history of DXF is tied closely to the history of AutoCAD.

The first version of AutoCAD to support 3D in any way was Release 2.1, which was released in May, 1985. Prior to this, AutoCAD was strictly a 2D application. Market interest influenced the addition of minimal 3D support in this version. This support consisted of adding elevation and thickness parameters to 2D entities such as lines and circles. This type of 3D support is often referred to as 2½D.

This relatively minimal 3D support was actually very useful. At that time, AutoCAD was heavily used by architects. Architects work with floor plans that are 2D drawings with limited extrusion. This addition added the capability of 3D visualization of a floor plan. Because of this implementation strategy for 3D in AutoCAD, the *xy*-plane is always the "floor" and the *z*-axis is up.

Release 2.6, released in June, 1986, added the 3DLINE and 3DFACE entities. The next major version of AutoCAD was released in September, 1987. This release, rather than being Release 3, was called Release 9. No new 3D constructs were added to this version.

AutoCAD became a true 3D application with Release 10 in October, 1988. There are two big constraints as to how 3D was implemented in this version. First, 2½D constructs were being widely used and had to be backwards compatible.

The second big constraint was the severe memory restrictions caused by the DOS platform. Recall that in 1988, there was a 640K memory barrier and most DOS computers had 2M or less of memory. Because of these limitations, the Entity Coordinate System (ECS) was born. ECS allowed 2½D constructs to be displayed in other coordinate systems. I discuss ECS in detail in this chapter.

This version also added more 3D constructs, including the polygon mesh entity, which isn't truly a new entity. It was added simply as a special case to the POLYLINE entity.

Subsequent versions of AutoCAD added minor additions to its 3D capabilities. AutoCAD Release 11 (October, 1990) added the POLYFACE MESH entity. This entity is a set of vertices and faces. It was added as another special case of the POLYLINE entity.

AutoCAD Release 12 (June, 1992) added no new 3D entities; however, it offered a solid modeling plug-in application. This offered some problems for DXF. However, the solids can be easily converted into polyface meshes.

AutoCAD Release 13 (November, 1994) added the ability for third parties to create their own entities. This ability makes it difficult to know what type of entities might be found in a Release 13 DXF file. Arbitrary entities are impossible for a general program to deal with. An example of this is the ACIS solids native to AutoCAD Release 13. ACIS solids are very useful constructs. However, in a DXF file they are specified as a 3DBODY entity, which requires a very expensive ACIS license to decode. Hence, getting transportable information out of AutoCAD Release 13 often means saving a drawing as a 3D Studio file (this can be done using the 3DSOUT command).

Overview of DXF File Format

If you were to view an ASCII DXF file with your text editor, you would discover that, unlike VRML, this format is not intended to be human readable. It's indecipherable computer gibberish. However, DXF files do have a very regular organization.

Group Entity Codes

At the lowest level, all DXF files are simply a series of group entity codes. A group entity code defines the contents of a DXF file. It is a numeric value on a single line, followed by an argument on the subsequent line. For example, a comment is group code 999 followed by a string. Here's an example:

```
999
This is a comment
```

In this example, the group code 999 denotes that a string will be found on the line that follows and that it will be a comment in the DXF file. All group codes follow this organization.

Table 7.1 describes the ranges and types for the group codes used in the DXF file format.

Table 7.1. DXF group code values

Group Value	Type of Value That Follows
xx00–xx09	String
xx10–xx39	Floating-point values (parts of points 1x=X, 2x=Y, 3x=Z)
xx140–xx59	Floating-point value
xx60–xx79	Integer value
999	Comment
210–239	Floating-point value
999	Comment

Data with a group value of 1000 or larger is an Extended Entity Data (XDATA) element, which is inserted by an AutoCAD plug-in application. These values are defined by the application that put them in the DXF file. Some integral parts of AutoCAD use XDATA elements to store information. Other programs may use empty blocks as data containers, so it's a good idea for DXF readers to be able to filter out empty blocks.

Most DXF group entity codes appear only once per entity, but XDATA codes may appear several times. In Release 13, some string data may appear several times. The most common group code that does this is 100, which is used to define the C++ class name for a third-party entity.

File Sections

A DXF file is divided into sections. Each starts with a section definition—a group code of 0 followed by the literal string `SECTION`. Next comes a section type and a body. Each section is closed by an end section (`ENDSEC`) construct. A section declaration looks like this:

```
 0
SECTION
 <Section Body>
 0
ENDSEC
```

Section Definitions

There are four types of sections:

1. HEADER
2. TABLES
3. BLOCKS
4. ENTITIES

The organization of the sections in a DXF file follows:

```
0
SECTION
2
HEADER
<Header Section Contents>
0
ENDSEC
0
SECTION
2
TABLES
<Tables Section Contents>
0
ENDSEC
0
SECTION
2
BLOCKS
<Blocks Section Contents>
0
ENDSEC
0
SECTION
2
ENTITIES
<Entities Section Contexts>
0
ENDSEC
0
EOF
```

Notice that each section begins with a group code of 0 and an entity name of SECTION. It is followed by a group code of 2 and the name of the section. Each section is terminated with a group code of 0 and an entity name of ENDSEC. The entire file is closed with a group code of 0 and an entity name of EOF.

The HEADER Section

The HEADER section contains variables that define the settings to be reloaded by AutoCad when a drawing is loaded. These settings include data such as whether the snap mode is on and what the grid units are. Most of this data is useful primarily to AutoCAD; other programs can safely ignore it. Since the focus of this chapter is on reading and writing the geometry in a DXF file, you can ignore this section in your implementation. A HEADER section has the following organization:

```
0
SECTION
2
HEADER
<Header Section Contents>
0
ENDSEC
```

The TABLES Section

The TABLES section contains data such as the viewport settings, line types, and layer information. Since the focus of this chapter is on reading and writing the geometry in a DXF file, you can ignore most of the data in this section in your implementation. The only data required is that concerning layers, which is needed to correctly determine an entity's color.

A TABLES section has the following organization:

```
0
SECTION
2
TABLES
<Tables Section Contents>
0
ENDSEC
```

A layer is a type of table. Each table begins with a group code of 0 followed by the string "TABLE." Following that is always a group code of 2. Next comes a string that defines the table type, in the case of layers, "LAYER." A group code value of 70 follows the table type identifier. This value defines the number of entries for this table. This table is followed with that number of layer entries.

Each layer entry begins with a group code with the value LAYER. It is followed with a group code 2 and the name of the layer. The group code 62 defines the color index for the layer. The layer name and its color index are important to preserve because this information is needed to correctly determine the color for subsequent entity definitions. The layer definition is terminated with a group code 0 with the value ENDTAB.

The following is a short example of a layer definition.

```
 0
TABLE
  2
LAYER
 70
      3
  0
LAYER
  2
0
 70
      0
 62
      7
  6
CONTINUOUS
  0
LAYER
  2
OBJECT
 70
     64
 62
      1
  6
CONTINUOUS
  0
LAYER
  2
SURFACE
 70
     64
 62
      2
  6
CONTINUOUS
  0
ENDTAB
```

The BLOCKS Section

A BLOCKS section is used to define objects that may be referenced later in the CAD drawing. It contains zero or more BLOCK entities. Items defined in a BLOCKS section are not considered items in the drawing unless they are inserted in the ENTITIES section. A BLOCKS section has the following organization:

```
  0
SECTION
  2
BLOCKS
  0
BLOCK
<The Entities that represent the Block>
 0
ENDBLK
<Additional Block Entities my be repeated>
  0
ENDSEC
```

A BLOCK entity defined in the BLOCKS section contains entities that represent components of a CAD drawing. Once defined in the BLOCKS section, these components may be inserted many times in the ENTITIES section. The entities that define the body of the BLOCK entity are composed of the same graphical entities that appear in the ENTITIES section. BLOCK entities cannot be nested, although they can contain other predefined blocks inserted with the DXF INSERT entity. In other words, BLOCK entities can refer to existing block definitions, but the definitions cannot be nested.

The ENTITIES Section

The ENTITIES section defines the contents of the drawing. All of the previous sections in the DXF file deal with setting up the environment so that the graphical elements defined in the ENTITIES section can adequately represent the CAD drawing. This section is usually the largest in most DXF files. It has the following organization:

```
  0
SECTION
  2
ENTITIES
<The entities that represent the CAD Drawing>
 0
ENDSEC
```

Colors and Layers

Colors and layers are important elements in defining how an entity appears in an AutoCAD drawing. Both are defined in an entity using group codes. The color group code is 62, and the layer group code is 8.

The layer value indexes into a list of layers that are obtained from the layer table, which is found in the TABLES section. The color value ranges from 0 to 255 and usually refers to one of the colors from AutoCAD's standard color system. However, there are rules that should be followed to correctly determine an entity's color.

Color Rules

If the group code 62 is omitted or the underlying color value is 0, the color is "by layer." That is, the color information will be obtained from the layer information. A color value of 255 means the color is "by block." That is, if the entity is located in the ENTITIES section, then its color is white and if the color is found in a BLOCKS section, then the entity's color is that of the block insertion entity.

The AutoCAD Standard Color System

The AutoCAD standard color system is used by DXF to determine the color of each entity. The system has seven standard base colors: 1 = red, 2 = yellow, 3 = green, 4 = cyan, 5 = blue, 6 = magenta, and 7 = white.

Each multiple of 10 of the color value represents a fully saturated color that is also defined along the rainbow. Some key values are 10 = red, 50 = yellow, 90 = green, 130 = cyan, 170 = blue, and 210 = magenta.

Colors that are multiples of 10 that fall in between these numbers are mixes of these colors. For example: 10 is 100% red, 20 is 75% red and 25% yellow, 30 is 50% red and 50% yellow, 40 is 25% red and 75% yellow. This color system wraps from magenta (210) back to red. This means the value 220 is 25% red and 75% magenta.

Putting even numbers in the ones digit space darkens the color. For example: 10, 12, 14, 16, and 18 are proportionally darker versions of red. An odd number in the ones digit space means the color is mixed 50% with white.

Colors in the range of 250–255 are grayscale values that move from dark gray to white. The leftover values 8 and 9 are undefined.

The Entity Coordinate System

AutoCAD Release 10 moved DXF into the third dimension. This was done by adding a *z*-axis vector, which is defined by the 210, 220, and 230 group codes.

From an AutoCAD user's viewpoint, a drawing is defined using the User Coordinate System (UCS). However, entities are actually stored using Entity Coordinate System (ECS) coordinates. This was originally done to save memory (recall that AutoCAD Release 10 occurred in October, 1988, when DOS-based computers had 640K memory barriers).

For any entity drawn in the *xy*-plane, the ECS is the same as the World Coordinate System (WCS). However, for entities that are positioned outside of that plane, the coordinates are specified in the ECS.

The ECS and WCS share the same origin with an entity. When the ECS is (0, 0, 1), both the WCS and ECS for the entity are the same. The ECS value defines the rotation that must be applied to the entity to orient it correctly. This saves AutoCAD storage space because an entity doesn't require that a full transformation be defined. However, simply defining one axis in a coordinate system doesn't supply enough information to recreate the entire coordinate system. How does AutoCAD create a coordinate system from this?

The answer is, arbitrarily but consistently. AutoCAD's designers arbitrarily chose one of many possible algorithms to create the coordinate system. Because everyone uses it, the results are consistent. Here's the algorithm:

```
if (fabs(z_axis.X()) < (1.0/64.0) &&
    fabs(z_axis.Y()) < (1.0/64.0))
{
    x_axis = SFVec3f(z_axis.Z(), 0.0, -z_axis.X());
} else {
    x_axis = SFVec3f(-z_axis.Y(), z_axis.X(), 0.0);
}

x_axis = Normalize(x_axis);
y_axis = Cross(z_axis, x_axis);
```

This algorithm may look strange, but it is actually very clever. The number 1.0/64.0 (first line of the algorithm) was chosen because it can be represented exactly as an IEEE floating-point value. So there is never any question about round-off error in the comparison.

Using this algorithm, you calculate the *x*-axis. Next, you simply normalize *x* and calculate the value for the *y*-axis by taking the cross product of the *z*-axis and the *x*-axis. This result can be used by constructing a 4×4 transformation matrix as follows:

```
transform = SFMatrix(
    x_axis.X(), x_axis.Y(), x_axis.Z(), 0.0,
    y_axis.X(), y_axis.Y(), y_axis.Z(), 0.0,
    z_axis.X(), z_axis.Y(), z_axis.Z(), 0.0,
    0.0,        0.0,        0.0,        1.0);
```

Each point defined in the ECS is multiplied by this matrix to find the actual coordinate for the point. It is important to note that these transformations can be nested. That is, inserting a block that in turn contains another inserted block will cause the transformations to be propagated.

AutoCAD deals with 2½D entities similarly. For example, a circle entity with a given "thickness" in some ECS could be used to represent a cylinder. The extrusion direction is always the *z*-axis. The base of the cylinder is always perpendicular to the *z*-axis. In other words, the *z*-axis doesn't skew the base of cylinder.

Some entities that always define their coordinates in the WCS are not affected by this transform. An example is the 3DFACE entity, which will never have the 210, 220, and 230 group codes. There also are some entities that have these group codes and still not be defined in the ECS. In these cases, the *z*-axis defines only the extrusion direction. An example is the LINE entity, the only entity discussed in this chapter that uses the *z*-axis exclusively as an extrusion direction.

Any 2D entity can become a 3D entity when a "thickness" is defined. These types of 3D entities are common in 2D floor plans, where a thickness is a simple way to extrude a 2D floor plan into a 3D drawing.

Entity Definitions

Two types of entities are defined in a DXF file: graphical and nongraphical. Graphical entities define the visible components in a CAD drawing, such as lines, circles, faces, and vertices. Nongraphical entities are components such as BLOCK entities.

This section defines a subset of the entities that may appear in a DXF file. All of the graphical entities that appear in this chapter have 3D components and so are useful in many 3D applications.

The 3DFACE Entity

A 3DFACE entity defines a polygon with either three or four vertices. The entity starts with a group code of 0. Next is the string "3DFACE" followed by several group codes that describe the polygon vertices, colors, layers, and visibility. These parameters are defined by the group codes given in Table 7.2.

Table 7.2. 3DFACE entity group code definitions

Group Codes	Description
8 (optional)	Defines the layer of which this polygon is a member.
10, 20, 30	Define the first vertex of the polygon. The float value following the group code 10 is the *x*-value. The float value following the group code 20 is the *y*-value. The float value following the group code 30 is the *z*-value.
11, 21, 31	Define the second vertex of the polygon. The float value following the group code 11 is the *x*-value. The float value following the group code 21 is the *y*-value. The float value following the group code 31 is the *z*-value.
12, 22, 32	Define the third vertex of the polygon. The float value following the group code 12 is the *x*-value. The float value following the group code 22 is the *y*-value. The float value following the group code 32 is the *z*-value.
13, 23, 33	Define the fourth vertex of the polygon. The float value following the group code 13 is the *x*-value. The float value following the group code 23 is the *y*-value. The float value following the group code 33 is the *z*-value. If this vertex equals the third vertex, then only three vertices have been defined and the fourth vertex can be ignored.
62 (optional)	The color index of the polygon.
70 (optional)	The edge flags. Bit 0 set means the first edge is visible. Bit 1 set means the second edge is visible. Bit 2 set means the third edge is visible. Bit 3 set means the fourth edge is visible.

Example of a 3DFACE Entity

The following example of a 3DFACE entity defines a triangle with the vertices (1.453219, –0.554065, –0.862826), (1.516323, –0.433194, –0.882400), and (1.634241, –0.339341, –0.841105). Even though the entity defines four vertices, the last is the same as the previous. Here is how a 3D triangle is defined in DXF:

```
0
3DFACE
8
0
  62
44
10
```

```
1.453219
20
-0.554065
30
-0.862826
11
1.516323
21
-0.433194
31
-0.882400
12
1.634241
22
-0.339341
32
-0.841105
13
1.634241
23
-0.339341
33
-0.841105
```

The LINE Entity

The LINE entity defines a 3D line. Every LINE entity has a starting point and ending point. It also has several optional entities, including a layer assignment, a color assignment, a thickness, and an extrusion direction. The entity starts with a group code of 0 followed by the string "LINE." Table 7.3 defines the group codes that may be used as parameters to a LINE entity.

Table 7.3. LINE entity group code definitions

Group Codes	Description
8 (optional)	Defines the layer to which the line is assigned.
10, 20, 30	The starting point of the line.
11, 21, 31	The ending point of the line.
39 (optional)	The line thickness. The default value is 0.
62 (optional)	The color index of the line.
210, 220, 230 (optional)	The extrusion direction. Note that a line is not defined in the ECS.

Example of a LINE Entity

The following example of a LINE entity defines a line in layer SURFACE that is displayed using color index 10. This line is defined by the two points (94.596821, 92.066485, 17.0) and (59.596821, 92.066485, 17.0).

```
  0
LINE
  8
SURFACE
 62
     10
 10
94.596821
 20
92.066485
 30
17.0
 11
59.596821
 21
92.066485
 31
17.0
```

If this line were to have an extrusion direction and a thickness, it would become a 3D polygon.

The VERTEX Entity

The VERTEX entity defines a 3D point. This entity exists only within a POLYLINE entity. It starts with a group code of 0 followed by the string "VERTEX." Table 7.4 gives the group codes that may be used in the VERTEX entity.

Table 7.4. VERTEX entity group code definitions

Group Codes	Description
8 (optional)	Defines the layer to which the line is assigned.
10, 20, 30	Define the *x*, *y*, and *z* locations for the entity.
40 (optional)	The starting width. The default is 0.
41 (optional)	The ending width. The default is 0.
50 (optional)	The curve fit tangent direction. The default is 0.

Table 7.4. VERTEX entity group code definitions *(continued)*

Group Codes	Description
62 (optional)	The color index of the line.
70	The vertex flag. The default is 0. The meaning of each bit when set to 1 in the vertex flag is as follows: bit 0 = Extra vertex bit 1 = Curve fit tangent bit 3 = Spline vertex created by spline-fitting bit 4 = Spline frame control point bit 5 = 3D POLYLINE vertex bit 6 = 3D polygon mesh vertex bit 7 = Polyface mesh
71, 72, 73, 74	Vertices indexes for vertex 1, 2, 3, and 4 of a face. These values are defined only for vertices defined in a POLYLINE entity. These group codes are defined only when bit 7 is 1 and bit 6 is 0 in the vertex flag.

Example of a VERTEX Entity

The following example of a VERTEX entity defines a 3D point of (29.261667, 77.066485, 20.0):

```
  0
VERTEX
  8
SURFACE
 62
     2
 10
29.261667
 20
77.066485
 30
20.0
 70
    64
```

The POLYLINE Entity

The POLYLINE entity is complicated. It can have several flavors, depending on the settings of its group code 70 value. It has a header that is followed by several vertices, and possibly faces, that describe a polygon. Table 7.5 defines the group codes that may be used as parameters to a POLYLINE entity.

Table 7.5. POLYLINE entity group code definitions

Group Codes	Description
8 (optional)	Defines the layer to which the line is assigned.
10, 20, 30	Define the elevation of the entity. The *x*- and *y*-values are always 0, and the *z*-value provides the elevation.
39 (optional)	The thickness of the POLYLINE. The default value is 0.
40 (optional)	The starting width. The default is 0.
41 (optional)	The ending width. The default is 0.
62 (optional)	The color index of the line.
66	The vertices-follow flag. This should always be 1 for POLYLINES. This flag is an internal AutoCAD flag that specifies that an entity is followed by a series of entities which are terminated by the SEQEND entity.
70	The POLYLINE bitfield. Bit 0 set means the POLYLINE is closed. Bit 1 set means curve-fit vertices have been added. Bit 2 set means spline-fit vertices have been added. Bit 3 set means this is a 3D POLYLINE. Bit 4 set means this is a 3D mesh. Bit 5 set means the POLYLINE is closed in the N direction. Bit 6 set means this is a polyface mesh. Bit 7 set means the linetype pattern is generated continuously around the vertices of the POLYLINE.
71 (optional)	The polygon mesh M vertex count. The default value is 0.
72 (optional)	The polygon mesh N vertex count. The default value is 0.
73 (optional)	The smooth surface M density. The default value is 0.
74 (optional)	The smooth surface N density. The default value is 0.
75 (optional)	The curves and smooth surfaces type. The values are 0 = no smooth surface, 5 = quadratic B-spline surface, 6 = cubic B-spline surface, and 8 = Bezier surface. The default value is 0.
210, 220, 230 (optional)	The extrusion direction.

There are three categories of POLYLINE entities, each radically different from the others:

1. Contains the original definition of a POLYLINE, that is, a set of connected 3D lines and arcs. I don't discuss 2D POLYLINES in this book.
2. Contains a series of vertices that are stitched together into a polygon's surface.
3. A set of polygon vertices followed by polygon faces.

Because the POLYLINE entity is so overloaded with meaning, it is the most complicated entity discussed in this chapter. Don't be discouraged if you have to read its description a few times to understand its definition.

Stitching Vertices Together

One type of POLYLINE entity is described by a series of M × N vertices that are stitched together to produce a polygon surface. The organization of this type of POLYLINE entity follows:

```
0
POLYLINE        <Begin Polyline Entity>
8
SURFACE         <Assign Polyline to SURFACE layer>
62
2               <Assign Color index 2 to Polyline>
66
1               <Vertices Follow>
10
0.0             <X insert location>
20
0.0             <Y insert location>
30
0.0             <Z insert location>
70
16              <This is a 3D polygon mesh>
71
<M value here>
72
<N value here>
<M by N Vertices Defined here>
0
SEQEND          <Close the Polyline entity>
```

Notice that the organization of this type of POLYLINE entity is straightforward. The tricky part to dealing with it is how to handle the group code 70 bit 0 and bit 6. These bits specify whether the POLYLINE wraps in the M or

N direction. The implementation of the reader defined later in this chapter will show you exactly what this means. In a nutshell, these group code 70 values specify whether the edges of the polygon created by the rectangular series of vertices are connected in the M or N direction. This allows shapes like Cylinders to be easily created.

Example of a 2 × 2 POLYLINE Entity

The following DXF example shows the definition of a 2 × 2 POLYLINE entity. Notice that here the group code 70 value indicates that the group is closed in the N direction.

```
  0
POLYLINE
  8
SURFACE
 62
     2
 66
     1
 10
0.0
 20
0.0
 30
0.0
 70
    48
 71
     2
 72
     2
  0
VERTEX
  8
SURFACE
 62
     2
 10
29.261667
 20
77.066485
 30
20.0
 70
    64
  0
```

```
VERTEX
  8
SURFACE
 62
     2
 10
28.923057
 20
77.883962
 30
20.0
 70
    64
  0
VERTEX
  8
SURFACE
 62
     2
 10
28.10558
 20
78.222572
 30
20.0
 70
    64
  0
VERTEX
  8
SURFACE
 62
     2
 10
27.288104
 20
77.883962
 30
20.0
 70
    64
 0
SEQEND
```

Another case to look out for is when the POLYLINE mesh is spline-fitted. A spline-fitted mesh is defined if bit 2 of the group 70 value is set. It is really two tangled meshes in one. The first is a control polygon, which is the base mesh. It has M × N vertices defined by the 71 and 72 group codes. The second is the spline-fitted mesh. It has M × N vertices defined by the 73 and 74 group codes.

A DXF reader should ignore the control polygon and read only the smoothed polygon. That is, it should read only group 73 and 74 vertices and should ignore the rest. Also, it must look at each vertex to see to which group it belongs. Vertices in the control polygon have bit 4 for group code 70 set and should be ignored.

Defining a Polyface Mesh

The most widely used form of the POLYLINE entity is the polyface mesh. This entity defines a set of vertices followed by a set of faces. It is the only form of POLYLINE whose faces may have their own layers and colors. The organization of this type of POLYLINE entity follows:

```
0
POLYLINE        <Begin Polyline Entity>
66
1               <Vertices Follow>
8
2               <Assign Polyline to layer 0>
62
2               <Assign Color index 2 to Polyline>
70
64              <Defines this as a polyface mesh>
0
VERTEX          <This is an example of a vertex declaration>
8
2
10
0.482118
20
0.482118
30
0
70
192             <Defines this entity as a polymesh vertex>

<Followed by many more vertices>

0
VERTEX          <This is an example of a face declaration>
8
2
62
```

```
2
10
0
20
0
30
0
70
128             <Defines this entity as a polymesh face>
71
1               <Face index 1>
72
5               <Face index 2>
73
6               <Face index 3>
74
2               <Face index 4>

<Followed by more faces>

0
SEQEND
```

Note that in this type of POLYLINE entity, the VERTEX entity fills two roles: It defines both the vertices and the faces of the polymesh.

Example of a Polyface Mesh

The following example of a POLYLINE entity comes from from an actual DXF file of a polymesh:

```
0
POLYLINE
66
1
8
2
62
2
70
64
0
VERTEX
8
2
10
0.482118
```

```
20
0.482118
30
0
70
192
0
VERTEX
8
2
10
0.482118
20
-0.482118
30
0
70
192
0
VERTEX
8
2
10
-0.482118
20
-0.482118
30
0
70
192
0
VERTEX
8
2
10
-0.482118
20
0.482118
30
0
70
192
0
VERTEX
8
2
10
0.482118
```

```
20
0.482118
30
9.09091
70
192
0
VERTEX
8
2
10
0.482118
20
-0.482118
30
9.09091
70
192
0
VERTEX
8
2
10
-0.482118
20
-0.482118
30
9.09091
70
192
0
VERTEX
8
2
10
-0.482118
20
0.482118
30
9.09091
70
192
0
VERTEX
8
2
62
2
```

```
10
0
20
0
30
0
70
128
71
1
72
5
73
6
74
2
0
VERTEX
8
2
62
2
10
0
20
0
30
0
70
128
71
2
72
6
73
7
74
3
0
VERTEX
8
2
62
2
10
0
20
```

```
0
30
0
70
128
71
3
72
7
73
8
74
4
0
VERTEX
8
2
62
2
10
0
20
0
30
0
70
128
71
4
72
8
73
5
74
1
0
VERTEX
8
2
62
2
10
0
20
0
30
0
```

```
70
128
71
1
72
2
73
3
74
4
0
VERTEX
8
2
62
2
10
0
20
0
30
0
70
128
71
8
72
7
73
6
74
5
0
SEQEND
```

The BLOCK Entity

A BLOCK entity is a nongraphical entity, that is, it does not directly appear in the drawing. However, a BLOCK entity can be referenced in a drawing. Such a reference in the ENTITY section instantiates the contents of the BLOCK into the drawing. The entity starts with a group code of 0 followed by the string "BLOCK." Table 7.6 shows the group codes used to define the BLOCK entity parameters.

Table 7.6. BLOCK entity group code definitions

Group Codes	Description
2	The BLOCK name.
3	The BLOCK name.
8 (optional)	Defines the layer to which the BLOCK is assigned.
10, 20, 30	The BLOCK base point. In any drawing created in versions of AutoCAD greater than 2.5, a BLOCK is reoriented upon creation to have a (0, 0, 0) base point. This means a BLOCK's base point is always (0, 0, 0).
62 (optional)	The color index of the BLOCK.
70 (optional)	The integer value that follows this code is the BLOCK type flag. The integer values are 1=an anonymous BLOCK, 2=the BLOCK has attributes, 4=the BLOCK is an external reference, 16=the BLOCK is external-dependent, 32=the BLOCK is a resolved external reference or is a dependent of an external reference, and 64=this BLOCK is referenced.

A BLOCK entity actually consists of several entities. Its organization follows:

```
0
BLOCK       <start of block entity>
8
SURFACE     <layer name>
62
1           <color definition>
2
FORK        <block name>
70
64          <block type flag>
10
0.0         <X component of block base point>
20
0.0         <Y component of block base point>
30
0.0         <Z component of block base point>
3
FORK        <block name>
<Additional Entities>
0
ENDBLK      <close block>
```

Notice that the BLOCK entity encloses many entity definitions. One way to think of this type of entity is as a named macro. It defines a named macro with a base location and many graphical entities. You can refer to a BLOCK entity by name by using an INSERT entity. An INSERT entity expands, in-line, the content of the BLOCK at the INSERT entity's position. This allows drawing components to be defined once and then replicated many times in a drawing.

Example of a BLOCK Entity

The following example of a BLOCK entity is defined as the BLOCK FORK and contains one LINE entity:

```
  0
BLOCK
  8
SURFACE
 62
     1
  2
FORK
 70
    64
 10
0.0
 20
0.0
 30
0.0
  3
FORK
  0
LINE
  8
SURFACE
 62
     1
 10
-3.5
 20
0.0
 30
0.0
 11
0.0
 21
0.0
```

```
 31
0.0
  0
  0
ENDBLK
```

The INSERT Entity

The INSERT entity is used to insert a BLOCK defined in the BLOCKS section in place of the INSERT entity. It starts with a group code of 0 that is followed by the string "INSERT." Table 7.7 defines the group codes that may be used as INSERT entity parameters.

Table 7.7. INSERT entity group code definitions

Group Codes	Description
2	The BLOCK name to be inserted.
8 (optional)	Defines the layer to which the polygon is assigned.
10, 20, 30	The location at which to place the BLOCK.
41, 42, 43 (optional)	The floating-point values that define the *x*-, *y*-, and *z*-scale factors for the BLOCK. The default value is (1.0, 1.0, 1.0).
50 (optional)	A floating-point value that defines the rotation of the BLOCK around the up direction in degrees. The default value is 0.
62 (optional)	The color index of the polygon.
70 (optional)	Is followed by an integer value that is the column count. The column count is the number of BLOCKs to add in the column direction. If a specific value is omitted, the value is assumed to be 1.
71 (optional)	Is followed by an integer value that is the row count. The row count is the number of BLOCKs to add in the column direction. If a specific value is omitted, the value is assumed to be 1.
44 (optional)	Is followed by a floating-point value that is the column spacing. The column spacing is the distance between the repeated column elements.
45 (optional)	Is followed by a floating-point value that is the row spacing definition. The row spacing is the distance between the repeated row elements.

(*continued*)

Table 7.7. INSERT entity group code definitions *(continued)*

Group Codes	Description
210, 220, 230 (optional)	The up direction of the BLOCK and is defined in the ECS. If these codes are omitted, the BLOCK is assumed to be oriented using the WCS. The default value is (0.0, 0.0, 1.0).

Example of an INSERT Entity

The following example of an INSERT entity inserts the contents of the BLOCK entity named FORK at the location (24.5, –5.0, 3.0):

```
 0
INSERT
  8
SURFACE
 62
     1
  2
FORK
 10
24.5
 20
-5.0
 30
3.0
```

Implementing a DXF Reader

The DXF reader described in this chapter will recognize only a subset of the entire DXF file definition. This is not a problem for implementing a DXF reader because unrecognized DXF entities are easily ignored.

Several interesting things can be noted about the DXF reader implementation. First, the DXF reader maintains a symbol table of defined BLOCKs. For it to do this, you must place graphical entities into an instance of the *DXFObject* class. This instance then represents all graphical entities in the reader. Each BLOCK entity will create an instance of the class *DXFObject* that is then placed in the BLOCK entity symbol table. Additionally, the ENTITIES section has an instance of a *DXFObject* associated with it. It is this instance that will be converted into the internal representation.

The DXFObject Class

The *DXFObject* class is used internally to represent the DXF graphical entities. As an entity is encountered, its components are added to a *DXFObject* instance. The class allows triangles and rectangles to be added. Also, it can merge one *DXFObject* instance into another. It further can re-represent a *DXFObject* instance into a *MeshCompactor* instance.

```
class DXFObject {
public:
    DXFObject(void);

    void AddTriangle(SFVec3f p1, SFVec3f p2,
         SFVec3f p3, SFVec3f color, char* layer);

    void AddRectangle(SFVec3f p1, SFVec3f p2,
         SFVec3f p3, SFVec3f p4,
         SFVec3f color, char* layer);

    void Merge(DXFObject* obj, SFVec3f scale,
         double rotation,
         SFVec3f direction, SFVec3f offset,
         SFVec3f color, char* layer);

    void Output(MeshCompactor*);
};
```

Reading Entity Parameters

The core of the DXF file format is the DXF entity. All entities start with a group code of 0. Most DXF entities also have parameters that are group codes, except they begin with some value other than 0.

This information is useful when you are writing software that parses a DXF entity. In most entities, the DXF reader can read group codes until it reaches a group code of 0. The nonzero group codes are parameters to the current entity. The group codes encountered are parsed, and the underlying values are saved using a switch statement. This allows either group code values to be read in any order or group codes to be optional.

Several C/C++ macros defined in the DXF source file detect and read the common entity parameters. These must be used in a switch statement. The macro identifies the targeted group code and reads the corresponding group code argument. The following source code shows some examples of the macros and their usage.

```
#define COLOR(fp, x)  case 62: \
    if (!DXFReadInt(fp, x)) \
        return FALSE; \
    break;
#define LAYER(fp, x)  case 8: \
    if (!DXFReadString(fp, x)) \
        return FALSE; \
    break;

.
.
.

// Example reading contents of an entity.
retval = DXFReadInt(fp, code);

// Read Entity parameters until another
// Entity is encountered.
while (retval && code != 0) {
    switch (code) {
        COLOR(fp, colorIndex);
        LAYER(fp, layer);
    default:
        // Ignore unknown group codes
        DXFReadString(fp, trash);
    }
    retval = DXFReadInt(fp, code);
}

// Put back the group code zero value
DXFUnreadInt(fp, code);
```

Reading a DXF File

The function `DXFReader()` is available for use by external functions. This function takes in a *GNode* object and a character string that represents the filename. The *GNode* object will contain the objects read from the DXF file when the reading is complete.

`DXFReader()` creates the storage for the DXF representation. It opens the file, reads the DXF files, and then converts it into the internal representation, as shown by the following code:

```
int DXFReader(GNode* obj, char* filename)
{
    DXFObject*         dxf = new DXFObject;
    MeshCompactor*     mesh  = new MeshCompactor;
```

```
    FILE*               fp;

    ASSERT(dxf != NULL && mesh != NULL);

    // Makes the StatusMessage function work.
    InitMessage(obj);

    // Open File
    if ((fp = fopen(filename, "r")) == NULL) {
        obj->ErrorMessage("Unable to open file '%s'",
             filename);
        return -1;
    }

    // Read the file.
    DXFReadFile(dxf, fp);

    // Close the file
    fclose(fp);

    // Emit a status message for the user
    obj->StatusMessage("Converting to internal
representation");

    // Remove storage for the Blocks
    CleanUp();

    // Convert our representation into a mesh.
    dxf->Output(mesh);
    delete dxf;

    // Convert the mesh into our internal format.
    mesh->AddTo(obj);
    delete mesh;

    return TRUE;
}
```

The DXFReadFile() Function

The `DXFReadFile()` function performs only one task: It reads the DXF file, looking for the start of each DXF section entity. When an entity is encountered, the `DXFReadSection()` function is called (see the next section). When the end of file is reached, this function returns.

Notice that this function calls the function `DXFReadGroup()`, which reads the group code and its string argument. The `DXFReadGroup` function is primarily used to read the group code 0 items (see three sections ahead).

```
int
DXFReadFile(DXFObject* obj, FILE* fp)
{
    int     retval;
    int     code;
    char    string[256];

    retval = DXFReadGroup(fp, code, string);
    while (retval && strcmp(string, "EOF") != 0) {
        if (strcmp(string, "SECTION") == 0) {
            DXFReadSection(obj, fp);
        } else if (strcmp(string, "EOF") == 0) {
            return TRUE;
        }
        retval = DXFReadGroup(fp, code, string);

    }

    return TRUE;
}
```

The DXFReadSection() Function

The `DXFReadSection()` function scans the DXF file for each of the four sections. A HEADER section or TABLES section is ignored. A BLOCKS section results in a call to the `DXFReadBlocks()` function (see the next section). An ENTITIES section results in a call to the `DXFReadEntities()` function (see three sections ahead).

Following is the `DXFReadSection()` function:

```
int DXFReadSection(DXFObject* obj, FILE* fp)
{
    int     retval;
    int     code;
    char    string[256];

    retval = DXFReadGroup(fp, code, string);
    while (retval && strcmp(string, "ENDSEC") != 0) {
        if (strcmp(string, "HEADER") == 0 ||
                strcmp(string, "TABLES") == 0) {
                // Ignore Headers && tables
                do {
```

```
                retval = DXFReadGroup(fp, code, string);
            } while (retval && (code != 0 ||
                strcmp(string, "ENDSEC") !=0));
            return retval;
        } else if (strcmp(string, "BLOCKS") == 0) {
            return DXFReadBlocks(obj, fp);
        } else if (strcmp(string, "ENTITIES") == 0) {
            return DXFReadEntities(obj, fp);
        }
        retval = DXFReadGroup(fp, code, string);
    }

    return TRUE;
}
```

The DXFReadBlocks() Function

The `DXFReadBlocks()` function scans for BLOCK entities in the BLOCKS section. When a new BLOCK entity is encountered, the `DXFReadBlock()` function is called (see the next section). The BLOCKS section is scanned for BLOCK entities until the ENDSEC entity is found.

```
int
DXFReadBlocks(DXFObject* obj, FILE* fp)
{
    int     retval;
    int     code;
    char    string[256];

    retval = DXFReadGroup(fp, code, string);
    while (retval && strcmp(string, "ENDSEC") != 0) {
        if (strcmp(string, "BLOCK") == 0) {
            retval = DXFReadBlock(obj, fp);
            ASSERT(retval);
        }
        retval = DXFReadGroup(fp, code, string);
    }

    return (strcmp(string, "ENDSEC") == 0);
}
```

The DXFReadBlock() Function

The `DXFReadBlock()` function reads a BLOCK entity. This entity contains a header that describes some information about the BLOCK, such as its name, color, layer, position, and group 70 code.

The header is followed by the entities that are contained in the BLOCK. These entities can include 3DFACE, POLYLINE, LINE, and INSERT entities. The BLOCK is closed with an ENDBLK entity. After the BLOCK is read, it is added to the block symbol table using the `AddSymbol()` function.

```
int
DXFReadBlock(DXFObject* obj, FILE* fp)
{
    int         retval, code, colorIndex, group70;
    SFVec3f     offset;
    char        string[256], layer[256],
                BLOCKname[256], trash[256];
    DXFObject* block = new DXFObject;

    // Read the block entities info.
    if (!DXFReadInt(fp, code)) return FALSE;

    while (code != 0) {
        switch (code) {
            COLOR(fp, colorIndex);
            LAYER(fp, layer);
            BLOCKNAME(fp, blockname);
            GROUP70(fp, group70);
            VERTEX1(fp, offset.X(), offset.Y(), offset.Z());
        default:
            DXFReadString(fp, trash);
        }
        DXFReadInt(fp, code);
    }
    DXFUnreadInt(fp, code); // Pushback last group code read

    // Read the entities associated with the block entity.
    retval = DXFReadGroup(fp, code, string);
    ASSERT(code == 0);
    while (retval && strcmp(string, "ENDBLK") != 0) {
        if (code == 0 && strcmp(string, "LINE") == 0) {
            retval = DXFReadLine(block, fp);
        } else if (code == 0 &&
                strcmp(string, "POLYLINE") == 0) {
            retval = DXFReadPolyline(block, fp);
        } else if (code == 0 &&
                strcmp(string, "3DFACE") == 0) {
            retval = DXFRead3DFace(block, fp);
        } else if (code == 0 &&
                strcmp(string, "INSERT") == 0) {
            retval = DXFReadInsert(block, fp);
        }
```

```
        retval = DXFReadGroup(fp, code, string);
    }

    // Save this block in the block symbol table.
    AddSymbol(blockname, block, offset);

    return retval;
}
```

The DXFReadEntities() Function

The `DXFReadEntities()` function reads the graphical and nongraphical entities found in the ENTITIES section. This function recognizes 3DFACE, POLYLINE, LINE, and INSERT entities and ignores all others.

```
int
DXFReadEntities(DXFObject* obj, FILE* fp)
{
    int     retval;
    int     code;
    char    string[256];

    retval = DXFReadGroup(fp, code, string);
    while (retval && strcmp(string, "ENDSEC") != 0) {
        if (strcmp(string, "LINE") == 0) {
            retval = DXFReadLine(obj, fp);
        } else if (strcmp(string, "INSERT") == 0) {
            retval = DXFReadInsert(obj, fp);
        } else if (strcmp(string, "POLYLINE") == 0) {
            retval = DXFReadPolyline(obj, fp);
        } else if (strcmp(string, "3DFACE") == 0) {
            retval = DXFRead3DFace(obj, fp);
        }

        retval = DXFReadGroup(fp, code, string);
    }

    return (strcmp(string, "ENDSEC") == 0);
}
```

The DXFReadInsert() Function

The `DXFReadInsert()` function reads the INSERT entity and places the BLOCK specified inline in the *DXFObject* instance passed in as the first argument. The INSERT entity has several parameters. These include the

BLOCK name, the insertion location, the number of items to insert in the row and column direction, and the spacing between multiple inserted items.

The BLOCK name is used to look up the definition of the BLOCK in the block symbol table. If the BLOCK is found in the symbol table, its contents are inserted into the *DXFObject* passed into `DXFReadInsert()` in place of the INSERT entity. (If the BLOCK is not found, the construct that looked up the BLOCK is ignored; this shouldn't happen.) The BLOCK may be inserted several times depending on the row and column count found in the INSERT entity.

```
int
DXFReadInsert(DXFObject* obj, FILE* fp)
{
    int         code, colorIndex;
    char        trash[256], layer[256], blockname[256];
    SFVec3f     insert, direction, scale(1.0, 1.0, 1.0);
    int         row = 1, col = 1;
    double      rowSpacing = 0.0, colSpacing = 0.0;
    double      rotation = 0.0;
    DXFObject* block;

    colorIndex = 0;
    strcpy(layer, "");

    // Read the Insert Entity
    if (!DXFReadInt(fp, code)) return FALSE;
    while (code != 0) {
        switch (code) {
            COLOR(fp, colorIndex);
            LAYER(fp, layer);
            BLOCKNAME(fp, blockname);
            VERTEX1(fp, insert.X(), insert.Y(),insert.Z());
            SCALE(fp, scale.X(), scale.Y(), scale.Z());
            DIRECTION(fp, direction.X(), direction.Y(),
                direction.Z());
            ROTATION(fp, rotation);
            INSERT_ROW(fp, row);
            INSERT_COL(fp, col);
            INSERT_ROW_SPACING(fp, rowSpacing);
            INSERT_COL_SPACING(fp, colSpacing);
        default:
            if (!DXFReadString(fp, trash)) return FALSE;
        }
        if (!DXFReadInt(fp, code)) return FALSE;
    }
    DXFUnreadInt(fp, code); // Pushback last code read
```

```
    // Lookup the associated BLOCK entity
    block = LookupObject(blockname, insert);

    // If the block entity is found, then insert the
    // contents of the block in place of the insert entity.
    if (block != NULL) {
        for (int i = 0; i < row; i++) {
            for (int j = 0; j < col; j++) {
                SFVec3f location = insert+
                                        SFVec3f(colSpacing*j,
                                        rowSpacing*i, 0.0);
                obj->Merge(block, scale, rotation,
                                        direction, location,
                                        Index2Color(colorIndex),
                                        blockname);
            }
        }
    }
    return TRUE;
}
```

The DXFReadPolyline() Function

The `DXFReadPolyline()` function reads the body of a DXF POLYLINE entity. This entity defines a polygon mesh. There are two major types of polygon meshes. One is defined with vertices and polygon faces. The other consists of a series of vertices stitched together to form the mesh. `DXFReadPolyline()` can read both types.

A POLYLINE entity, which defines a mesh, has two parts: the entity definition followed by several VERTEX entities. It is closed with a SEQEND entity.

The POLYLINE entity definition specifies which type of polygon mesh the entity defines. Group code 70 returns a parameter that defines which type to expect. If bit 6 of the group code 70 value is 1, then the vertices that follow will be stitched together into a mesh. If bit 7 is 1 and bit 6 is 0, then the polygon mesh is defined by vertices and faces.

The following code reads the body of the DXF POLYLINE entity and adds the polygon mesh to the *DXFObject* passed in the first argument:

```
int
DXFReadPolyline(DXFObject* obj, FILE* fp)
{
    MFVec3f     vertices;
    SFVec3f     offset;
    int         code, colorIndex, polycode,
                vertexcode, retval;
```

```
int         m_dim = 0, n_dim = 0, follow = 0;
char        trash[256], layer[256], string[256];

colorIndex = 0;
strcpy(layer, "");

// Read Polyline header
if (!DXFReadInt(fp, code)) return FALSE;

while (code != 0) {
    switch (code) {
        COLOR(fp, colorIndex);
        LAYER(fp, layer);
        GROUP70(fp, polycode);
        VERTICES_FOLLOW(fp, follow);
        VERTEX1(fp, offset.X(), offset.Y(), offset.Z());
        M_DIM(fp, m_dim);
        N_DIM(fp, n_dim);
    default:
        if (!DXFReadString(fp, trash)) return FALSE;
    }
    if (!DXFReadInt(fp, code)) return FALSE;
}
DXFUnreadInt(fp, code); // Pushback last code read

// Now read the vertices

retval = DXFReadGroup(fp, code, string);
while (retval && strcmp(string, "SEQEND") != 0) {
    if (strcmp(string, "VERTEX") == 0) {
        SFVec3f     p;
        int         face[4] = {0, 0, 0, 0};

        // Read VERTEX
        if (!DXFReadInt(fp, code)) return FALSE;

        while (code != 0) {
            switch (code) {
                COLOR(fp, colorIndex);
                LAYER(fp, layer);
                GROUP70(fp, vertexcode);
                VERTEX1(fp, p.X(), p.Y(), p.Z());
                FACE(fp, 0, face[0]);
                FACE(fp, 1, face[1]);
                FACE(fp, 2, face[2]);
                FACE(fp, 3, face[3]);
            default:
                if (!DXFReadString(fp, trash))
```

```
                    return FALSE;
                }
                if (!DXFReadInt(fp, code)) return FALSE;
            }
            DXFUnreadInt(fp, code); // Pushback last

            if (follow && (vertexcode & 64)) {
                // We've found a vertex
                vertices.Add(p+offset);
            } else if (follow && !(vertexcode & 64) &&
                    vertexcode & 128) {
                // We've found a face
                if (face[0] != face[1] && face[1] != face[2] &&
                        face[0] && face[2]) {
                    if (face[3] != face[2]) {
                        obj->AddRectangle(
                        vertices[abs(face[0])-1],
                        vertices[abs(face[1])-1],
                        vertices[abs(face[2])-1],
                        vertices[abs(face[3])-1],
                        Index2Color(colorIndex),
                        layer);
                    } else {
                        obj->AddTriangle(
                        vertices[abs(face[0])-1],
                        vertices[abs(face[1])-1],
                        vertices[abs(face[2])-1],
                        Index2Color(colorIndex),
                        layer);
                    }
                }
            }
        }
        retval = DXFReadGroup(fp, code, string);
}
// If we are stitching together a mesh then here's
// where we do it.
if (follow && (polycode & 16)) {
    int     m_wrap = (polycode & 1) != 0;
    int     n_wrap = (polycode & 32) != 0;

    for (int i = 0; i < m_dim+m_wrap-1; i++) {
        for (int j = 0; j < n_dim+n_wrap-1; j++) {
            obj->AddRectangle(
            vertices[(i%m_dim)*n_dim+(j%n_dim)],
            vertices[(i%m_dim)*n_dim+(j+1)%n_dim],
            vertices[((i+1)%m_dim)*n_dim+
                        (j+1)%n_dim],
```

```
                    vertices[((i+1)%m_dim)*n_dim+j%n_dim],
                    Index2Color(colorIndex), layer);
            }
        }
    }

    return retval;
}
```

The DXFReadLine() Function

The `DXFReadLine()` function reads the body of a DXF LINE entity. A LINE entity consists of two vertices that define each end of the line segment. A layer and color assignment may be optionally assigned.

Because the underlying representation recognizes only triangles and rectangles, this function converts the lines encountered into very narrow rectangles. These rectangles are added to the *DXFObject* passed in the first argument.

```
int
DXFReadLine(DXFObject* obj, FILE* fp)
{
    int         colorIndex;
    int         code, retval;
    char        trash[256], layer[256];
    SFVec3f     p1, p2, p3, p4;
    SFVec3f     delta(0.0, 0.0, 0.00001);

    colorIndex = 0;
    strcpy(layer, "");

    // Read the LINE Entity
    retval = DXFReadInt(fp, code);

    while (retval && code != 0) {
        switch (code) {
            COLOR(fp, colorIndex);
            LAYER(fp, layer);
            VERTEX1(fp, p1.X(), p1.Y(), p1.Z());
            VERTEX2(fp, p3.X(), p3.Y(), p3.Z());
        default:
            if (!DXFReadString(fp, trash)) return FALSE;
        }
        retval = DXFReadInt(fp, code);
    }
```

```
    DXFUnreadInt(fp, code); // Pushback last code read

    obj->AddRectangle(p1, p1+delta, p3, p3+delta,
        Index2Color(colorIndex), layer);

    return retval;
}
```

Implementing a DXF Writer

To create a DXF file format writer, you have to write a small amount of C++ code to convert the internal representation of 3D objects into polygons. This conversion is very easy to accomplish because the internal representation of 3D objects is very similar to that of a DXF file.

The `GNode::Write()` member function traverses the scene, and the appropriate member function of a *GWrite* derived class is called for each recognized *GNode* instance encountered. This allows implementers to write DXF file format writers without having to know the details of the internal representation of 3D objects. Also, the internal representation allows 3D objects to be converted to polygons. So all you need to do to implement a DXF writer is tell the internal representation that you want only polygons and then write out the polygons as triangles.

Because of this internal support for polygons, writing a capable DXF writer is not nearly as challenging as writing a DXF reader. The writer needs only to convert polygons converted from the internal representation into 3DFACE entities.

The following class definition describes the *GWriteDXF* derived *GWrite* class:

```
class GWriteDXF : public GWrite {
private:
    char   m_name[256];

public:
    GWriteDXF(void) : GWrite() {strcpy(m_name, "");}

    // Tell internal representation that we only
    // want to see polygons.
    Short   PolygonSupported(void)  {return TRUE;}

    // Overridden member functions
    void    Prolog(GNode*, GState&);
    void    Epilog(GNode*, GState&);
    void    StartPolygons(GState&, char*);
```

```
    void    Polygon(GState&, long, MFVec3f*,
                    MFVec3f* = NULL,
                    GWriteMaterial* = NULL);
};
```

Writing the DXF Header

After the DXF file has been opened, the `GWriteDXF::Prolog()` member function is called. The layer name is set to the default, and an empty HEADER section is written. An ENTITY section is opened so that polygons encountered during the traversal of internal 3D objects can be directly written.

```
void GWriteDXF::Prolog(GNode* gp, GState&)
{
    // Save a default layer name.
    strcpy(m_name, "Default");

    // Write a Default Header section and open the
    // Entities section
    fprintf(m_fp, "0\nSECTION\n2\nHEADER\n0\nENDSEC\n");
    fprintf(m_fp, "0\nSECTION\n2\nENTITIES\n" );
}
```

Closing the DXF File

The `GWriteDXF::Epilog()` member function closes the ENTITIES section and then writes an EOF entity:

```
void GWriteDXF::Epilog(GNode*, GState&)
{
    // Close the Entities section and mark the end
    // of the file.
    fprintf(m_fp, "0\nENDSEC\n0\nEOF\n" );
}
```

Keeping Track of Layers

The `GWriteDXF::StartPolygon()` member function is encountered whenever a polygon mesh is about to be emitted. This function announces the name of the layer with which the object is associated.

```
void GWriteDXF::
StartPolygons(GState& state, char* name)
{
```

```
    // Save the current layer name
    if (state.HeirName() != NULL &&
            strcmp(m_name, state.HeirName()) != 0) {
        strcpy(m_name, state.HeirName());
    }
}
```

Writing the Polygons

The `GWriteDXF::Polygon()` member function is called for every polygon encountered during the traversal of the 3D objects being traversed. It is passed the vertex list in the third argument and the material associated with the polygon in the last argument. The material is converted into a color, and the color is converted into a DXF color index.

Next, the polygon is converted into one or more 3DFACE entities, depending on the number of faces in the polygon. This implementation converts the polygon into `sides-2` triangles, which are emitted as 3DFACE entities.

```
void GWriteDXF::
Polygon(GState& state, long faceNum, MFVec3f* v, MFVec3f* n,
    GWriteMaterial* m)
{
    // Get the current color
    SFVec3f    color = m->Color();

    // Write the polygon
    if (m_fp != NULL && v->Elements() >= 3) {
        SFVec3f    triangle[3];
        triangle[0] = (*v)[0];

        // Convert the polygon into triangles
        for (int i = 2; i < v->Elements(); i++) {
            triangle[1] = (*v)[i-1];
            triangle[2] = (*v)[i];

            // Write each triangle as a 3DFACE Entity.
            fprintf(m_fp, "0\n3DFACE\n8\n%s\n", m_name);

            // Convert the color of the polygon into the
            // closest matching color in the AutoCAD
            // default color palette.
            fprintf(m_fp, "62\n%d\n",
                Color2Index(color.Red(),
                    color.Green(), color.Blue()) );

            // Write each vertex in the triangle
```

```
                fprintf(m_fp, "10\n%f\n20\n%f\n30\n%f\n",
                        triangle[0].X(), triangle[0].Y(),
                        triangle[0].Z());
                fprintf(m_fp, "11\n%f\n21\n%f\n31\n%f\n",
                        triangle[1].X(), triangle[1].Y(),
                        triangle[1].Z());
                fprintf(m_fp, "12\n%f\n22\n%f\n32\n%f\n",
                        triangle[2].X(), triangle[2].Y(),
                        triangle[2].Z());
                // Repeat the vertex because DXF always
                // wants four.
                fprintf(m_fp, "13\n%f\n23\n%f\n33\n%f\n",
                        triangle[2].X(), triangle[2].Y(),
                        triangle[2].Z());
            }
        }
    }
```

References

AutoCAD Reference Manual. 1990. San Rafael, Calif.: AutoDesk, Inc.

Bourke, Paul. "Minimum Requirements for Creating a DXF of a 3D Model." 1993. http://www.auckland.ac.nz/arch/pdbourke/interchange/min3d.html.

Chapter 8

3D Studio R2/R3/R4

3D Studio is a 3D modeling and animation application program from AutoDesk for PCs running DOS or Windows NT. AutoDesk also produces the very popular CAD program AutoCAD. These programs complement each other; they can import and export each other's files.

3D Studio has been a real workhorse for 3D visualization and animation on the PC. It is a very feature-rich environment that has been used by many successful artists to create a wide variety of images and animation. It also has been used in multimedia projects and to help create special effects for television and movies.

Most competitors of 3D Studio have acknowledged that software's popularity by including the capability to import and export its files. AutoDesk encourages this by selling a 3D Studio File Toolkit, which includes a set of C libraries for most common PC C/C++ compilers. The Toolkit also contains a comprehensive description of the components of the 3D Studio binary file format. This documentation is highly recommended for anyone writing a commercial import/export utility for 3D Studio.

In this chapter, I discuss a subset of the 3D Studio format. This subset describes named objects, triangle meshes, and surface materials. Other features, such as Keyframe data, bitmap textures, and texture mapping, are not addressed.

The 3D Studio file format has two file suffixes: 3DS and PRJ. Both have the same underlying format. They differ in that the PRJ file contains one or more object definitions plus lighting, camera, and animation specifications. In the following description of the 3D Studio file format, I focus on the 3DS version of the format, since it's what most people want to import.

Overview of the 3DS File Format

The 3DS file format is binary. As mentioned in Chapter 6, binary file formats require special consideration because extra design effort is needed to make the source for a binary file portable. This is because the integer formats of different computer processors may differ in their byte ordering. The implementation described in this chapter is designed to make porting as easy as reasonably possible. However, it has not been ported. Some porting issues are discussed in the implementation section in this chapter.

A 3DS file's content is primarily a series of triangles. The file also contains data about grouping, textures, lights, cameras, and animation. Even though 3DS Studio supports more exotic shapes, all are converted into polygons in the 3D Studio file format.

Byte Ordering Considerations

One issue regarding the 3D Studio file format requires special consideration if you are planning to write your own format reader or writer. It is byte ordering. Binary files can be a very space efficient and fast means of storing data to files. However, the same basic numeric data types are often represented differently on different types of computer systems. This difference derives from how bytes in multibyte values are stored on different processors. The byte representation comes in two flavors: little-endian and big-endian. The "endianness" of values has to do with the byte ordering of values.

Chapter 6 discusses the details of "endianness" in more depth. To summarize that discussion, you must encapsulate the binary read and write functions. For example, by defining `ReadLong(FILE*, long&)` and `WriteLong(FILE*, long)` functions, you can ensure that all binary writes of long integers are enclosed in a set of functions. These functions can be altered to match the binary representation of the target machine without anyone's having to alter any other portion of the software.

Overview of the 3D Studio Format

A 3D Studio file is organized as a series of binary chunks. These chunks are simply a generic way of defining the individual components of the format. By using chunks, you make it possible for a program to to read a file and deal only with the components that your program recognizes. Unrecognized components are easily ignored.

Each chunk has a header. Most also have a body. The chunk header is 6 bytes long and is composed of a 16-bit integer (a short) and a 32-bit integer (a long).

The short value contains a unique identification value that identifies the type of the chunk. The long value defines the length of the chunk including the header.

Syntax of the 3D Studio File

The syntax of the 3D Studio binary file (*.3DS) is straightforward. At the top level are only three chunks that the reader deals with:

1. M3DMAGIC identifies the file as a 3DS file rather than a PRJ file.
2. M3D_VERSION identifies the version of the 3DS file.
3. MDATA defines all of the mesh data.

In this chapter, I focus on MDATA and its subchunks.

The Chunk Header

Each 3DS binary file is composed of many chunk headers. Table 8.1 describes the parts of the chunk header.

Table 8.1 3D Studio chunk header

Data Type	Size	Starting Position	Description
Short	2	0	The identifier for the chunk. For example, the first chunk in a 3DS file is always M3DMAGIC, which has an identifier value of 0x4d4d.
Long	4	2	The length of the chunk, including this header.

Commonly Used Chunks

Several types of chunks are used repeatedly throughout a 3DS file. These are COLOR_F, LIN_COLOR_F, COLOR_24, LIN_COLOR_24, INT_PERCENTAGE, and FLOAT_PERCENTAGE. These chunks are used often in MDATA sections.

COLOR_F Chunk

The COLOR_F chunk contains three floating-point values that define an RGB color. It is used in 3D Studio R1 and R2 but has been superseded in 3D Studio R3 with LIN_COLOR_F. Table 8.2 describes the COLOR_F chunk.

Table 8.2 COLOR_F chunk

Data Type	Size	Starting Position	Description
Header	6	0	The header ID value for COLOR_F is 0x0010. The total size of this chunk is 18.
Float	4	6	A 32-bit floating-point value. This value represents the color red and may range from 0.0 (no red component) to 1.0 (maximum red component).
Float	4	10	A 32-bit floating-point value. This value represents the color green and may range from 0.0 (no green component) to 1.0 (maximum green component).
Float	4	14	A 32-bit floating-point value. This value represents the color blue and may range from 0.0 (no blue component) to 1.0 (maximum blue component).

LIN_COLOR_F Chunk

The LIN_COLOR_F chunk contains three floating-point values that define a linear RGB color. This chunk is used in 3D Studio R3. Table 8.3 describes the LIN_COLOR_F chunk.

Table 8.3. LIN_COLOR_F chunk

Data Type	Size	Starting Position	Description
Header	6	0	The header ID value for LIN_COLOR_F is 0x0013. The total size of this chunk is 18.
Float	4	6	A 32-bit floating-point value. This value represents the color red and may range from 0.0 (no red component) to 1.0 (maximum red component).
Float	4	10	A 32-bit floating-point value. This value represents the color green and may range from 0.0 (no green component) to 1.0 (maximum green component).

Table 8.3. LIN_COLOR_F chunk *(continued)*

Data Type	Size	Starting Position	Description
Float	4	14	A 32-bit floating-point value. This value represents the color blue and may range from 0.0 (no blue component) to 1.0 (maximum blue component).

COLOR_24 Chunk

The COLOR_24 chunk contains three single-byte values that define an RGB color. This chunk is used in 3D Studio R1 and R2 and has been superseded in 3D Studio R3 by LIN_COLOR_24. Table 8.4 describes the COLOR_24 chunk.

Table 8.4. COLOR_24 chunk

Data Type	Size	Starting Position	Description
Header	6	0	The header ID value for COLOR_24 is 0x0011. The total size of this chunk is 9.
Unsigned char	1	6	A byte value. This value represents the color red and may range from 0 (no red component) to 255 (maximum red component).
Unsigned char	1	7	A byte value. This value represents the color green and may range from 0 (no green component) to 255 (maximum green component).
Unsigned char	1	8	A byte value. This value represents the color blue and may range from 0 (no blue component) to 255 (maximum blue component).

LIN_COLOR_24 Chunk

The LIN_COLOR_24 chunk contains three single-byte values that define a linear RGB color. This chunk is used in 3D Studio R3. Table 8.5 describes the LIN_COLOR_24 chunk.

Table 8.5. LIN_COLOR_24 chunk

Data Type	Size	Starting Position	Description
Header	6	0	The header ID value for LIN_COLOR_24 is 0x0012. The total size of this chunk is 9.
Unsigned char	1	6	A byte value. This value represents the color red and may range from 0 (no red component) to 255 (maximum red component).
Unsigned char	1	7	A byte value. This value represents the color green and may range from 0 (no green component) to 255 (maximum green component).
Unsigned char	1	8	A byte value. This value represents the color blue and may range from 0 (no blue component) to 255 (maximum blue component).

INT_PERCENTAGE Chunk

The INT_PERCENTAGE chunk defines an integer percentage. This type of value is often used in surface material definitions. Table 8.6 describes the INT_PERCENTAGE chunk.

Table 8.6. INT_PERCENTAGE chunk

Data Type	Size	Starting Position	Description
Header	6	0	The header ID value for INT_PERCENTAGE is 0x0030. The total size of this chunk is 8.
Short	2	6	Contains an integer percentage value. This value can range from 0 to 100. In some cases, it may be negative.

FLOAT_PERCENTAGE Chunk

The FLOAT_PERCENTAGE chunk defines a float percentage value. Table 8.7 describes this chunk.

Table 8.7. FLOAT_PERCENTAGE chunk

Data Type	Size	Starting Position	Description
Header	6	0	The header ID value for FLOAT_PERCENTAGE is 0x0031. The total size of this chunk is 10.
Float	4	6	Contains a floating-point percentage value. This value can range from 0.0 to 1.0. In some cases, it may be negative.

File Header Chunks

All 3D Studio files begin with a special chunk that identifies the file. For the 3DS file, this is the M3DMAGIC chunk. This chunk has a variable length. Table 8.8 describes the M3DMAGIC chunk.

Table 8.8. M3DMAGIC chunk

Data Type	Size	Starting Position	Description
Header	6	0	The header ID value for M3DMAGIC is 0x4d4d. The total size of this chunk is variable.
M3D_VERSION	10	6	Defines the version of the 3DS file. Currently the value 3 is used.
MDATA	Variable	16	Defines the objects in the 3DS file.

M3D_VERSION Chunk

The M3D_VERSION chunk defines the version of the 3DS file. Table 8.9 describes this chunk.

Table 8.9. M3D_VERSION chunk

Data Type	Size	Starting Position	Description
Header	6	0	The header ID value for M3D_VERSION is 0x0002. The total size of this chunk is 10.
Long	4	6	Defines the version of the file. The current value is 3.

MDATA Chunk

The MDATA chunk is the largest chunk in most 3D Studio files. Each MDATA chunk contains many subchunks. In this section, I define only the subset of chunks necessary for reading or writing individual objects. Other chunks either can be ignored when reading or are not necessary when writing the file and so are optional. Table 8.10 describes the MDATA chunk.

Table 8.10. MDATA chunk

Data Type	Size	Starting Position	Description
Header	6	0	The header ID value for MDATA is 0x3d3d. The total size of this chunk is variable.
MESH_VERSION	10	6	The chunk that contains the current revision of the 3DS file format.
MAT_ENTRY	Variable	16	One or more of these chunks define the materials that will be used by the polygons in the mesh.
MASTER_SCALE	10	Undefined	Defines the scale of the factor for all geometric coordinates.
NAME_OBJECT	Variable	Undefined	One or more of these chunks define the objects, such as meshes, cameras, and lights, that populate a 3DS file.

MESH_VERSION Chunk

The MESH_VERSION chunk defines the revision of 3D Studio with which the MDATA section is compatible. The legal values are 1 for Release 1, 2 for Release 2, and 3 for Release 3. Table 8.11 describes the MESH_VERSION chunk.

Table 8.11. MESH_VERSION chunk

Data Type	Size	Starting Position	Description
Header	6	0	The header ID value for MESH_VERSION is 0x3d3e. The total size of this chunk is 10.
Long	4	6	Specifies the revision of 3D Studio with which the MDATA section is compatible.

MASTER_SCALE Chunk

The MASTER_SCALE chunk defines the scale for all of the geometric coordinates in the file. For example, a master value of 1.0 means there is one unit per inch. Table 8.12 describes the MASTER_SCALE chunk.

Table 8.12. MASTER_SCALE chunk

Data Type	Size	Starting Position	Description
Header	6	0	The header ID value for MASTER_SCALE is 0x0100. The total size of this chunk is 10.
Float	4	6	Specifies the scale. For example, a value of 1.0 means there is one unit per inch.

Material Chunks

MAT_ENTRY Chunk

The MAT_ENTRY chunk defines a named material that may be reused throughout the MDATA definition. One chunk is defined for each named material, so there may be several MAT_ENTRY chunks defined in a 3DS file. Each name in the MAT_ENTRY chunk must be unique. Table 8.13 describes the MAT_ENTRY chunk.

Table 8.13. MAT_ENTRY chunk

Data Type	Size	Starting Position	Description
Header	6	0	The header ID value for MAT_ENTRY is 0xafff. The total size of this chunk is variable.
MAT_NAME	Variable	6	Defines the name of the material. This chunk may appear only once in the MAT_ENTRY chunk. The name must be unique from other MAT_ENTRY chunks.
MAT_AMBIENT	15	Undefined	Defines the ambient color of the surface material. This attribute must be defined only once in the MAT_ENTRY chunk.
MAT_DIFFUSE	15	Undefined	Defines the diffuse color of the surface material. This attribute must be defined only once in the MAT_ENTRY chunk.
MAT_SPECULAR	15	Undefined	Defines the specular color of the surface material. This attribute must be defined only once in the MAT_ENTRY chunk.
MAT_SHININESS	14	Undefined	Defines the shininess of the surface material. This attribute must be defined only once in the MAT_ENTRY chunk.
MAT_TRANSPARENCY	14	Undefined	Defines the transparency of the current material. This attribute must be defined only once in the MAT_ENTRY chunk.
MAT_SHADING	8	Undefined	Defines the shading of the current material. This attribute must be defined only once in the MAT_ENTRY chunk.

MAT_NAME Chunk

The MAT_NAME chunk defines the name of the material. Each chunk must define a name. The length of the name string may be from 1 to 15 characters, with one additional character reserved for the `NULL` terminator. The name string defined in the chunk must be unique for all MAT_ENTRY chunks. Table 8.14 describes the MAT_NAME chunk.

Table 8.14. MAT_NAME chunk

Data Type	Size	Starting Position	Description
Header	6	0	The header ID value for MAT_NAME is 0xa000. The total size of this chunk is variable but is between 8 and 22 bytes.
String	Between 1 and 15 characters, with one additional character reserved for the `NULL` terminator.	6	Contains the name of the material.

MAT_AMBIENT Chunk

The MAT_AMBIENT chunk defines the ambient color for the material. It can be either 15 or 24 characters long, depending on the version of the 3DS file. Table 8.15 describes the MAT_AMBIENT chunk.

Table 8.15. MAT_AMBIENT chunk

Data Type	Size	Starting Position	Description
Header	6	0	The header ID value for MAT_AMBIENT is 0xa010. The total size of this chunk is either 15 or 24, depending on the version of the 3DS file.
COLOR_24	9	6	The color of the ambient light (R1 & R2).
LIN_COLOR_24 (optional)	9	15	The linear color of ambient light (R3).

MAT_DIFFUSE Chunk

The MAT_DIFFUSE chunk defines the diffuse color for the material. It can be either 15 or 24 characters long, depending on the version of the 3DS file. Table 8.16 describes the MAT_DIFFUSE chunk.

Table 8.16. MAT_DIFFUSE chunk

Data Type	Size	Starting Position	Description
Header	6	0	The header ID value for MAT_DIFFUSE is 0xa020. The total size of this chunk is either 15 or 24, depending on the version of the 3DS file.
COLOR_24	9	6	The color of the diffuse light (R1 & R2)
LIN_COLOR_24 (optional)	9	15	The linear color of diffuse light (R3).

MAT_SPECULAR Chunk

The MAT_SPECULAR chunk defines the specular color for the material. It can be either 15 or 24 characters long, depending on the version of the 3DS file. Table 8.17 describes the MAT_SPECULAR chunk.

Table 8.17. MAT_SPECULAR chunk

Data Type	Size	Starting Position	Description
Header	6	0	The header ID value for MAT_SPECULAR is 0xa030. The total size of this chunk is either 15 or 24, depending on the version of the 3DS file.
COLOR_24	9	6	The color of the specular light (R1 & R2).
LIN_COLOR_24 (optional)	9	15	The linear color of specular light (R3).

MAT_SHININESS Chunk

The MAT_SHININESS chunk defines the shininess for the material. The MAT_SHININESS chunk is 14 bytes long and defines the shininess ratio of the material. The shininess value ranges from 0 (matte) to 100 (shiny). Table 8.18 describes the MAT_SHININESS chunk.

Table 8.18. MAT_SHININESS chunk

Data Type	Size	Starting Position	Description
Header	6	0	The header ID value for MAT_SHININESS is 0xa040. The total size of this chunk is 14.
INT_PERCENTAGE	8	6	Contains the integer percentage value for shininess. The legal values are 0 (matte) to 100 (shiny).

MAT_TRANSPARENCY Chunk

The MAT_TRANSPARENCY chunk defines the opacity of the material. It is 14 bytes long and defines the transparency ratio of the material. The transparency value ranges from 100 (transparent) to 0 (opaque). Table 8.19 describes the MAT_TRANSPARENCY chunk.

Table 8.19. MAT_TRANSPARENCY chunk

Data Type	Size	Starting Position	Description
Header	6	0	The header ID value for MAT_TRANSPARENCY is 0xa040. The total size of this chunk is 14.
INT_PERCENTAGE	8	6	Contains the integer percentage value for transparency. The legal values are 100 (transparent) to 0 (opaque).

MAT_SHADING Chunk

The MAT_SHADING chunk defines the method of display for the material. It is 8 bytes long and defines the shading method of the material. The legal values for shading are 0 (wireframe), 1 (flat shading), 2 (Gouraud), 3 (Phong), and 4 (Metal). Table 8.20 describes the MAT_SHADING chunk.

Table 8.20. MAT_SHADING chunk

Data Type	Size	Starting Position	Description
Header	6	0	The header ID value for MAT_SHADING is 0xa100. The total size of this chunk is 8.
Short	2	6	Defines the display method for the material. The legal values are 0 (wireframe), 1 (flat shading), 2 (Gouraud), 3 (Phong), and 4 (Metal).

Object Chunks

Only one chunk in a 3DS file defines objects: NAMED_OBJECT. This chunk can define either a polygon mesh, a camera, or a light. For our purposes, I define only the polygon mesh version of this chunk, the N_TRI_OBJECT chunk. Table 8.21 describes the NAMED_OBJECT chunk.

Table 8.21. NAMED_OBJECT chunk

Data Type	Size	Starting Position	Description
Header	6	0	The header ID value for NAMED_OBJECT is 0x4000. The total size of this chunk is variable.
N_TRI_OBJECT	Variable	6	Defines a polygon mesh and the mesh's texture.

N_TRI_OBJECT Chunk

The N_TRI_OBJECT chunk defines a polygon mesh object. The mesh is composed of a vertex list, a face list, and a list that maps the defined materials to the faces. Each face is a triangle. This means that when you are writing a N_TRI_OBJECT, any polygons that are written must be tesselated to a series of triangles. Table 8.22 describes the N_TRI_OBJECT chunk.

Table 8.22. N_TRI_OBJECT chunk

Data Type	Size	Starting Position	Description
Header	6	0	The header ID value for N_TRI_OBJECT is 0x4100. The total size of this chunk is variable.
POINT_ARRAY	Variable	6	Defines the vertices to the polygon mesh.
FACE_ARRAY	Variable	Undefined	Defines the faces of the mesh.
MSH_MAT_GROUP	Variable	Undefined	Assigns materials to each face of the mesh.

POINT_ARRAY Chunk

The POINT_ARRAY chunk defines the list of vertices used by N_TRI_OBJECT to define a polygon mesh. This chunk is variable in length, ranging from 44 to 786,428 bytes, depending on whether POINT_ARRAY defines only the minimum legal vertices of 3 or the maximum of 65,535. Table 8.23 describes the POINT_ARRAY chunk.

Table 8.23. POINT_ARRAY chunk

Data Type	Size	Starting Position	Description
Header	6	0	The header ID value for POINT_ARRAY is 0x4110. The total size of this chunk is variable.
Unsigned short	2	6	Contains the number of points in the vertex list. The legal range is 3–65535.

(*continued*)

Table 8.23. POINT_ARRAY chunk *(continued)*

Data Type	Size	Starting Position	Description
(Point list)	3*sizeof(float)* vertex_count	8	A series of vertices and variable in length. Each vertex is composed of three float values that represent an (*x*, *y*, *z*) location. The number of vertices in this field is specified by the previous field in this chunk.

FACE_ARRAY Chunk

The FACE_ARRAY chunk defines the list of triangles that compose the list of faces. Each triangle is specified as four unsigned shorts. The first three define the indexes into the vertex list for the actual points used in the triangle. The fourth defines edge visibility. The face list is followed optionally by one or more MSH_MAT_GROUP chunks, which apply materials to the faces. Table 8.24 describes the FACE_ARRAY chunk.

Table 8.24. FACE_ARRAY chunk

Data Type	Size	Starting Position	Description
Header	6	0	The header ID value for FACE_ARRAY is 0x4120. The total size of this chunk is variable.
Unsigned short	2	6	Contains the number of faces in the face list. The legal range is 3–65535.
(face_list)	4*sizeof(unsigned short)*face_count	8	A series of faces and variable in length. Each face is composed of four unsigned short values. The first three are the indexes into the vertex list that define the points in the face. They are denoted by A, B, and C.

Table 8.24. FACE_ARRAY chunk *(continued)*

Data Type	Size	Starting Position	Description
(face_list)	4*sizeof(unsigned short)*face_count	8	The fourth value defines the edge visibility of the face. Its legal values are bit 0=edge CA visible, bit 1=edge BC visible, bit 2=edge AB visible, bit 3=U-axis texture wrap, and bit 4=V-axis texture wrap. The number of faces in this field is specified by the previous field in this chunk.
MSH_MAT_GROUP	Variable	Undefined	Can occur zero or more times. It defines the mapping of the material definitions to the mesh faces.

MSH_MAT_GROUP Chunk

The MSH_MAT_GROUP chunk maps materials to faces. It contains the name of the material to map, a count of the faces that will be assigned this material, and a list of material faces. Table 8.25 describes the MSH_MAT_GROUP chunk.

Table 8.25. MSH_MAT_GROUP chunk

Data Type	Size	Starting Position	Description
Header	6	0	The header ID value for MSH_MAT_GROUP is 0x4130. The total size of this chunk is variable.
String	Between 1 and 15 plus one character for the `NULL` terminator	6	Contains the name of the material that will be mapped to the specified faces.

(continued)

Table 8.25. MSH_MAT_GROUP chunk *(continued)*

Data Type	Size	Starting Position	Description
Unsigned short	2	Undefined	The number of faces that will be assigned this material.
Array of short	sizeof(short) *num_faces	Undefined	Contains a list of indexes into the face list. Each index assigns the specified material name to the face corresponding to the index.

Implementing a 3DS Reader

The 3DS reader recognizes only part of all chunks defined in the 3DS file format. The components are named objects (groups), triangle meshes (polygons), and materials. The *MeshCompactor* class is used in the implementation to help convert the 3DS components into the internal representation.

Reading a Chunk

The chunk is the fundamental component of a 3DS file. It denotes the beginning of a new component. Each chunk identifies its type with an unsigned short value that is unique for each chunk type. The chunk identifier is followed by a long value that defines the size of the chunk. The implementation of a chunk reader for 3DS follows:

```
// Declare Chunk structure
typedef struct {
    unsigned short          id;
    long                    len;
} Chunk3DS;

// Read Chunk into Chunk structure
int Read3DSChunk(GNode* root, FILE* fp, Chunk3DS& chunk)
{
    if (!ReadUShort(fp, chunk.id)) return FALSE;
    if (!ReadLong(fp, chunk.len)) return FALSE;
    return TRUE;
}
```

Verifying the File Type

It is important to verify that the file being read is actually the file type expected. The function `Is3DSFile()` reads the current chunk and verifies that the file is a 3DS file. The function saves the current position, reads the chunk, repositions the file location to the starting position, and returns the result. The repositioning of the file location ensures the function `_3ds_reader()` will be undisturbed by the verification function.

```
// Verifies that the current file is a 3ds file.
int
Is3DSFile(GNode* root, FILE* fp)
{
    Chunk3DS    chunk;
    long        pos = ftell(fp);

    if (!Read3DSChunk(root, fp, chunk)) {
        fseek(fp, pos, SEEK_SET);
        return FALSE;
    }

    fseek(fp, pos, SEEK_SET);
    return (chunk.id == M3DMAGIC);
}
```

Reading Basic Data Types

A 3DS file has several basic data types, including strings, colors, and percentages. The following source shows how each of these types is read:

```
// Read string and truncate if buffer is shorter than
// actual string.
int Read3DSString(GNode* root, FILE* fp,
                      char* name, int len = 256)
{
    int c;

    for (int i=0; (c = fgetc(fp)) != EOF &&
            c != '\0'; i++) {
        if (i < len) {
            name[i] = c;
        }
    }
    if (i < len) {
        name[i] = '\0';
    } else {
        name[len-1] = '\0';
    }
```

```
    return (c != EOF);
}

// Read a Percent Chunk
int ReadPercentage(GNode* root, FILE* fp, float& value)
{
    Chunk3DS    chunk;
    long        chunkStart = ftell(fp);

    if (!Read3DSChunk(root, fp, chunk)) return FALSE;

    if (chunk.id == INT_PERCENTAGE) {
          short svalue;
          if (!ReadShort(fp, svalue)) return FALSE;
          value = (float) svalue/ (float) 100.0;
          return TRUE;
    } else if (chunk.id == FLOAT_PERCENTAGE) {
          if (!ReadFloat(fp, value)) return FALSE;
          return TRUE;
    }

    // Skip the chunk
    fseek(fp, chunkStart + chunk.len, SEEK_SET);
    return FALSE;
}

// Read a color definition
int ReadColor(GNode* root, FILE* fp;
        float& red, float& green, float& blue)
{
    Chunk3DS            chunk;
    long                chunkStart = ftell(fp);
    unsigned char       tmp;

    if (!Read3DSChunk(root, fp, chunk)) return FALSE;
    switch (chunk.id) {
    case COLOR_F:
          if (!ReadFloat(fp, red)) return FALSE;
          if (!ReadFloat(fp, green)) return FALSE;
          if (!ReadFloat(fp, blue)) return FALSE;
          break;
    case COLOR_24:
          if (!ReadUByte(fp, tmp)) return FALSE;
          red = (float) tmp / (float) 255.0;
          if (!ReadUByte(fp, tmp)) return FALSE;
          green = (float) tmp / (float) 255.0;
          if (!ReadUByte(fp, tmp)) return FALSE;
          blue = (float) tmp / (float) 255.0;
```

```
            break;
        default:
            fseek(fp, chunkStart + chunk.len, SEEK_SET);
            return FALSE;
    }

    return TRUE;
}
```

Reading the M3DMAGIC Chunk

The M3DMAGIC chunk identifies the file as 3DS, so it should be the first chunk found in the 3DS file.

The function `_3ds_reader()` opens the specified 3DS file as a binary file and proceeds to read its contents, encountering first the M3DMAGIC chunk. The function `Read3DSFile()` reads the contents of that chunk and creates an instance of the class *MaterialDict*. This class then creates an instance of the material dictionary that is filled in when the MAT_ENTRY chunks are parsed. Later, the material dictionary is used in the N_TRI_OBJECT chunk to map the faces to the defined materials.

```
// External entry for reading 3ds file.
void _3ds_reader(GNode* root, char* filename)
{
    FILE*       fp;
    long        fileSize;
    Chunk3DS    chunk;

    // Open 3DS file (remember it's binary!)
    if ((fp = fopen(filename, "rb")) != NULL) {
        long  chunkStart = ftell(fp)

        // Get File Size
        fseek(fp, 0, SEEK_END);
        fileSize = ftell(fp);
        fseek(fp, 0, SEEK_SET);

        // Verify file type
        if (!Is3DSFile(root, fp)) {
            root->ErrorMessage("File '%s' is not a 3ds
                               binary file.", filename);
            return;
        }

        // Loop through the chunks
        while (chunkStart < fileSize &&
```

```
                    Read3DSChunk(root, fp, chunk)) {
                    switch (chunk.id) {
                    case M3DMAGIC:
                          if (!Read3DSFile(root, fileSize,
                                chunkStart, chunk.len, fp)) {
                                root->ErrorMessage("Read failed
                                      for 3ds file '%s'", filename);
                                return;
                          }
                          break;
                    default:
                          // Skip past unexpected chunks
                          fseek(fp, chunkStart + chunk.len,
                                SEEK_SET);
                    }
                    chunkStart = ftell(fp);
              }
        }
}
// Read 3ds file
int Read3DSFile(GNode* root, long fileSize, long fileStart,
      long fileLen, FILE* fp)
{
      long                chunkStart = ftell(fp);
      Chunk3DS            chunk;
      MaterialDict        *matdict = new MaterialDict;
      unsigned long       version;

      while (chunkStart < fileStart + fileLen &&
            Read3DSChunk(root, fp, chunk)) {
            switch (chunk.id) {
            case M3D_VERSION:
                  if (!ReadULong(fp, version)) goto error;
                  break;
            case MDATA:
                  if (!ReadMDATA(root, matdict, fileSize,
                        chunkStart, chunk.len, fp))
                              goto error;
                  break;
            default;
                  // Skip past unexpected chunks
                  fseek(fp, chunkStart + chunk.len, SEEK_SET);
            }
            chunkStart = ftell(fp);
      }

      if (matdict != NULL) delete matdict;
      return TRUE;
```

```
error:
    // Clean up the mess and report the error.
    if (matdict != NULL) delete matdict;
    return FALSE;
}
```

Reading the MDATA Chunk

`Read3DSFile()` encounters the MDATA chunk header, thereby causing the function `ReadMDATA()` to be called. Notice that the MDATA chunk is followed by the MESH_VERSION, MASTER_SCALE, MAT_ENTRY, and NAMED_OBJECT chunks. MAT_ENTRY is repeated one or more times and defines the material used in the 3DS file. It is followed by the NAMED_OBJECT definitions. There may be zero or more NAMED_OBJECTS in the file.

```
// Read toplevel objects
int ReadMDATA(GNode* root, MaterialDict* matdict,
        long fileSize, long mdataStart, long mdataSize,
        FILE* fp)
{
    long                  chunkStart = ftell(fp);
    Chunk3DS              chunk;
    unsigned long         version;
    float                 scale;

    while (chunkStart < mdataStart + mdataSize &&
          Read3DSChunk(root, fp, chunk)) {
          switch (chunk.id) {
          case MESH_VERSION:
                if (!ReadULong(fp, version)) {
                      return FALSE;
                }
                break;
          case MAT_ENTRY:
                if (!ReadMatEntry(root, matdict, fileSize,
                            chunkStart, chunk.len, fp)) {
                      return FALSE;
                }
                break;
          case MASTER_SCALE:
                if (!ReadFloat(fp, scale)) {
                      return FALSE;
                }
                break;
          case NAMED_OBJECT:
                if (!ReadNamedObject(root, matdict,
                            fileSize, chunkStart, chunk.len,
                            fp)) {
```

```
                    return FALSE;
                }
                break;
            default:
                // Skip past unexpected chunks
                fseek(fp, chunkStart + chunk.len, SEEK_SET);
            }
            chunkStart = ftell(fp);
        }
        return TRUE;
}
```

Reading the MAT_ENTRY Chunk

`ReadMDATA()` is the function that encounters the MAT_ENTRY chunk headers. When it reads MAT_ENTRY, the `ReadMatEntry()` function is called. This function reads the material definition from the MAT_ENTRY chunk and places it into a new entry in the material dictionary. The materials in the material dictionary will be referenced in the N_TRI_OBJECT when materials are mapped to the faces in the mesh.

```
// Read a material definition, add it to the
// material dictionary.
int
ReadMatEntry(GNode* root, MaterialDict* matdict,
    long fileSize, long matStart, long matSize, FILE* fp)
{
    long                chunkStart = ftell(fp);
    Chunk3DS            chunk;
    char                name[256];
    float               red, green, blue;
    float               percentage;
    GWriteMaterial      material;

    ASSERT(matdict != NULL);

    while (chunkStart < matStart + matSize &&
            Read3DSChunk(root, fp, chunk)) {
            switch (chunk.id) {
            case MAT_NAME:
                    if (!Read3DSString(root, fp, name, 256))
                            return FALSE;
                    root->StatusMessage("Reading material '%s'",
                            name);
                    break;
            case MAT_AMBIENT:
                    if (!ReadColor(root, fp, red, green, blue))
```

```
                    return FALSE;
                material.AmbientColor(
                    SFVec3f(red, green, blue));
                break;
            case MAT_DIFFUSE:
                if (!ReadColor(root, fp, red, green, blue))
                    return FALSE;
                material.DiffuseColor(
                    SFVec3f(red, green, blue));
                break;
            case MAT_SPECULAR:
                if (!ReadColor(root, fp, red, green, blue))
                    return FALSE;
                material.SpecularColor(
                    SFVec3f(red, green, blue));
                break;
            case MAT_SHININESS;
                if (!ReadPercentage(root, fp, percentage))
                    return FALSE;
                material.Shininess(percentage);
                break;
            case MAT_TRANSPARENCY:
                if (!ReadPercentage(root, fp, percentage))
                    return FALSE;
                material.Transparency(percentage);
                break;
            default
                // Skip past unexpected chunks
                fseek(fp, chunkStart + chunk.len, SEEK_SET);
            }
            chunkStart = ftell(fp);
}

matdict->Add(name, material);

return TRUE;
}
```

Reading the NAMED_OBJECT Chunk

`ReadMDATA()` is the function that encounters the NAMED_OBJECT chunk headers. When it reads NAMED_OBJECT, the `ReadNamedObject()` function is called. `ReadNamedObject()` reads the name of the NAMED_OBJECT and then reads the subsequent chunks. When an N_TRI_OBJECT is encountered, the `ReadTriObject()` function is called and reads the polygon mesh associated with this chunk.

```
// Read the Named Mesh (other named objects are ignored).
Int ReadNamedObject(GNode* root, MaterialDict* matdict, long
    fileSize, long namedStart, long namedSize, FILE* fp)
{
    char         groupName[256];
    Chunk3DS     chunk;
    long         chunkStart;

    if (!Read3DSString(root, fp, groupName, 256))
        return FALSE;

    root->StatusMessage("Reading object '%s'", groupName);

    chunkStart = ftell(fp);

    while (chunkStart < namedStart+namedSize &&
          Read3DSChunk(root, fp, chunk)) {
          switch (chunk.id) {
          case N_TRI_OBJECT:
                if (!ReadTriObject(root, matdict, fileSize,
                      fp, chunkStart, chunk.len, groupName))
                      return FALSE;
                break;
          default:
                // Skip past unexpected chunks
                fseek(fp, chunkStart + chunk.len, SEEK_SET);
          }
          chunkStart = ftell(fp);
    }

    return TRUE;
}
```

Reading the N_TRI_OBJECT Chunk

`ReadTriObject()` reads the body of the N_TRI_OBJECT chunk. All of the conversion of 3DS to the internal format is done in this function.

`ReadTriObject()` reads the POINT_ARRAY chunk and calls the `ReadPointArray()` function, which returns the vertex list in the internal format. `ReadTriObject()` also reads the FACE_ARRAY chunk and calls the `ReadFaceArray()` function, which returns the faces in the internal format.

The materials associated with the faces in the mesh are defined using the MSH_MAT_GROUP chunk. When this chunk is encountered, the `MeshMatGroup()` function is called, which in turn returns the materials and the material indexes in the internal format.

After all the chunks have been encountered, the data returned from each function associated with the chunks is used to construct the internal representation of the mesh.

The first step in doing this is to create a Separator in which to place the mesh. This Separator is added as a child to the *GNode** that is passed into the function. All of the components of the mesh are added to this Separator.

Next, the string passed into the function as 'groupName' has any non-alphanumeric characters removed and then is attached to the Separator. Removing these characters prevents problems with other formats that restrict names to alphanumeric values.

The default material binding can be used if only one material is associated with this mesh. Using this binding requires no additional constructs to the internal representation. If more than one material is associated with this mesh, then you must add a MaterialBinding construct with the value `PER_PART_INDEXED`. The materials are added after the MaterialBinding

Finally, add the vertices, the faces, and the material indexes to the internal representation.

```
// Read the Mesh
int ReadTriObject(GNode* root, MaterialDict* matdict,
        long fileSize, FILE* fp, long triStart,
        long triSize, char* groupName)
{
    Chunk3DS                chunk;
    long                    chunkStart = ftell(fp);
    short                   firstMaterialFlag = TRUE;
    short                   matcount = 0;

    MFVec3f*                vertices = new MFVec3f;
    MFLong*                 faces = new MFLong;
    GMaterial*              material = new GMaterial;
    GSeparator*             sep = new GSeparator;
    GCoordinate3*           coords = new GCoordinate3;
    GIndexedFaceSet*        poly = new GIndexedFaceSet;
    MFLong*                 matfaces = new MFLong;
    SFMatrix                matrix;
    unsigned int            i;

    if (vertices == NULL || faces == NULL || sep == NULL ||
          poly == NULL || coords == NULL ||
          material == NULL || matfaces == NULL) {
          goto error;
    }
```

```
    matrix = Identity();

    while (chunkStart < triStart + triSize &&
          Read3DSChunk(root, fp, chunk)) {
          switch (chunk.id) {
          case POINT_ARRAY:
                if (!ReadPointArray(vertices, fileSize, fp))
                      goto error;
                break;
          case FACE_ARRAY:
                if (!ReadFaceArray(faces, fileSize, fp))
                      goto error;
                break;
          case MSH_MAT_GROUP:
                if (firstMaterialFlag) {
                      for (int i = 0; i < faces->Elements();
                                  i++) {
                            matfaces->Add(0L);
                      }
                      firstMaterialFlag = FALSE;
                }
                matcount++;
                if (!ReadMeshMatGroup(root, matdict,
                      material, *matfaces, fileSize, fp))
                      goto error;
                break;
          default:
                // Skip past unexpected chunks
                fseek(fp, chunkStart + chunk.len, SEEK_SET);
          }
          chunkStart = ftell(fp);
}

// Create a new separator
root->AddChild(sep);

// Sanitize the string
for (i = 0; i < strlen(groupName); i++) {
      if (!isalnum(groupName[i])) {
            groupName[i] = '_';
      }
}

// Set the name of the separator to the name of
// the group
sep->SetName(groupName);
```

```
// If more than one material, then change the
// material binding
if (matcount > 1) {
      GMaterialBinding* mbinding = new GMaterialBinding
      mbinding->Value(G_PER_PART_INDEXED);
      sep->AddChild((GNode*) mbinding);
}

// Add material
sep->AddChild((GNode*) material)

// Add the points to the current group
coords->Point(vertices);
sep->AddChild((GNode*) coords);

// Add the faces to the current group
poly->CoordIndex(faces);

    // Add material indexes if necessary.
    if (matcount > 1) {
          poly->MaterialIndex(matfaces);
    } else {
          delete matfaces;
    }

    // Add the faces to the separator
    sep->AddChild((GNode*) poly);

    return TRUE;

error:
    // Clean up the mess and report the error.
    if (vertices != NULL) delete vertices;
    if (faces != NULL) delete faces;
    if (sep != NULL) delete sep;
    if (coords != NULL) delete coords;
    if (poly != NULL) delete poly;
    if (coords != NULL) delete coords;
    if (material != NULL) delete material;
    if (matfaces != NULL) delete matfaces;
    return FALSE;
}
```

Reading the POINT_ARRAY chunk

The `ReadPointArray()` function reads the vertex list of the mesh. The POINT_ARRAY chunk body consists of an unsigned short *count* that specifies the number of 3D points in the list, followed by that number of points.

Each point consists of three floating-point values. `ReadPointArray()` reads the values and then adds them to the *MFVec3f* list passed into this function.

```
// Read vertices
int ReadPointArray (MFVec3f* vertices, long fileSize,
            FILE *fp)
{
    unsigned short    count;
    SFVec3f           vec;

    if (!ReadUShort(fp, count)) return FALSE;
    while (count-- > 0) {
            for (int i = 0; i < 3; i++) {
                    float value;
                    if (!ReadFloat(fp, value)) return FALSE;
                    vec[i] = value;
            }
            vertices->Add(vec);
    }
    return TRUE;
}
```

Reading the FACE_ARRAY Chunk

The `ReadFaceArray()` function reads the triangle faces of the FACE_ARRAY chunk body. The body consists of an unsigned short *count* that specifies the number of faces to read, followed by that number of faces.

Each point consists of four unsigned shorts. The first three are the indexes of the vertices in the vertex face list. The fourth describes the visible edges. The first three values are added to the *MFLong* that is passed into `ReadFaceArray()` and a value of –1 is added to terminate the triangle face.

```
// Read polygons
int ReadFaceArray (MFLong* faces, long unsigned fileSize,
FILE* fp)
{
    unsigned short    count
    unsigned short    value;
```

```
    // Read the count
    if (!ReadUShort(fp, count)) return FALSE;

    // Read the faces
    while (count-- > 0) {
          // Read the triangle
          for (int i = 0; i < 3; i++) {
                if (!ReadUShort(fp, value)) return FALSE;
                faces->Add(value);
          }
          // Close the face
          faces->Add(-1);

          // Read the visable edges
          if (!ReadUShort(fp, value)) return FALSE;
    }

    return TRUE;
}
```

Reading the MSH_MAT_GROUP Chunk

The `ReadMeshMatGroup()` function reads the material mapping of the current N_TRI_OBJECT. This function is called whenever a MSH_MAT_GROUP chunk is encountered. This chunk's body consists of a string that corresponds to the name of the material being mapped, followed by a list of face indexes that use that material. The material index is placed into the *MFLong* value passed into `ReadMeshMatGroup()`, which contains the mapping of each face to its corresponding material.

```
// Read the materials used by the group
int ReadMeshMatGroup(GNode* root, MaterialDict* matdict,
        GMaterial* material, MFLong& matfaces,
        long fileSize, FILE* fp)
{
    unsigned short    count, face
    char              name[256];
    GWriteMaterial*   lookup, defaultMat;
    long              index = 0;

    // Read the material name
    if (!Read3DSString(root, fp, name, 256)) return FALSE;

    // Convert it to a material index
    if ((lookup = matdict->Lookup(name)) != NULL) {
          index = material->Add(lookup);
```

```
    } else {
        index = material->Add(&defaultMat);
    }

    // Read the number of faces to map
    if (!ReadUShort(fp, count)) return FALSE;

    // Map each of the faces
    while (count-- > 0) {
        if (!ReadUShort(fp, face)) return FALSE;
        matfaces[face] = index;
    }

    return TRUE;
}
```

Implementing a 3DS Writer

Creating a 3DS file format writer requires writing a C++ class, *GWrite3DS*, that can convert from the internal representation into the 3DS file format. The process of creating this class is fairly straightforward, with the help of the *GWrite* class.

The `GNode::Write(GState&, GWrite&)` member function traverses the current scene. As the internal representation is traversed, the appropriate member functions of the *GWrite* derived class are called for each *GNode* instance encountered during traversal. As a result, implementers of a format writer do not have to understand all of the details of the internal representation. Instead, they need to address in the *GWrite* derived class only the details that they consider important for the specific file format. This mechanism allows the *GWrite* class to be overridden by the *GWrite3DS* class and only the functionality that is needed to write a 3DS file to be implemented.

Following is the definition of the *GWrite3DS* class:

```
class GWrite3DS : public GWrite {
private:
    char                m_name[256];
    MeshCompactor       m_mesh;

public:
    GWrite3DS(void) : GWrite() {strcpy(m_name, "");}
    // Overridden Member Functions
    short PolygonSupported(void)  {return TRUE;}

    void  Polygon(GState&, long, MFVec3f*, MFVec3f* = NULL,
                GWriteMaterial* = NULL);
```

```
    void  Epilog(GNode*, GState&);
    void  Prolog(GNode*, GState&);
    short FileMode(void)    {return GWriteBinaryFile;}

private:
    // Internal member functions used to write
    // the 3DS chunks
    long  WriteMData(void);
    long  WriteMeshVersion(long);
    long  WriteMatEntries(void);
    long  WriteNamedObjects(void);
    long  WriteColor(float red, float green, float blue);
    long  WriteTriObject(GMaterial*, MeshCompactor&);
    long  WritePointArray(MeshCompactor&);
    long  WriteFaceArray(GMaterial*, MeshCompactor&,
                MFLong&, MFLong&);
    long  WriteMaterial(MFLong&, MFLong&);
    long  WriteChunk(unsigned short, long);
    long  WritePatch(long data, long location);
};
```

Notice that few of the functions defined in the *GWrite* base class need to be overwritten. This is because the 3DS file format supports only polygons; the internal representation will tessellate all other shapes into the equivalent polygon representation. This process reduces the number of functions that are needed to be overridden to the `Polygon()` and the `Epilog()` member functions. Most of the other member functions defined in the *GWrite3DS* class definition actually write the 3D Studio chunks to the destination file.

Saving a 3D Studio File

The *GWrite3DS* class can be used just like any other *GWrite* derived class. This means that the C++ source to write a 3D Studio file is almost identical to the source required to write the TrueSpace file, the DXF file, or another *GWrite* derived class. An example of how a 3D Studio file is actually written using the *GWrite3DS* class follows. Notice that only the name of the member function, the *CFileDialog* definition, and the declaration of *GWrite3DS* are different from similar examples in the other chapters in this book.

```
void C3DviewDoc::OnFileSave3DS()
{
    CFileDialog fileDlg( FALSE, NULL, NULL,
                OFN_HIDEREADONLY | OFN_OVERWRITEPROMPT,
                "3D Studio (*.3ds)|*.3ds||");
```

```
    if (fileDlg.DoModal() == IDOK) {
        char  buffer[256];

        strcpy(buffer, fileDlg.GetPathName());

        FILE* fp = fopen(buffer, "wb");

        if (fp != NULL) {
            GWrite3DS   write
            GState      state

            // Display hourglass cursor
            StartBusy();

            // Open the output file
            write.Open(this, state, buffer);

            // Traverse the internal database, calling
            // the write class as appropriate.
            Write(state, write);

            // Close the write class, flushing any
            // remaining information.
            write.Close(this, state);

            // Restore previous cursor
            EndBusy();

            // Update current file name
            SetPathName( fileDlg.GetPathName() );
        }
    }
}
```

From an external viewpoint, all that is required to make the 3D Studio writer complete is to fill in the `GWrite3DS::Prolog()`, `GWrite3DS::Polygon()`, and `GWrite3DS::Epilog()` member functions. These three are the only functions that haven't been defined in the class definitions that are publicly available. The remaining functions are used privately, either directly or indirectly, by the `GWrite3DS::Epilog()` member function.

Implementing the GWrite3DS::Prolog() Member Function

The `GWrite3DS::Prolog(GNode*, GState&)` member function is called immediately after the 3DS file has been opened. For this implementation, it is used only to report to the user that the conversion process has started.

```
// Called when the 3DS file is opened.
void GWrite3DS::
Prolog(GNode* root, GState& state)
{
    root->StatusMessage("Converting internal format into a
3DS file.");
}
```

Implementing the GWrite3DS::Polygon() Member Function

The `GWrite3DS::Polygon()` member function uses the *MeshCompactor* class that has been instantiated in the *GWrite3DS* instance. The *MeshCompactor* instance will convert a series of polygons into a group of vertices and faces. It compacts the polygons into a single vertex list and converts the faces into a series of faces lists organized by group name. After the traversal of the internal representation is complete, the *MeshCompactor* instance will contain a re-representation of the entire object that will be used by the `Epilog()` member function to emit the 3D Studio file.

This re-representation of the object data may seem wasteful, since it results in the same object's being stored in memory twice. However, the representation that the 3D Studio writer needs is different than the internal representation of the object, so the re-representation is necessary.

The following source code is the implementation of the `GWrite3DS::Polygon()` member function:

```
// Called for every polygon in the internal representation
void GWrite3DS::
Polygon(GState& state, long faceNum, MFVec3f* v, MFVec3f* n,
        GWriteMaterial* m)
{
    // Notice Name changes
    if (state.HeirName() != NULL &&
                strcmp(m_name, state.HeirName()) != 0) {
          m_mesh.Name(state.HeirName());
          strcpy(m_name, state.HeirName());
    }

    // Add polygon
    m_mesh.BeginPolygon(m);
    for (int i = 0; i < v->Elements(); i++) {
          m_mesh.AddVertex((*v)[i]);
    }
    m_mesh.EndPolygon();
}
```

Implementing the GWrite3DS::Epilog() Member Function

The `GWrite3DS::Epilog()` member function actually starts and finishes the writing of a 3D Studio file. It writes the M3DMAGIC chunk, which identifies the file as a 3D Studio file, the version of the file, and the MDATA section. Although this member function is small, there is a lot going on with it.

Notice that the size of the M3DMAGIC chunk is being calculated as the 3D Studio file is written. This value will be used when the 3D Studio file has been written in order to back-patch the size of the M3DMAGIC chunk to the correct value.

Writing a chunk can be a dicey affair. Many chunk types have variable lengths, so it is very difficult to predict the size of the chunk before the chunk header has to be written. One solution to this problem is to back-patch. Back-patching means the unknown element is written with some bogus value. The location of that bogus value is saved and then later, when the contents of that element are known, the bogus value is overwritten with the correct value.

Only four functions are called in this function:

- `WriteChunk()`. Writes the current chunk identifier and chunk size and returns the location of the size element so that it may be back-patched later if necessary.
- `WriteLong()`. One of the many functions that encapsulates the writes of binary data elements.
- `WriteMDATA()`. Writes the MDATA section to the 3D Studio file.
- `WritePatch()`. Moves the current file location to the location of the M3DMAGIC size and overwrites the new size value. The original file location is returned after the overwrite has completed.

```
// Called after all the polygons have been read.
void GWrite3DS::
Epilog(GNode* root, GState& state)
{
    long  bpatch;
    long  size = 0;

    // Write the M3DMAGIC chunk header w/bogus size
    bpatch = WriteChunk(M3DMAGIC, 0);
    size += SizeofChunk;

    // Write the Version
    WriteChunk(M3D_VERSION, SizeofChunk+sizeof(long));
    WriteLong(m_fp, 2);
    size += SizeofChunk+sizeof(long);
```

```
    // Write the Object
    size += WriteMData();

    // Fill in the correct size for the M3DMAGIC chunk
    WritePatch(bpatch, size);

    root->StatusMessage("Write Complete");
}
```

The following two functions deal with writing the chunk and back-patching the size of the chunk:

```
// Write the chunk id and size, return the location
// of the size value so that it may be back-patched if
// necessary.
long GWrite3DS::
WriteChunk(unsigned short id, long size)
{
    long retval

    // Write chunk id
    WriteUShort(m_fp, id);

    // Save location of size value
    retval = ftell(m_fp);

    // Write size value
    WriteULong(m_fp, (unsigned long) size);

    // Return file location of size data in case
    // backpatching is necessary.
    return retval;
}

// Move the location of the file to the
// back-patch location, overwrite the old data
// with the new data, and move back to our previous
// location.
long GWrite3DS::
WritePatch(long location, long data)
{
    long current = ftell(m_fp);
    fseek(m_fp, location, SEEK_SET);
    WriteLong(m_fp, data);
    fseek(m_fp, current, SEEK_SET);
    return current;
}
```

Implementing the GWrite3DS::WriteMDATA() Member Function

The `GWrite3DS::WriteMDATA()` member function deals with the details for writing the current 3D object as a 3D Studio file. It writes the MDATA chunk, which is of variable length and must be back-patched. It also writes the mesh version, the material data, and the polygon groups as named objects. The functions `WriteMeshVersion()`, `WriteMatEntries()`, and `WriteNamedObjects()` write the underlying subchunks. Each of these functions returns the size of the saved data. The returned values are used to calculate the size of the parent MDATA chunk.

```
// This function writes the MDATA chunk. This
// Chunk contains the MeshVersion, the material
// entries, and the named objects that define
// the 3d object.
long GWrite3DS::
WriteMData(void)
{
    long size = 0, bpatch;

    // Write the chunk header for MDATA w/bogus size
    bpatch = WriteChunk(MDATA, 0);
    size += SizeofChunk;

    size += WriteMeshVersion(2L);
    size += WriteMatEntries();
    size += WriteNamedObjects();

    // Overwrite the bogus size with the actual size
    WritePatch(bpatch, size);

    return size;
}
```

Implementing the GWrite3DS::WriteMeshVersion( ) Member Function

The `GWrite3DS::WriteMeshVersion()` member function writes the mesh version. The version number of the mesh corresponds to the release of 3D Studio with which the file complies.

```
// Writes the current MeshVersion. The legal
// values are 1, 2, or 3. These values correspond
// to the release of 3D Studio that the 3DS file
// complies with.
long GWrite3DS::
WriteMeshVersion(long version)
{
```

```
    WriteChunk(MESH_VERSION, SizeofChunk+sizeof(long));
    WriteLong(m_fp, version);
    return SizeofChunk+sizeof(long);
}
```

Implementing the GWrite3DS::WriteMatEntries Member Function

The `GWrite3DS::WriteMatEntries()` member function writes the material found in the *MeshCompactor* instance as a series of 3D Studio MAT_ENTRY chunks. Notice that each chunk consists of these chunks: ambient color, diffuse color, specular color, shininess value, transparency value, and shading value.

```
// This function converts the MeshCompactor's
// GMaterial instance into a 3D Studio material
// definition.
long GWrite3DS::
WriteMatEntries(void)
{
    const long SizeofColor = SizeofChunk+3;

    GMaterial*  mat = m_mesh.Material();
    char        buffer[256];
    long        size = 0, itemSize, bpatch;

    ASSERT(mat != NULL);

    for (int i = 0; i < mat->Elements(); i++) {
          GWriteMaterial     material = (*mat)[i];
          SFVec3f            color;
          float              shininess, transparency;

          itemSize = 0;

          bpatch = WriteChunk(MAT_ENTRY, 0);
          itemSize += SizeofChunk;

          sprintf(buffer, "Mat%d", i);

          // Write Material Name
          WriteChunk(MAT_NAME,
               SizeofChunk+strlen(buffer)+1);
          itemSize += SizeofChunk+strlen(buffer)+1;
          for (unsigned int j = 0; j < strlen(buffer); j++)
          {
                WriteByte(m_fp, buffer[j]);
```

```
}
WriteByte(m_fp, '\0');

// Write Ambient
color = material.AmbientColor();
WriteChunk(MAT_AMBIENT, SizeofChunk+SizeofColor);
WriteColor((float) color.X(), (float) color.Y(),
            (float) color.Z());
itemSize += SizeofChunk+SizeofColor;

// Write Diffuse
color = material.DiffuseColor();
WriteChunk(MAT_DIFFUSE, SizeofChunk+SizeofColor);
WriteColor((float) color.X(), (float) color.Y(),
            (float) color.Z());
itemSize += SizeofChunk+SizeofColor;

// Write Specular
color = material.SpecularColor();
WriteChunk(MAT_SPECULAR, SizeofChunk+SizeofColor);
WriteColor((float) color.X(), (float) color.Y(),
            (float) color.Z());
itemSize += SizeofChunk+SizeofColor;

// Write Shininess
shininess = (float) material.Shininess();
WriteChunk(MAT_SHININESS,
      SizeofChunk*2+sizeof(short));
WriteChunk(INT_PERCENTAGE,
      SizeofChunk+sizeof(short));
WriteShort(m_fp, (short) (shininess*100.0+0.5));
itemSize += SizeofChunk*2+sizeof(short);

// Write Transparency
transparency = (float) material.Transparency();
WriteChunk(MAT_TRANSPARENCY,
      SizeofChunk*2+sizeof(short));
WriteChunk(INT_PERCENTAGE,
      SizeofChunk+sizeof(short));
WriteShort(m_fp, (short) (shininess*100.0+0.5));
itemSize += SizeofChunk*2+sizeof(short);

// Write Shading - default to Gouraud
WriteChunk(MAT_SHADING,
      SizeofChunk+sizeof(short));
WriteShort(m_fp, 2);
itemSize += SizeofChunk+sizeof(short);
```

```
            // Write Size
            WritePatch(bpatch, itemSize);

            size += itemSize;
        }

    return size;
}
```

Implementing the GWrite3DS::WriteColor Member Function

The `GSWrite3DS::WriteColor()` member function writes a COLOR_24 chunk, which is used by many of the subelements of the MAT_ENTRY chunk.

```
// Writes a color chunk. This function is used
// by WriteMatEntries to specify the surface colors
// for the 3D Studio material.
long GWrite3DS::
WriteColor(float red, float green, float blue)
{
    WriteChunk(COLOR_24, SizeofChunk+3);
    WriteUByte(m_fp, (unsigned char) (red*255.0+0.5));
    WriteUByte(m_fp, (unsigned char) (green*255.0+0.5));
    WriteUByte(m_fp, (unsigned char) (blue*255.0+0.5));
    return SizeofChunk+3;
}
```

Implementing the GWrite3DS::WriteNamedObjects Member Function

The `GWrite3DS::WriteNamedObjects()` member function iterates through all of the groups defined for the *MeshCompactor* instance that is held by the *GWrite3DS* instance. Each *MeshCompactor* instance is converted into smaller meshes. This is done to separate the vertices in the groups from the vertices of the larger mesh. The mesh of each group is passed to the function `WriteTriObject()`, which writes the mesh as a 3D Studio N_TRI_OBJECT chunk.

```
// This function writes each of the groups defined
// in the MeshCompactor instance as a NAMED_OBJECT
// chunk.
long GWrite3DS::
WriteNamedObjects(void)
```

```
{
    long        size = 0, bpatch;
    MFVec3f*    coords = m_mesh.Coordinates();
    char        name[256];

    for (long group = 0; group < m_mesh.Groups(); group++) {
          SFLong       faceCnt;
          SFLong*      faces = m_mesh.Faces(group);
          MFLong       mat_list;

          if (m_mesh.Name(group) == NULL) {
                sprintf(name, "NoName%d", group);
          } else {
                strcpy(name, m_mesh.Name(group));
          }

          // Output Polygons for group
          if (faces->Elements() > 0) {
                MeshCompactor*    sub_mesh =
                                        new MeshCompactor;
                MFVec3f*          sub_coords = NULL;
                short             sub_polyOpen = TRUE;
                long              itemSize = 0;

                // Compact and count vertices and faces
                sub_mesh->BeginPolygon(
                      &m_mesh.FaceIndex2Material(
                                  group, faceCnt));
                for (long i = 0; i < faces->Elements(); i++)
                {
                      SFLong      face = (*faces)[i];
                      if (face >= 0) {
                            SFVec3f vertex =
                                  (*coords)[face];
                            sub_mesh->AddVertex(vertex);
                      } else {
                            sub_mesh->EndPolygon();
                            sub_polyOpen = FALSE;
                            faceCnt++;
                            if (i+1 < faces->Elements()) {
                                  sub_mesh->BeginPolygon(
                                        &m_mesh.FaceIndex2Ma
                                  terial(group, faceCnt));
                                  sub_polyOpen = TRUE;
                            }
                      }
                }
```

```
                if (sub_polyOpen) {
                      sub_mesh->EndPolygon();
                }

                // Write NAMED_OBJECT chunk header
                // w/bogus size
                bpatch = WriteChunk(NAMED_OBJECT, 0);
                itemSize = SizeofChunk;

                // Write the name of the group. Remember
                // we can only write names of a maximum of
                // 10 characters. Let's hope they're unique.
                for (i = 0; name[i] && i < 10; i++) {
                      WriteByte(m_fp, name[i]);
                }
                WriteByte(m_fp, '\0');

                itemSize += i+1;

                itemSize +=
                      WriteTriObject(m_mesh.Material(),
                            *sub_mesh);

                // Save the actual size of the
                // NAMED_OBJECT chunk
                WritePatch(bpatch, itemSize);

                size += itemSize;

                delete sub_mesh;
          }
    }

    return size;
}
```

Implementing the GWrite3DS::WriteTriObject Member Function

The `GWrite3DS::WriteTriObject()` member function writes the mesh passed in as an argument as an N_TRI_OBJECT chunk. This chunk will write three or more subchunks by using the functions `WritePointArray()`, `WriteFaceArray()`, and `WriteMaterial()`.

`WritePointArray()` writes the vertex list of the mesh. `WriteFaceArray()` tessellates each of the polygons into triangles and then writes the triangles as a series of indexes into the vertex list. `WriteMaterial()` writes the materials used by the mesh as a series of one or more MSH_MAT_GROUP chunks.

```
// This function writes the specified mesh as a
// N_TRI_OBJECT chunk.
long GWrite3DS::
WriteTriObject(GMaterial* savedMaterial,
               MeshCompactor& mesh)
{
    long        size = 0, faceCnt = 0, triangleCnt = 0;
    long        tripatch;
    MFLong      uniqueMatindex, faceMatindex;

    // Write N_TRI_OBJECT w/bogus size
    tripatch = WriteChunk(N_TRI_OBJECT, 0);
    size += SizeofChunk;

    // Save the subcomponents
    size += WritePointArray(mesh);
    size += WriteFaceArray(savedMaterial, mesh,
               faceMatindex, uniqueMatindex);
    size += WriteMaterial(faceMatindex, uniqueMatindex);

    // Save the actual size of the chunk
    WritePatch(tripatch, size);

    return size;
}
```

Implementing the GWrite3DS::WritePointArray Member Function

The `GWrite3DS::WritePointArray()` member function writes the vertex list of the specified mesh as a POINT_ARRAY chunk. This chunk contains a chunk header, a count of vertices, and a series of three floating-point values that represent each vertex.

```
// This function writes the vertex list of the
// mesh out as a POINT_ARRAY chunk.
long GWrite3DS::
WritePointArray(MeshCompactor& mesh)
{
    MFVec3f*    coords = mesh.Coordinates();
    long        size = SizeofChunk+sizeof(short)+
                       sizeof(float)*3*coords->Elements();

    // Write POINT_ARRAY
    WriteChunk(POINT_ARRAY, size);
```

```
    WriteUShort(m_fp, (unsigned short) coords->Elements());
    for (long i=0; i < coords->Elements(); i++) {
          SFVec3f vec = (*coords)[i];
          WriteFloat(m_fp, (float) vec.X());
          WriteFloat(m_fp, (float) vec.Y());
          WriteFloat(m_fp, (float) vec.Z());
    }
    return size;
}
```

Implementing the GWrite3DS::WriteFaceArray Member Function

The `GWrite3DS::WriteFaceArray()` member function writes the polygons passed into it as a series of triangle faces. These faces are written to the FACE_ARRAY chunk.

This function also collects the materials that are used by each face and the total number of materials used. This information is returned to the calling function so that it can be passed to the `WriteMaterial()` member function. `WriteMaterial()` writes the MSH_MAT_GROUP chunk, which associates 3D Studio materials (these have already been written) with each face in the face array.

```
// This member function writes the faces associated
// with the specified mesh. It also stores information
// about the materials used for each face for use by the
// WriteMaterial function. The matindex argument will
// contain the material indexes used by each face, and
// the uniqueMatindex argument will contain
// a list of the materials used by the mesh.
long GWrite3DS::
WriteFaceArray(GMaterial* savedMaterial,
        MeshCompactor& mesh, MFLong& matindex,
        MFLong& uniqueMatindex)
{
    MFLong*      faces = mesh.Faces();
    GMaterial*   materials = mesh.Material();
    MFLong       face;
    long         facepatch, current,
                 size = 0, faceCnt = 0, triangleCnt = 0;

    // Write FACE_ARRAY
    facepatch = WriteChunk(FACE_ARRAY, 0);

    // Write Bogus Triangle Count;
    WriteShort(m_fp, 0);

    size += SizeofChunk+sizeof(short);
```

```
    // Convert the Face list into faces.
    for (int i=0; i < faces->Elements(); i++) {
          MFLong       value = (*faces)[i];
          if (value >= 0) {
                face.Add(value);
          } else {
                SFLong matvalue = savedMaterial->Lookup(
                      &mesh.FaceIndex2Material(0,
                                  faceCnt++));

                uniqueMatindex.Add(matvalue, TRUE);

                // 3DS only allows triangles. This routine
                // writes the current face as triangles.
                for (long j=1; j < face.Elements()-1; j++) {
                      matindex.Add(matvalue);
                      WriteUShort(m_fp, (short) face[0]);
                      WriteUShort(m_fp, (short) face[j]);
                      WriteUShort(m_fp, (short) face[j+1]);
                      WriteUShort(m_fp, (short) 1);
                      size += sizeof(short)*4;
                      triangleCnt++;
                }
                face.Clear();
          }
    }

    // Save current position
    current = ftell(m_fp);

    // Go to saved location
    fseek(m_fp, facepatch, SEEK_SET);

    // Update size
    WriteLong(m_fp, size);
    //Update face count
    WriteShort(m_fp, (short) triangleCnt);

    // Go back to the current position
    fseek(m_fp, current, SEEK_SET);

    return size;
}
```

Implementing the GWrite3DS::WriteMaterial Member Function

The `GWrite3DS::WriteMaterial()` member function writes one or more MSH_MAT_GROUP chunks. These chunks associate the faces defined in the face array with the named materials that were saved earlier in the file. A face array may use many different materials for the faces in the array, so this function may emit several MSH_MAT_GROUP chunks. One of these chunks is written for each material used in the face array.

The function is passed two *MFLong* values, which were filled in by the `WriteFaceArray()` function. The first, `faceMatindex`, maps materials to faces. This is accomplished by having each index of the `faceMatindex` elements correspond to the equivalent face index. Hence, the material index in `faceMatindex[0]` corresponds to first face in the face array list. The second value, `uniqueMatindex`, is a list of all of the materials used in the face array.

`WriteMaterial()` iterates through each of the unique materials and a MSH_MAT_GROUP chunk is written for each. This chunk consists of the name of the material to associate with the face array and a list of the faces (by index value) that use the material.

```
// This member function writes the MSH_MAT_GROUP
// chunk which associates the 3D Studio material
// with each of the faces in the face array.
long GWrite3DS::
WriteMaterial(MFLong& faceMatindex, MFLong& uniqueMatindex)
{
    long  size = 0, matpatch, fcountPatch;

    // Write MSH_MAT_GROUP
    for (int i=0; i < uniqueMatindex.Elements(); i++) {
          SFLong      mvalue = uniqueMatindex[i];
          char  buffer[256];
          long  facesAssigned = 0;

          // Create a material name that matches our saved
          // materials
          sprintf(buffer, "Mat%d", mvalue);

          matpatch = WriteChunk(MSH_MAT_GROUP, 0);
          size += SizeofChunk;

          // Write the name of the material. Remember
          // we can only write names of a maximum of
          // 15 characters. Let's hope they're unique.
          for (i = 0; buffer[i] && i < 16; i++) {
                WriteByte(m_fp, buffer[i]);
          }
          WriteByte(m_fp, '\0');
```

```
            size += i+1;

            fcountPatch = ftell(m_fp);
            WriteShort(m_fp, 0);
            size += sizeof(short);

            // Write material indexes
            for (int j=0; j < faceMatindex.Elements(); j++) {
                  if (faceMatindex[j] == mvalue) {
                        facesAssigned++;
                        WriteUShort(m_fp, j);
                        size += sizeof(short);
                  }
            }

            // Save the updated face count
            WritePatch(fcountPatch, facesAssigned);

            // Save the correct size
            WritePatch(matpatch, size);
      }

      return size;
}
```

Reference

3D Studio Release 3 File Toolkit: Reference Manual. June 7, 1994. San Rafael, Calif.: AutoDesk, Inc.

Chapter 9

WTK-NFF Version 2.1

WorldToolKit is a cross-platform application development system for creating virtual reality (VR) applications. It is available on many platforms, including Windows 95, Windows NT, DEC Alpha workstations, and many UNIX workstations.

Most VR development systems focus on polygon primitives. This is because polygons can be quickly manipulated, and speed is a key requirement of most VR systems. Amazing things can be done in a VR environment using only polygons, surface materials, and texture mapping. For this reason, WorldToolKit's file format, Neutral File Format, defines only polygon meshes.

The WorldToolKit Neutral File Format (WTK-NFF) is an ASCII file format that represents polygon geometry. This file contains one or more named polygon objects composed of vertices and faces. The file format allows color and textures to be specified for the polygons.

Overview of the WTK-NFF

The WTK-NFF closely resembles several of the formats I've already discussed. It consists of one or more named groups of polygon objects composed of vertices and faces. Each face has a defined color and an optional material definition.

A WTK-NFF file supports C++ style comments. A comment begins with the characters // and continues until the end of the current line is encountered.

The file begins with an NFF header. This header always begins with a file identifier that may be either the literal string 'nff' or the literal string 's8'. A version declaration may optionally appear after the NFF header. This chapter describes Version 2.1 of the WTK-NFF, but the reader discussed is backwards compatible with its earlier versions.

The WTK-NFF file identifier and versions may optionally be followed by a viewpoint definition. This definition is composed of *viewpos* and *viewdir* commands that specify the position and direction, respectively, of the specified viewpoint.

The rest of the WTK-NFF file is devoted to the definition of one or more polygon objects. Each polygon object has the following organization:

```
<object name>
<vertex count>
<vertex>
     .
     .
     .
<polygon face count>
<face>
     .
     .
     .
```

The syntax for a WTK-NFF file is short and simple. It is defined using the following BNF grammar.

```
// <name>   is a non-terminal
// ::=      is an assignment
// ...|...  means either this construct OR that construct
// [...]    means the bracketed construct is repeated one
//          or more times.
// '...'    is a literal string definition.

<Start>             ::=    <FileID>
                           [<Version>]
                           [<ViewPosition>]
                           [<ViewDirection>]
                           [<Object>}
                    ;

// Identify file format. The value 'nff'
// denotes the current format, the value
// 's8' was used in some early versions.
<FileID>            ::=    'nff' | 's8'
                    ;

// Current version is 2.1
<Version>           ::=    'version' <Float>
                    ;
```

```
// Viewpoint location
<ViewPosition>    ::=    'viewpos' <Point3D>
                  ;

// Viewpoint direction
<ViewDirection>   ::=    'viewdir' <Point3D>
                  ;

// An object is a polygon mesh. The mesh is made up
// of a Mesh Name, a set of vertices, and
// a set of faces.
<Object>          ::=    <Identifier>      // Name of mesh
                         <Integer>         // Vertex Count
                         {<Vertex>}        // Vertices
                         <Integer>         // Face Count
                         {<Face>}          // Faces
                  ;

// A 3D point.
<Point3D>         ::=    <Float> <Float> <Float>
                  ;

// A 3D point with an optional Normal, Color, and Texture
Coordinate
<Vertex>  ::=     <Point3D> [<Normal>] [<RGB>] [<UV>]
                  ;

// A definition of a normal vector
<Normal>          ::=    'norm' <Float> <Float> <Float>
                  ;

// A color is a 12 bit value or a 24 bit value.
// You can tell by the length of the hex string.
// It will be >= 5 characters for a 12 bit value.
// The value is always 0xrgb. The rgb values are 4 bits
// each for the 12 bit value and 8 bits each for the 16 bit
// value.
<RGB>             ::=    'rgb' <Color>
                  ;

// A texture map UV position point.
<UV>              ::=    'uv' <Float> <Float>
                  ;

// The first value in a face is the number of vertices in
// the polygon. The integers following are integer indices
// into the vertex list that make up the polygon. The face
```

```
// must have a 12 or 24 bit color definition. The value
// 'both' defines that both sides of the polygon are
// visible. The optional <Texture> defines the name of the
// texture. The 'id' '=' defines an optional face
// identification value.
<Face>              ::=  <Integer> {<Integer>} <Color>
                         ['both'] [<Texture>]
                         ['id' '=' <Integer>]
                         [<Portal>]
                    ;

<Color>             ::=  <Hex>
                    ;

<Float>             ::= ['-']{'0'..'9'}['.' {'0'..'9'}]
                    ;

<Integer>           ::= ['-'] {'0'..'9'}
                    ;

<Texture>           ::=   '_'{'A'..'Z' | 'a'..'z' | '0'..'9'}
                    ;

<Portal>            ::=   '-'{'A'..'Z' | 'a'..'z' | '0'..'9'}
                    ;

<Identifier>        ::=   {'a'..'z' | 'A'..'Z' | '0'..'9'
                               | '_' | '.' | ':'}
                    ;

<Hex>               ::=   '0x' {'0'..'9' | 'a'..'f' | 'A'..'F'}
                    ;
```

Syntax of the WTK-NFF

WTK-NFF has only a few commands. It doesn't have a lot of bells and whistles. It just gets down to business defining the key components that a VR application needs. Most VR applications define just polygons, surface materials, and texture mapping. But it's amazing what can be done with small polygon models and the right materials or texture maps. This section defines each of the components of the WTK-NFF.

Comments

The WTK-NFF allows C++ style comments to be defined, as the following snippet of code shows:

```
// This is an example WTK-NFF definition
nff
// Define the version (optional)
version 2.1
```

File Type Identifier

Every WTK-NFF file begins with a line containing 'nff' or 's8'. This allows easy identification of the file as a WorldToolKit file and is necessary because there is more than one 3D file format with the *.nff file suffix. An example of the first few lines of a WTK-NFF file, including a header definition, follows:

```
nff
version 1.60
viewpos  0.000000 0.000000 0.000000
viewdir  0.000000 0.000000 1.000000
```

Version Information

Immediately following the WTK-NFF file identifier may optionally be a command that specifies the version of the WTK-NFF file format definition with which the file complies. The version is specified by the literal string 'version', which is followed by a float value of 1.6 or higher. The WTK-NFF format described in this chapter is Version 2.1. An example version command follows:

```
version 2.1
```

Viewpoint

A viewpoint may optionally be included in the WTK-NFF file. It is described with two commands. The first is the *viewpos* command, which is followed by three floating-point values that describe the location of the viewpoint. The second is the *viewdir* command, which is followed by three floating-point values that describe the view direction. The following WTK-NFF file fragment illustrates how these commands may be used. It describes a viewpoint at position (0, 0, 0) looking up the z-axis.

```
s8

viewpos  0.000000 0.000000 0.000000
viewdir  0.000000 0.000000 1.000000
```

WTK-NFF Object

Most of a WTK-NFF file consists of one or more object definitions. An object definition contains a name, a list of vertices, and a list of faces.

The Object's Name

The name of the object is composed mostly of alphanumeric characters; a few special characters are allowed. Following the name is an integer value that describes the number of vertices defined for the object. That number is the number of vertices expected after the count. Next, the polygon faces are defined. Each polygon face definition begins with the count of faces in the object. That number of face definitions follow.

Here's an example of a WTK-NFF object definition:

```
Example
4
0.000000 0.000000 0.000000
0.000000 -10.000000 0.000000
15.000000 -10.000000 0.000000
15.000000 0.000000 0.000000
1
4 3 2 1 0 0xf00 both
```

This example object, named 'Example,' contains four vertices and one polygon face. The face consists of four vertices that define a rectangle with the 12-bit color definition of red. The option 'both' specifies that both sides of the polygon are visible.

Definitions of the Vertices

The vertex count follows the object name. The count is an integer value that specifics the total number of vertices defined for this object. Each vertex is defined in a single Textual line and always contains three floating-point values that define the 3D location of the vertex.

The following is an example of several vertices:

```
366.029114 -268.516113 222.487091
374.819092 -268.516113 222.487045
366.029144 -239.216049 222.487045
```

```
374.819031 -239.216034 222.487030
366.029114 -239.216125 -96.149658
366.029053 -268.516113 -96.149628
```

The vertex definition may also specify a normal direction, a color, and/or a texture map UV coordinate.

The syntax of a vertex definition is

```
Vertex        :=    <Float> <Float> <Float>
                    ['norm' <Float> <Float> <Float>]
                    ['rgb' <Hex>]
                    ['uv' <Float> <Float>]
```

The definition may optionally contain a normal definition. A normal defines the direction in which the surface of the object is pointing. By defining normals as part of a vertex, you can give an object a smoother appearance. Following is an example of vertices with normals:

```
0.0 0.0 0.0 norm 0 0 0
-1.0 0.0 0.0 norm 0.0 .707 .707
0.0 1.0 0.0 norm 0.707 0.0 0.707
```

A definition also may optionally contain a color definition. If all the vertices in a polygon have color definitions, then the color definition in the vertex definition is used rather than the color definitions for the polygons. A color definition included with a vertex looks like this:

```
0.0 1.0 0.0 rgb 0xff0000 // a red vertex
```

A vertex definition may also optionally include a UV value for mapping a texture onto the polygons. An example of a vertex with a UV value is

```
0.0 1.0 0.0 uv 0.25 0.5
```

Definitions of the Faces

After all the vertices have been defined, the polygon faces are defined. The syntax of a polygon face is

```
<Face>             ::=   <Integer> {<Integer>}
                         'rgb' <Hex>
                         ['both']
                         [<Texture>]
                         ['id' '=' <Integer>]
                         [<Portal>]
                   ;
```

The first item in a polygon face entry is the vertices count. The count is followed by that number of integer values that are indexed into the vertex list of the object. Each integer represents a vertex in the polygon.

The faces are followed by an RGB color definition. The color is either a 12-bit hexadecimal value or a 24-bit hexadecimal value. If the value is 12 bits, then the hex digits are 0xrgb. If the value is 24 bits, then the hex digits are 0xrrggbb.

A polygon face is usually visible only on the front side. The front is the side to which the normal for the polygon is perpendicular. To make a polygon face visible on both sides, specify the token 'both' in the polygon face definition.

A polygon face may also define a texture map, an identifier value, and/or a portal. To optionally define a texture map, specify the type of texture along with the texture name. Following are the types of textures:

```
_v_       - plain texture
_s_       - shaded texture
_t_       - transparent texture
_u_       - shaded and transparent texture
```

The type of the texture is concatenated to the texture name. For example, if the texture was from a file named "stone" and was shaded, the texture type would be `_s_stone`.

A polygon face may also define an optional identifier value. This value allows a polygon to be assigned an integer value. Here's an example of a polygon face definition that allows the polygon to be identified with the integer value 123:

```
4 1 3 4 2 0xf00 id=123
```

A polygon face may also define an optional portal. A portal specifies a universe to be loaded when the polygon is crossed. It consists of a hyphen followed by the name of the universe. Here's an example of a polygon face with a portal:

```
4 1 3 4 2 0xf0f -homeworld
```

Implementing a WTK-NFF Reader

The WTK-NFF is relatively small, so the reader for the format is short.

The reader is implemented using a GNU Bison parser generator and a GNU Flex lexical analyzer. These tools are used to parse very complicated computer languages such as C++. They are also very useful for quickly putting together parsers for smaller languages such as this one.

The ReadWTKNFF() Function

The `ReadWTKNFF()` function is the only function available outside of the reader itself. As the file is parsed, its components are added to the global *MeshCompactor* variable *yymesh*, thereby enabling an intermediate representation to be saved. To read a WTK-NFF file, an external function need only pass in the top-level *GNode* instance (probably a *GSeparator*) and the file name of the WTK-NFF file being read.

This function opens the filed specified, initializes the lexical analyzer and parser, and then parses the file. The parsed file is converted into the internal representation by using the `AddTo()` member function of the *MeshCompactor* class. This function converts the *MeshCompactor* representation into the representation of the internal 3D objects.

```
int ReadWTKNFF(GNode* obj, char* filename)
{
    MeshCompactor     mesh;

    // Open the specified file.
    FILE* fp = fopen(filename, "r");

    // Return an error if unable to open file.
    if (fp == NULL) {
         return FALSE;
    }

    // Make sure that the GNode* is legal.
    if (obj == NULL) {
         return FALSE;
    }

    // Initialize the lexer
       yyinit(fp);

    // Make the MeshCompactor available to
    // the BNF productions.
    yymesh = &mesh;

    // Make the GNode* object available to
    // the BNF productions.
    yyobject = obj;
```

```
    // Parse the file.
    yyparse();

    // Convert the file into our internal
    // format.
    mesh.AddTo(obj);

    // Cleanup and exit.
    fclose(fp);

    return TRUE;
}
```

The Parser

The Bison parser defines the possible types that can be passed back from the lexer or from other productions in the `%union` construct. The `%union` defines the integer, float, string, and color types. These are the only types that productions and the lexer can return. The `%union` construct is defined as:

```
%union {
    double      real;
    long        integer;
    char        string[MaxStringLen+1];
    ColorType   color;
}
```

Because `%unions` don't allow classes to be defined in them, a `ColorType` must be used to pass colors from the lexer and from productions instead of an *SFVec3f*.

The next section in the parser defines tokens and types. Here a token identifier or production is associated with a return type. All identifiers and productions that return values are defined in Table 9.1.

Table 9.1. The parser/lexical analyzer tokens

Identifier/Production	Data Type	Return Type	Comment
INTVAL_TOK	Identifier	Integer	An integer value.
HEXVAL_TOK	Identifier	Integer	A hexadecimal value that starts with the characters 0x.

Table 9.1. The parser/lexical analyzer tokens *(continued)*

Identifier/Production	Data Type	Return Type	Comment
FLOATVAL_TOK	Identifier	Float	A floating-point value.
ID_TOK	Identifier	String	An unrecognized string.
NFF_TOK	Identifier	None	'nff' or 's8'.
VERSION_TOK	Identifier	None	'version'
VIEWPOS_TOK	Identifier	None	'viewpos'
VIEWDIR_TOK	Identifier	None	'viewdir'
NORM_TOK	Identifier	None	'norm'
RGB_TOK	Identifier	None	'rgb'
UV_TOK	Identifier	None	'uv'
BOTH_TOK	Identifier	None	'both'
TEXTURE_TOK	Identifier	None	A texture definition string.
PORTAL_TOK	Identifier	None	A portal definition string.
IDTOK_TOK	Identifier	None	'id'
Color	Production	Color	The production color that converts a hexadecimal value into a color.

The Bison Productions Code

A Bison parser is constructed of BNF-like productions that specify how the file is organized and allows C/C++ code to be attached to the productions. The productions in the WTK-NFF parser use these global variables:

- `vertices`. Contains a list of the vertices for the current object.
- `face`. Contains the indexes into the vertex list that defines the current polygon.
- `ObjectName`. Contains the name of the current object.
- `CheckColor`. Forces a material to be created when it is set to `TRUE`.

The WTK-NFF Bison parser has four key productions: `Start`, `Object`, `Polygon`, and `Color`. Most of the work in the parser is handled in these.

The parser starts with the first production defined, `Start`. This production defines the overall layout of the WTK-NFF. It is the link to the other productions through the `Object` production, which is referenced in the `Start` production.

The `Object` production initializes a new object and initiates the parsing of the vertex list and the faces.

The `Polygon` object converts each polygon into a polygon in the global *MeshCompactor* instance.

The `Color` production converts a hexadecimal color value into a `ColorType` value for use by the `Polygon` production.

The source code for the Bison parser follows:

```
/* Parsing starts with this production. It     */
/* recognizes the WTK-NFF header by checking   */
/* for the NFF_TOK. It looks for the optional */
/* version, viewpos, and viewdir productions, */
/* and then parses the underlying objects.     */
/* After parsing is completed the globals      */
/* vertices and face are cleared.              */

Start:          NFF_TOK
                OptVersion
                OptViewpos
                OptViewdir
                Objects
                {
                      // Cleanup storage
                      vertices.Clear();
                      face.Clear();
                }
    ;

OptVersion:     /* empty */
    |           VERSION_TOK FLOATVAL_TOK
    ;

OptViewpos:     /* empty */
    |           VIEWPOS_TOK FLOATVAL_TOK
                      FLOATVAL_TOK FLOATVAL_TOK
    ;

OptViewdir:     /* empty */
    |           VIEWDIR_TOK FLOATVAL_TOK
                      FLOATVAL_TOK FLOATVAL_TOK
    ;

Objects:        Object
    |           Objects Object
    ;

/* Parse the 3D object. Initialize the new             */
```

```
/* object when its name is encountered and          */
/* then parse the vertices and faces of the object. */
Object:          ID_TOK
                 {
                        // Delete previous vertices and faces
                        vertices.Clear();
                        face.Clear();

                        // Save new object name.
                        strcpy(ObjectName, $1);

                        // Start a new group with the new name
                        yymesh->Name($1);

                        // Force the create of a new material
                        CheckColor = FALSE;
                 }
                 INTVAL_TOK
                 Vertices
                 INTVAL_TOK
                 Polygons
    ;

Vertices: Vertex
    |            Vertices Vertex
    ;

/* Add the vertex to the global vertex list. */
Vertex:          FLOATVAL_TOK FLOATVAL_TOK
                        FLOATVAL_TOK OptNorm OptRGB OptUV
                 {
                        // Add vertex to local vertex list
                        vertices.Add(SFVec3f($1, $2, $3));
                 }
    ;

OptNorm:         /* empty */
    |            NORM_TOK FLOATVAL_TOK
                        FLOATVAL_TOK FLOATVAL_TOK
    ;

OptRGB:          /* empty */
    |            RGB_TOK HEXVAL_TOK
    ;

OptUV:          /* empty */
    |           UV_TOK FLOATVAL_TOK FLOATVAL_TOK
    ;
```

```
Polygons: Polygon
    |           Polygons Polygon
    ;

/* Add the polygon face to the MeshCompactor object  */
/* defined globally. */
Polygon:        PolyFaces Color OptBoth OptTexture
                       OptID OptPortal
                {
                       if (!CheckColor ||
                              $2.x != PrevColor.x ||
                              $2.y != PrevColor.y ||
                              $2.z != PrevColor.z) {
                              char groupName[256];

                              // Update the materail
                              material.Color($2.x, $2.y,
                                           $2.z);
                              yymesh->Name(ObjectName);
                              PrevColor = $2;
                              CheckColor = TRUE;
                       }

                       // Add current material to the polygon
                       yymesh->BeginPolygon(&material);
                       for (int i = 0; i < face.Elements();
                                          i++) {
                              // save each vertex.
                              yymesh->AddVertex(
                                    vertices[face[i]]);
                       }

                       // Close polygon and clear the face.
                       yymesh->EndPolygon();
                       face.Clear();
                }
    ;

PolyFaces:      INTVAL_TOK
                Faces
    ;

/* Save the faces in the faces global varible. These      */
/* values are used by the Polygon production to construct */
/* the object.                                            */
Faces:          INTVAL_TOK        {face.Add($1);}
    |           Faces INTVAL_TOK  {face.Add($2);}
    ;
```

```
/* Convert a hex color to an ColorType.                        */
Color:          HEXVAL_TOK
                {
                      ColorType color;
                      long value = $1;

                      // Convert hex value into a color

                      if (value < 0) {
                            // 24 bit value
                            value = -value;
                            color.z = (float)
                                        (value%256)/256.0;
                            value /= 256;
                            color.y = (float)
                                        (value%256))/256.0;
                            value /= 256;
                            color.x = (float)
                                        (value%256)/256.0;
                            $$ = color;
                      } else {
                            // 12 bit value
                            color.z = (float)
                                        (value%16)/16.0;
                            value /= 16;
                            color.y = (float)
                                        (value%16)/16.0;
                            value /= 16;
                            color.x = (float)
                                        (value%16)/16.0;
                            $$ = color;
                      }
                }
    ;

OptBoth:        /* empty */
    |           BOTH_TOK
    ;

OptTexture:     /* empty */
    |           TEXTURE_TOK
    ;

OptID:          /* empty */
    |           IDTOK_TOK '=' INTVAL_TOK
    ;
```

```
OptPortal:          /* empty */
        |           PORTAL_TOK
        ;
```

The Lexical Analyzer

The GNU Flex lexical analyzer is composed of nine regular expressions that tokenize the file stream for the parser. Table 9.2 defines each regular expression and its action.

Table 9.2. The lexical analyzer's regular expressions and actions

<table>
<tr><th>Expression</th><th>Action</th><th>Comments</th></tr>
<tr><td>W[^\n]*</td><td>None</td><td>Recognizes C++ style comments.</td></tr>
<tr><td>[\t]+</td><td>None</td><td>Recognizes whitespace.</td></tr>
<tr><td>“\n” | “\r” |
“\r\n” |“\n\r”</td><td>None</td><td>Recognizes all permutations of newlines.</td></tr>
<tr><td>_[A-Za-z_][A-Za-z0-9_]*</td><td>Returns TEXTURE_TOK</td><td>Recognizes texture tokens.</td></tr>
<tr><td>-[A-Za-z_][A-Za-z0-9_]*</td><td>Returns PORTAL_TOK</td><td>Recognizes the portal token.</td></tr>
<tr><td>-?[0-9]+(\.([0-9]+)?)?[Ee][\+\-]?[0-9]+ |
-?([0-9]+)?\.[0-9]+[Ee][\+\-]?[0-9]+ |
-?([0-9]+)?\.[0-9]+ |
-?[0-9]+\.([0-9]+)?</td><td>Returns FLOATVAL_TOK</td><td>Recognizes all the permutations of a floating-point value.</td></tr>
<tr><td>-?[0-9]+</td><td>Returns INTVAL_TOK</td><td>Recognizes an integer value.</td></tr>
<tr><td>“0x”[0-9a-fA-F]+</td><td>Return HEXVAL_TOK</td><td>Recognizes a hexadecimal string.</td></tr>
<tr><td>[a-zA-Z0-9_\.\:]+</td><td>Returns either ID_TOK or a keyword token</td><td>First checks to see if the string is a keyword by looking up the string in the keyword table. If it is a keyword, the associated token is returned. If it is not a keyword, then the token ID_TOK is returned.</td></tr>
</table>

The following GNU Flex code performs the actions described in Table 9.2.

```
// Line number
int yylineno = 1;

// Current object (declared in nff_gram.y)
extern GNode*   yyobject;

// Keyword table definition.
typedef struct KEYWORD {
    char        *name;
    int         value;
    struct KEYWORD    *next;
} KEYWORD;

static KEYWORD *yylookUp(char*);

/*
 *  This array of symbols contains the key words for
 *  the ewav file. A yyhash table is created out of these
 *  values and checked each time an identifier is found.
 *  The result of doing this is a smaller and faster lexer.
 */
static KEYWORD  yysymbols[] = {
    "nff",      NFF_TOK,            (KEYWORD *) NULL,
    "s8",       NFF_TOK,            (KEYWORD *) NULL,
    "version",  VERSION_TOK,        (KEYWORD *) NULL,
    "viewpos",  VIEWPOS_TOK,        (KEYWORD *) NULL,
    "viewdir",  VIEWDIR_TOK,        (KEYWORD *) NULL,
    "norm",     NORM_TOK,           (KEYWORD *) NULL,
    "rgb",      RGB_TOK,            (KEYWORD *) NULL,
    "uv",       UV_TOK,             (KEYWORD *) NULL,
    "id",       IDTOK_TOK,          (KEYWORD *) NULL
};

#define NUMOFKEYWORDS (sizeof(yysymbols)/sizeof(KEYWORD))
#define LEX_HASHSIZE  (NUMOFKEYWORDS+NUMOFKEYWORDS/4)
KEYWORD               *yyhashTbl[LEX_HASHSIZE] = {NULL};

%}

%%

\/\/[^\n]*      {/* ignore comments */;}
[ \t]+          {/* ignore whitespace */;}
"\n" |
"\r" |
"\r\n" |
```

```
"\n\r"          {
                        yylineno++;
                        if (yylineno % 100 == 0) {
                              if (yyobject != NULL) {
                                    yyobject-
>StatusMessage("Reading Line %d", yylineno);
                              }
                        }
                }
_[A-Za-z_][A-Za-z0-9_]*          {return TEXTURE_TOK;}
-[A-Za-z_][A-Za-z0-9_]*          {return PORTAL_TOK;}

-?[0-9]+(\.([0-9]+)?)?[Ee][\+\-]?[0-9]+ |
-?([0-9]+)?\.[0-9]+[Ee][\+\-]?[0-9]+  |
-?([0-9]+)?\.[0-9]+ |
-?[0-9]+\.([0-9]+)?     {
                        yylval.real = atof(yytext);
                        return FLOATVAL_TOK;

                }

-?[0-9]+        {
                        sscanf(yytext, "%ld",
                              &yylval.integer);
                        return INTVAL_TOK;
                }

"0x"[0-9a-fA-F]+        {
                        char* sp = &yytext[2];
                        yylval.integer = 0;

                        while (*sp) {
                              if (isdigit(*sp)) {
                                    yylval.integer *= 16;
                                    yylval.integer +=
                                          *sp - '0';
                              } else if (*sp >= 'a' &&
                                          *sp <= 'f') {
                                    yylval.integer *= 16;
                                    yylval.integer +=
                                          *sp - 'a' + 10;
                              } else if (*sp >= 'A' &&
                                          *sp <= 'F') {
                                    yylval.integer *= 16;
                                    yylval.integer +=
                                          *sp - 'A' + 10;
                              }
```

```
                        sp++;
                }

                if (strlen(yytext) > 5) {
                        yylval.integer =
                                -yylval.integer;
                }
                return HEXVAL_TOK;
        }

[a-zA-Z0-9_\.\:]+               {
                KEYWORD         *np;

                strcpy(yylval.string , yytext);

                if ((np=yylookUp((char *) yytext)) !=
                                (KEYWORD *) NULL) {
                        strcpy(yylval.string, "");
                        return np->value;
                }

                return ID_TOK;
        }

.       {
                return yytext[0];
        }

%%
```

Implementing a WTK-NFF Writer

To create a WTK-NFF writer, you need to write a small amount of C++ code that will convert the internal representation of 3D objects into polygons. This conversion process is very easy to accomplish because the internal representation of 3D objects closely resembles that of a WTK-NFF file.

The `GNode::Write()` member function traverses the scene, and the appropriate member function of a *GWrite* derived class is called for each recognized *GNode* instance encountered. This arrangement allows implementers to write WTK-NFF file format writers without having to know the details of the internal representation of 3D objects. Also, the internal representation allows 3D objects to be converted to polygons. So to implement a WTK-NFF writer, you need only tell the internal representation that we want only polygons and then write out the polygons.

The following class definition describes the *GWriteNFF* derived *GWrite* class:

```
class GWriteNFF : public GWrite {
private:
    MeshCompactor       m_mesh;
    char                m_name[256];

public:
    GWriteNFF(void) : GWrite() {m_name[0] = '\0';}
    short PolygonSupported(void)   {return TRUE;}

    void  Polygon(GState&, long, MFVec3f*,
          MFVec3f* = NULL, GWriteMaterial* = NULL);
    void  Epilog(GNode*, GState&);
};
```

Handling Polygons

The `Polygon()` member function is called for every polygon encountered during the traversal of the 3D representation for the current objects. Since the WTK-NFF file is composed of individual objects, each of which has its own vertex list and face list, the polygons must be saved in a *MeshCompactor* construct so that each group can later be emitted individually. The groups need to be converted from having a single vertex list across all groups, as in the representation of a *MeshCompactor* instance, to having one vertex list per object. This conversion is handled in the `Epilog()` member function.

```
// Called for every polygon in the internal representation
void GWriteNFF::
Polygon(GState& state, long faceNum, MFVec3f* v,
      MFVec3f* n, GWriteMaterial* m)
{
    char  *pHeirName, heirName[256];

    pHeirName = state.HeirName();

    if (pHeirName != NULL) {
          strcpy(heirName, pHeirName);
    }

    // Notice Name changes
    if (pHeirName != NULL &&
                strcmp(m_name, heirName) != 0) {
          m_mesh.Name(heirName);
          strcpy(m_name, heirName);
```

```
        }

        // Add polygon
        m_mesh.BeginPolygon(m);
        for (int i = 0; i < v->Elements(); i++) {
              m_mesh.AddVertex((*v)[i]);
        }
        m_mesh.EndPolygon();
}
```

Emitting the WTK-NFF File

After the 3D objects in the internal representation have been completely traversed, the `Epilog()` member function is called. At this point, the internal representation for the 3D objects are available in the *MeshCompactor* instance *m_mesh*.

Converting the representation into the form needed for the WTK-NFF file requires that each group found in the *MeshCompactor* instance associated with the *GWriteNFF* instance be converted into a local *MeshCompactor* instance. After the polygons from the group have been placed in the local *MeshCompactor* instance, that instance is written as a WTK-NFF object. This process is repeated for every group in the *MeshCompactor* instance associated with the *GWriteNFF* instance.

```
// Called after all the polygons have been read.
void GWriteNFF::
Epilog(GNode* root, GState& state)
{
    MeshCompactor*     mesh = new MeshCompactor;

    if (mesh == NULL) {
          return;
    }
    // Write the preface
    fprintf(m_fp, "nff\nversion 2.1\n\n");

    // Cycle through each of the groups
    for (long group = 0; group < m_mesh.Groups(); group++) {
          MFVec3f*     coords = m_mesh.Coordinates();
          MFLong*      faces = m_mesh.Faces(group);
          SFLong       vertices;

          mesh->Reset();

          if (faces->Elements() > 0) {
                long                 faceCnt = 0;
```

```
GWriteMaterial      material =
                    m_mesh.FaceIndex2Material(
                          group, faceCnt);

// Write the group name
fprintf(m_fp, "%s\n", m_mesh.Name(group));

// Create a mesh out of the group
mesh->BeginPolygon(&material);
for (long i = 0; i < faces->Elements(); i++)
{
      SFLong       face = (*faces)[i];
      if (face >= 0) {
            mesh->AddVertex(
                  (*coords)[face]);
      } else {
            mesh->EndPolygon();
            faceCnt++;
            material =
m_mesh.FaceIndex2Material(group, faceCnt);
            mesh->BeginPolygon(&material);
      }
}
mesh->EndPolygon();

// Convert the mesh into the WTK-NFF
// group information.
MFVec3f* group_coords = mesh->Coordinates();
MFLong*  group_faces = mesh->Faces();

// Output vertices
fprintf(m_fp, "%d\n",
      group_coords->Elements());
for (i = 0; i < group_coords->Elements();
            i++) {
      SFVec3f value = (*group_coords)[i];
      fprintf(m_fp, "%f %f %f\n",
            value.X(), value.Y(),
            value.Z());
}

// Output faces
fprintf(m_fp, "\n%d\n", faceCnt);

for (faceCnt = i = 0;
      i < group_faces->Elements();
      i += vertices+1, faceCnt++) {
      material = mesh->FaceIndex2Material(
```

```
                        0, faceCnt);
               SFVec3f      color = material.Color();

               for (vertices = 0;
                      (*group_faces)[i+vertices] >= 0;
                      vertices++)
                      ;

               if (vertices > 0) {
                      fprintf(m_fp, "%d ", vertices);

               for (long j = 0; j < vertices;
                             j++) {
                      fprintf(m_fp, "%d ",
                         (*group_faces)[i+j]);
               }
                      fprintf(m_fp, "0x%02x%02x%02x
both\n",
                        (long)(color.Red()*255.0),
                        (long) (color.Green()*255.0),
                        (long) (color.Blue()*255.0));
               }
          }
       }
   }
   if (mesh != NULL) {
          delete mesh;
   }
}
```

Reference

WorldToolKit Neutral File Format Version 2.1. 1995. Mill Valley, Calif.: Sense8 Corporation.

Chapter 10

POVRay V2.2

POVRay is a cross-platform, copyrighted freeware raytracer. Very feature-rich, it originated from David Buck's DKB-Trace ray tracer and is being actively developed and supported by many people on CompuServe's Graphics Developers' Forum and on the Internet. The development of POVRay is coordinated by Chris Young. It is available for free from the ftp site ftp.povray.org and the Web site www.povray.org.

POVRay is easily the most-discussed software package on several of the Usenet comp.graphics newsgroups. A very capable package overall, it has two features that make it stand out. One, it's free, and two, the source code is available.

You might wonder why, when the source code to POVRay is available, I would devote a chapter to reading and writing the POVRay format. You might expect that you could "borrow" the source and place it into your application. Unfortunately, this isn't possible. The POVRay development team has placed on it a very restrictive licensing agreement that doesn't allow this type of usage. It is trying to balance user availability of source with protection of their intellectual property. They are concerned that unscrupulous individuals will repackage and sell their work if they don't protect it. It is my understanding that they've actually had a couple of incidents that have reinforced this concern. So, you can look at the source, but you must keep it out of your applications.

In this chapter, I focus on reading and writing the POVRay V2.2 file format. As I'm writing this chapter, V3.0 is in beta test. However, neither the source nor a precise description of the language changes is available, so I can discuss only V2.2. This should not be a problem, since V3.0 will be a superset of V2.2. So it should be relatively easy for you to extend the BNF once the documentation for V3.0 is available.

Overview of the POVRay Format

POVRay is intended to be a human readable format for describing a 3D scene. It can describe triangles, many types of objects, boolean operations on objects, and a very rich procedural definition for textures.

The POVRay file format definition is large. The book *Ray Tracing Creations—Second Edition*, by Chris Young and Drew Wells, devotes more than half of its 571 pages to describing this format. It is not feasible to describe POVRay to that level of detail here, so I heartily recommend that book. It is helpful if you want to learn the details of each command in the format or want a thorough discussion of the documents that accompany the application's distribution. In this chapter, I focus on what's missing from the descriptions of POVRay that are currently available.

And what's missing is a precise description of the POVRay language. The descriptions that do exist focus on the newer syntax of POVRay V2.*x*. However, this syntax comprises only a small portion of the actual V2.2 language syntax. Most POVRay files, including the example files included with POVRay V2.2, are actually a combination of POVRay V2.*x* syntax and the earlier POVRay syntax. The lack of a precise definition of the POVRay language makes writing a parser for POVRay a nightmare.

So here I give a pragmatic description of the POVRay file format. I include a description that will allow most, but not necessarily all, legal POVRay files to be read. Also, the BNF and source code in this chapter will allow most POVRay V2.2 files to be parsed.

Parsing Issues

The source included here is written using GNU Bison and Flex. Bison has some limitations when it comes to parsing certain types of grammars. One is that it can handle only one level of look-ahead. But the POVRay V2.2 syntax requires more than one token look-ahead to unambiguously decide how to parse some constructs. So there are some ambiguities that cannot be resolved with Bison. You may think then that Bison is not suitable for building a POVRay V2.2 reader. Fortunately, most such ambiguities can be easily dealt with or are very unlikely to occur in the first place.

Two major problems arise with reading V2.2 files. First, the difficulty of merging the syntax of POVRay V1.0 with the documented syntax of POVRay V2.2. Second, dealing with ambiguities that arise when merging the two different languages.

POVRay allows the parser to switch modes while parsing so that POVRay V1.0 syntax can be read. This was useful for helping folks migrate from V1.0

to V2.*x*. However, it caused serious headaches for the implementer of a POVRay file reader.

V1.0 has a different syntax for many language components than does V2.2. The most difficult of these two problems is how 3D points and normals (which I call vectors) are really handled in V2.*x*. A vector in V1.0 uses whitespace to separate the three floating-point values; V2.x syntax uses commas as separators. Also, scalar values and vectors are separated by whitespace in V1.0, but by commas in V2.*x*. These differences may seem minor, but they cause some serious problems when trying to parse a file. Consider this example:

```
sphere { <3 -2 9> 4 }
```

which specifies a sphere at location (3, –2, 9) with a radius of 4 using the V1.0 syntax. V2.*x* has added the notation of expressions on scalar values and vectors. So the expression <3 –2 9> has two possible interpretations: <3 –2, 9> or <3, –2, 9>. To deal with this problem, the POVRay design team added the comma separator to V2.*x* so that users can unambiguously define expressions.

However, if you've used V2.*x* much you've probably discovered that it allows the newer syntax to be intermixed with the old syntax. How did the POVRay design team resolve the ambiguities? They didn't. They simplified the problem. Consider this example:

```
#include "colors.inc"
#include "textures.inc"

camera {
   location  <0, 0,-6>
   look_at   <0, 0, 0>
}

light_source {<10, 20, -30> color White}
background {rgb <0.75, 0.75, 0.75>}

sphere { <1 -1 0>, 0.75
   pigment {Red}
   finish {ambient 0.3 phong 1}
}

sphere { <1, -1, 0>, 0.75
   pigment {Red}
   finish {ambient 0.3 phong 1}
}
```

If all the ambiguities were resolved, there should be only one sphere visible located to the right and below the center. Figure 10.1 shows the image that is generated.

Figure 10.1. Two spheres when there should be one.

Notice that there are two spheres visible, one apparently at <1, –1, 0> and another at <0, 0, 0>. What's going on here?

It appears that the point <1, –1, 0> has been converted to <1–1, 0, 0> or <0, 0, 0>. By implication, expressions are always evaluated and zeros fill in any missing parameters. The POVRay team seems to have come up with a reasonable compromise here. The compromise will break some older code but will allow many older POVRay files to load and run without modification. From this, it appears that a vector in V2.2 is defined by the following BNF grammar fragment:

```
<Vector>   ::=    '<' <Double> [[','] <Double>]
                          [[','] <Double>] '>'
           ;
```

The POVRay V2.2 BNF

The following BNF describes the grammar for V2.2. The grammar is quite large and still growing. Using this grammar as a basis, you should be able to write a parser for V2.2.

```
// <name>   is a non-terminal
// ::=      is an assignment
// ...|...  means either this construct OR that construct
// [...]    means the bracketed construct is optional
// {...}    means the bracketed construct is repeated one
//          or more times.
// '...'    is a literal string definition.

<Start>     ::=   {<SceneItem>}
            ;

<SceneItem>::=    <Background>
            |     <Camera>
            |     <Fog>
            |     <LanguageDirective>
            |     <Shape>
            ;

<Background>::= 'background' '{' <Color> '}'
            ;

<Camera>    ::=  'camera' '{' {<CameraItem>} '}'
            ;

<CameraItem>::= 'location' <Vector>
            |    'direction' <Vector>
            |    'up' <Vector>
            |    'right' <Vector>
            |    'sky' <Vector>
            |    'look_at' <Vector>
            |    <Transformation>
            |    <CameraIdentifier>
            ;

<Fog>       ::=  'fog' '{' {<FogItem>} '}'
            ;

<FogItem>   ::=  <Color>
            |    <Double>
            |    'distance' <Double>
            ;

<LanguageDirective>::=['#'] 'declare' <ID> '=' <Camera>
            |     ['#'] 'declare' <ID> '=' <Color>
            |     ['#'] 'declare' <ID> '=' <ColorMap>
            |     ['#'] 'declare' <ID> '=' <Double>
            |     ['#'] 'declare' <ID> '=' <Shape>
            |     ['#'] 'declare' <ID> '=' {<Texture>}
```

```
                |     ['#'] 'declare' <ID> '=' <Vector>
                |     ['#'] 'declare' <ID> '=' <Finish>
                |     ['#'] 'declare' <ID> '=' 'version'
                |     ['#'] 'default' '{' {<Default>} '}'
                |     ['#'] 'max_trace_level' <Double>
                |     ['#'] 'version' <Double>
                ;

<Include>       ::=   ['#'] 'include' <String>
                ;

<Default>       ::=   <Texture>
                |     <Color>
                |     <Finish>
                ;

<Shape>         ::=   <BicubicPatch>
                |     <Blob>
                |     <Box>
                |     <Cubic>
                |     <Cone>
                |     <Composite>
                |     <Cylinder>
                |     <Disc>
                |     <HeightField>
                |     <LightSource>
                |     <Object>
                |     <Plane>
                |     <Poly>
                |     <Quadric>
                |     <Quartic>
                |     <SmoothTriangle>
                |     <Sphere>
                |     <Torus>
                |     <Triangle>
                |     <CSGShape>
                |     <ShapeIdentifier>
                |     <Include>
                ;

<Composite>::=        'composite' '{' {<Shape>}
                            [{<ShapeModifier>}] '}'
                ;

<CSGShape>::=         <Intersection>
                |     <Difference>
                |     <Union>
                |     <Merge>
```

```
            ;

<Intersection>::=     'intersection' '{' {<Shape>}
                            [{<ShapeModifier>}] '}'
            ;

<Difference>::= 'difference' '{' {<Shape>}
                      [{<ShapeModifier>}] '}'
            ;

<Union>       ::= 'union' '{' {<Shape>}
                      [{<ShapeModifier>}] '}'
              ;

<Merge>       ::= 'merge' '{' {<Shape>}
                      [{<ShapeModifier>}] '}'
              ;

<BicubicPatch>::='bicubic_patch' '{' <ShapeIdentifier>
                      [{<ShapeModifier>}] '}'
              |   'bicubic_patch' '{'
                   [{<BicubicKeyword>}]
                   <NextVector> <NextVector>
                   <NextVector> <NextVector>
                   <NextVector> <NextVector>
                   <NextVector> <NextVector>
                   <NextVector> <NextVector>
                   <NextVector> <NextVector>
                   <NextVector> <NextVector>
                   <NextVector> <NextVector>
                   [{<ShapeModifier>}] '}'
              ;

<BicubicKeyword>::=      'type' <Double>
              |    'flatness' <Double>
              |    'u_steps' <Double>
              |    'v_steps> <Double>
              |    <Double> <NextDouble> <NextDouble>
              |    <Double> <NextDouble> <NextDouble>
              |          <NextDouble>
              ;

<Blob>        ::=  'blob' '{' <ShapeIdentifier>
                         [{<ShapeModifier>}] '}'
              |    'blob' '{' {<BlobItem>}
                         [{<ShapeModifier>}] '}'
              ;
```

```
<BlobItem>::=     'component' <Double> <NextDouble>
                        <NextVector>
            |     'threshold' <Double>
            ;

<Box>       ::=   'box' '{' <ShapeIdentifier>
                        [{<ShapeModifier>}] '}'
            |     'box''{' <Vector> <NextVector>
                        [{<ShapeModifier>}] '}'
            ;

<Cone>      ::=   'cone' '{' <Vector> <NextDouble>
                        <NextVector> <NextDouble> ['open']
                        [','] [{<ShapeModifier>}] '}'
            ;

<Cylinder>  ::=     'cylinder' '{' <Vector> <NextVector>
                        <NextDouble> ['open'] [',']
                        [{<ShapeModifier>}] '}'
            ;

<Cubic>     ::=     'cubic' '{' <ShapeIdentifier>
                        [{<ShapeModifier>}] '}'
            |       'cubic' '{'
                        ['<'] <FloatList> ['>'] [',']
                        [{<ShapeModifier>}] '}
            ;

<Disc>      ::=     'disk' '{' <Vector> <NextVector>
                        <NextDouble> [<NextDouble>] [',']
                        [{<ShapeModifier>}] '}'
            ;

<HeightField>::='height_field' '{' <ShapeIdentifier>
                        [{<HeightFieldModifier>}] '}'
            |   'height_field' '{'
                        <HeightFieldType> <String>
                        [{<HeightFieldModifier>}] '}'
            ;

<HeightFieldType>::=  'gif' | 'pot' | 'tga'
            ;

<HeightFieldModifier>::=<ShapeModifier>
            |   'water_level' <Double>
            |   'smooth'
            ;
```

```
<LightSource>::='light_source' '{' <LightSourceIdentifier>
                        [{<LightSourceModifier>}] '}'
            |   'light_source' '{' <Vector> <Color>
                        [{<LightSourceModifier>}] '}'
            ;

<LightSourceModifier>::='spotlight'
            |   'point_at' <Vector>
            |   'falloff' <Double>
            |   'radius' <Double>
            |   'tightness' <Double>
            |   <Transformation>
            |   'looks_like' '{' <Shape> '}'
            |   'area_light' <Vector> <NextVector>
                           <NextDouble>  <NextDouble>
            |   'adaptive' <Double>
            |   'jitter'
            |   <Color>
            ;

<Object>    ::= 'object' '{' <Shape> [{<ShapeModifier>}] '}'
            ;

<Plane>     ::= 'plane' '{' <ShapeIdentifier>
                      [{<ShapeModifier>}] '}'
            |   'plane' '{' <Vector> <NextDouble> [',']
                      [{<ShapeModifier>}] '}
            ;

<Poly>      ::= 'poly' '{' <ShapeIdentifier>
                      [{<ShapeModifier>}] '}'
            |   'poly' '{' <Double> [','] '<' FloatList '>'
                      [','] [{<ShapeModifier>}] '}'
            ;

<FloatList> ::=  <Double> [{<NextDouble>}]
            ;

<Quadric>   ::=  'quadric' '{' <ShapeIdentifier>
                       [{<ShapeModifier>}] '}'
            |    'quadric' '{' <Vector> <NextVector>
                       <NextVector> <NextDouble>
                       [{<ShapeModifier>}] '}'
            ;

<Quartic>   ::=  'quartic' '{' <ShapeIdentifier>
                       [{<ShapeModifier>}] '}'
            |    'quartic' '{' '<' <FloatList> '>'
```

```
                        [{<ShapeModifier>}] '}'
            ;

<SmoothTriangle>::=     'smooth_triangle' '{'
                              <ShapeIdentifier>
                              [{<ShapeModifier>}] '}'
            |     'smooth_triangle' '{'
                        <Vector> <NextVector> <NextVector>
                        <NextVector> <NextVector> <NextVector>
                        [{<ShapeModifier>}] '}'
            ;

<Sphere>    ::=   'sphere' '{' <ShapeIdentifier>
                        [{<ShapeModifier>}] '}'
            |     'sphere' '{' <Vector> <NextDouble>
                        [{<ShapeModifier>}] '}'
            ;

<Torus>     ::=   'torus' '{' <Double> <NextDouble> [',']
                        [{<ShapeModifier>}] '}'
            |     'torus' '{' <ShapeIdentifier>
                        [{<ShapeModifier>}] '}
            ;

<Triangle>  ::=   'triangle' '{' <ShapeIdentifier>
                        [{<ShapeModifier>}] '}'
            |     'triangle' '{' <Vector> <NextVector>
                        <NextVector>
                        [{<ShapeModifier>}] '}'
            ;

<ShapeModifier>::=<Transformation>
            |   <Color>
            |   {<Texture>}
            |   <FinishParameter>
            |   <ClippedBy>
            |   <BoundedBy>
            |   'inverse'
            |   'no_shadow'
            |   'sturm'
            ;

<ClippedBy>::=   'clipped_by' '{' {<Shape>} '}'
         ;

<BoundedBy> ::= 'bounded_by' '{' {<Shape>} '}'
         ;
```

```
<Texture>    ::= 'texture' '{' {<TextureItem>} '}'
             |   <TextureIdentifier>
             ;

<TextureItem>::=<ColorPattern>
             |   <NormalPattern>
             |   <NormalPatternModifier>
             |   <FinishParameter>
             |   <SpecialTexture>
             |   <TextureIdentifier
             ;

<ColorPattern>::='agate'
             |    'bozo'
             |    'granite'
             |    'leopard
             |    'marble'
             |    'mandel'
             |    'radial'
             |    'onion'
             |    'spotted'
             |    'wood'
             |    'checker' <Color> <Color>
             |    'gradient' <Vector>
             |    <Color>
             |    'image_map' '{' [{<MapPrefix>}]
                        <MapFileType> <String>
                        [{<ImageMapModifier>}] '}'
             |    <ColorPatternModifier>
             ;

<ColorPatternModifier>::= 'turbulence' <Double>
             |    'octaves' <Double>
             |    'lambda' <Double>
             |    <ColorMap>
             |    <ColorMapIdentifier>
             |    <Transformation>
             ;

<NormalPattern>::=     'bumps' <Double>
             |    'dents' <Double>
             |    'ripples' <Double>
             |    'waves' <Double>
             |    'wrinkles' <Double>
             |    'bump_map' '{' [{<MapPrefix>}]
                        <MapFileType> <String>
                        [{<BumpMapModifier>}] '}'
             ;
```

```
<NormalPatternModifier>::=  'phase' <Double>
           |    'frequency' <Double>
           ;

<FinishParameter>::=  <Double>
           |    'metallic'
           |    'ambient' <Double>
           |    'diffuse' <Double>
           |    'specular' <Double>
           |    'roughness' <Double>
           |    'phong'      <Double>
           |    'phong_size' <Double>
           |    'brilliance' <Double>
           |    'ior' <Double>
           |    'refraction' <Double>
           |    'reflection' <Double>
           |    <Finish>
           |    'crand'      <Double>
           |    'normal' '{' <NormalPattern>
                     [{<NormalPatternModifier>}] '}'
           ;

<Finish>     ::=  'finish' '{' {<FinishParameter>} '}'
           |     <FinishIdentifier>
           ;

<SpecialTexture>::='tiles' '{' {<Texture>} 'tile2'
                     {<Texture>} '}'
           |    'material_map' '{' [{<MapPrefix>}]
                     <MapFileType> <String> {<Texture>}
                     [{<MaterialMapModifier>}] '}'
           ;

<ImageMapModifier>::= 'once'
           |    'interpolate' <Double>
           |    'map_type' <Double>
           |    'alpha' ['all'] <Double>
           |    'filter' ['all'] <Double> [<NextDouble>]
           ;

<BumpMapModifier>::=  'once'
           |    'interpolate'<Double>
           |    'map_type' <Double>
           |    ('use_color' | 'use_colour')
           |    'use_index'
           |    'bump_size' <Double>
           ;
```

```
<MaterialMapModifier>::='once'
            |    'interpolate' <Double>
            |    'map_type' <Double>
            ;

<MapPrefix> ::=  <Double>
            |    <Vector>
            ;

<MapFileType>::='iff' | 'gif' | 'dump' | 'tga'
            ;

<Color:>    ::= 'pigment' '{' {<ColorPattern>}
                     [{<PigmentModifier>}] '}'
            |   <ColorCommand>] {<ColorComponent>}
            ;

<ColorCommand>::='color' | 'colour'
            |   'quick_color' | 'quick_colour'
            ;

<PigmentModifier>::= <FinishParameter>
            ;

<ColorComponent>::='red' <Double>
            |    'green' <Double>
            |    'blue' <Double>
            |    'alpha' <Double>
            |    'filter' <Double>
            |    'rgbf' '<' <Double> <NextDouble>
                       <NextDouble> <NextDouble> '>'
            |    'rgb' <Vector>
            |    <ColorIdentifier>
            ;

<ColorMap>  ::=  ('color_map' | 'colour_map')
                      '{' [{<ColorMapEntry>}] '}'
            |    ('color_map' | 'colour_map')
                      '{' [{<ColorMapIdentifier>}] '}'
            ;

<ColorMapEntry>::='[' <Double> <NextDouble> [',']
                      <Color> [<Color>] ']'
            |     '[' <Double> [','] <Color> ']'
            ;
```

```
<Transformation>::='translate' <Vector>
            |    'rotate'  (<Double> | <Vector>)
            |    'scale'   (<Double> | <Vector>)
            ;

<NextVector>::=  ',' <Vector>
            |    '<' <Double> [<NextDouble>]
                        [<NextDouble>] '>'
            ;

<Vector>    ::=  '<' <Double> [<NextDouble>]
                        [<NextDouble>] '>'
            |    <VectorIdentifier>
            |    <Vector> '+' <Vector>
            |    <Vector> '-' <Vector>
            |    <Vector> '*' <Vector>
            |    <Vector> '*' <Double>
            |    <Double> '*' <Vector>
            |    <Vector> '/' <Vector>
            |    <Double> '/' <Vector>
            |    <Vector> '/' <Double>
            |    '(' <Vector> ')'
            |    ('-' | '+') <Vector>
            ;

<NextDouble>::=  ',' <Double>
            |    <DoubleToken>
            |    <DoubleIdentifier>
            ;

<Double>    ::=  <DoubleToken>
            |    <DoubleIdentifier>
            |    <Double> '+' <Double>
            |    <Double> '-' <Double>
            |    <Double> '*' <Double>
            |    <Double> '/' <Double>
            |    '(' <Double> ')'
            |    ('-' | '+') <Double>
            ;

<DoubleToken>::= {'0'..'9'} ['.' {'0'..'9'}
                        ['e' ['-' | '+'] {'0'..'9'}]]
            |    [{'0'..'9'}] '.' {'0'..'9'}
                        ['e' ['-' | '+'] {'0'..'9'}]
            ;

<String>    ::=  '"' {'a'..'z' | 'A'..'Z' | '0'..'9' | '~' |
                 '!' | '/' | '@' | '#' | '$' | '%' | '^' |
```

```
                 '&' | '*' | '(' | ')' | '-' | '_' | '+' |
                 '=' | '{' | '}' | '[' | ']' | ':' | ';' |
                 '\'' | '|' | '<' | '>' | ',' | '.' | '?'}
                 '"'
            ;

<ID>        ::=  ('a'..'z' | 'A'..'Z') {['a'..'z' |
                      'A'..'Z' | '0'..'9']}
            ;
```

Syntax of POVRay

This section gives a very terse description of each language keyword defined in the POVRay V2.2 BNF. These descriptions are not suitable for learning POVRay. The documentation that accompanies POVRay is better as a learning tool.

Table 10.1 is intended as a cross reference for each keyword in V2.2 and the BNF production in which it is used. It also includes a short description of how each keyword is used.

Table 10.1 POVRay keywords

Keyword	BNF Production References	Usage
adaptive	LightSourceModifier	An optional specification to light_source that speeds up the calculation of an area light.
agate	ColorPattern	A pigment lookup function. It uses a sine function to map the colors.
all	ImageMapModifier	A modifier to the filter keyword that specifies that the filter value applies to all colors.
alpha	ImageMapModifier, ColorComponent	An obsolete language construct replaced by the filter construct.
ambient	FinishParameter	Defines the amount of ambient light to apply to the texture.
area_light	LightSourceModifier	Defines a softer edge to light from a light source.
background	SceneItem	Defines the background color of the scene.

(continued)

Table 10.1 POVRay keywords *(continued)*

Keyword	BNF Production References	Usage
bicubic_patch	Shape	A bezier patch created from 16 points.
blob	Shape	A sphere that is attracted or repelled from other blob objects to give a liquid effect.
blue	ColorComponent	Defines the amount of blue in a color.
bounded_by	Boundedby	An optional construct that is defined to help speed up ray intersection calculations of complex objects.
box	Shape	Defines a box shape.
bozo	ColorPattern	A pigment lookup function. It uses a random-number generator to map the colors. The result is a blotchy look.
brilliance	FinishParameter	Specifies the size of the diffuse reflection in a texture.
bump_map	NormalPattern	Uses an image file to specify the bump pattern on a texture.
bump_size	BumpMapModifier	Specifies the apparent depth of the bumps defined in the bump_map.
bumps	NormalPattern	Allows a texture to have a bumpy-looking surface that is specified using random values.
camera	Camera	The object that specifies the viewpoint for the scene.
checker	ColorPattern	A pigment lookup function that toggles between two colors to produce a tile-like pattern.
clipped_by	ClippedBy	Similar to the CSG intersection operation except that it doesn't fill in areas that were cut away.
color	ColorCommand	Denotes the beginning of a color specification.

Table 10.1 POVRay keywords *(continued)*

Keyword	BNF Production References	Usage
color_map	ColorMap	Begins the definition of a color map that is the definition of one or more colors in a table. The colors can be defined to blend between entries in the table to produce a color gradient.
colour	ColorCommand	Denotes the beginning of a color specification.
colour_map	ColorMap	Begins the definition of a color map that is the definition of one or more colors in a table. The colors can be defined to blend between entries in the table to produce a color gradient.
component	BlobItem	A modifier to the blob keyword.
composite	Composite	An obsolete term that performs the same function as a union.
cone	Cone	Specifies a Cone object.
crand	FinishParameter	Adds a random, grainy effect to a texture.
cubic	Cubic	Defines objects using a third-order polynomial function.
cylinder	Cylinder	Defines a Cylinder object.
declare	LanguageDirective	Used when assigning an item to a global symbol name.
default	Default	Defines a default texture to be used on all objects that don't have an explicit texture definition.
dents	NormalPattern	Used much like the bumps keyword. It defines random dents on the surface of an object.
difference	Difference	A CSG operation that creates an object that is the difference of two or more objects.
diffuse	FinishParameter	Defines how light from light sources is diffused from the object.
direction	CameraItem	Specifies the direction in which the camera is pointed.
disc	Disc	Defines a flat, circular disc.

Table 10.1 POVRay keywords *(continued)*

Keyword	BNF Production References	Usage
distance	FogItem	A modifier to the fog keyword.
dump	MapFiletype	Defines the graphical file format dump that will be used by the image map, bump map, or material_map construct.
falloff	LightSourceModifier	A modifier to the spotlight option.
filter	ColorComponent	Specifies how transparent a color will be.
finish	Finish	Defines the noncolor-related components of a texture.
flatness	BicubicKeyword	A modifier for a bicubic_patch construct.
fog	SceneItem	Defines the fog effect on a scene.
frequency	NormalPatternModifier	Specifies the frequency of the ripples in a normal pattern.
gif	MapFileType	Defines the graphical file format gif that will be used by the image_ map, bump_map, or material_map construct.
gradient	ColorPattern	A pigment lookup function. It uses a ramp function to map the colors.
granite	ColorPattern	A pigment lookup function. It uses a random-number generator to map the color.
green	ColorComponent	Defines the amount of green in a color.
height_field	HeightField	Uses an image to create a three-dimensional shape.
iff	MapFileType	Defines the graphical file format iff that will be used by the image_map, bump_map, or material_map construct.
image_map	ColorPattern	Specifies a graphics file to be used as a pigment pattern.
include	Include	Inserts an external file into the currently parsed file.

Table 10.1 POVRay keywords *(continued)*

Keyword	BNF Production References	Usage
interpolate	BumpMapModifier, ImageMapModifier	Smooths transitions in a graphics file when they are enlarged.
intersection	Intersection	A CSG operation that creates an object that is the intersection of two or more objects.
inverse	ShapeModifier	Inverts the inside and outside definitions of an object. This modifier is useful only to CSG operations.
ior	FinishParameter	Specifies the index of refraction for an object.
jitter	LightSourceModifier	A modifier to the area_light option.
lambda	ColorPatternModifier	A modifier to the turbulence function.
leopard	ColorPattern	A pigment lookup function. It produces a spotting effect.
light_source	LightSource	Defines lights in a scene file.
location	CameraItem	Defines the position of a camera.
look_at	CameraItem	Defines a position at which the camera is pointing.
looks_like	LightSourceModifier	Applies a shape to a light_source.
mandel	ColorPattern	A pigment lookup function that uses Mandelbrot fractals to map the colors.
map_type	ImageMapModifier, BumpMapModifier, MaterialMapModifier	Specifies how an image map is applied to a surface.
marble	ColorPattern	A pigment lookup function that produces the banding effect that makes marble textures look convincing.
material_map	SpecialTexture	Allows an image file to be applied to a texture definition.
max_trace_level	LanguageDirective	Defines the maximum number of reflections that will be allowed when raytracing the image.
merge	Merge	Similar to the `%union` operation, except internal surfaces are removed.

Table 10.1 POVRay keywords *(continued)*

Keyword	BNF Production References	Usage
metallic	FinishParameter	Specifies that the highlighting of the object will use the surface color.
no_shadow	ShapeModifier	Specifies that an object casts no shadows.
normal	FinishParameter	Defines variations in the surface of an object to give it a more realistic appearance.
object	Object	A container for a shape definition.
octaves	ColorPatternModifier	Modifies the turbulence applied to a pattern.
once	ImageMapModifier, BumpMapModifier, MaterialMapModifier	Tells a image_map, bump_map, or texture_map that the image will be repeated only once.
onion	ColorPattern	A pigment lookup function that maps colors to concentric spheres.
open	Cylinder, Cone	Specifies that the Cylinder or Cone is open rather than having caps on the ends.
phase	NormalPatternModifier	Changes the phase of ripples defined for a normal.
phong	FinishParameter	Allows the Phong highlighting to be specified.
phong_size	FinishParameter	Allows the Phong highlighting to be specified.
pigment	Color	Specifies the color component of a material.
plane	Plane	Defines an infinite plane.
point_at	LightSourceModifier	Specifies the position toward which a spotlight is pointed.
poly	Poly	Defines an object by using a seventh-order polynomial.
pot	MapFileType	Defines the graphical file format pot that will be used by the image_map, bump_map, or material_map construct.

Table 10.1 POVRay keywords *(continued)*

Keyword	BNF Production References	Usage
quadric	Quadric	Defines an object by using a second-order polynomial.
quartic	Quartic	Defines an object by using a fourth-order polynomial.
quick_color	ColorCommand	Defines a color that is used only for the texture when rendering in low-quality modes.
quick_colour	ColorCommand	Defines a color that is used only for the texture when rendering in low-quality modes.
radial	ColorPattern	A pigment lookup function that maps the colors in a radial wedge pattern as it moves from one color in the color map to another.
radius	LightSourceModifier	Modifies the spotlight option.
red	ColorComponent	Defines the amount of red in a color.
reflection	FinishParameter	Specifies the amount of reflection from a surface.
refraction	FinishParameter	Turns refraction on or off.
rgb	ColorComponent	Defines the red, green, and blue values of a color.
rgbf	ColorComponent	Defines the red, green, blue, and filter components of a color.
right	CameraItem	Specifies the horizontal direction of the camera view.
ripples	NormalPattern	Enables a wave pattern that looks like concentric ripples in a liquid.
rotate	Transformation	Specifies the amount of rotation in degrees in the *x*-, *y*-, and *z*-directions. If a single floating-point value is specified, it is applied to all three directions.
roughness	FinishParameter	Controls the highlights defined for a texture.

Table 10.1 POVRay keywords *(continued)*

Keyword	BNF Production References	Usage
scale	Transformation	Specifies the amount that an object is scaled in the *x*-, *y*-, and *z*-directions. If a single floating-point value is specified, it is applied to all three directions.
sky	CameraItem	Defines the panning and tilting axes of the camera.
smooth	HeightFieldModifier	Specifies that the surface normals of a *Height* field be modified to give a smoother appearance.
smooth_triangle	SmoothTriangle	Defines a Triangle with surface normals for each of its vertices.
specular	FinishParameter	Controls the amount of specular highlighting on a surface.
sphere	Sphere	Defines a Sphere object.
spotlight	LightSourceModifier	Modifies the light_source command that specifies that the light is a spot_light rather than a point light or area light.
spotted	ColorPattern	A pigment lookup function that produces a spotting effect.
sturm	ShapeModifier	Specifies that a more accurate root solver be used. This can make some objects render more precisely.
texture	Texture	Defines both the pigment and surface parameters of a texture.
tga	MapFileType	Defines the graphical file format tga that will be used by the image_map, bump_map, or material_map construct.
threshold	BlobItem	Modifies the blob command.
tightness	LightSourceModifier	Modifies a spotlight.
tile2	SpecialTexture	Defines the second texture of two tiled textures.
tiles	SpecialTexture	Defines the first texture of two tiled textures.

Table 10.1 POVRay keywords *(continued)*

Keyword	BNF Production References	Usage
torus	Torus	Defines a torus-shaped object.
translate	Transformation	Moves the specified object by the specified amount.
triangle	Triangle	Defines a polygon with three points.
turbulence	ColorPatternModifier	Modifies the amount of randomness.
type	BicubicKeyword	Specifies the type of the bicubic_patch construct.
u_steps	BicubicKeyword	Specifies the number of rows of subpatches in a bicubic_patch.
union	Union	A CSG operation that creates an object that is the union of two or more objects.
up	CameraItem	Specifies the up direction for the camera.
use_color	BumpMapModifier	Specifies whether a color value is used in a bump_map.
use_colour	BumpMapModifier	Specifies whether a color value is used in a bump_map.
use_index	BumpMapModifier	Specifies whether a color value is used in a bump_map.
v_steps	BumpMapModifier	Specifies the number of columns of subpatches in a bicubic_patch.
version	LanguageDirection	Sets or returns the current version mode.
water_level	HeightFieldModifier	Defines the lowest visible area in a *Height* field.
waves	NormalPattern	Specifies a normal pattern that looks like concentric waves in a liquid.
wood	ColorPattern	A pigment lookup function that maps colors in concentric rings around the *z*-axis.
wrinkles	NormalPattern	Specifies a normal pattern that looks like wrinkles on a cloth.

Implementing a POVRay Reader

As you've probably noticed from the BNF and the previous discussion, the POVRay is large. Very few 3D modeling or rendering packages come close to the breadth of features available in this language. As a result, most implementations of a POVRay reader will tackle only a subset of the entire POVRay language.

For this implementation, I parse the entire language but convert only a small portion of the encountered language constructs into the internal format. These recognized constructs include spheres, triangles, smooth_triangles, transformations, and a subset of the texture definition.

Local Representation

One important difference between the internal representation, which is based on the VRML language, and the POVRay language is how transformations are handled. In POVRay, a transformation is usually part of the *ShapeModifier* production. Thus a transformation for an object is defined within the object. In contrast, VRML uses the notion of a transformation stack that is applied to all subsequent objects.

Hence, there is no one-for-one conversion of the constructs in POVRay and the internal representation. The entire POVRay file must be parsed before the transformation information is known for certain. As a result, the POVRay file needs to be held while it is parsed and then converted into the internal format.

This conversion is handled by the local representation class *Object* and its derived classes. Since this implementation supports only spheres and triangles, the only defined derived classes are *Triangle* and *Sphere*. The *Object* class has the following definition:

```
class Object {
public
    // Constructor
    Object(void);

    // Destructor
        ~Object(void);

    // Appends object to the child list
    void                AppendChild(Object*);

    // Append object to the next list
    void                AppendNext(Object*);
```

```
// Returns the Next item
Object*             Next(void);

// Returns the child item
Object*             Child(void);

// Copy the specified object into this object
virtual void        Copy(Object*);

// Create a new instance of the current object
virtual Object*     Copy(void);

// Insert the equivalent transform into the
// internal representation.
virtual void LoadTransformsTo(GNode* gp);

// Convert the transforms into a matrix
virtual SFMatrix Transform(void);

// Returns TRUE if a material is attached to this
// object
int MaterialFlag(void);

// Convert the material attached to this object
// to a material useful to the internal representation.
virtual GWriteMaterial Material(void);

// Traverse Child and Next items and convert them
// into the internal representation.
virtual GNode*      ConvertAll(MeshCompactor*);

// Traverse the Child items and convert them into
// the internal representation.
virtual GNode*      Convert(MeshCompactor*);

// Apply transformations to the object.
virtual void        Translate(double, double, double);
virtual void        Rotate(double, double, double);
virtual void        Scale(double, double, double);

// Apply a color to the object
virtual void        SetColor(double, double,
                            double, double = 0.0);
virtual void        SetColor(POVColor&);

// Return the color applied to the object
virtual POVColor    SetColor(void);
```

```
    // Set the surface material properties (ambient,
    // diffuse, specular, and reflection).
    virtual void        Material(double, double,
                                 double, double);

    // Set and get for Ambient property.
    virtual void        Ambient(double a);
    virtual double      Ambient(void);

    // Set and get for Diffuse property.
    virtual void        Diffuse(double);
    virtual double      Diffuse(void);

    // Set and get for Specular property.
    virtual void        Specular(double);
    virtual double      Specular(void);

    // Set and get for Reflection property.
    virtual void        Reflection(double);
    virtual double      Reflection(void);
};
```

This class and its derived classes are used to create the local representation of the POVRay file, which is then converted into the VRML-style internal format. The following example from the file pov_gram.y, which contains the Bison BNF representation, illustrates how this class is used to create the local representation of the POVRay file:

```
Sphere:     SPHERE_TOK '{' ShapeIdentifier
            {
                  if ($3 != NULL && $3->ovalue != NULL) {
                        yyPush($3->ovalue->Copy());
                  } else {
                        yyPush(NULL);
                  }
            }
            ShapeModifiers '}'
            {
                  $$ = yyCurrentObject();
                  yyPop();
            }
      |     SPHERE_TOK '{' Vector NextDouble
            {
                  yyPush(new Sphere($3.x, $3.y, $3.z, $4));
            }
            ShapeModifiers '}'
            {
```

```
                $$ = yyCurrentObject();
                yyPop();
            }
    ;
```

This production defines the implementation for the POVRay Sphere language construct. Two cases are handled in this production. First, the case in which the Sphere is actually a reference to a predefined Sphere object that is saved in the global POVRay symbol table. Second, the case in which a standalone definition of a Sphere is handled.

Both implementations have a similar runtime action. A new object is created, in this case a Sphere, and this object is pushed onto the current object hierarchy stack. This stack allows nested object definitions to be saved by placing them on the object stack. The top element of the stack will have operations applied to it, such as transformations or the application of a texture. Once the productions within the Sphere definition have completely parsed the construct, the newly created object is popped; this restores the object stack to the previous state. That object is returned to the invoking production.

The Sphere object is passed back up to the production that initiated the evaluation of the Sphere construct, the *Shape* production. The following BNF is a portion of that production:

```
Shape:          BicubicPatch        {$$ = $1;}
    |           Blob                {$$ = $1;}
    |           Box                 {$$ = $1;}
                .
                .
                .
    |           Sphere              {$$ = $1;}
                .
                .
                .
```

Notice that the productions simply pass the object returned to the production that invoke the *Shape* production. In most cases, this is the *SceneItem* production. This production handles parsing the language constructs of the POVRay BNF:

```
SceneItem:      Camera              {$$ = $1;}
    |           Fog                 {$$ = NULL;}
    |           LanguageDirective   {$$ = NULL;}
    |           Shape               {$$ = $1;}
    |           Background          {$$=NULL;}
    ;
```

The result of the *SceneItem* production is returned to the *SceneItems* production and then up to the initial production *Start*. The *SceneItems* production combines the returning objects into a list of objects that is returned to the *Start* production. The *Start* production places the object list in the global variable `pov_root`. The `pov_root` variable contains the local representation after the POVRay file has been read.

```
Start:          SceneItems          {pov_root = $1;}
    ;

SceneItems:     SceneItem           {$$ = $1;}
    |           SceneItems SceneItem
                {
                        if ($1 != NULL) {
                                $1->AppendNext($2);
                                $$ = $1;
                        } else {
                                $$ = $2;
                        }
                }
    ;
```

The povray_reader() Function

The `povray_reader()` function is one of two functions that are available externally from the parser. The other is `povray_searchdir()`. This latter function is used to specify the search path for the include directories used by POVRay. For example, c:\povray2\docs;c:\povray2\scenes. Following is the definition of `povray_searchdir()`:

```
void
povray_searchdir(const char* paths)
{
    char  buffer[256];
    int   i = 0, j = 0;

    incIndex = 0;

    while (strlen(&paths[i]) > 0) {
           j = 0;
           for (; paths[i] && paths[i] != ';'; i++, j++) {
                  buffer[j] = paths[i];
           }
```

```
            buffer[j] = '\0';

            if (paths[i] == ';') {
                  i++;
            }

            if (strlen(buffer) > 0) {
                  AddSearchDir(buffer);
            }
      }
}
```

As the file is parsed, its components are added to the local representation of the POVRay file. This allows an intermediate representation to be saved. To read a POVRay file, an external function need only pass in the top-level *GNode* instance (probably a *GSeparator*) and the file name of the POVRay file being read.

The reader first initializes some global variables for the parser and then creates the variables *x, y, z,* and *clock* for the symbol table that is kept for POVRay. These values are built into POVRay and must be defined to be able to correctly read many POVRay files. After the parser is initialized, the file is opened and read. The function `yyparse()` invokes the parser.

If the file is read in correctly, the local representation of the POVRay file is in the global variable *`pov_root`*. This representation can be converted to the VRML-style internal representation by invoking the `ConvertAll()` member function of the *`pov_root`* instance. The value returned is an equivalent representation in the internal representation.

```
int

povray_reader(GNode* root, const char* name)
{
    Symbol*      sym;
    char         buffer[256];

    strcpy(buffer, name);

    // Initialize globals for bison
    symtable = NULL;
    errorFlag = FALSE;
    base = root;

    // Add the symbols x, y, z, and clock
    // to the symbol table.
    AddSymbol( "x",  VectorIdentifier );
```

```
if ((sym = LookupSymbol("x")) != NULL) {
      sym->vvalue.x = 1.0;
      sym->vvalue.y = 0.0;
      sym->vvalue.z = 0.0;
}

AddSymbol( "y",  VectorIdentifier );
if ((sym = LookupSymbol("y")) != NULL) {
      sym->vvalue.x = 0.0;
      sym->vvalue.y = 1.0;
      sym->vvalue.z = 0.0;
}

AddSymbol( "z",  VectorIdentifier );
if ((sym = LookupSymbol("z")) != NULL) {
      sym->vvalue.x = 0.0;
      sym->vvalue.y = 0.0;
      sym->vvalue.z = 1.0;
}

AddSymbol( "clock",  DoubleIdentifier );

// Open the file
if ((yyin = fopen(buffer, "r")) != NULL) {
      // Read the file
      yyinit();
      initFile(buffer, yyin, 1);
      yyparse();
      fclose( yyin );

      if (pov_root != NULL) {
            // Convert the file into our internal format
            root->AddChild(pov_root->ConvertAll());
      }
} else {
      yyerror("Unable to open file '%s'\n", buffer);
      DeleteSymbolTable();
      return FALSE;
}

// Clean up
DeleteSymbolTable();
if (pov_root != NULL) {
      delete pov_root;
      pov_root = NULL;

}
```

```
    if (!errorFlag) {
          yyStatusMessage("Reading Complete");
    }

    return (!errorFlag);
}
```

Highlights of the POVRay Parser

The Bison BNF described in the file pov_gram.y is large. You have seen several Bison BNF files described in gory detail in previous chapters. Since this file is so large, and the signal-to-noise ratio is low, I focus on the portions of the grammar that are necessary to convey the overall organization of the parser.

Supported Shapes

Three shapes are supported for conversion into the VRML-style internal format: a smooth triangle, a triangle, and sphere. All shapes have a similar definition, which consists of two parts. The first part recognizes the shape specified with a predefined identifier. Thus shapes can be defined using the declare statement and reused throughout the POVRay file. The second part is the definition of an instance of that shape.

The definition of a shape causes an instance of that shape to be pushed onto the shape stack. The object at the top of the shape stack becomes the target of subsequent definitions when resolving the *ShapeModifier* production. When the shape has been parsed, the top of the shape stack is popped and that value is returned as the result of the shape production.

```
SmoothTriangle: SMOOTHTRIANGLE_TOK '{' ShapeIdentifier
    {
          if ($3 != NULL && $3->ovalue != NULL) {
                yyPush($3->ovalue->Copy());
          } else {
                yyPush(NULL);
          }
    }
    ShapeModifiers '}'
    {
          $$ = yyCurrentObject();
          yyPop();
    }

|   SMOOTHTRIANGLE_TOK '{'
          Vector NextVector NextVector
```

```
            NextVector NextVector NextVector
        {
            Vector v1, v2, v3, v4, v5, v6;

            v1 = $3; v2 = $4; v3 = $5;
            v4 = $6; v5 = $7; v6 = $8;
            Triangle* bp = new Triangle(
                  v1.x, v1.y, v1.z,
                  v3.x, v3.y, v3.z,
                  v5.x, v5.y, v5.z);
            yyPush(bp);
        }
        ShapeModifiers '}'
        {
            $$ = yyCurrentObject();
            yyPop();
        }
;

Sphere:         SPHERE_TOK '{' ShapeIdentifier
        {
            if ($3 != NULL && $3->ovalue != NULL) {
                  yyPush($3->ovalue->Copy());
            } else {
                  yyPush(NULL);
            }
        }
        ShapeModifiers '}'
        {
            $$ = yyCurrentObject();
            yyPop();
        }

|       SPHERE_TOK '{' Vector NextDouble
        {
            yyPush(new Sphere($3.x, $3.y, $3.z, $4));
        }
        ShapeModifiers '}'
        {
            $$ = yyCurrentObject();
            yyPop();
        }
;

Triangle: TRIANGLE_TOK '{' ShapeIdentifier
        {
            if ($3 != NULL && $3->ovalue != NULL) {
                  yyPush($3->ovalue->Copy());
```

```
                } else {
                        yyPush(NULL);
                }
        }
        ShapeModifiers '}'
        {
                $$ = yyCurrentObject();
                yyPop();
        }
;

|       TRIANGLE_TOK '{' Vector NextVector NextVector
        {
                yyPush(new Triangle(
                        $3.x, $3.y, $3.z,
                        $4.x, $4.y, $4.z,
                        $5.x, $5.y, $5.z));
        }
        ShapeModifiers '}'
        {
                $$ = yyCurrentObject();
                yyPop();
        }
;
```

Textures

Textures are applied to the object that is on the top of the object stack. This is the object that is currently being defined in the POVRay parser.

Textures are defined as part of the *ShapeModifier* production. A texture has two possible components: a pigment or color and a finish. The *ShapeModifier* production defines both of these components and applies them to the current object.

```
ShapeModifier:
                .
                .
                .
|               Color
                {
                        Object* bp = yyCurrentObject();
                        if (bp != NULL) {
                                bp->SetColor($1);
                        }
                }
|               Textures
                {
```

```
                Object* bp = yyCurrentObject();
                if (bp != NULL && $1 != NULL) {
                        bp->Ambient($1->Ambient());
                        bp->Diffuse($1->Diffuse());
                        bp->Specular($1->Specular());
                        bp->Reflection($1->Reflection());
                        bp->SetColor($1->GetColor());
                }
                if ($1 != NULL) {
                        delete $1;
                }
        }
        .
        .
        .
;
```

The color components are defined using the production *ColorComponents*, which resolves multiple color definitions, and *ColorComponent*, which defines a color component. For this implementation, only simple color definitions are supported, thereby allowing the implementation of a simple mechanism for handling multiple color entries. All that needs to be done is to add the color components together. For example, consider this color definition:

```
color red 1.0 green 0.4 blue 0.6
```

This definition has three color components. If each is summed with the previous color component, the final result is the expected color value of (1.0, 0.4, 0.6).

```
ColorComponents: ColorComponent    {$$ = $1;}
|         ColorComponents ColorComponent
          {
                $$.r = $1.r + $2.r;
                $$.g = $1.g + $2.g;
                $$.b = $1.b + $2.b;
                $$.f = $1.f + $2.f;
          }
;
```

Each color component is defined using the *ColorComponent* production. This production returns the color that corresponds to the detected component.

```
ColorComponent: RED_TOK Double
          {
```

```
                $$.r = $2;
                $$.g = $$.b = $$.f = 0.0;
          }
|         GREEN_TOK Double
          {
                $$.g = $2;
                $$.r = $$.b = $$.f = 0.0;
          }
|         BLUE_TOK Double
          {
                $$.b = $2;
                $$.g = $$.r = $$.f = 0.0;
          }
|         RGBF_TOK '<' Double NextDouble
                      NextDouble NextDouble '>'
          {
                $$.r = $3;
                $$.g = $4;
                $$.b = $5;
                $$.f = $6;
          }
|         RGB_TOK Vector
          {
                $$.r = $2.x;
                $$.g = $2.y;
                $$.b = $2.z;
                $$.f = 0.0;
          }
|         ColorIdentifier
          {
                $$ = $1->cvalue;
          }
          .
          .
          .
;
```

The *FinishParameter* production defines the surface properties of the texture, including the ambient, diffuse, specular, and reflection properties. The values encountered are directly applied to the current object on the stack.

```
FinishParameter:
          .
          .
          .
    |     AMBIENT_TOK Double
          {
```

```
                if (yyCurrentObject() != NULL) {
                        yyCurrentObject()->Ambient($2);
                }
        }
    |   DIFFUSE_TOK Double
        {
                if (yyCurrentObject() != NULL) {
                        yyCurrentObject()->Diffuse($2);
                }
        }
    |   SPECULAR_TOK Double
        {
                if (yyCurrentObject() != NULL) {
                        yyCurrentObject()->Specular($2);
                }
        }
    |   REFLECTION_TOK Double
        {
                if (yyCurrentObject()!=NULL) {
                        yyCurrentObject()->Specular($2);
                }
        }
    |   Finish
        {
                Object* bp = yyCurrentObject();
                if ($1 != NULL) {
                        if (bp != NULL) {
                                bp->Ambient($1->Ambient());
                                bp->Diffuse($1->Diffuse());
                                bp->Specular($1->Specular());
                                bp->Reflection($1-
>Reflection());
                        }
                        delete $1;
                }
        }
        .
        .
        .
    ;
```

Transformations

Transformations are applied to individual objects in POVRay. They are defined using the *Transformation* production, which causes the transformation to be read and then attached to the current object. The transformations supported by POVRay are translate, rotate, and scale.

```
Transformation: TRANSLATE_TOK  Vector
    {
          if (yyCurrentObject() != NULL) {
                yyCurrentObject()->Translate($2.x, $2.y,
$2.z);
          }
    }
|   ROTATE_TOK Double
    {
          if (yyCurrentObject() != NULL) {
                yyCurrentObject()->Rotate($2, $2, $2);
          }
    }
|   ROTATE_TOK Vector
    {
          if (yyCurrentObject() != NULL) {
                yyCurrentObject()->Rotate($2.x, $2.y, $2.z);
          }
    }
|   SCALE_TOK Double
    {
          if (yyCurrentObject() != NULL) {
                yyCurrentObject()->Scale($2, $2, $2);
          }
    }
|   SCALE_TOK Vector
    {
          if (yyCurrentObject() != NULL) {
                yyCurrentObject()->Scale($2.x, $2.y, $2.z);
          }
    }
;
```

Scalar and Vector Definitions

The definition of the scalar and vector expressions is key to the backwards compatibility of POVRay V2.2 with earlier versions. The POVRay grammar defined in the reader evaluates the expressions encountered as they are read. This process simplifies the definition of the expression, since parse trees do not have to be defined for the expression.

Using a Bison grammar to define the expression will allow the expression to be easily extended as POVRay continues to develop.

Notice that a vector definition may contain one, two, or three double values. This allows the evaluation of expressions and the evaluation of earlier POVRay syntax in the same definition. However, the price paid for this ability is the possibly incorrect evaluation of earlier POVRay vectors.

The following defines the expression productions found in the file pov_gram.y:

```
Vector:    '<' Double OptNextDouble OptNextDouble '>'
           {
                  $$.x = $2; $$.y = $3; $$.z = $4;
           }
|          VectorIdentifier {$$ = $1->vvalue;}
|          Vector '+' Vector
           {
                  $$.x = $1.x + $3.x;
                  $$.y = $1.y + $3.y;
                  $$.z = $1.z + $3.z;
           }
|          Vector '-' Vector
           {
                  $$.x = $1.x - $3.x;
                  $$.y = $1.y - $3.y;
                  $$.z = $1.z - $3.z;
           }
|          Vector '*' Vector
           {
                  $$.x = $1.x * $3.x;
                  $$.y = $1.y * $3.y;
                  $$.z = $1.z * $3.z;
           }
|          Vector '*' Double
           {
                  $$.x = $1.x * $3;
                  $$.y = $1.y * $3;
                  $$.z = $1.z * $3;
           }
|          Double '*' Vector
           {
                  $$.x = $1 * $3.x;
                  $$.y = $1 * $3.y;
                  $$.z = $1 * $3.z;
           }
|          Vector '/' Vector
           {
                  $$.x = $1.x / $3.x;
                  $$.y = $1.y / $3.y;
                  $$.z = $1.z / $3.z;
           }
|          Double '/' Vector
           {
                  $$.x = $1 / $3.x;
                  $$.y = $1 / $3.y;
```

```
                $$.z = $1 / $3.z;
            }
|           Vector '/' Double
            {
                $$.x = $1.x / $3;
                $$.y = $1.y / $3;
                $$.z = $1.z / $3;
            }
|           '(' Vector ')' {$$ = $2;}
|           '-' Vector %prec UNARY
            {
                $$.x = -2.x;
                $$.y = -2.y;
                $$.z = -2.z;
            }
|           '+' Vector %prec UNARY
            {
                $$.x = 2.x;
                $$.y = 2.y;
                $$.z = 2.z;
            }
;

OptNextDouble:  /* empty */ {$$ = 0.0;}
    |           NextDouble  {$$ = $1;}
    ;

NextDouble:     ',' Double
                {$$ = $2;}
    |           DOUBLEVAL_TOK
                {$$=$1;}
    |           DoubleIdentifier
                {$$ = $1->dvalue;}
    ;

Double:         DOUBLEVAL_TOK                {$$=$1;}
    |           DoubleIdentifier             {$$ = $1->dvalue;}
    |           Double '+' Double            {$$ = $1 + $3;}
    |           Double '-' Double            {$$ = $1 - $3;}
    |           Double '*' Double            {$$ = $1 * $3;}
    |           Double '/' Double            {$$ = $1 - $3;}
    |           '(' Double ')'               {$$ = $2;}
    |           '-' Double %prec UNARY       {$$ = -$2;}
    |           '+' Double %prec UNARY       {$$ = $2;}
    ;
```

The POVRay Lexical Analyzer

The POVRay lexical analyzer is found in the file pov_lex.l. Its organization is very similar to that of other Flex-based lexical analyzers described in this book. However, it has one unique feature: It can handle inline include files.

An inline include file is a POVRay language construct that specifies that a specific file is to be inserted into the file and the contents read as if they were a part of the current file. This capability is implemented by creating a file stack in the lexical analyzer.

The following production from pov_gram.y demonstrates how the lexical analyzer is called to initiate the reading of an include file. The function `pushFile()` is called with the full include file pathname. This function saves the current parse state, opens the new file, and resets the lexical analyzer to continue parsing at the beginning of the new file.

```
Include:        OptPound INCLUDE_TOK STRINGVAL_TOK
    {
            FILE  *fp = NULL;
            char  buffer[256];
            long i;

            // Check the povray path list
            for (i=0; i < incIndex; i++) {
                  sprintf(buffer, "%s\\%s", incList[i], $3);
                  if ((fp = fopen(buffer, "r")) != NULL) {
                        break;
                  }
            }

            if (fp != NULL) {
                  // Found the file, now load it.
                  fclose(fp);
                  pushFile(buffer);
            } else {
                  // Oops, didn't find the file.
                  YYERROR;
            }
    }
    ;
```

When the end of the include file is encountered, the command `yywrap()` is called. `yywrap()` calls the function `popFile()`, which closes the current file and replaces the lexical analyzer state with the previously saved state. Parsing then continues from the point after the include statement was encountered. The definition of `yywrap()` follows:

```
// Handle the End-Of-File for the current file.
int yywrap(void)
{
    return popFile();
}
```

The Lexical Analyzer Expressions

Table 10.2 defines the regular expressions of the lexical analyzer and the actions that result. Note that some expressions may execute one of several possible actions depending on the current value of the matched expression.

Table 10.2. Regular expressions and actions of the lexical analyzer

<table>
<tr><th>Expression</th><th>Action</th><th>Comments</th></tr>
<tr><td>/*</td><td>None</td><td>Recognizes a C-style comment. The rest of this comment is parsed using the function <code>yycomment()</code>. This allows arbitrarily large comments that can be read without having to enlarge the lexical analyzer's input buffer.</td></tr>
<tr><td>“//”[^\n\r]*</td><td>None</td><td>Recognizes C++-style comments.</td></tr>
<tr><td>[\t]+</td><td>None</td><td>Recognizes whitespace.</td></tr>
<tr><td>“\n”|“\r”|“\r\n”|“\n\r”</td><td>None</td><td>Recognizes all permutations of a newline.</td></tr>
<tr><td>[0-9]+(\.[0-9]*)?[Ee][\+\-]?[0-9]+|
[0-9]+\.[0-9]+[Ee][\+\-]?[0-9]+|
([0-9]*)\.[0-9]+|
[0-9]+</td><td>DOUBLEVAL_TOK</td><td>Recognizes floating-point numbers, which are returned as the type DOUBLEVAL_TOK.</td></tr>
<tr><td>[a-zA-Z0-9_]+</td><td>Keyword token, an identifier, or an ID_TOK</td><td>Recognizes alphanumeric strings. The string is first checked against the keywords in the keyword table. If a match is found, then the token value associated with the keyword is returned. If no keyword match is found, then the global symbol table is checked to see if a symbol with that current string has been defined. If it has, then that associated identifier token is returned. If no matches</td></tr>
</table>

(*continued*)

Table 10.2. Regular expressions and actions of the lexical analyzer *(continued)*

Expression	Action	Comments
		are found in either table, the ID_TOK value is returned.
\"(\\.|[^\n\\"])*\"	STRINGVAL_TOK	Recognizes double-quoted strings and returns the token STRING-VAL_TOK.

Implementing a POVRay Writer

To create a POVRay file format writer, you have to write a small amount of C++ code that will convert the internal representation of 3D objects into polygons. This conversion may not take full advantage of POVRay's capabilities. However, it is very easy to do and will allow POVRay to read and render the internal representation.

For each recognized *GNode* instance encountered, the `GNode::Write()` member function traverses the scene and the appropriate member function of a *GWrite* derived class is called. This process allows implementers to write POVRay file format writers without having to know the details of the internal representation of 3D objects. Also, the internal representation allows 3D objects to be converted to polygons. So to implement a POVRay writer, you need only tell the internal representation that the POVRay writer implementer supports only polygons and then writes out the polygons as POVRay triangles.

The following class definition describes the *GWritePOVRay* derived *GWrite* class:

```
class GWritePOVRay : public GWrite {
private:
    char               m_name[256];
    MeshCompactor      m_mesh;

public:
    GWritePOVRay(void)  : GWrite() {strcpy(m_name, "");}
    short PolygonSupported(void)   {return TRUE;}
    void  Epilog(GNode*, GState&);

    void  Polygon(GState&, long, MFVec3f*, MFVec3f* = NULL,
           GWriteMaterial* = NULL);
};
```

Handling Polygons

The `Polygon()` member function is called for every polygon encountered during the traversal of the 3D representation for the current objects. The polygons are placed into a *MeshCompactor* instance so that each group can later be emitted individually. The conversion into a POVRay file is handled in the `Epilog()` member function.

```
void GWritePOVRay::
Polygon(GState& state, long faceNum, MFVec3f* v,
                MFVec3f* n, GWriteMaterial* m)
{
    // Notice Name changes
    if (state.HeirName() != NULL &&
                strcmp(m_name, state.HeirName()) != 0) {
          m_mesh.Name(state.HeirName());
          strcpy(m_name, state.HeirName());
    }

    // Add polygon
    m_mesh.BeginPolygon(m);
    for (int i = 0; i < v->Elements(); i++) {
          m_mesh.AddVertex((*v)[i]);
    }
    m_mesh.EndPolygon();
}
```

Emitting the POVRay File

The `Epilog()` member function is called after the 3D objects in the internal representation have been completely traversed. At this point, the internal representation for the 3D objects are now available in the *MeshCompactor* instance *m_mesh*.

For converting the representation into the form required for the POVRay file, several items must be emitted. First, a default camera position is calculated and emitted. Then the materials used are converted into an equivalent POVRay representation and emitted. Finally, the groups are emitted. Each polygon in a group is converted into one or more Triangle objects so that they can be written as a POVRay *Triangle* command.

```
void GWritePOVRay::
Epilog(GNode* root, GState& state)
{
    MFVec3f*    coords = m_mesh.Coordinates();
    GMaterial*  material = m_mesh.Material();
```

```
GState      lstate;
SFVec3f     lookat, position, up, direction;
SFVec3f     minRange(1000000.0, 1000000.0, 1000000.0);
SFVec3f     maxRange(-1000000.0, -100000.0, -1000000.0);

// Write info about converted object.
fprintf(m_fp, "/* Object converted by 3D Crossroads
        library */\n");

// Find range of 3D objects
root->Range(lstate, minRange, maxRange);

// Print Range information
fprintf(m_fp, "/* minimum range of the object (%f, %f,
        %f) */\n",
            minRange.X(), minRange.Y(), minRange.Z());
fprintf(m_fp, "/* maxiumum range of the object (%f, %f,
        %f) */\n",
            maxRange.X(), maxRange.Y(), maxRange.Z());

// Calculate a camera location
DefaultCamera(root, lookat, position, up);
direction = Normalize(lookat - position);

// Write the camera location
fprintf(m_fp, "camera {\n");
Indent(m_fp, 1);
fprintf(m_fp, "look_at <%f, %f, %f>\n",
            lookat.X(), lookat.Y(), lookat.Z());
Indent(m_fp, 1);
fprintf(m_fp, "location <%f, %f, %f>\n",
            position.X(), position.Y(), position.Z());
Indent(m_fp, 1);
fprintf(m_fp, "direction <%f, %f, %f>\n",
            direction.X(), direction.Y(),
direction.Z());
Indent(m_fp, 1);
fprintf(m_fp, "up <%f, %f, %f>\n",
            up.X(), up.Y(), up.Z());
Indent(m_fp, 1);
fprintf(m_fp, "right <640/480, 0, 0>\n");
fprintf(m_fp, "}\n\n");

// Create some default lights
fprintf(m_fp, "light_source {<%f, %f, %f> color rgb <1,
        1, 1>}\n",
            position.X(), position.Y(), position.Z());
fprintf(m_fp, "light_source {<%f, %f, %f> color rgb <1,
        1, 1>}\n\n",
```

```
                lookat.X(), lookat.Y() + position.Z(),
lookat.Z());

    // Write Materials
    if (material != NULL && material->Elements() > 0) {
          int   elements = material->Elements();

          // Look through each of the material
          for (int i = 0; i < elements; i++) {
                GWriteMaterial wmat =   (*material)[i];
                SFVec3f      color;
                SFFloat      diffuseValue, ambientValue,
                             transparency;

                // Convert material to an approximation
                // of that material in POVRay.
                color = wmat.Color();
                diffuseValue = (SFFloat) 1.0;
                ambientValue = wmat.AmbientCoefficient();
                transparency = wmat.Transparency();

                fprintf(m_fp, "#declare _Mat%d = texture
                        {\n", i);
                Indent(m_fp, 1);
                fprintf(m_fp, "pigment {rgbf <%f, %f, %f,
                        %f>}\n",
                             color.Red(), color.Green(),
                             color.Blue(),
                             transparency);
                Indent(m_fp, 1);
                fprintf(m_fp, "finish {ambient %f diffuse
                        %f}\n",
                             ambientValue, diffuseValue);
                fprintf(m_fp, "}\n");
          }
    }

    // Write Objects
    if (m_mesh.Groups() > 1) {
          fprintf(m_fp, "union {\n");
    } else {
          fprintf(m_fp, "object {\n");
    }

    // Cycle through each of the groups
    for (long group = 0; group < m_mesh.Groups(); group++) {
          MFLong*     faces = m_mesh.Faces(group);
```

```
MFLong* matIndex = m_mesh.MaterialIndex(group);
SFLong      faceCnt = 0;
SFLong      elements = (faces != NULL ? faces->
                          Elements() : 0);
short objflag;

// Print the name of the group
if (m_mesh.Name(group) != NULL) {
      Indent(m_fp, 1);
      fprintf(m_fp, "/* Group %s */\n",
             m_mesh.Name(group));
}

Indent(m_fp, 1);
for (int i = 0; i < elements; i++) {
      if ((*faces)[i] < 0) {
            faceCnt++;
      }
}
if (faceCnt > 1) {
      fprintf(m_fp, "union {\n");
      objflag = TRUE;
} else if (faceCnt > 0) {
      fprintf(m_fp, "object {\n");
      objflag = TRUE;
} else {
      objflag = FALSE;
}
faceCnt = 0;

// Print the face lists
if (elements > 0) {
      MFVec3f     polygon;
      for (int i = 0; i < elements; i++) {
            SFLong      face = (*faces)[i];
            if (face < 0) {
                  SFLong           polySize =
                  polygon.Elements();
                  SFLong      mat = 0;
                  if (matIndex != NULL) {
                        mat =
                  (*matIndex)[faceCnt];
                  }

                  for (int j = 2; j < polySize;
                  j++) {
                        SFVec3f     base  =
                  polygon[0],
```

```
                                                  first =
polygon[j-1],
                                                  second =
polygon[j];
                                        Indent(m_fp, 2);
                                        fprintf(m_fp, "triangle
{\n");
                                        Indent(m_fp, 3);
                                        fprintf(m_fp,"<%g, %g,
%g>,\n",
                                             base.X(), base.Y(),
base.Z());
                                        Indent(m_fp, 3);
                                        fprintf(m_fp,"<%g, %g,
%g>,\n",
                                             first.X(),
first.Y(), first.Z());
                                        Indent(m_fp, 3);
                                        fprintf(m_fp,"<%g, %g,
%g>\n",
                                             second.X(),
second.Y(), second.Z());
                                        if (matIndex != NULL) {
                                             Indent(m_fp, 3);
                                             fprintf(m_fp,
"texture {_Mat%d}\n", mat);
                                        }
                                        Indent(m_fp, 2);
                                        fprintf(m_fp, "}\n");
                                   }

                                   polygon.Clear();
                                   faceCnt++;
                              } else {
                                   SFVec3f     vertex =
(*coords)[face];
                                   polygon.Add(vertex);
                              }
                    }
          }
          if (objflag) {
                    Indent(m_fp, 1);
                    fprintf(m_fp, "}\n");
          }
     }
     fprintf(m_fp, "}\n");
}
```

References

Persistence of Vision Ray Tracer Version 2.0—User's Documentation. 1993. POV-Ray Team.

Young, Chris, and Drew Wells. *Ray Tracing Creations, Second Edition*. 1994. Corte Madera, Calif.: Waite Group Press.

Chapter 11

Building the Crossroads Class Library

In this chapter, I explain the organization of the directories found on the CD-ROM included with this book and describe how to recompile the *Crossroads* class library.

The CD-ROM contains the source code for the *Crossroads* class library, a 3D file conversion 32-bit Windows application with source, and a graphical 3D file conversion 32-bit OCX custom control. Using the *Crossroads* library does not require that you recompile the library's source. Precompiled versions of the library are on the CD-ROM and may be used directly with Visual C++. The source code is provided to allow the library to be ported to other environments, to be enhanced, or to be recompiled using different compilation flags.

The CD-ROM Directory Structure

The three items on the CD-ROM are in the following directories:

- `[CD-ROM]:\INCLUDE`. C++ headers for the *Crossroads* library.
- `[CD-ROM]:\LIB`. Visual C++ libraries for the *Crossroads* library.
- `[CD-ROM]:\XROAD`. Source code and Visual C++ project for the *Crossroads* library.
- `[CD-ROM]:\APPL`. Visual C++/MFC application that uses the *Crossroads* class library. This directory contains the Visual C++/MFC project for a 3D file format conversion application that can read 3D files, view them, and allow them to be written in another 3D file format.
- `[CD-ROM]:\OCX`. Visual C++ OCX custom control project. This directory contains a Visual C++ project for an OCX custom control that can read, write, and view 3D files. The resulting OCX control can be used in

Visual Basic, Delphi, Visual C++, or any other development language that supports 32-bit OCX custom controls.

- `[CD-ROM]:\TOOLS`. This directory contains the Windows 95 and Windows NT versions of the free GNU tools Bison, Flex, and Sed. These tools are required if you wish to change the BNF grammar or lexical analyzer associated with the VRML, POVRay, or World-Toolkit file formats. They are console applications with a UNIX-style interface. Their installation is a bit quirky (due to my laziness). Both Bison and Flex require a specific directory to exist on the drive on which you are installing. The installation script (found in `[CD-ROM]:\TOOLS\INSTALL.BAT`) describes the installation procedure. In most situations, executing `INSTALL.BAT` will cause the files to be installed properly.
- `[CD-ROM]:\INSTALL`. A setup application that will install a precompiled version of the 3D conversion application and the OCX custom control. Executing this setup application makes these items available in Windows 95 or Windows NT.

[CD-ROM]:\INCLUDE Directory Contents

The INCLUDE directory contains the C++ header files needed to recompile and use the *Crossroads* library. It contains the following files:

```
3DS.H          - 3DS Studio Reader/Writer Definition
BASE.H         - Defines GNode class library
CALIGARI.H     - TrueSpace Reader/Writer Definition
CAMERA.H       - Defines Camera Class
DXF.H          - DXF Reader/Writer Definition
LIGHT.H        - Defines Light Class
MATERIAL.H     - Defines Material Class
OBJ.H          - Wavefront OBJ Reader/Writer Definition
POLYMESH.H     - Defines Classes to define a polymesh
POVRAY.H       - POVRay Reader/Writer Definition
RAW.H          - RAW Reader/Writer Definition
SEPARATO.H     - Defines Separator Class
SHAPES.H       - Defines Shape Classes
TRANSFOR.H     - Defines Transformation Classes
VALUE.H        - Defines types for Class Library
WRITE.H        - Classes to aid in writing formats
WRL.H          - VRML Writer Definition
WTK.H          - WorldToolkit Reader/Writer Definition
XROADS.H       - Crossroads Class Library Include
```

[CD-ROM]:\LIB Directory Contents

The LIB directory contains these precompiled *Crossroads* libraries:

```
XROAD32D.LIB      - Visual C++ debug class library.
XROAD32.LIB       - Visual C++ release class library.
```

[CD-ROM]:\XROAD Directory Contents

The XROAD directory contains all of the files that implement the *Crossroads* library. Some are in subdirectories that correspond to each of the supported file formats. Following is a list of those files:

```
3DS <DIR>              - Files for 3DS Reader/Writer
3DS\3DS.CPP            - 3DS Reader/Writer Implementation

BASE <DIR>             - Base Crossroads support files
BASE\BASE.CPP          - GNode Class Implementation
BASE\CAMERA.CPP        - Camera Classes Implementation
BASE\LIGHT.CPP         - Light Classes Implementation
BASE\MATERIAL.CPP      - Material Classes Implementation
BASE\POLYMESH.CPP      - Mesh Classes Implementation
BASE\SEPARATO.CPP      - Separator Classes Implementation
BASE\SHAPES.CPP        - Shape Classes Implementation
BASE\TRANSFOR.CPP      - Transform Classes Implementation
BASE\VALUE.CPP         - Value Classes Implementation

DXF <DIR>              - Files for DXF Reader/Writer
DXF\DXF.CPP            - DXF Reader/Writer Implementation

POVRAY <DIR>           - Files for POVRay Reader/Writer
POVRAY\POV_GRAM.CPP    - C++ version of POVRay Grammar
POVRAY\POV_GRAM.H      - Grammar Include File
POVRAY\POV_GRAM.Y      - Bison Grammar Definition
POVRAY\POV_LEX.CPP     - C++ Lexical Analyzer
POVRAY\POV_LEX.L       - Flex Lexical Analyzer Definition
POVRAY\POVRAY.CPP      - POVRay Writer Implementation
POVRAY\SYMBOL.H        - POVRay Symbol Table
POVRAY\UPDATE.BAT      - Turns POV_GRAM.Y & POV_LEX.L to C++

RAW <DIR>              - Files for RAW Reader/Writer
RAW\RAW.CPP            - RAW Reader/Writer Implementation

TRUSPACE <DIR>         - Files for COB Reader/Writer
CALIGAR.CPP            - COB Reader/Writer Implementation
```

```
VRML <DIR>              - Files for VRML Reader
VRML\SYMTBL.CPP         - Symbol Table Implementation
VRML\SYMTBL.H           - Symbol Table Definition
VRML\UPDATE.BAT         - Turns WRL_GRAM.Y & WRL_LEX.L into C++
VRML\WRL.CPP            - VRML Reader/Writer Entry Points
VRML\WRL_GRAM.CPP       - VRML Grammar Implementation in C++
VRML\WRL_GRAM.H         - VRML Grammar Header
VRML\WRL_GRAM.Y         - VRML Bison Grammar Description
VRML\WRL_LEX.CPP        - VRML Lexical Analyzer in C++
VRML\WRL_LEX.L          - VRML Lexical Analyzer Definition

WAVEFNT <DIR>           - Files for OBJ Reader/Writer
WAVEFNT\OBJ.CPP         - OBJ Reader/Writer Implementation

WTK_NFF <DIR>           - Files for NFF Reader/Writer
NFF_GRAM.CPP            - NFF Grammar Implementation in C++
NFF_GRAM.H              - NFF Grammar Header
NFF_GRAM.Y              - NFF Bison Grammar Description
NFF_LEX.CPP             - NFF Lexical Analyzer in C++
NFF_LEX.L               - NFF Lexical Analyzer Definition
UPDATE.BAT              - Turns NFF_GRAM.Y & NFF_LEX.L into C++
WTK.CPP                 - NFF Writer Implementation

XROADS.CPP              - Functions to aid access to library
XROAD.MDP               - Crossroads Visual C++ Project
XROAD.MAK               - Crossroads Visual C++ Makefile
```

Recompiling the Crossroads Class Library

Recompiling the *Crossroads* library is very straightforward. If you follow the steps in the subsequent sections, recompiling should take only a few minutes.

Requirements

The *Crossroads* library included with the source code on the CD-ROM was created using Visual C++ 4.0, so recompiling the library requires Visual C++ 4.0 or later. The library's source code requires about 1M of disk space. Compiling both the debug and release versions of the library requires approximately 20M.

Rebuilding the Crossroads Release Version

To rebuild the release version of the *Crossroads* library, recursively copy the INCLUDE and XROAD directories so that all of the subdirectories and files from the CD-ROM are placed in an equivalent directory structure on your hard drive. With Windows 95, you do this by using the Explorer. With Windows NT, you do it with the File Manager.

Next, invoke the Visual C++ 4.0 or later compiler. Select the project XROAD\XROAD.MDP, ensuring it is set to Release. Then start the build by selecting the menu item Build/Rebuild All or pressing Alt-F8. The build should complete with only a handful of warnings (from unused variables generated in the Bison parser). Figure 11.1 shows the build environment of Visual C++.

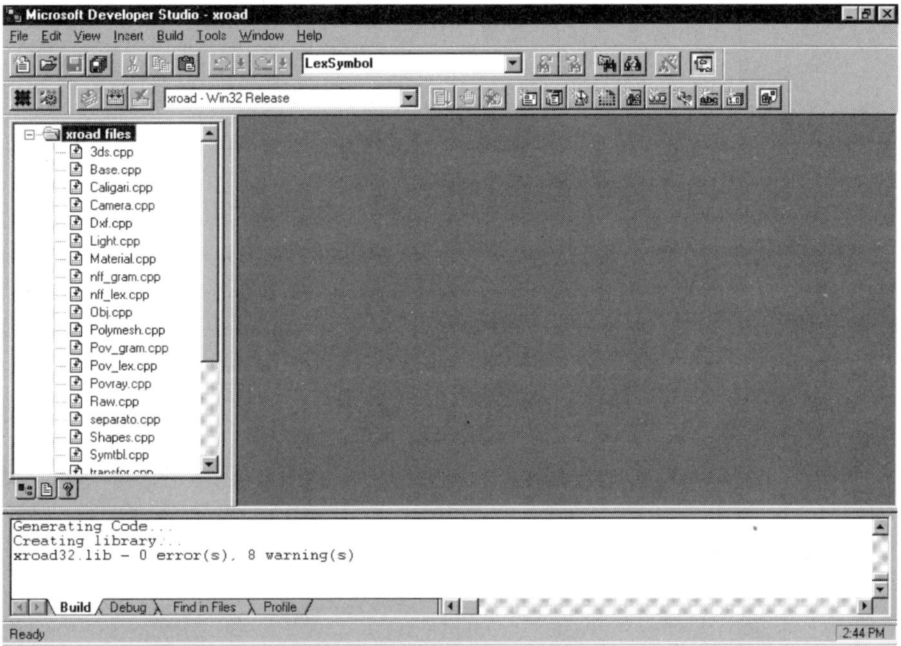

Figure 11.1. Visual C++ build environment.

After compilation, the resultant library is placed in the LIB directory as XROAD32.LIB. This directory is at the same level as the INCLUDE directory. Placing the library here makes it immediately available to other projects. If you want to make a local version of the library, select Build/Settings/Link.

To select a working directory for the library, you need to replace the output file name of ..\LIB\XROAD32.LIB with some other path and filename (see Figure 11.2). I usually use Release\XROAD32.LIB, which places the library in the current release's working directory. However, you can place the file wherever is most convenient for you.

The XROAD\XROAD.MDP project has several preprocessor definitions that may be altered (see Figure 11.3). Most used in this project are common

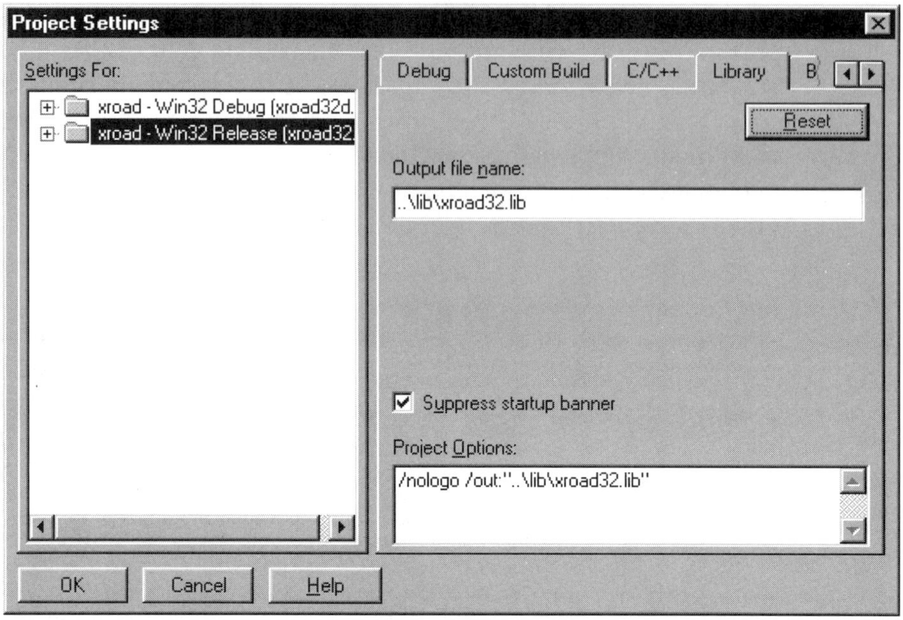

Figure 11.2. Project settings for the Visual C++ build library.

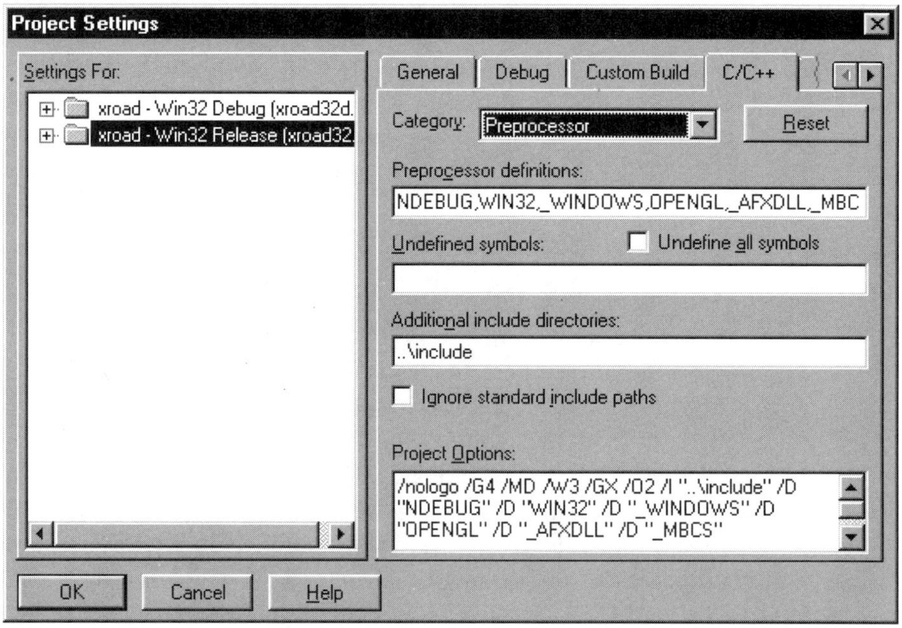

Figure 11.3. Preprocessor settings for the Visual C++ building preprocessor.

to static libraries. The OPENGL preprocessor flag, however, is unique to this project. This flag inserts or removes the OpenGL calls that are used to display a 3D scene. When it is present, the library is compiled with OpenGL function calls; otherwise, the library omits any OpenGL calls. This allows programs like console applications that do not require the scene represented by the *Crossroads* library to be drawn to simply omit that code. By default, the OPENGL preprocessor definition is defined in the project.

The *Crossroads* library has been written so as to not use any MFC specific classes or functions. This was done to increase the chances of the library's being ported to other environments. However, if the library is going to be used with an MFC application, it should be compiled as if it used the MFC class library. This will ensure that the C++ functions `new` and `delete` that are used in the *Crossroads* library are compatible with the MFC application.

To use the MFC class library, select Build/Settings/General. Then in the Microsoft Foundation Class combo box, choose "Use MFC in a Shared DLL" (the default). See Figure 11.4.

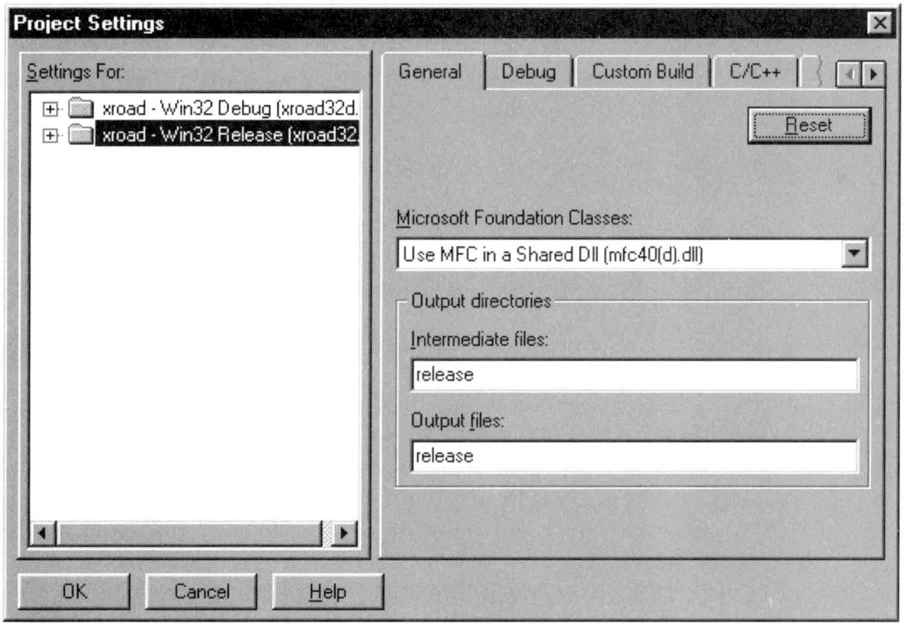

Figure 11.4. General project settings for the Visual C++ build.

Rebuilding the Crossroads Debug Version

Rebuilding the debug version of the *Crossroads* library is very similar to rebuilding the release version. If you haven't already copied the *Crossroads* class library source to your hard drive, do this by recursively copying the INCLUDE and XROAD directories so that all of the subdirectories and files from the CD-ROM are placed in an equivalent directory structure on your hard drive. With Windows 95, do this by using the Explorer. With Windows NT, do it with the File Manager.

Next, invoke the Visual C++ 4.0 or later compiler. Select the project XROAD\XROAD.MDP. Then select the combo box on the project toolbar and choose the subproject "xroad - W32 Debug" to make it the active project.

To recompile, chose the Build-all icon from the project toolbar or the Build/Rebuild All menu item.

After compilation, the resultant library is placed in the LIB directory as XROAD32D.LIB. This is at the same level as the INCLUDE directory. Placing the library here makes it immediately available to other projects. If you want to make a local version of the library, select Build/Settings/Link.

To select a working directory for the library you need to replace the output file name of ..\LIB\XROAD32D.LIB with some other path and filename. I usually use Debug\XROAD32D.LIB, which places the library in the current release's working directory. However, you can place the file wherever is most convenient for you.

As with the release version of the *Crossroads* class library, the preprocessor definition OPENGL is defined by default. To remove it, select Build/Settings.../C/C++ and then the Preprocessor category. From there, select the definition in the *Definition* field and delete it. When the project is rebuilt after this change, all OpenGL function calls will have been removed.

The *Crossroads* class library has been written so as to not require any MFC specific classes or functions. This was done to increase the chances of the library's being ported to other environments. However, if the library is going to be used with an MFC application, it should be compiled as if it used the MFC class library. This will ensure that the C++ functions `new` and `delete` that are used in the *Crossroads* library are compatible with the MFC application.

To use the MFC class library, select Build/Settings/General. Then in the Microsoft Foundation Class combo box, choose "Use MFC in a Shared DLL" (the default).

Special Considerations

Like VRML and WTK-NFF, POVRay uses a Bison parser and Flex lexical analyzer. To recompile the XROAD\XROAD.MDP project after changing a Bison or Flex file requires the corresponding parser and lexical analyzer C/C++ source code to be regenerated. This is done using the UPDATE.BAT file in each subdirectory. This batch file must be run whenever you change the Bison or Flex file.

The UPDATE.BAT file performs several operations. First, it converts the Bison parser definition into a C/C++ file. That file is run through the GNU Sed program, which substitutes the symbol POV for all occurrences of yy or YY in the source code. This substitution is done because several Bison parsers and Flex lexical analyzers are going to be compiled into the same application. Running these Sed scripts allows each Bison and Flex source code to have a unique set of variable and function names so that there is no name collision at compile or link time.

After the Sed program has processed and renamed the file, the file created by Bison is erased. A similar series of steps is performed on the header file that was produced by Bison from the parser definition.

The final set of operations converts the Flex lexical analyzer description to a C/C++ file. It then creates unique variable and function names for the source by running the same Sed script on it as was run on the Bison parser. These variable and function names match those in the parser.

```
bison -dv pov_gram.y
sed -e s/yy/POV/g -e s/YY/POV/g < POV_gram.tab.c >
pov_gram.cpp
erase pov_gram.tab.c
sed -e s/yy/POV/g -e s/YY/POV/g < POV_gram.tab.h >
pov_gram.h
erase pov_gram.tab.h
flex pov_lex.l
sed -e s/yy/POV/g -e s/YY/POV/g < lex.yy.c > pov_lex.cpp
erase lex.yy.c
erase pov_gram.output
```

Portability Issues

The source code for the C++ class library is intended to be portable. However, it has not been ported to any other C++ development environment or computer platform. The rule-of-thumb that many people use with supposedly portable code is that "it ain't portable unless you've ported it." I believe the changes required to port the *Crossroads* class library to another development environment (like Borland C++) or to another computer platform (like the Macintosh) are minimal, but I'm not making any promises. If you do port source to another platform, please let me (keithr@europa.com) know about it so that I can make the changes available to other users.

Byte Ordering Issues

The *Crossroads* class library supports two binary file formats: 3D Studio (3DS) and TrueSpace (COB). Some computer platforms use a different ordering for integer and floating-point values than do Intel-based PCs. If you intend to port the source code to another computer platform where the byte ordering differs from an Intel processor's, you will need to modify the *Crossroads* source code that reads and writes numeric values. This code is isolated in a series of inline functions that are defined in the C++ header file `[CD-ROM]:\include\write.h`. If you are familiar with byte-ordering issues, the changes should be straightforward. For more information on byte ordering, see Chapters 6 and 8.

Chapter 12

Building a 3D File Conversion Windows Application

In this chapter, I discuss the steps for creating an application using the *Crossroads* class library that can open, view, and save 3D files. These steps are:

1. create a skeleton application,
2. create a *CDocument* class,
3. add file open and save capabilities, and
4. create an OpenGL CView.

The application was created with Visual C++ 4.0 and uses the Microsoft Foundation Class (MFC) class library. It is an SDI (single document interface) application that uses MFC's Document/View model for representing and displaying a 3D model or scene. The document is derived from the MFC *CDocument* class. The *Crossroads* class library is added to a *CDocument* derived class. The *CView* derived class uses OpenGL to display the contents of the *CDocument* class as a wireframe.

This is a "cookbook" approach to building this project. It is not intended as a tutorial on OpenGL, Visual C++, or MFC. If you want more information on these topics, see the references listed at the end of the chapter.

Creating a Skeleton Application

Invoke the Microsoft Developers Studio (MDS). This brings up the workspace for the Visual C++ 4.0 compiler. To start a new application, select File/New... . The New dialog appears showing several possible selections. Select "Project Workspace." The "New Project Workspace" dialog appears (see Figure 12.1). Select a type of "MFC AppWizard (exe)" and a project name of "xroad."

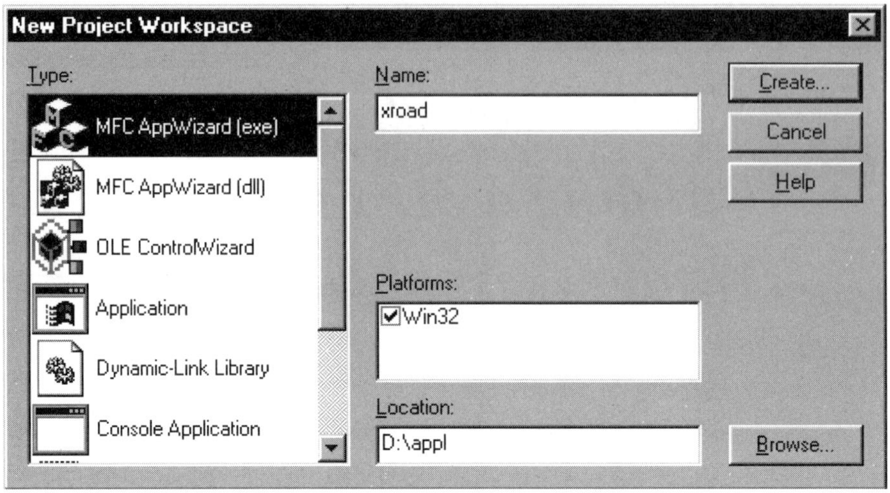

Figure 12.1. New Project Workspace.

Click the Create… button and Step 1 of the AppWizard appears (see Figure 12.2). This step allows you to select the type of project you want to build. In this case, select "Single document" and click Next>.

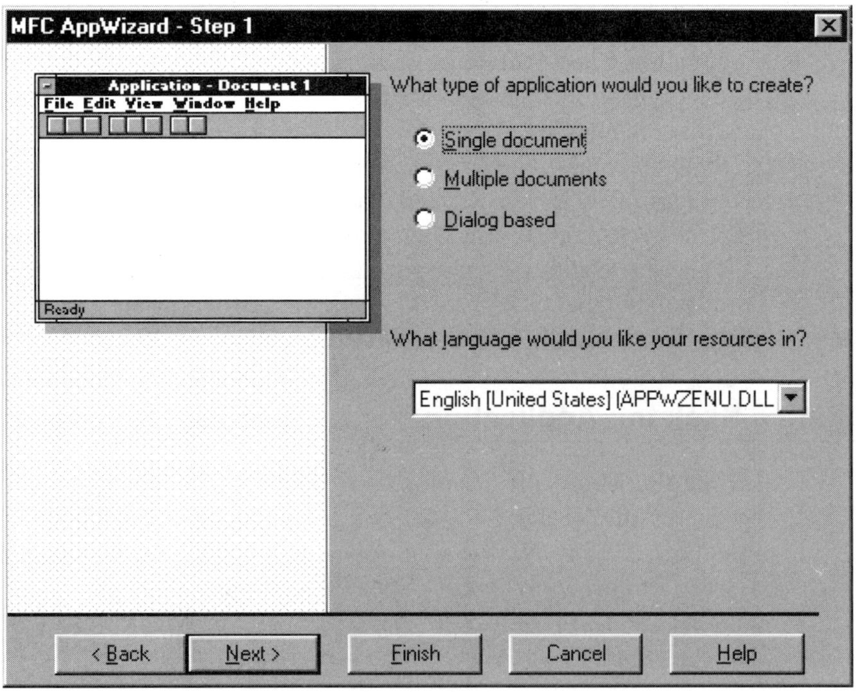

Figure 12.2. Step 1 of the AppWizard: Selecting the type of project.

Step 2 of the AppWizard allows you to select the type of database support an application needs (see Figure 12.3). You don't need database support for this application, so leave the default setting of "None." To move to the next screen, click Next>.

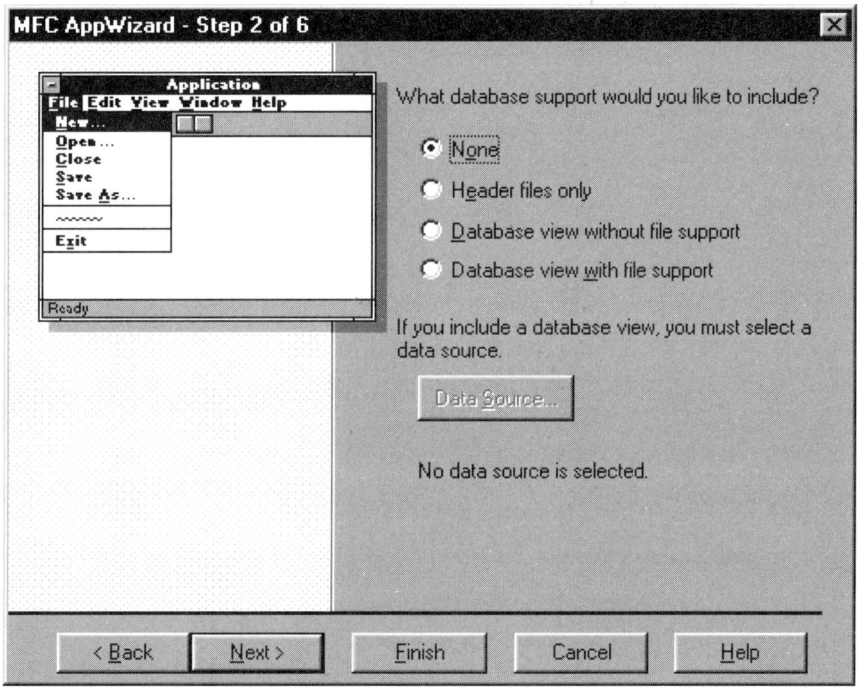

Figure 12.3. Step 2 of the AppWizard: Selecting the type of database support.

With step 3 of the AppWizard, you select the type of OLE support for the application (see Figure 12.4). This application will not be an OLE server or container, so set the type of document support to "None." However, although OLE automation and OLE controls are not needed for this application, I usually enable them for all applications I build. OLE automation allows you to define an external programming interface to your application. I like to use it to write test scripts for my applications. OLE controls support allows you to use OCX custom controls in the application.

After you make these selections, click Next>.

Step 4 of the AppWizard allows you to select several features of the application (see Figure 12.5). In this case, you want to support a toolbar, a status bar, and 3D controls. After you make these selections, click Next>.

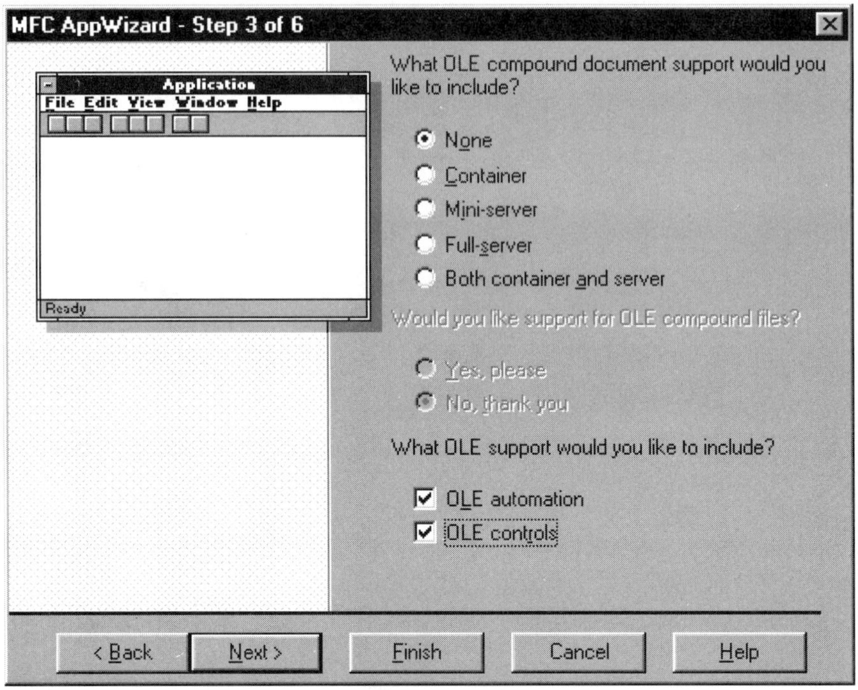

Figure 12.4. Step 3 of the AppWizard: Selecting the type of OLE support.

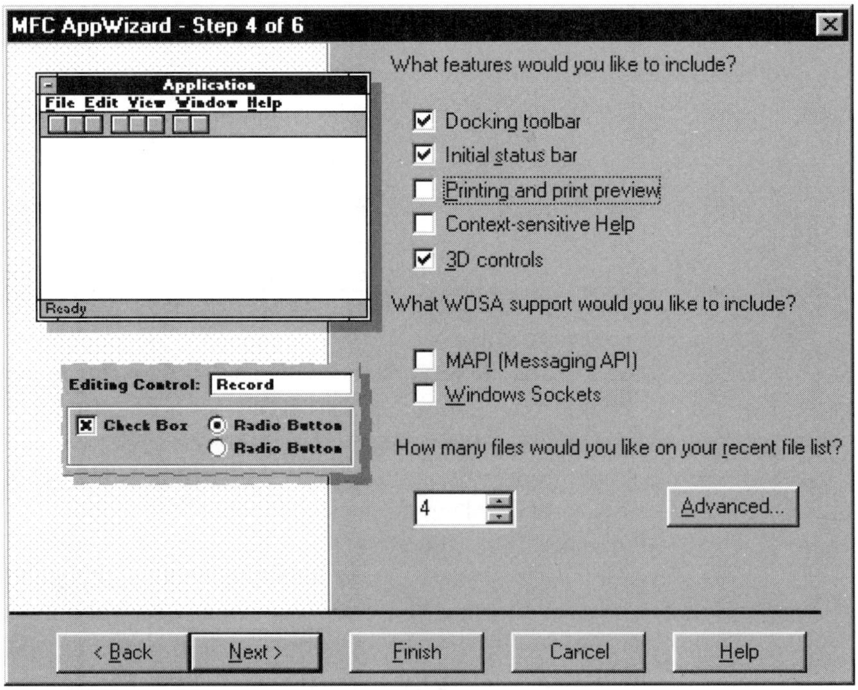

Figure 12.5. Step 4 of the AppWizard: Selecting features.

Step 5 of the AppWizard allows you to generate comments and to decide which type of MFC library to use (see Figure 12.6). Select the default settings of "Yes" and "As a shared DLL." Click Next> to continue.

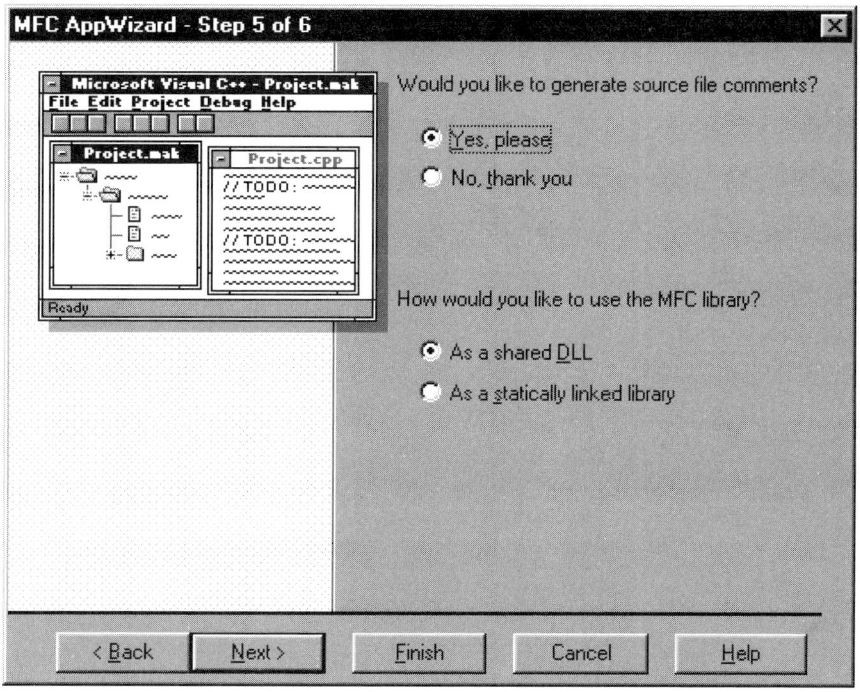

Figure 12.6. Step 5 of the AppWizard: Generating comments and selecting the type of library.

With Step 6 of the AppWizard, you enable the renaming of the classes and files that are automatically generated for the skeleton project (see Figure 12.7). The names generated for the project are adequate, so click Finish to continue.

The New Project Information window appears, summarizing the selections that were made (see Figure 12.8). Click OK to continue.

Now the MDS has a skeleton project on which you can base your development. It took only a minute or so to create and contains over 700 lines of C++ code and comments.

Next, start the build by clicking the Build icon on the MDS toolbar or pressing Shift+F8. The build should complete without any errors.

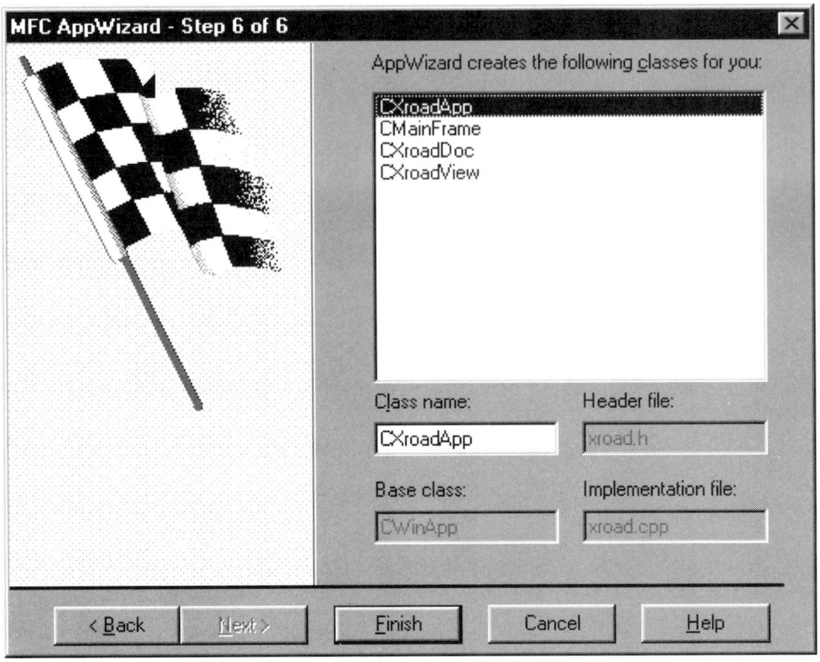

Figure 12.7. Step 6 of the AppWizard: Renaming classes and files.

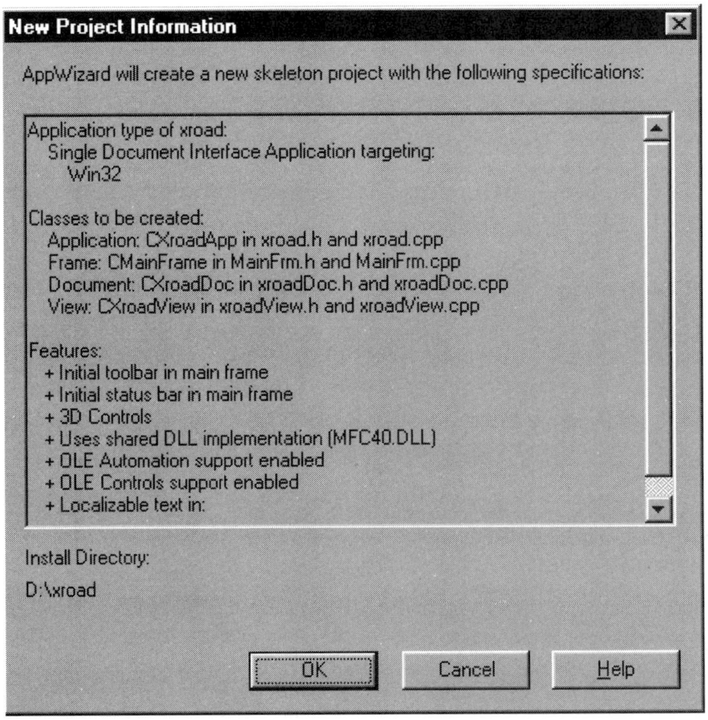

Figure 12.8. Summary of the new skeleton project.

Creating a CDocument Derived Class for the Crossroads Library

The next major task is to add the *Crossroads* library to the *CDocument* class derived class *CXroadDoc*, which was defined by the AppWizard.

Modifying the XRoadDoc.h File

To make the class a *Crossroads* library derived class, add the C++ code (in bold characters in the following code) to the XRoadDoc.h file:

```
// xroadDoc.h : interface of the CXroadDoc class
//
/////////////////////////////////////////////////////////////////
#include <XRoads.H>
class CXroadDoc : public CDocument, public GSeparator
{
protected: // create from serialization only
    CXroadDoc();
    DECLARE_DYNCREATE(CXroadDoc)

// Attributes
public:

// Operations
public:
    void StatusMessage( char* fmt, ... )
    void ErrorMessage( char* fmt, ... );
    void StartBusy( void );
    void EndBusy(void);
```

The include file XRoad.h is a single include that embodies the entire *Crossroads* class library. All files that use this library should include this header file. The *GSeparator* class is added to the inheritance list for the *XRoadDoc* class. This addition allows the behavior of a *GSeparator* class, which is functionally equivalent to the VRML Separator construct, to be added to the *XRoadDoc* class.

Also, four member functions defined for the *GSeparator* class should be overridden in the *XRoadDoc* class: `StatusMessage()`, `ErrorMessage()`, `StartBusy()`, and `EndBusy()`. These member functions are used to present information to the user about a current operation.

`StatusMessage()` is used to inform a user of the current progress of an operation. The implementation for the *XRoadDoc* class causes this message to be displayed on the status bar.

`ErrorMessage()` is used to inform the user of an error that occurred while performing an operation. These errors can include syntax errors in the file format.

`StartBusy()` and `EndBusy()` are used to turn the hourglass cursor on and off. Calls to these functions enclose long operations.

Updating XRoadDoc.cpp

Add the following implementations for the four derived member functions defined in the XRoadDoc.h. Place these at the end of the XRoadDoc.cpp file.

```
void CXroadDoc::
StatusMessage( char* fmt, ... )
{
    if (AfxGetApp() != NULL &&
        AfxGetApp()->m_pMainWnd != NULL) {
          char  buffer[256];
          CStatusBar* pStatus = (CStatusBar*)
          AfxGetApp()->m_pMainWnd->GetDescendantWindow(
                      AFX_IDW_STATUS_BAR);
          va_list     argptr;

          va_start(argptr, fmt);
          vsprintf( buffer, fmt, argptr );
          va_end(argptr);

        if (pStatus != NULL) {
                pStatus->SetPaneText(0, buffer);
                pStatus->UpdateWindow();
          }
    }
    return;
}

void CXroadDoc::
ErrorMessage( char* fmt, ... )
{
    va_list     argptr;
    char  buffer[256];

    va_start(argptr, fmt);
    vsprintf( buffer, fmt, argptr );
    va_end(argptr);

    MessageBox(NULL, buffer, "Error Message", MB_OK |
          MB_ICONEXCLAMATION);
}

void CXroadDoc::
StartBusy(void)
{
    BeginWaitCursor();
}
```

```
void CXroadDoc::
EndBusy(void)
{
    EndWaitCursor();
}
```

Project Settings

With the additions described in the previous section, the *CXroadDoc* class is now able to represent 3D objects and scenes. It also can read and write all of the supported 3D file formats. To compile these additions, you need only add

- the *Crossroads* include directory to the include search path,
- the *Crossroads* libraries to the debug and release subprojects, and
- the OpenGL libraries to the project.

To add the *Crossroads* include directory to the projects search directory, select Build/Settings... . This brings up a tabbed dialog box. You add another directory to the search path by selecting the "C/C++" tab and then the "Preprocessor" category. I place the project directory at the same level as the *Crossroads* include and library directories. To add the include directory to the project, select both subprojects in the "Settings For:" list. Then type "..\include" or the correct path location on your machine for the *Crossroads* class library includes into the "Additional include directories:" field and click OK. See Figure 12.9.

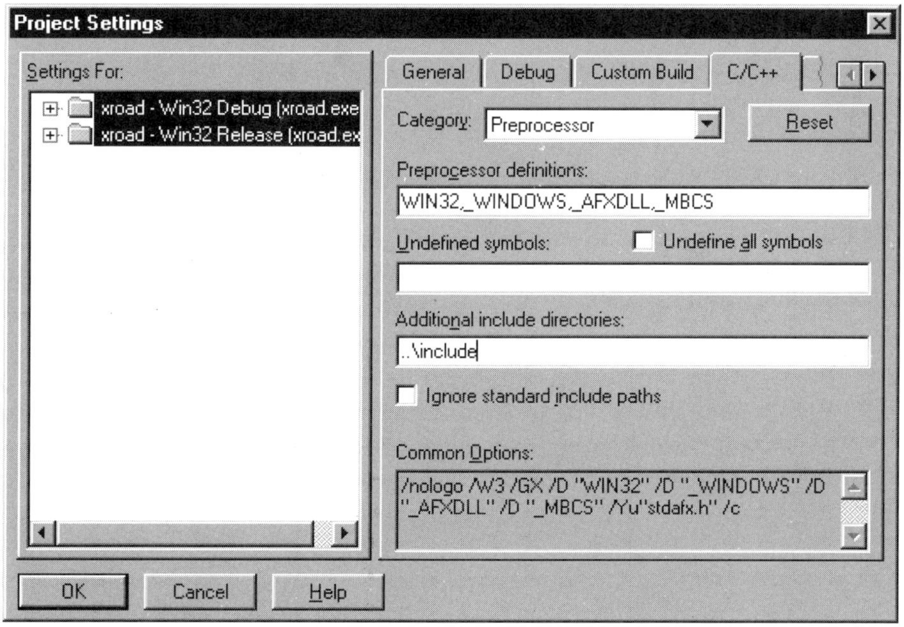

Figure 12.9. Adding the *Crossroads* include directory to the project settings.

To add the *Crossroads* debug library to the project, select Build/Settings.../Link. Then select the debug subproject in the "Settings For:" list and type the path to the *Crossroads* debug library in the "Object/library modules:" field. See Figure 12.10.

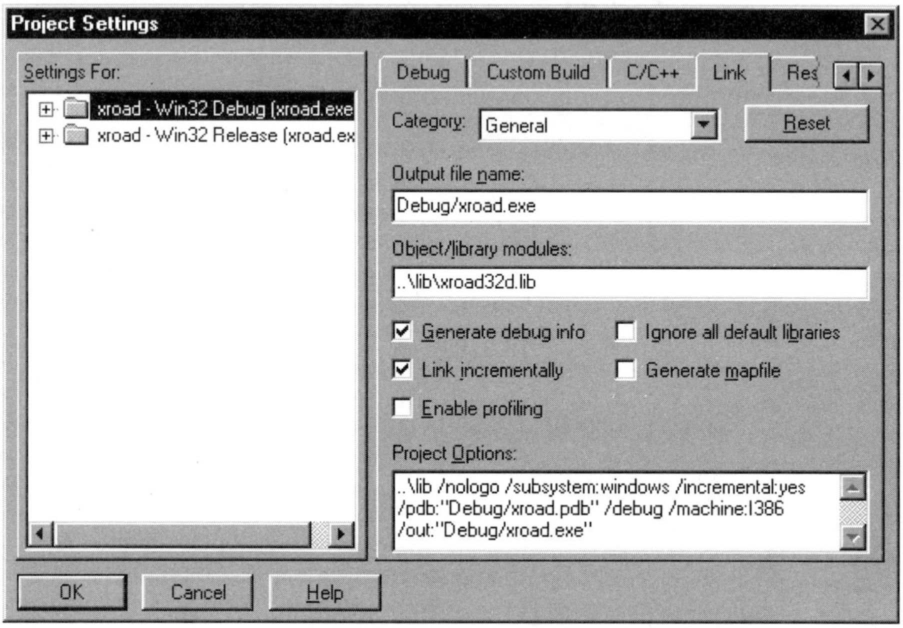

Figure 12.10. Adding the debug library to the project.

Next, select the release subproject in the "Settings For:" list and type the release *Crossroads* library location into the "Object/library module:" field. See Figure 12.11.

The final step is to add the OpenGL libraries to the project. Select both projects in the "Settings For:" list. Then in the "Object/library modules:" field, type in gluax.lib, glu32.lib, and opengl32.lib (see Figure 12.12). Click OK.

The project now has been updated and should compile correctly. Click the Build icon on the toolbar or press Shift+F8 to build the project. If it doesn't build correctly, correct any problems before continuing.

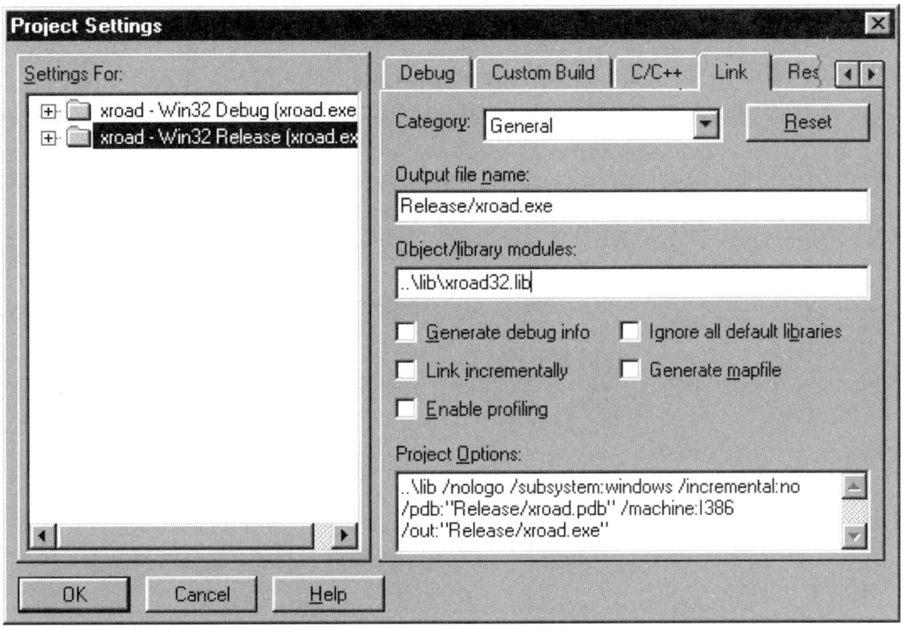

Figure 12.11. Adding the release subproject to the project.

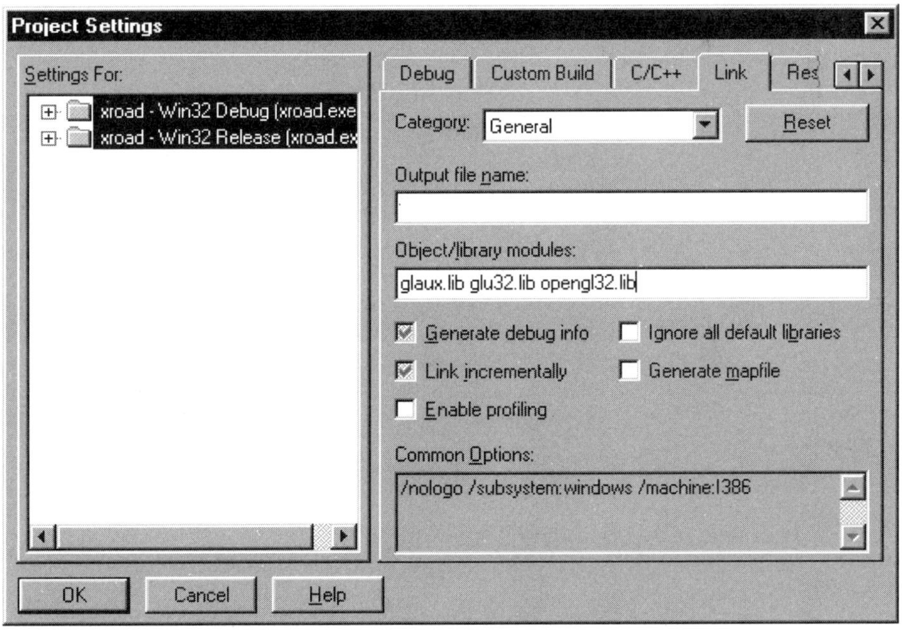

Figure 12.12. Adding the OpenGL Libraries to the project.

Adding File Open and Save Capabilities

Most Windows applications have File/Open... and File/Save As... menu items. The next step to creating the application is to route these menu items to the *CXroadDoc* class. Normally in MFC, the *CView* derived class handles most of the user interface messages in an application. However, since this is a small SDI application you can cheat a bit and route the File/Open... and File/Save As... items directly to the *CXroadDoc* class. This is done via the ClassWizard. Invoke the ClassWizard by selecting View/ClassWizard… or pressing Ctrl+W. To add a member function that is called when File/Open… is selected, select the Message Maps tab. Then select the *CXroadDoc* class in the “Class name:” field and ID_FILE_OPEN in the “Object IDs:” field. Finally, select COMMAND in the “Messages:” field. Click Add Function... and then click OK on the confirmation dialog. See Figure 12.13.

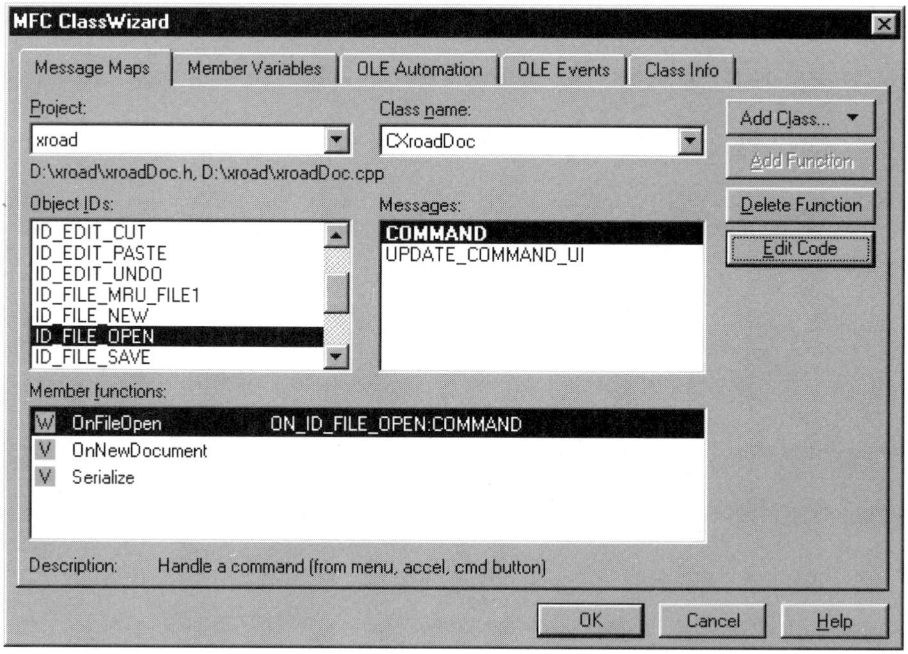

Figure 12.13. Adding a member function for File/Open....

To add a member function that is called when File/Save As… is selected, select the *CXroadDoc* class in the “Class name:” field. Then select ID_FILE_SAVE_AS in the “Object IDs:” field. Finally, select COMMAND in the "Messages:" field. Click Add Function... and then click OK on the confirmation dialog. See Figure 12.14.

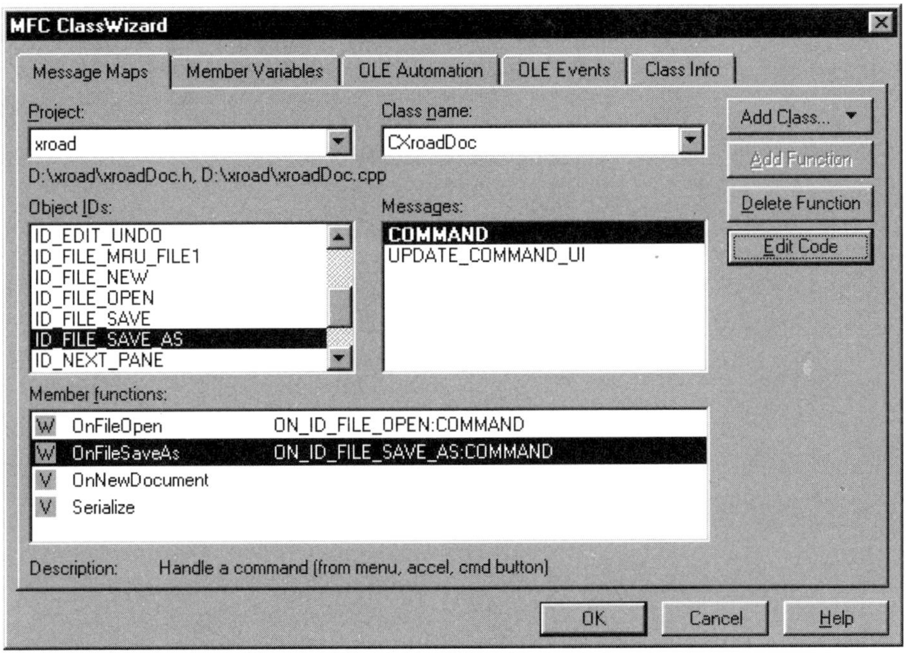

Figure 12.14. Adding a member function for File/Save As... .

Next, add the following implementation to the `OnFileOpen()` and `OnFileSaveAs()` *CXroadDoc* member functions:

```
void CXroadDoc::OnFileOpen()
{
    char  buffer[512];

    // Get path to POVRay includes
    CString     povray_path =
                AfxGetApp()->GetProfileString(
                      "POVRay", "Path", ".\\");

    // Get filter string for CFileDialog
    XRoad_CFileDialog_String(buffer);

    // Create Open Dialog box
    CFileDialog fileDlg(TRUE, NULL, NULL,
          OFN_HIDEREADONLY | OFN_PATHMUSTEXIST, buffer);
```

```
    // Display Open Dialog box
    if (fileDlg.DoModal() == IDOK) {
          // OK chosen, erase the current objects
          Clear();

         // Read the file and update view if successful
         if (XRoad_Reader((GNode*) this,
                     fileDlg.GetPathName(), povray_path)) {
              UpdateAllViews(NULL);
              SetPathName(fileDlg.GetPathName());
         }
    }

    return;
}

void CXroadDoc::OnFileSaveAs()
{
    char buffer[512];

    // Get filter string for CFileDialog
    XRoad_CFileDialog_String(buffer);

    // Create SaveAs Dialog box
    CFileDialog fileDlg(FALSE, NULL, NULL,
          OFN_HIDEREADONLY | OFN_OVERWRITEPROMPT, buffer);

    // Display SaveAs Dialog box
    if (fileDlg.DoModal() == IDOK) {
          // If OK chosen, then save the current 3D file
          XRoad_Writer((GNode*) this,
                      fileDlg.GetPathName());
    }
}
```

After `OnFileOpen()` and `OnFileSaveAs()` have been implemented, add a `Clear()` member function to the `OnNewDocument()` member function, as follows:

```
BOOL CXroadDoc::OnNewDocument()
{
    if (!CDocument::OnNewDocument())
          return FALSE;

    Clear();

    return TRUE;
}
```

At this point, you should compile your project to make sure the changes you made were successful. You've now completed the changes to the *CXroadDoc* class needed to support the *Crossroads* class library. The current application is able open 3D files and save them as any other file type.

Creating an OpenGL CView

The next task in this project is to enable the loaded file to be displayed. Most of the changes to the *CXroadView* class that you make here are required for MFC to support OpenGL.

First, you want to add an OpenGL *HGLRC* device context value to the *CXroadView* class. Do this by adding the bolded line, shown in the following code, to the *CXroadView* class declaration in the file XroadView.h:

```
class CXroadView : public CView
{
protected: // create from serialization only
    CCXroadView();
    DECLARE_DYNCREATE(CXroadView)

// Attributes
public:
    CXroadDoc* GetDocument();
    HGLRC         m_hRC;

// Operations
public:
```

Adding Windows Message Member Functions

The next step is to add three Windows message hooks to which the *CXroad-View* class must attach:

- WM_CREATE
- WM_DESTORY
- WM_SIZE

These are needed to initialize and update the OpenGL information correctly.

The code necessary to intercept the message is created using the Class-Wizard. Invoke the ClassWizard by selecting the View/ClassWizard... or pressing Ctrl+W.

To connect the WM_CREATE message, select *CXroadView* "Class Name:" field and WM_CREATE in the "Messages:" list. See Figure 12.15. Click Add Function... and then click OK on the confirmation dialog. You've now connected WM_CREATE to the `CXroadView::OnCreate()` member function.

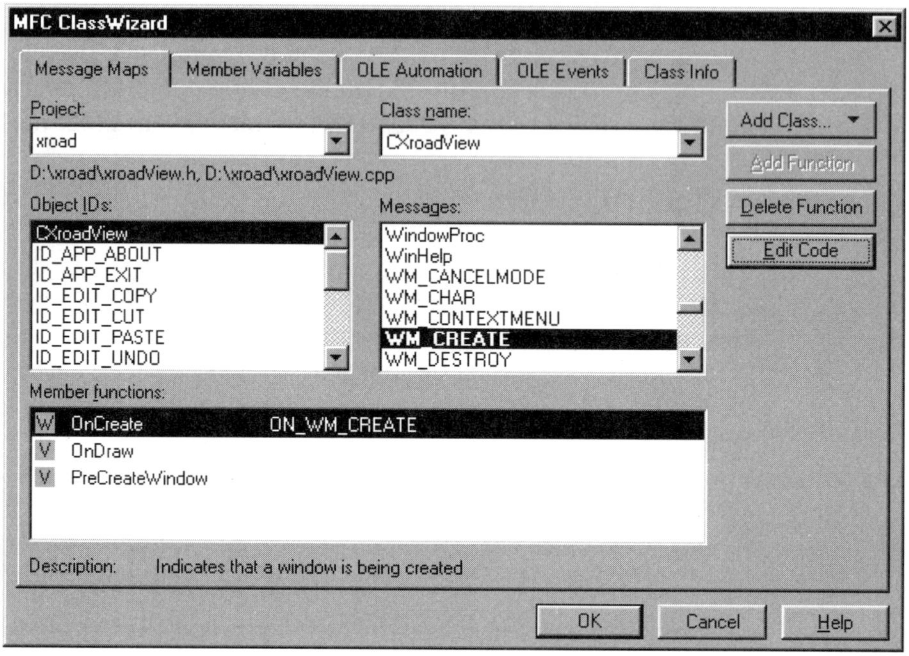

Figure 12.15. Connecting WM_CREATE to *CXroadView*.

To connect the WM_DESTROY message, select WM_DESTROY in the "Messages:" list and click Add Function... . See Figure 12.16. Then click OK on the confirmation dialog. WM_DESTROY is now connected to the `CXroadView::OnDestroy()` member function.

The last Windows message to connect is WM_SIZE. Select WM_SIZE in the "Messages:" list and click Add Function... . Select OK on the confirmation dialog. See Figure 12.17. WM_SIZE is now connected to the `CXroadView::OnSize()` member function.

Implementing the New CXroadView Member Functions

Next, you implement the new *CXroadView* member functions that you connected in the last section. The first *CXroadView* member function to update is `PreCreateWindow()`. This member function must set the `cs.style` bit values WS_CLIPCHILDREN and WS_CLIPSIBLINGS so that the OpenGL library can initialize properly. To implement it, add the bold lines shown in the following code to the function defined in the file XRoadView.cpp:

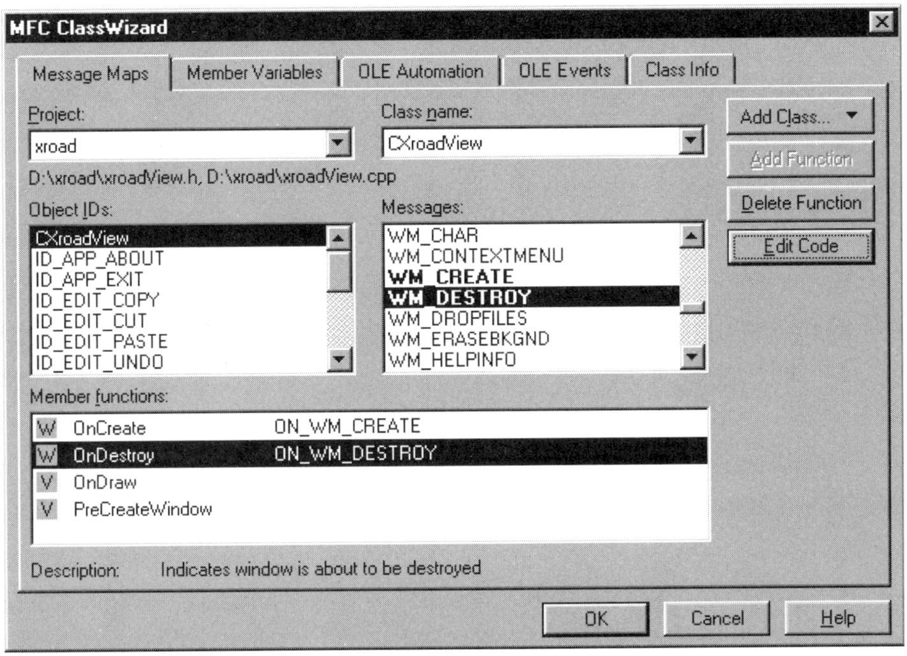

Figure 12.16. Connecting WM_DESTROY to *CXroadView*.

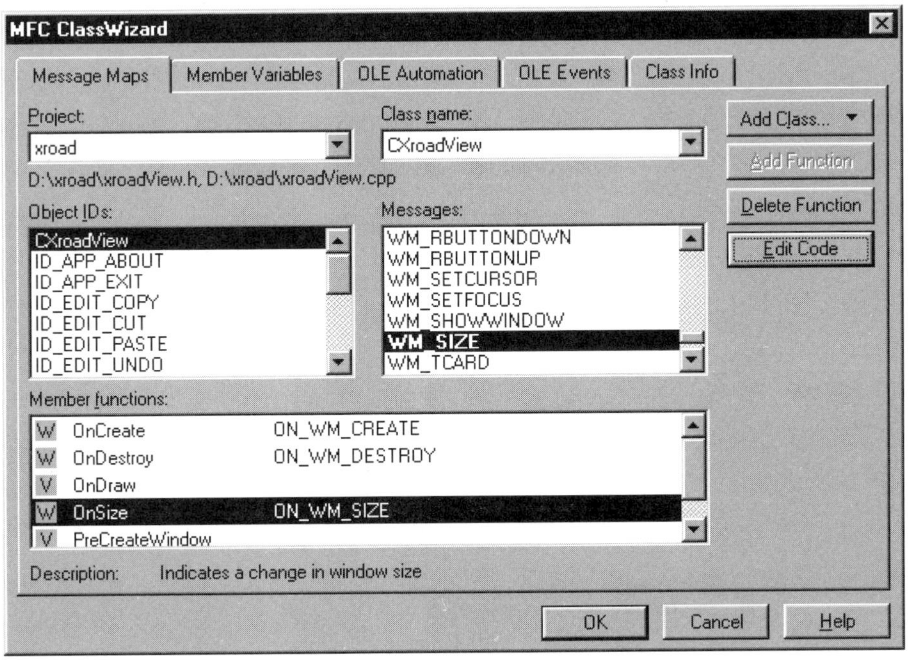

Figure 12.17. Connecting WM_SIZE to *CXroadView*.

```
BOOL CXroadView::PreCreateWindow(CREATESTRUCT& cs)
{
    // Required or OPENGL will fail to initialize!
    cs.style |= WS_CLIPCHILDREN | WS_CLIPSIBLINGS;
    return CView::PreCreateWindow(cs);
}
```

Next, fill in the `OnCreate()` member function. `OnCreate()` creates an OpenGL device context and places it in the member variable *m_hRC*. To implement `OnCreate()`, add the bold lines shown in the following code to your existing `OnCreate()` function:

```
int CXroadView::OnCreate(LPCREATESTRUCT lpCreateStruct)
{
    PIXELFORMATDESCRIPTOR pfd = {
          sizeof(PIXELFORMATDESCRIPTOR),// size of this pfd
          1,                      // version number
          PFD_DRAW_TO_WINDOW |    // Property Flags
                PFD_SUPPORT_OPENGL,
          PFD_TYPE_RGBA,          // RGBA type
          24,                     // 24-bit color depth
          0, 0, 0, 0, 0, 0,       // color bits ignored
          0,                      // no alpha buffer
          0,                      // shift bit ignored

          0,                      // no accumulation buffer
          0, 0, 0, 0,             // accum bits ignored
          32,                     // 32-bit z-buffer
          0,                      // no stencil buffer
          0,                      // no auxiliary buffer
          PFD_MAIN_PLANE,         // main layer
          0,                      // reserved
          0, 0, 0                 // layer masks ignored
    };

    CClientDC clientDC(this);

    int pixelFormat =
        ChoosePixelFormat(clientDC.m_hDC, &pfd);

    SetPixelFormat(clientDC.m_hDC, pixelFormat, &pfd)

    DescribePixelFormat(clientDC.m_hDC, pixelFormat,
              sizeof(pfd), &pfd);

    m_hRC = wglCreateContext(clientDC.m_hDC);
```

```
    if (CView::OnCreate(lpCreateStruct) == -1)
        return -1;

    return 0;
}
```

To the current `OnDestroy()` member function, add the bold lines shown in the following code:

```
void CXroadView::OnDestroy()

{
    CView::OnDestroy();
    wglDeleteContext(m_hRC);
    m_hRC = NULL;
}
```

To the current `OnSize()` member function, add the bold lines shown in the following code:

```
void CXroadView::OnSize(UINT nType, int cx, int cy)
{
    CView::OnSize(nType, cx, cy);
    CClientDC     clientDC(this);
    wglMakeCurrent(NULL, NULL);
}
```

The last member function to be filled in is `OnDraw()`. However, first you must write a function that can create some data from an existing scene. This data includes the center of the scene, a suggested camera position and light position, and the width, height, and depth of the scene. It is used to create the view of the scene.

The calculated camera position is used if the scene doesn't have a predefined camera. The following C++ function calculates this position:

```
void DefaultPositions(GNode* pDoc, SFFloat& width,
                      SFFloat& height, SFFloat& depth,
                      SFVec3f& objectCenter,
                      SFVec3f& cameraPosition,
                      SFVec3f& lightPosition)
{
    SFMatrix                matrix;
    float                   max = (float) 100000.0;
    SFVec3f                 minv(max, max, max);
    SFVec3f                 maxv(-max, -max, -max);
    SFFloat                 maxdimension;
    GState                  state;
```

```
    // Find max, and min position of scene objects
    pDoc->Range(state, minv, maxv);

    // Calculate depth, height, and width
    depth = maxv.Z() - minv.Z();
    height = maxv.Y() - minv.Y();
    width = maxv.X() - minv.X();

    // Find larger dimension of width & height
    if (width > height) {
          maxdimension = width;
    } else {
          maxdimension = height;
    }

    // Calculate center of 3D scene
    objectCenter.X((SFFloat) (width/2.0 + minv.X()));
    objectCenter.Y((SFFloat) (height/2.0 + minv.Y()));
    objectCenter.Z((SFFloat) (depth/2.0 + minv.Z()));

    // Calculate a default camera position
    cameraPosition.X((SFFloat) objectCenter.X());
    cameraPosition.Y((SFFloat) objectCenter.Y());
    cameraPosition.Z((SFFloat) (maxv.Z() + depth/2.0 +
        maxdimension));

    // Calculate a default light position
    lightPosition.X((SFFloat) objectCenter.X());
    lightPosition.Y((SFFloat) objectCenter.Y());
    lightPosition.Z((SFFloat) (maxv.Z() + depth/2.0 +
        maxdimension*200.0));
}
```

OnDraw() draws the current scene of the *CXroadView* class. The following source implements it:

```
void CXroadView::OnDraw(CDC* pDC)
{
    RECT                        rect;
    CXroadDoc*                  pDoc = GetDocument();
    GPerspectiveCamera*         camera;
    GState                      state, cameraState;
    long                        count = 0;
    SFFloat                     width, height, depth;
    SFVec3f                     objectCenter, cameraPosition;
    SFVec3f                     lightPosition;

    // Viewport rectangle
    GetClientRect(&rect);
```

```
// Write a message to the status bar
pDoc->StatusMessage("Drawing.");

// Set current OpenGL device context to viewport
wglMakeCurrent(pDC->m_hDC, m_hRC);

// Create some default settings for the scene
DefaultPositions((GNode*) pDoc, width, height, depth,
    objectCenter, cameraPosition, lightPosition);

// Setup OpenGL
glPolygonMode(GL_FRONT_AND_BACK, GL_LINE);
glDisable(GL_LIGHTING);
glClearColor(0.5f, 0.4f, 0.4f, 1.0f);
glEnable(GL_DEPTH_TEST);
glDepthFunc(GL_LESS);
glDepthRange(0.0, depth*100.0);
glClearDepth(depth*100.0);
glClear(GL_COLOR_BUFFER_BIT | GL_DEPTH_BUFFER_BIT);

// Search for a default camera
camera = (GPerspectiveCamera*)
            pDoc->FindTypeByIndex(cameraState,
                   GPerspectiveCameraType, count, 0);

if (camera == NULL) {
      // No camera was found in the scene so
      // create a default Camera
      SFLong      w = rect.right;
      SFLong      h = rect.bottom;
      SFFloat     aspectRatio = ((SFFloat) w)/
                                  ((SFFloat) h);

      glMatrixMode(GL_PROJECTION);
      glLoadIdentity();
      gluPerspective(Rad2Deg((SFFloat) 0.785398),
            aspectRatio, 0.0001, depth*100.0);
      gluLookAt(cameraPosition.X(), cameraPosition.Y(),
            cameraPosition.Z(), objectCenter.X(),
            objectCenter.Y(), objectCenter.Z(),
            0.0, 1.0, 0.0);
      glViewport(0, 0, w, h);
} else {
      // Use the camera found in the scene
      camera->SetCameraOpenGL(cameraState,
            rect.right, rect.bottom);
}
```

```
    // Switch to modelview mode
    glMatrixMode(GL_MODELVIEW);
    glLoadIdentity();

    // Draw the scene.
    pDoc->DrawOpenGL(state);

    // Emit the scene
    glFinish();

    // Set current OpenGL device context to NULL
    wglMakeCurrent(NULL, NULL);

    // Write Ready to the status bar.
    pDoc->StatusMessage("Ready.");
}
```

At this point, you should compile your project to make sure the changes you made were successful. You've now completed the changes to the *CXroadView* class needed to support the OpenGL library. The application will now allow 3D files to be opened, viewed, and saved. Figure 12.18 shows an example of this application with a 3D file loaded and displayed.

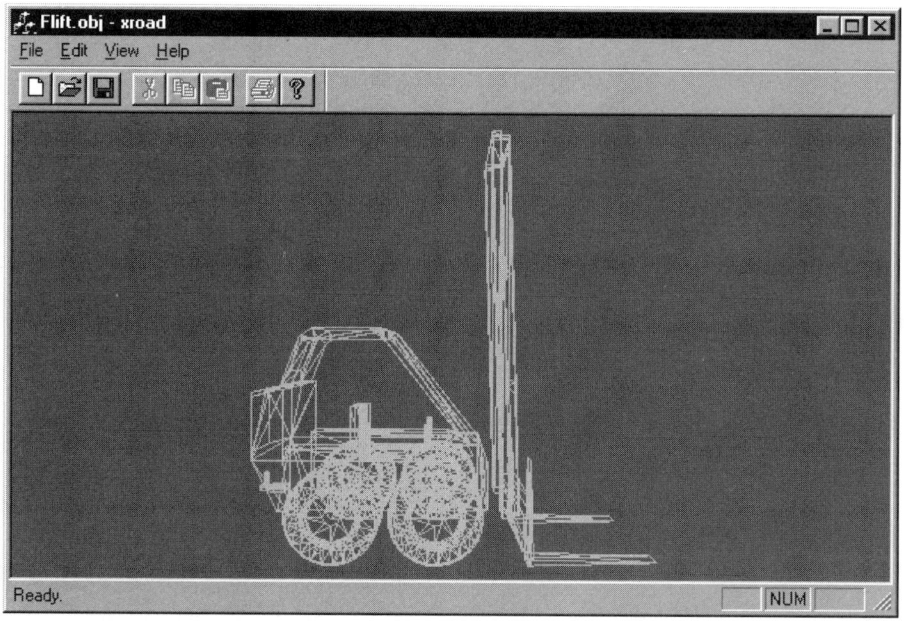

Figure 12.18. Example of a 3D file.

References

Crain, Dennis. "Windows NT OpenGL: Getting Started." April 1994. http://www.microsoft.com/msdn/library/technote/opengl9.htm.

Kruglinski, David J. *Inside Visual C++*. 1993. Redmond, WA: Microsoft Press.

Chapter 13

Building and Using an OCX Custom Control

In Chapter 12, you built a standalone Windows application from the *Crossroads* class library. In this chapter, you will build a 32-bit OLE custom control from that library.

An OLE custom control (OCX) is a program component that can be used in many environments such as Visual Basic, Excel, Visual C++, Delphi, and most other Windows application programming environments.

In this chapter, I discuss the steps for creating an OCX custom control using the *Crossroads* class library that can open, view, and save 3D files. The application was created with Visual C++ 4.0 and uses the Microsoft Foundation Class (MFC) class library.

This is a "cookbook" approach to building this project. It is not intended as a tutorial on OpenGL, Visual C++, or MFC. If you want more information of these topics, refer to the references listed at the end of the chapter.

For simplicity's sake, I do not address Windows bitmap palettes in this project. So this OCX will run correctly for display settings of greater than 256 colors. However, bitmap palettes are addressed in the OCX project included on the CD-ROM. Refer to that if you wish to add palette support to this project.

The following sections describe the steps to build a standalone application from the *Crossroads* class library. These steps are

1. create a skeleton OCX control,
2. create a *COleControl* derived class, and
3. add file open and save capabilities.

Creating a Skeleton OCX Control

Invoke the Microsoft Developers Studio (MDS). This brings up the workspace for the Visual C++ 4.0 compiler. To start a new application, select File/New... . The New dialog appears showing several possible selections. Select "Project Workspace" to bring up the "New Project Workspace" dialog (see Figure 13.1). Select a type of "OLE ControlWizard" and a project name of "xroad."

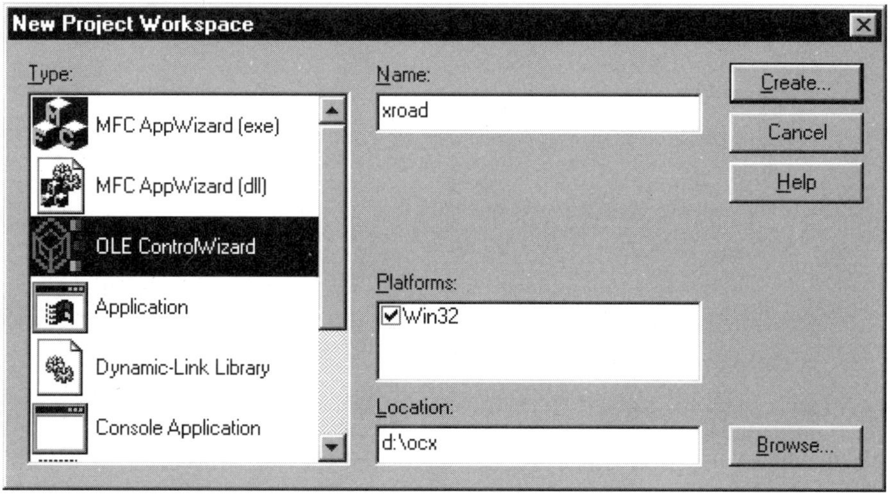

Figure 13.1. New Project Workspace.

Click Create... and Step 1 of the ControlWizard appears (see Figure 13.2). This step allows you to select options for the control. The default selections are satisfactory, so click Next> to continue.

Step 2 of the ControlWizard allows you to select several features the control may have (see Figure 13.3). Select the default selections, as well as "Acts as a simple frame control" and "Available in 'Insert Object' dialog." Then click Finish.

The New Project Information window appears, summarizing the selections that were made (see Figure 13.4). Click OK to continue.

Now the MDS has a skeleton OCX control on which you can base your development. It took only a minute or so to create and contains over 500 lines of C++ code and comments.

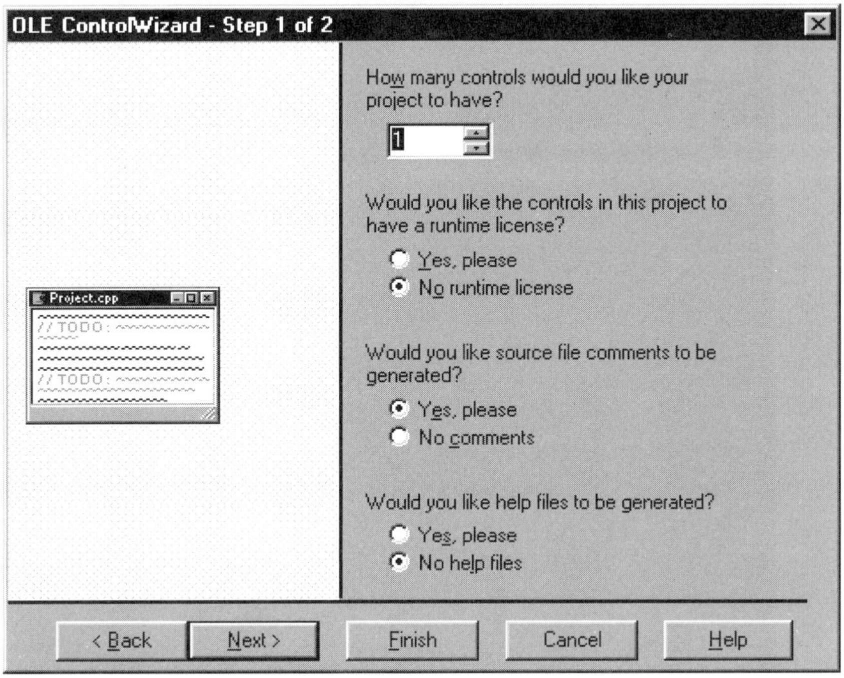

Figure 13.2. Step 1 of the ControlWizard: Selecting options.

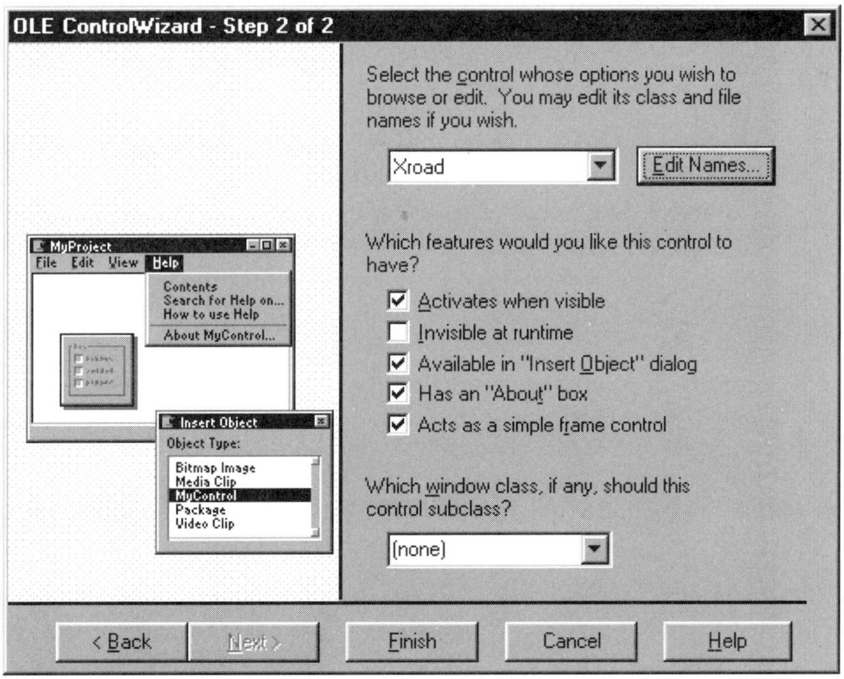

Figure 13.3. Selecting features.

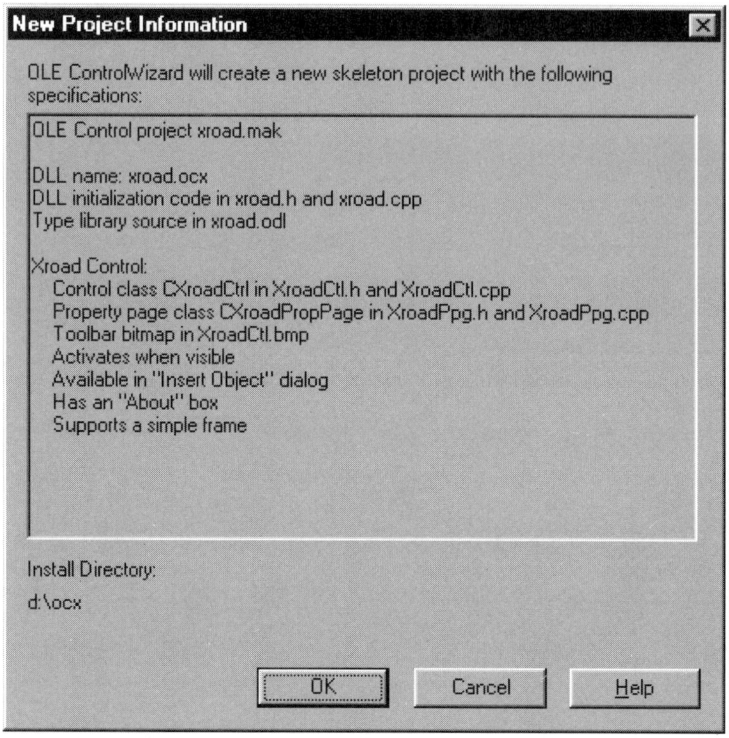

Figure 13.4. Summary of the new skeleton project.

Next, start the build by clicking the Build icon on the MDS toolbar or pressing Shift+F8. The build should complete without any errors.

Test the control after the build has completed. Select the Tools/OLE Control Test Container to bring up the OLE Test Container. This application allows you to place controls into it and to access the properties of the controls for testing. Insert your control into the test container by selecting Edit/Insert OLE Control. This brings up a list of OLE Controls to insert. Select the "Xroad Control" (probably the last selection in the list). The control is placed in the test container. "Xroad Control" isn't very interesting. It simply draws an ellipse in the control window, as shown in Figure 13.5.

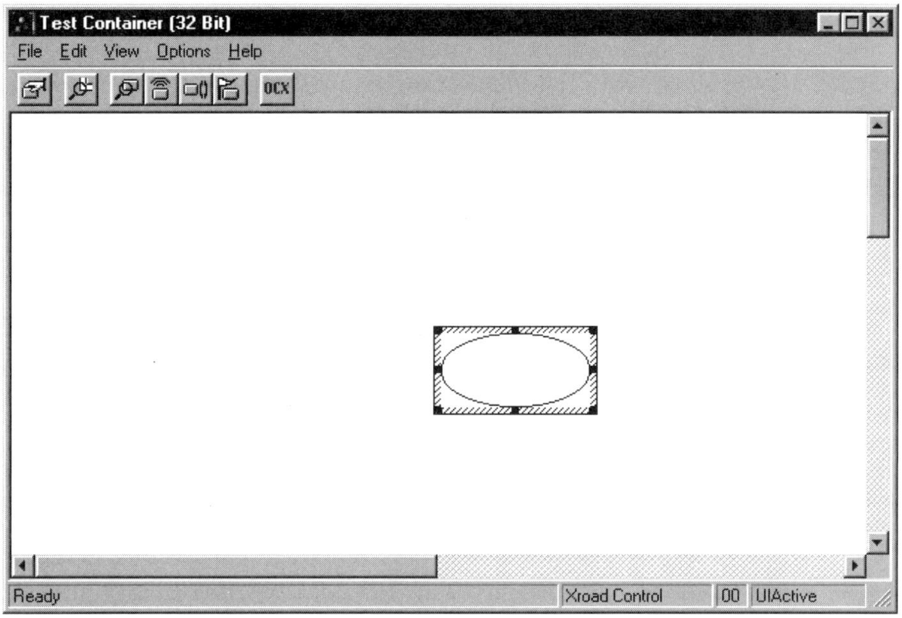

Figure 13.5. "Xroad Control."

Creating a COleControl Derived Class

The next major task is to add the *Crossroads* library to the *COleControl* derived class *CXroadCtrl*, which was defined by the ControlWizard.

Modifying the XRoadCtl.h File

To make the class a *Crossroads* library derived class, add the C++ code in bold characters in the following code to the XRoadCtl.h file:

```
#include <xroads.h>

class CXroadCtrl : public COleControl, public GSeparator
{
    DECLARE_DYNCREATE(CXroadCtrl)

// Constructor
public:
    CXroadCtrl();
    SFVec3f       m_objectCenter;
    CDC*          m_memdc;
    CRect         m_membounds;
```

```
    HGLRC           m_hrc;
    HPALETTE        m_hPalette;
    CBitmap*        m_bitmap;

// Overrides

    // Render opengl
    void StartBusy(void);
    void EndBusy(void);
    void StatusMessage(char*, ...);
    void ErrorMessage(char*, ...);

    void RenderOpenGL(CDC*, CRect&);
    void CreateRenderingContext(CDC*, const CRect&);
    void EndRenderingContext(CDC*, const CRect&);
    void SetupProjection(CDC*, const CRect&);
    void SetupBkColor(void);
```

The include file XRoad.h is a single include that embodies the entire *Crossroads* class library. All files that use this library should include this header file. The *GSeparator* class is added to the inheritance list for the *XRoadCtrl* class. This addition allows the behavior of a *GSeparator* class, which is functionally equivalent to the VRML Separator construct, to be added to the *XRoadCtrl* class.

Also, four member functions defined for the *GSeparator* class should be overridden in the *XRoadCtrl* class: `StatusMessage`, `ErrorMessage`, `StartBusy`, and `EndBusy`. These member functions are used to present information to the user about the current operation.

`StatusMessage()` is used to inform a user of the current progress of an operation. The implementation for the *XRoadCtrl* class causes this message to be emitted as a OLE event. This allows the message to be intercepted and used if needed in such programming languages as Visual Basic.

`ErrorMessage()` is used to inform the user of an error that occurred while the program is performing an operation. These errors can include syntax errors in the file format. The implementation causes this message to be emitted as a OLE event.

`StartBusy()` and `EndBusy()` are used to turn the hourglass cursor on and off. Calls to these functions enclose long operations.

In addition to the overloaded *GSeparator* member functions, five other member functions will be added for OpenGL support. Listed next, these assist the rendering of an OpenGL image:

1. `RenderOpenGL()` causes the current scene to be rendered by OpenGL. This function is always called from the `OnDraw()` member function.

2. `CreateRenderingContext()` creates the current OpenGL rendering context. OpenGL currently doesn't allow the device context that is passed to `OnDraw()` to be rendered directly. `CreateRenderingContext()` creates a device context from a bitmap. This allows OpenGL to render directly to this bitmap, which is later copied to the device context passed to `OnDraw()`.
3. `EndRenderingContext()` clears the current rendering context.
4. `SetupProjection()` initializes OpenGL and sets up the camera used when rendering the scene.
5. `SetupBkColor()` converts the OCX background color into the background color for the OpenGL rendered scene.

Adding the GSeparator Derived Member Functions to XRoadCtl.cpp

Add the following implementations for the four *GSeparator* derived member functions defined in the XRoadCtl.h:

```
void CXroadCtrl::
StartBusy( void )
{
    BeginWaitCursor();
}

void CXroadCtrl::
EndBusy( void )
{
    EndWaitCursor();
}

void CXroadCtrl::
StatusMessage( char* fmt, ... )
{
    va_list     argptr;
    char  buffer[256];

    va_start(argptr, fmt);
    vsprintf( buffer, fmt, argptr );
    va_end(argptr);

    //FireStatusMessage(buffer);

    return;
}
```

```
void CXroadCtrl::
ErrorMessage( char* fmt, ... )
{
    va_list     argptr;
    char  buffer[256];

    va_start(argptr, fmt);
    vsprintf( buffer, fmt, argptr );
    va_end(argptr);

    //FireErrorMessage(buffer);
}
```

Note that `StatusMessage()` and `ErrorMessage()` are only partially implemented. This is because you haven't yet added the OLE events required to complete the implementation. You'll do this later in the chapter.

Adding the OpenGL Member Functions to XRoadCtl.cpp

Add the following implementations for the OpenGL member functions defined in the XRoadCtl.h:

```
void CXroadCtrl::
CreateRenderingContext(CDC* pdc, const CRect& bounds)
{
    BITMAP      bmInfo;

    // Get the Bitmap associated with
    // OCX device context.
    CBitmap*    pBitmap = pdc->GetCurrentBitmap();

    // Extract info from the bitmap
    pBitmap->GetObject(sizeof(BITMAP), &bmInfo);

    PIXELFORMATDESCRIPTOR   pfd;

    // Clear the pfd variable
    memset(&pfd, 0, sizeof(PIXELFORMATDESCRIPTOR));

    pfd.nSize = sizeof(PIXELFORMATDESCRIPTOR);
    pfd.nVersion = 1;
    pfd.dwFlags =     PFD_DRAW_TO_BITMAP |
                          PFD_GENERIC_FORMAT |
                          PFD_SUPPORT_GDI |
                          PFD_SUPPORT_OPENGL;
    pfd.iPixelType = PFD_TYPE_RGBA;
    pfd.cColorBits = (BYTE) bmInfo.bmBitsPixel;
```

```
    pfd.cDepthBits = 32;
    pfd.iLayerType = PFD_MAIN_PLANE;

    // Setup the OpenGL rendering context
    int nPixelFormat = ChoosePixelFormat(pdc->GetSafeHdc(),
                             &pfd);

    SetPixelFormat(pdc->GetSafeHdc(), nPixelFormat, &pfd);
    m_hrc = wglCreateContext(pdc->GetSafeHdc());
    wglMakeCurrent(pdc->GetSafeHdc(), m_hrc);
}

void CXroadCtrl::SetupBkColor(void)
{
    // Get Background Color
    COLORREF clrBack = TranslateColor(GetBackColor());

    // Convert to floating point RGB values.
    float red = ((float) GetRValue(clrBack))/255.0f;
    float green = ((float) GetGValue(clrBack))/255.0f;
    float blue = ((float) GetBValue(clrBack))/255.0f;

    // Apply to OpenGL Background.
    glClearColor(red, green, blue, 0.0f);
}

void  CXroadCtrl::EndRenderingContext(CDC* pdc, const CRect&
                                    bounds)
{
    // Remove device context OpenGL current selection
    wglMakeCurrent(NULL, NULL);

    // Delete OpenGL device context.
    if (m_hrc != NULL) {
          wglDeleteContext(m_hrc);
          m_hrc = NULL;
    }
}

void DefaultPositions(GNode* node, SFFloat& width, SFFloat&
                    height, SFFloat& depth, SFVec3f&
                    objectCenter, SFVec3f& cameraPosition)
{
    const float       max = (float) 100000.0;
    SFVec3f           minv(max, max, max);
    SFVec3f           maxv(-max, -max, -max);
    GState            state;
```

```
    // Find Scene range
    node->Range(state, minv, maxv);

    // Convert range into depth, width, and height
    depth = maxv.Z() - minv.Z();
    height = maxv.Y() - minv.Y();
    width = maxv.X() - minv.X();

    // Calculate object center
    objectCenter.X((SFFloat) (width/2.0 + minv.X()));
    objectCenter.Y((SFFloat) (height/2.0 + minv.Y()));
    objectCenter.Z((SFFloat) (depth/2.0 + minv.Z()));

    // Calculate default camera position.
    cameraPosition.X((SFFloat) objectCenter.X());
    cameraPosition.Y((SFFloat) objectCenter.Y());
    cameraPosition.Z((SFFloat) (maxv.Z() + depth/2.0 +
                (width > height ? width : height)));
}

void CXroadCtrl::SetupProjection(CDC* pdc, const CRect&
                                  rect)
}
    GPerspectiveCamera*     camera;
    GState                  state, cameraState;
    SFFloat                 width, height, depth;
    SFVec3f                 cameraPosition;

    // Find object parameters and calculate
    // default camera position.
    DefaultPositions(this, width, height, depth,
                m_objectCenter, cameraPosition);

    // Setup OpenGL
    glPolygonMode(GL_FRONT_AND_BACK, GL_LINE);
    glDisable(GL_LIGHTING);
    glEnable(GL_DEPTH_TEST);
    glDepthFunc(GL_LESS);
    glDepthRange(0.0, depth*100.0);
    glClearDepth(depth*100.0);
    glClear(GL_COLOR_BUFFER_BIT | GL_DEPTH_BUFFER_BIT);

    // Look for a defined camera
    long count = 0;
    camera = (GPerspectiveCamera*)
                FindTypeByIndex(cameraState,
                GPerspectiveCameraType, count, 0);

    if (camera == NULL) {
```

```
            // Use default camera position
            SFLong        w = rect.right;
            SFLong        h = rect.bottom;
            SFFloat       aspectRatio = ((SFFloat) w)/((SFFloat)
h);

            // Set projection mode
            glMatrixMode(GL_PROJECTION);
            glLoadIdentity();

            // Create a window perspective
            gluPerspective(Rad2Deg((SFFloat) 0.785398),
                        aspectRatio, 0.0001, depth*100.0);

            // Create camera
            gluLookAt(cameraPosition.X(), cameraPosition.Y(),
                      cameraPosition.Z(), m_objectCenter.X(),
                      m_objectCenter.Y(), m_objectCenter.Z(),
                      0.0, 1.0, 0.0);
      } else {
            // Use defined camera position
            camera->SetCameraOpenGL(cameraState, rect.right,
                  rect.bottom);
      }

      // Set modelview mode
      glMatrixMode(GL_MODELVIEW);
      glLoadIdentity();
}

void CXroadCtrl::
RenderOpenGL(CDC* dc, CRect& bounds)
{
      GState      state;

      // Render the scene
      DrawOpenGL(state);
}
```

Updating CXroadCtrl Constructor, Destructor and OnDraw() Functions

The member functions however, already exist in the skeleton OCX control; their implementations need to be replaced with the following member functions:

- CXroadCtrl::CXroadCtrl
- CXroadCtrl::CXroadCtrl
- CXroadCtrl

```
CXroadCtrl::CXroadCtrl()
{
    InitializeIIDs(&IID_DXroad, &IID_DXroadEvents);

    EnableSimpleFrame();

    m_membounds = CRect(0, 0, 0, 0);
    m_memdc = NULL;

    m_hrc = NULL;
    m_hPalette = NULL;
    m_bitmap = NULL;
    SetModifiedFlag();
}

CXroadCtrl::~CXroadCtrl()
{
    Clear();

    if (m_hPalette) {
          DeleteObject(m_hPalette);
    }

    if (m_hrc != NULL) {
          EndRenderingContext(m_memdc, m_membounds);
    }

    if (m_bitmap != NULL) {
          delete m_bitmap;
    }

    if (m_memdc != NULL) {
          delete m_memdc;
    }

}

void CXroadCtrl::OnDraw(CDC* pdc, const
        CRect& rcBounds, const CRect& rcInvalid)
{
    CBitmap     *pOldBitmap = NULL;
    CRect       bounds (rcBounds);
    int         saveDC = pdc->SaveDC();

    ASSERT(pdc->GetMapMode() == MM_TEXT);

    // Force window to start at (0, 0)
    pdc->SetViewportOrg(bounds.left, bounds.top);
```

```
pdc->SetWindowOrg(0, 0);
pdc->SetWindowExt(bounds.Width(), bounds.Height());
bounds = CRect(0, 0, bounds.Width(), bounds.Height());

// Update memory CDC if some significant change
// has occured.
if (m_membounds != bounds || m_bitmap == NULL ||
      m_memdc == NULL || IsModified()) {

      m_membounds = bounds;

      if (m_memdc != NULL) delete m_memdc;

      m_memdc = new CDC;

      m_memdc->CreateCompatibleDC(pdc);

      if (m_bitmap != NULL) delete m_bitmap;

      m_bitmap = new CBitmap;

      m_bitmap->CreateCompatibleBitmap(pdc,
                  m_membounds.Width(),
                  m_membounds.Height());
}

pOldBitmap = m_memdc->SelectObject(m_bitmap);

if (IsModified()) {
      StartBusy();
      StatusMessage("Rendering");

      int   height = m_membounds.Height(),
            width = m_membounds.Width();

      // Render the Scene
      CreateRenderingContext(m_memdc, m_membounds);
      SetupBkColor();
      SetupProjection(m_memdc, m_membounds);
      RenderOpenGL(m_memdc, m_membounds); Render Scene
      glFlush();

      // Clean up rendering context
      EndRenderingContext(m_memdc, m_membounds);
      EndBusy();
      StatusMessage("Ready");
}
```

```
    // Blit the bitmap to the window
    pdc->BitBlt(bounds.left, bounds.top,
                bounds.Width(), bounds.Height(),
                m_memdc, m_membounds.left,
                m_membounds.top, SRCCOPY);

    // Clean up
    m_memdc->SelectObject(pOldBitmap);

    pdc->RestoreDC(saveDC);

    SetModifiedFlag(FALSE);
}
```

Project Settings

With the additions described in the previous sections, the *CXroadCtrl* class is now able to store 3D objects and scenes. It also can read and write all of the supported 3D file formats. To make the project ready for interim compilation, you need only add

- the *Crossroads* include directory to the include search path,
- the *Crossroads* libraries to the debug and release subprojects, and
- the OpenGL libraries to the project.

To add the *Crossroads* include directory to the project search directory select Build/Settings... . This brings up a tabbed dialog box. You add another directory to the search path by selecting the "C/C++" tab and then the "Preprocessor" category. I place the project directory at the same level as the *Crossroads* include and library directories.

To add the include directory to the project, select both subprojects in the "Settings For:" list. Then type "..\include" or the correct path location on your machine for the *Crossroads* class library includes into the "Additional include directories:" field and click OK. See Figure 13.6.

For the Xroad.h file to compile properly for this project, you must also add a OPENGL definition to the "Preprocessor definitions" field. This will ensure the OpenGL includes are made available for the project.

To add the *Crossroads* debug library to the project, select Build/settings.../Link. Then select the debug subproject in the "Settings For:" list and type the path to the *Crossroads* debug library in the "Object/library modules:" field. See Figure 13.7.

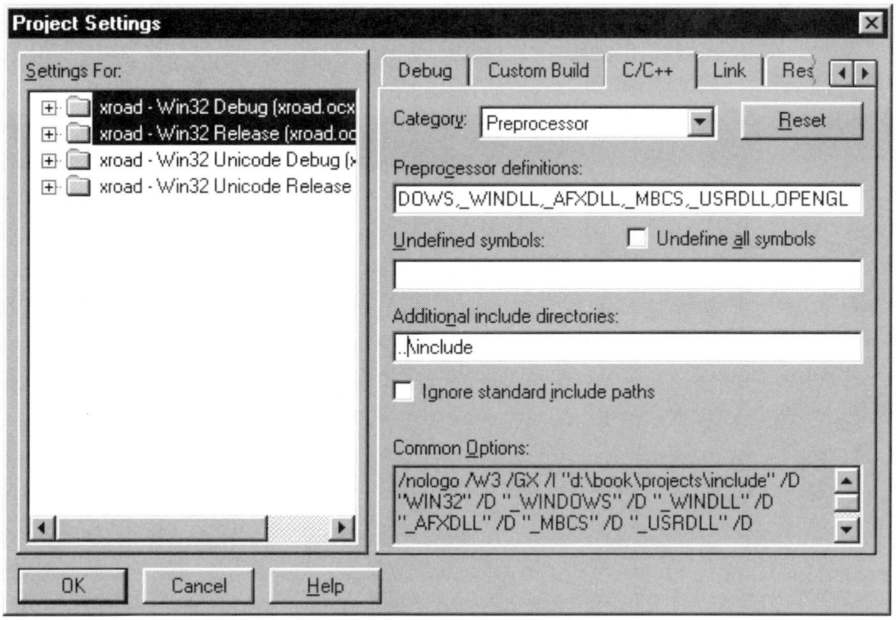

Figure 13.6. Adding the include directory to the project.

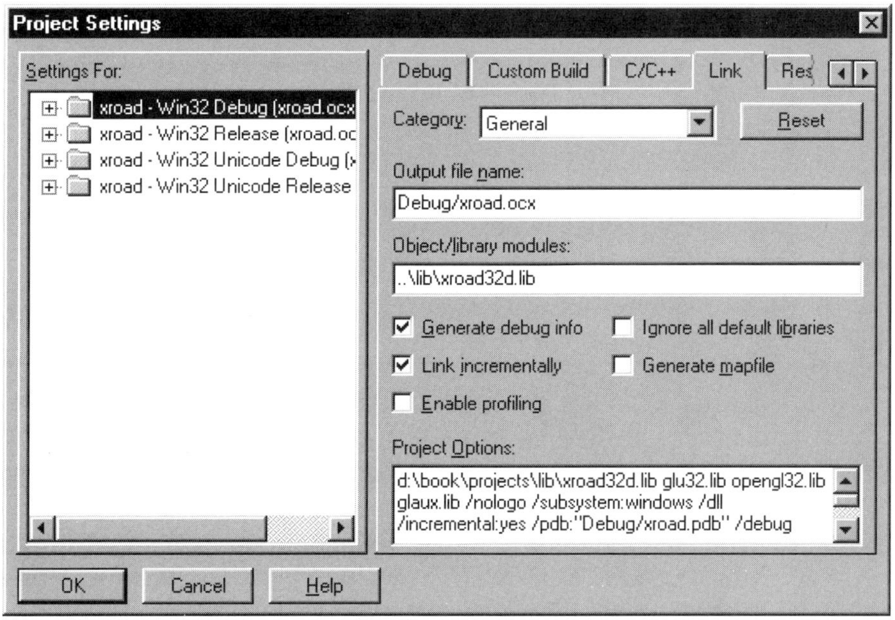

Figure 13.7. Adding the debug library to the project.

Next, select the release subproject in the "Settings For:" list and type the release *Crossroads* library location into the "Object/library modules:" field. See Figure 13.8.

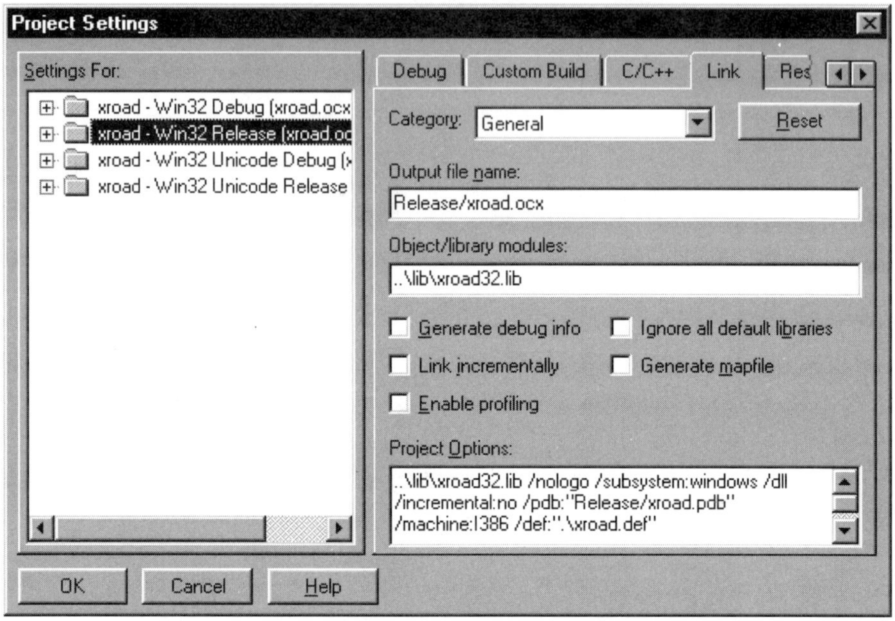

Figure 13.8. Adding the release subproject to the project.

The final step is to add the OpenGL libraries to the project. Select both projects in the "Settings For:" list. Then in the "Object/library modules:" field type in gluax.lib, glu32.lib, and opengl32.lib (see Figure 13.9). Click OK.

The project has now been updated and should compile correctly. Click the Build icon on the toolbar or press Shift+F8 to build the project. If it doesn't build correctly, correct any problems before continuing.

Adding File Open and Save Capabilities

The OCX control allows you to display 3D scenes. However, there currently is no way in the control to specify which file to load and render. In this section, you add the capability of opening and saving 3D scenes using three new properties that you will create.

To create a property for an OCX control, invoke the ClassWizard in your Visual C++ OCX project by selecting View/ClassWizard or pressing Ctrl+W. When the ClassWizard dialog appears, select the OLE Automation tab. This tab brings up the wizard that allows OLE properties and methods to be added to the currently selected class. Make sure that the *CXroadCtrl* class is selected in the "Class name:" field. See Figure 13.10.

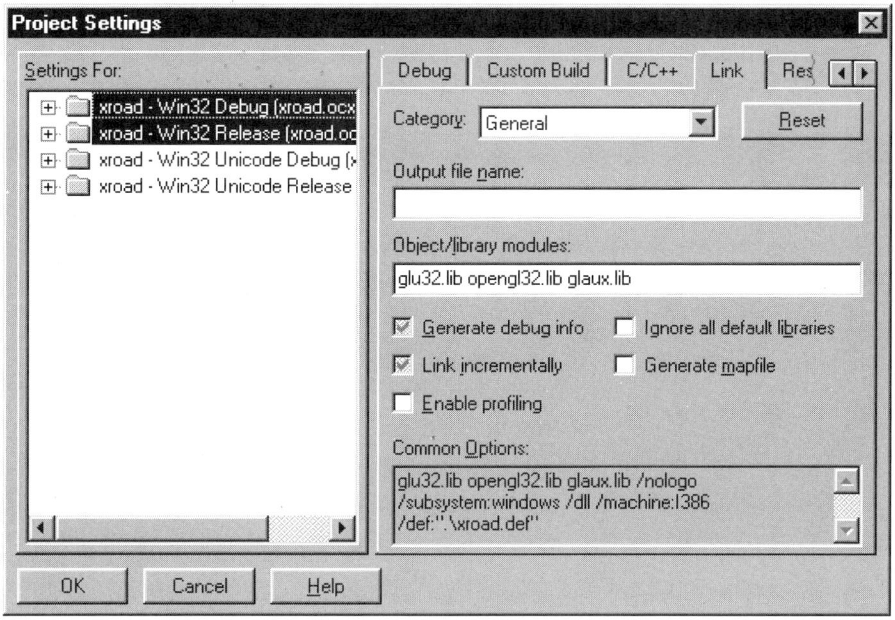

Figure 13.9. Adding the OpenGL libraries to the project.

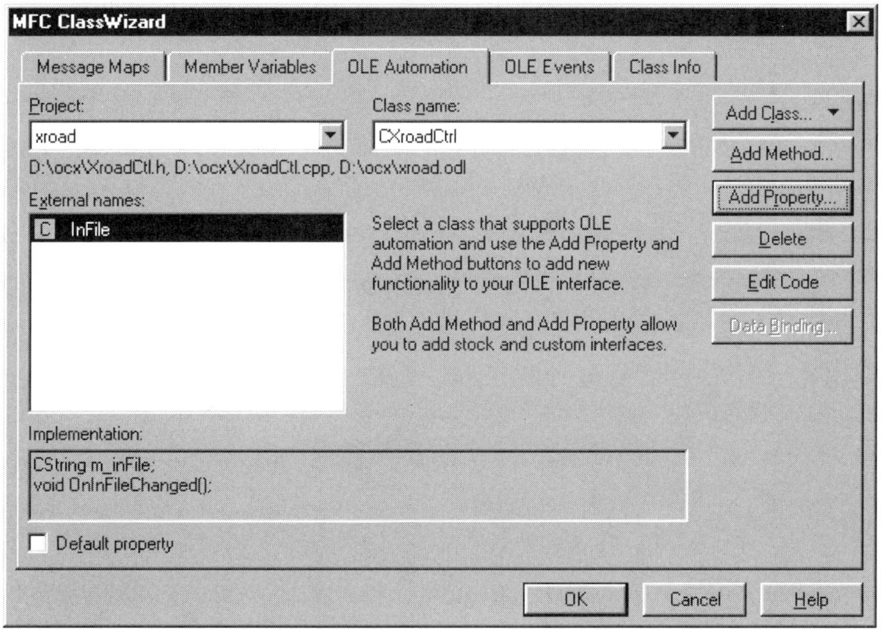

Figure 13.10. Adding OLE properties and methods.

To create a property, select Add Property... . This button brings up a dialog that allows you to create a OLE property (see Figure 13.11). In this case, you want to create a property that allows the specification of the filename of an input file. When a filename is assigned to this property in the running OLE control, that file will be read and placed as the current scene.

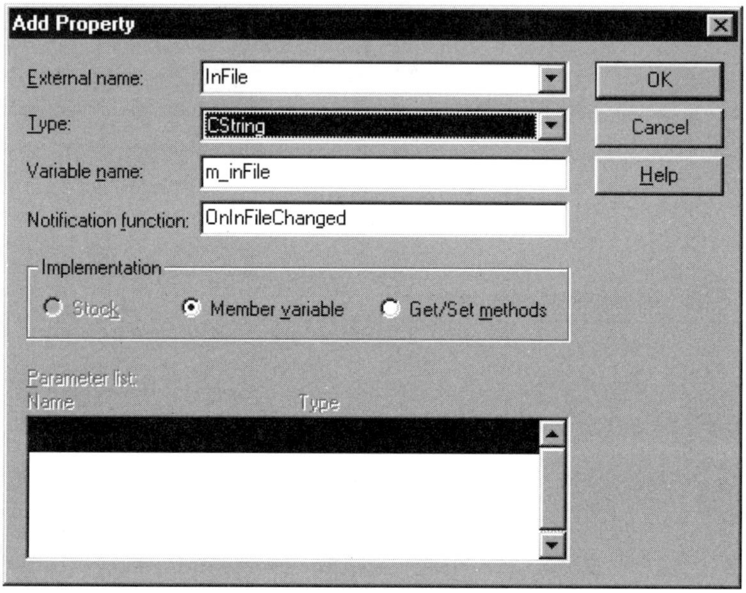

Figure 13.11. Specifying an input file name.

Name the property "InFile" and place the name into the "External name:" field. Select "CString" in the "Type:" field and set the implementation to "Member variable." Click OK.

You now have implemented an OLE property. If you select Edit Code on the ClassWizard, you will find that the following implementation has been added to XroadCtl.cpp:

```
void CXroadCtrl::OnInFileChanged()
{
    // TODO: Add notification handler code

    SetModifiedFlag();
}
```

The `OnInFileChanged()` member function is called whenever the "InFile" property is changed. This would be an ideal place to implement the file reader. To do this, add the bold lines shown in the following code to `OnInFileChanged()`:

```
void CXroadCtrl::OnInFileChanged()
{
    // Delete old scene
    Clear();

    // Read new scene
    XRoad_Reader(this, m_inFile);

    // Make sure that OnDraw() is called.
    InvalidateControl();

    SetModifiedFlag();
}
```

If you recompile your project now and run the test container, you will be able to read a 3D scene. First, bring up the OLE Test Container and add the "Xroad Control" to the container. Then view and set a property via View/Properties… . Finally, to view a supported 3D file, type the full path name into the "InFile" property. The file will be read and then rendered in the OCX control. See Figure 13.12.

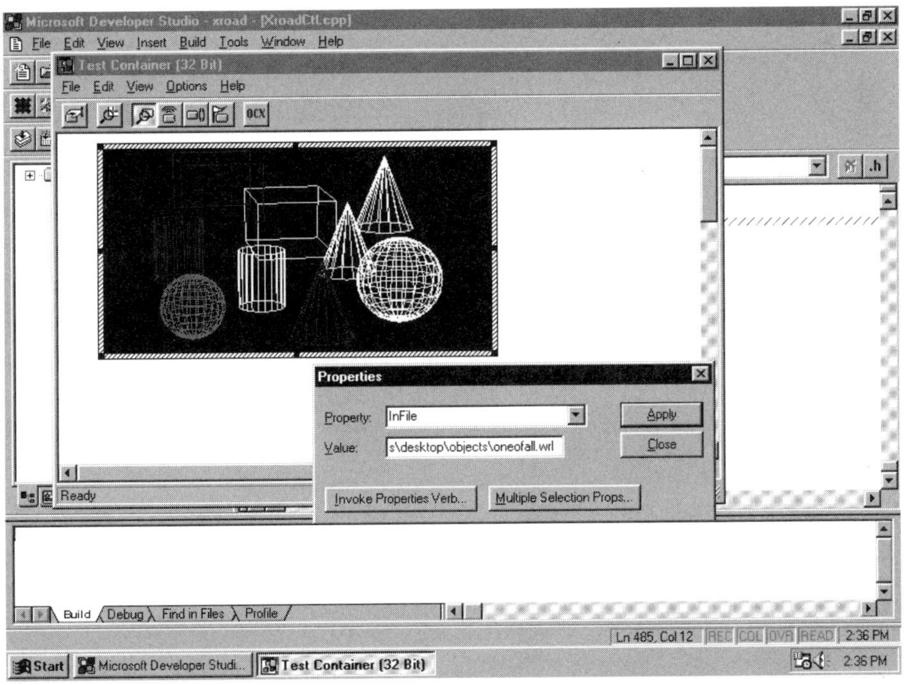

Figure 13.12. Example of OCX reading a VRML file in the test container.

Finishing the File Open Implementation

Although you now can read in 3D files, your file open implementation is incomplete. One 3D file format supported—POVRay—requires an include path.

The POVRay path string is a semicolon-separated list of full path names. To make the POVRay path available, add a "POVRayPath" property following the procedure in the previous section. Be sure the *XroadCtl* class is selected in the "Class name:" field and "POVRayPath" is in the "External name:" field. See Figure 13.13.

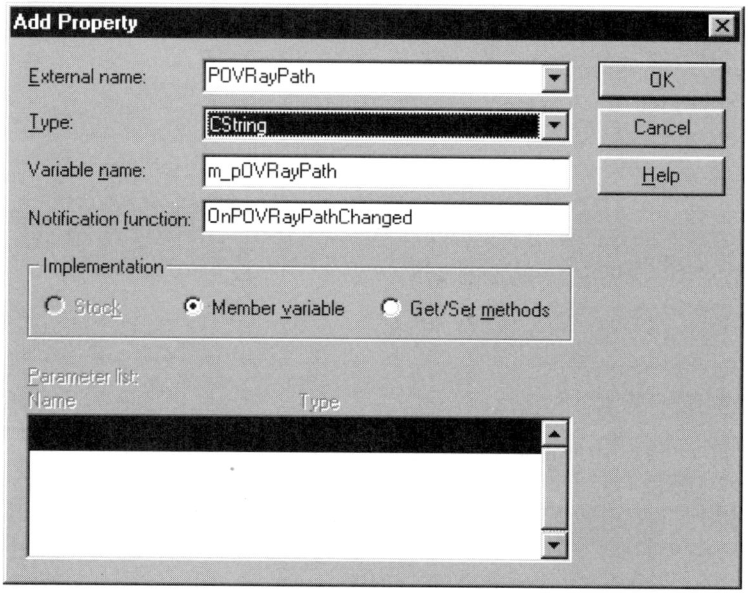

Figure 13.13. Adding a POVRayPath property.

You now have an implementation of the "POVRayPath" property. Note that the internal name for this property is `m_pOVRayPath`. To update the current code to read POVRay files correctly, you must add the bold code shown in the following to the `OnInFileChanged()` member function:

```
void CXroadCtrl::OnInFileChanged()
{
    // Delete old scene
    Clear();
```

```
    // Read new scene
    XRoad_Reader(this, m_inFile, m_pOVRayPath);

    // Make sure that OnDraw() is called.
    InvalidateControl();

    SetModifiedFlag();
}
```

No action must be performed when the POVRay path is changed, so there is no need to modify the `OnPOVRayPathChanged()` member function. We care about the path only when a POVRay file is to be read.

Implementing File Save

Implementing a file save property is nearly identical to implementing the file open property. The only difference is the few lines of code that are added to the `OnChanged()` member function that will be created by the ClassWizard.

To make the save file name, "OutFile," available, add an "OutFile" property following the procedure given in previous sections. Be sure the *XroadCtl* class is selected in the "Class name:" field and "OutFile" is in the "External name:" field. See Figure 13.14.

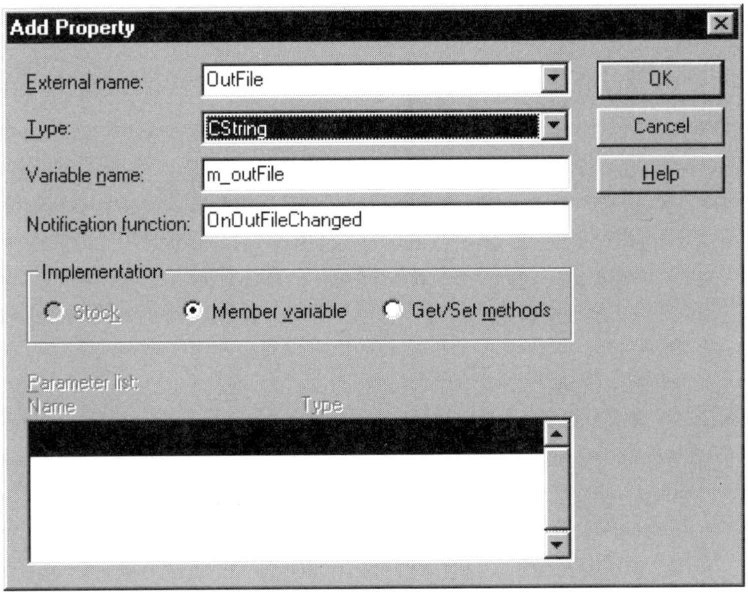

Figure 13.14. Adding the OutFile property.

You now have implemented this OLE property. If you select Edit Code on the ClassWizard, you will find that the following implementation has been added to XroadCtl.cpp:

```
void CXroadCtrl::OnOutFileChanged()
{
    // TODO: Add notification handler code

    SetModifiedFlag();
}
```

The `OnOutFileChanged()` member function is called whenever the "OutFile" property is changed. For this reason, this is a good place to add the file save implementation. To do that, add the bold lines shown in the following code to the `OnOutFileChanged()` member function:

```
void CXroadCtrl::OnOutFileChanged()
{
    // Write scene
    XRoad_Writer(this, m_outFile);
    SetModifiedFlag();
}
```

If you recompile your project now and run the test container, you will be able to write a 3D scene. First, bring up the OLE Test Container and add the "Xroad Control" to the container. Then view and set a property via View/Properties... . Finally, select a supported 3D file by typing the full path name into the "InFile" property. The file will be read and then rendered in the OCX control.

Now you can save the file as a new file by typing the full path name, along with the suffix of the 3D file format to which you wish to convert the scene. For example, to save the scene as a 3DS file named "test" in desktop, type "c:\windows\desktop\test.3ds" into the "OutFile" property.

Adding Some Details

Your program is now functionally complete, meaning it can read and write 3D files. However, there a few niceties that you should implement, for example, the OLE events for status messages and error messages and an OCX background color property.

Adding the OLE Events

To create an OLE event in your OCX control, bring up the ClassWizard in your Visual C++ OCX project by selecting View/ClassWizard or pressing Ctrl+W. When the ClassWizard dialog appears, select the OLE Events tab. This tab brings up the wizard that allows OLE events to be added to the currently selected class. Make sure that the *CXroadCtrl* class is selected in the "Class name" field. See Figure 13.15.

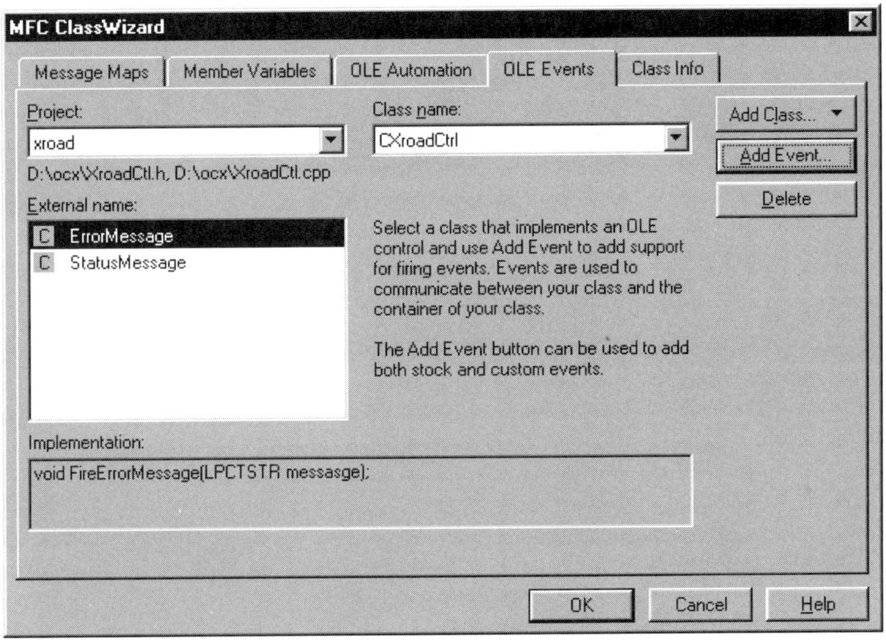

Figure 13.15. Creating an OLE event in the OCX control.

Next, click Add Event... . Type the name "StatusMessage" into the "External name:" field and add an argument named "message" with a type of "LPCTSTR." Click OK. See Figure 13.16.

Next, click Add Event again. Type the name "ErrorMessage" into the "External name:" field, add an argument named "message" with a type of "LPCTSTR", and click OK. See Figure 13.17.

Exit the ClassWizard. You can now finish the implementation of the `StatusMessage()` and `ErrorMessage()` member functions. Add the bold lines shown in the following code to the implementation of these functions. Doing this makes the messages available to programs using the OCX control.

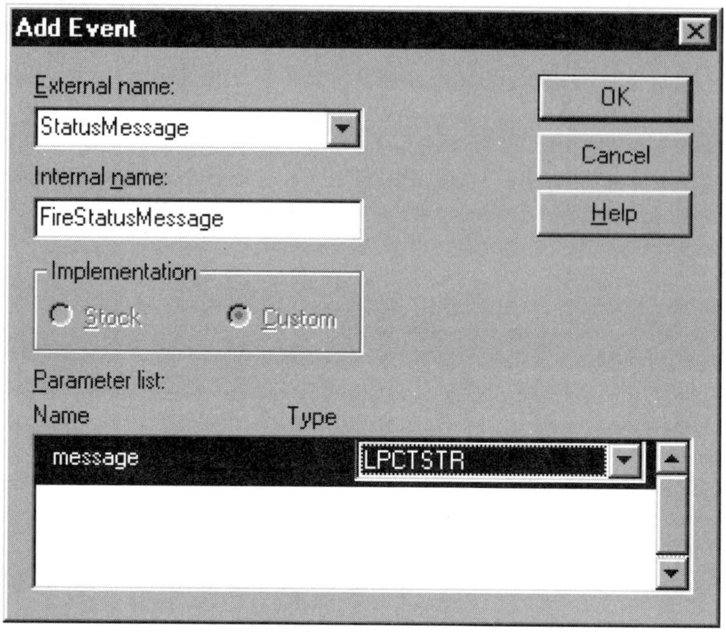

Figure 13.16. Adding the StatusMessage event.

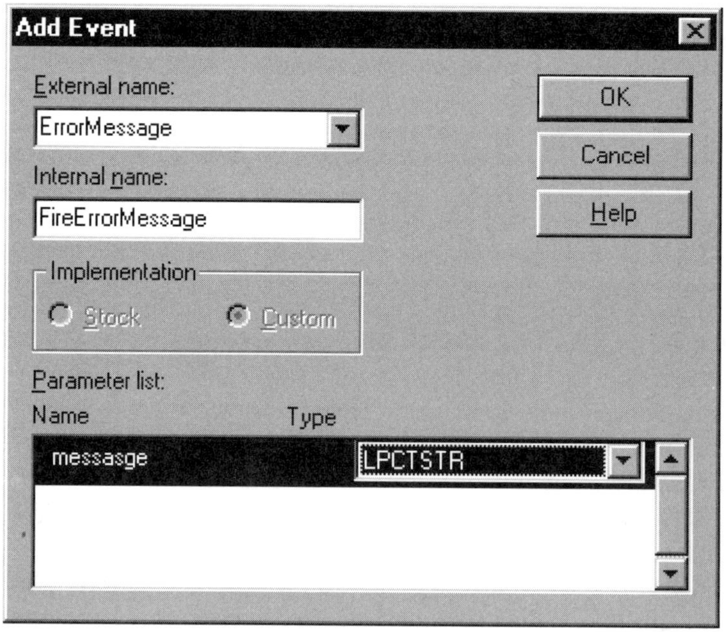

Figure 13.17. Adding the ErrorMessage event.

```
void CXroadCtrl::
StatusMessage( char* fmt, ... )
{
    va_list     argptr;
    char  buffer[256];

    va_start(argptr, fmt);
    vsprintf( buffer, fmt, argptr );
    va_end(argptr);

    FireStatusMessage(buffer);

    return;
}

void CXroadCtrl::
ErrorMessage( char* fmt, ... )
{
    va_list    argptr;
    char  buffer[256];

    va_start(argptr, fmt);
    vsprintf( buffer, fmt, argptr );
    va_end(argptr);

    FireErrorMessage(buffer);
}
```

Adding the Background Color Property

The background color property is a stock property for an OCX control. This means the implementation already exists. All you need to do is make the property available.

To do this, bring up the ClassWizard as before and select the OLE Automation tab. Click Add Property and then select "BackColor" from the "External Name:" combo box. Click OK. See Figure 13.18. You have added the BackColor implementation.

Your project is complete. After you compile this project you will have support of all of the features discussed. In the next section, I show you how to use some of these features.

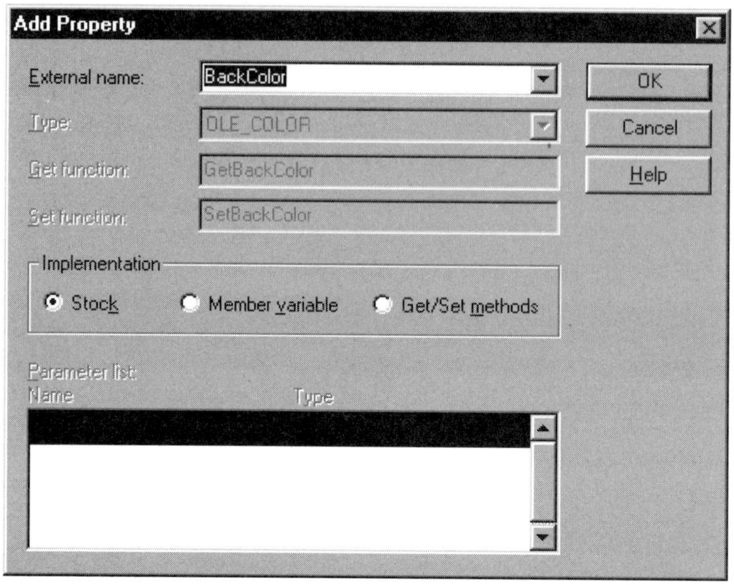

Figure 13.18. Adding the BackColor implementation.

Using the OCX Control with Visual Basic 4.0

Visual Basic is a very flexible and quick way to test the OCX control you created. Using that control, one additional Visual Basic control, and about 20 lines of Visual Basic code, you can create an application that can perform the same tasks as the standalone *Crossroads* application.

To build this Visual Basic application, first bring up the Visual Basic 4.0 32-bit development environment. This environment looks like Figure 13.19 when it is first invoked.

Next, add the *Crossroads* OCX control to the control palette. Select Tools/Custom Control… and then select the "xroad OLE Control Module." A new icon appears in the bottom right-hand corner of the control palette. Since you haven't defined the icon for this control, it uses the default icon, OCX. See Figure 13.20.

Select the OCX icon and place a *Crossroads* OCX on the default Form1 associated with the Visual Basic project. The resulting form and property sheet for the *Crossroads* OCX should look like Figure 13.21.

Note that the properties "BackColor," "InFile," "POVRayPath," and "OutFile" are visible on the property sheet for the OCX. If you were to type a legitimate filename of a supported 3D file into the "InFile" property, that file would be read and displayed on the current Visual Basic Form1.

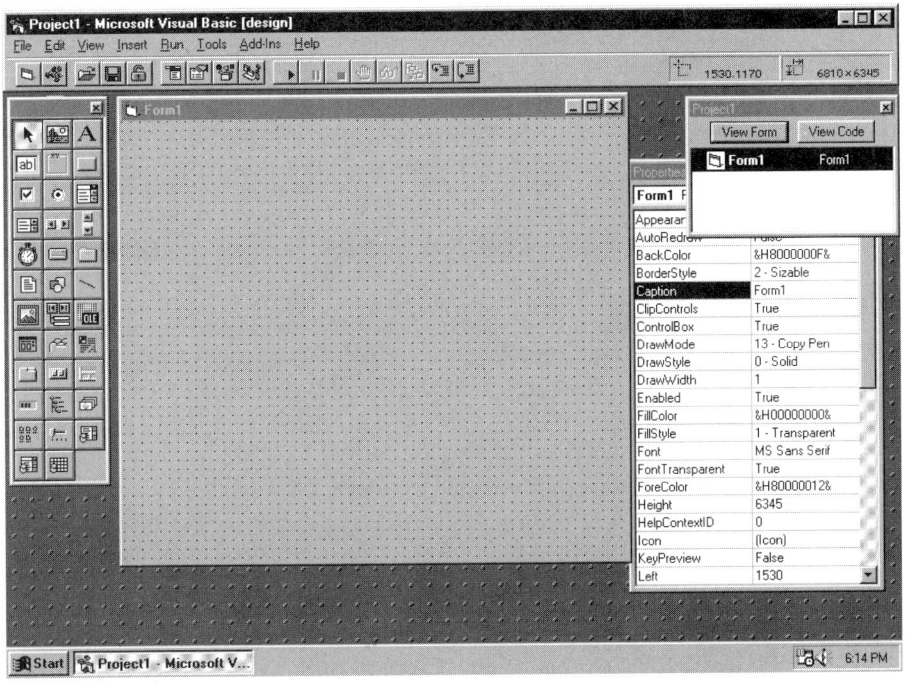

Figure 13.19. The default Visual Basic 4.0 development environment.

Figure 13.20. The Visual Basic control palette with OCX Control.

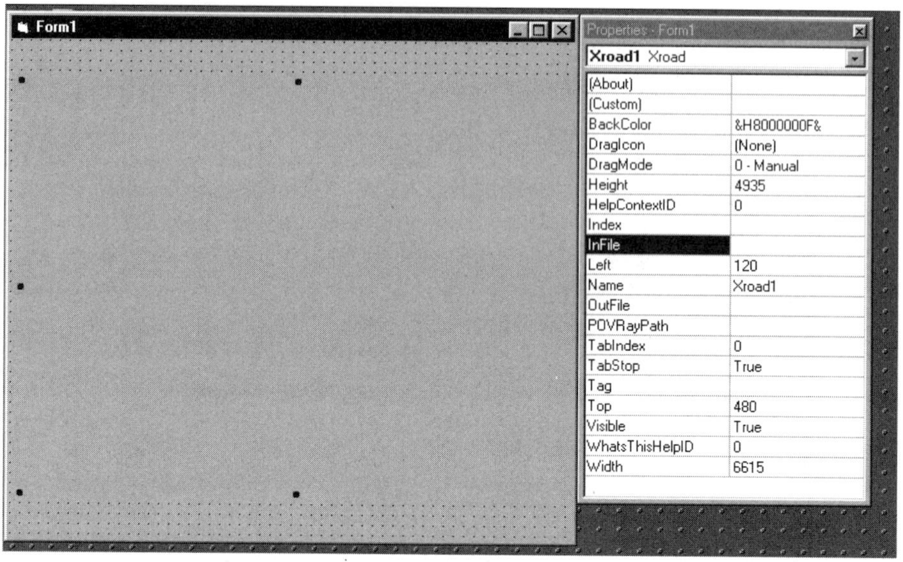

Figure 13.21. The Crossroads OCX and its property sheet.

The next step is to add a menu. Select Tools/Menu Editor to bring up the Menu Editor dialog. Add the top-level menu selection of "File" with the sub-selections "Open...," "Save As...," and "Exit." See Figure 13.22.

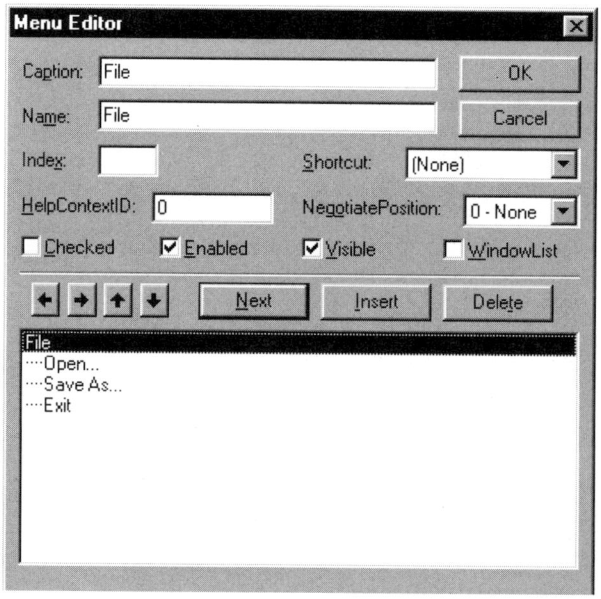

Figure 13.22. Adding a menu to the Visual Basic project.

Click OK. The top-level menu item “File” should now be visible on the form. Before you can add code to the menu items, you need to add a CommonDialog control to the form. To do this, select the CommonDialog control icon (see Figure 13.23) and place it on the form. In the property sheet of the CommonDialog control, change the “Name” property from “CommonDialog1” to “CD.”

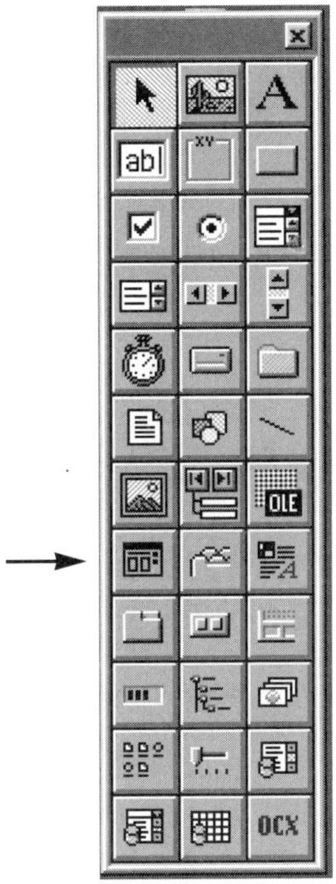

Figure 13.23. Adding a CommonDialog control.

Add code to the Open… menu item by selecting that menu entry. Visual Basic will bring up the code associated with the action. The function that appears is an empty `OpenMenu_Click()` function. Add the following code to that function:

```
Private Sub OpenMenu_Click()
    On Error GoTo Cancel
    CD.Filter = "3D Studio (*.3ds)|*.3ds|Autocad DXF
(*.dxf)|*.dxf|POVRay V2.2 (*.pov)|*.pov|RAW
(*.raw)|*.raw|TrueSpace (*.cob)|*.cob|Wavefront
(*.obj)|*.obj|WTK-NFF (*.nff)|*nff|VRML (*.wrl)|*.wrl"
    CD.ShowOpen
    Xroad1.InFile = CD.filename
```

```
    Exit Sub
Cancel:
    Exit Sub
End Sub
```

To start the project running, click Run or press F5. Select File/Open... and then a file to be read and rendered. Figure 13.24 shows an example program form.

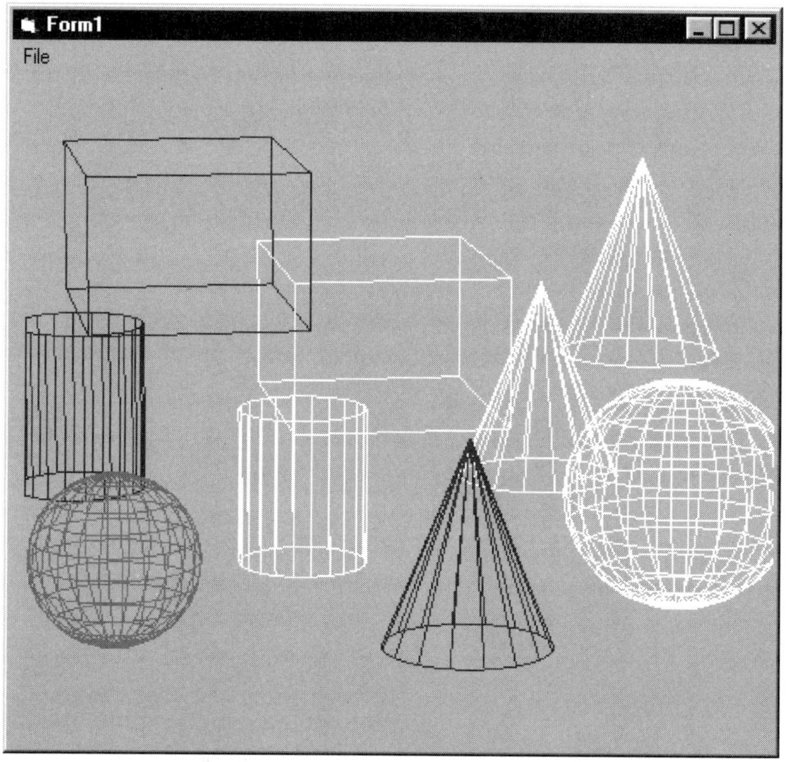

Figure 13.24. Example of a running Visual Basic program.

Adding the Save As... menu item support is just as easy. Add code to Save As... by selecting that menu entry. Visual Basic will bring up the code associated with the action. The function that appears is an empty `SaveAs_Click()` function. Add the following code to that function:

```
Private Sub SaveAs_Click()
    On Error GoTo Cancel
     CD.Filter = "3D Studio (*.3ds)|*.3ds|Autocad DXF
```

```
(*.dxf)|*.dxf|POVRay V2.2 (*.pov)|*.pov|RAW
(*.raw)|*.raw|TrueSpace (*.cob)|*.cob|Wavefront
(*.obj)|*.obj|WTK-NFF (*.nff)|*nff|VRML (*.wrl)|*.wrl"
    CD.ShowSave
    Xroad1.OutFile = CD.filename
    Exit Sub
Cancel:
    Exit Sub
End Sub
```

The last menu item to add to complete the functionality of this application is an Exit menu item. Add code to Exit by selecting that menu entry. Visual Basic will bring up the code associated with the action. The function that appears is an empty `Exit_Click()` function. Add the following code to that function:

```
Private Sub Exit_Click()
    End
End Sub
```

References

Crain, Dennis. "Windows NT OpenGL: Getting Started." April 1994. http://www.microsoft.com/msdn/library/technote/opengl9.htm.

Kruglinski, David J. *Inside Visual C++*. 1993. Redmond, WA: Microsoft Press.

Chapter 14

The Crossroads Class Library Reference

In this chapter, I define the representation of the 3D scenes found in the software in this book. The design goal is to make the *Crossroads* class library map as close to the equivalent VRML representation as possible.

Using VRML as the model for the design of the library has several advantages. First, VRML is straightforward to understand and reasonably well documented. This relieves some of the documentation needs, since reading a tutorial on VRML should be sufficient for understanding how these classes need to be instantiated to represent a scene.

Second, VRML-like representation has a very natural mapping into OpenGL calls. As a result, the internal representation can be easily displayed using the portable OpenGL 3D library. Third, VRML is a popular and fast-evolving standard. Having the *Crossroads* library track VRML closely means that dealing with the addition of new features to the VRML should be very straightforward.

Of course, this model has some disadvantages. One general problem is that the model used for representing data in VRML is more flexible than the model used in some of the other 3D file formats described in previous chapters. So while reading a less rich format into the *Crossroads* library should be easy, moving an arbitrary VRML representation into a less rich format can cause some interesting problems. You will see most of them are handled by using some of the helper classes included with the library.

Another general problem with the internal representation is that it doesn't represent all 3D constructs that are used in some 3D file formats. So there will be a loss of data when reading from these formats. An example of this can be seen when looking at the POVRay file format. POVRay is a very rich file format, but it has many constructs that cannot be directly represented in the *Crossroads* class library. For example, POVRay can represent objects as the boolean operation of several graphics primitives, but that concept is not yet a part of VRML.

As the developer of a 3D file format reader, you have several options when dealing with these problems. You could add the primitive operation to the class library, you could convert the constructs into a set of constructs that can be represented in the library, or you could simply ignore the construct.

In the file formats described in the previous chapters, missing functionality in the class library will cause data loss in the conversion process. Often this isn't a problem. We are all familiar with data loss during the conversion process. For example, when a CorelDRAW drawing is converted into a BMP file, you usually don't expect a paint program that reads the converted image to be able to perform the same operations on the image as CorelDRAW does. This conversion from a vector drawing format to a raster image format causes much data loss, but usually the loss is an acceptable trade-off for having the data where we need it. The same is true for converting 3D files.

How to Use This Chapter

This chapter documents each type and class in the *Crossroads* 3D internal representation class library. It is intended as a reference guide to each of the classes that make up the 3D class library.

The information in this chapter is key to your understanding the implementations of the 3D file formats described in previous chapters. However, it probably makes good sense to read the tutorial, found in Chapter 2, first and then use this chapter as a reference to the library.

Primitive Types and Classes and Helper Classes

Several types of primitive types and classes and helper classes are used in the internal representation. Data representation types include *SFMatrix*, *SFVec2f*, *SFVec3f*, *SFRotation*, class *MFArray<>*, *MFLong*, *MFFloat*, *MFString*, *MFVec2f*, *MFVec3f*, and *MFMatrix*. One class—*GState*—holds the traversal state of the 3D scene. The classes *GWrite* and *MeshCompactor* help in reading and writing the internal 3D representation. Figure 14.1 lists these primitive types and classes and helper classes.

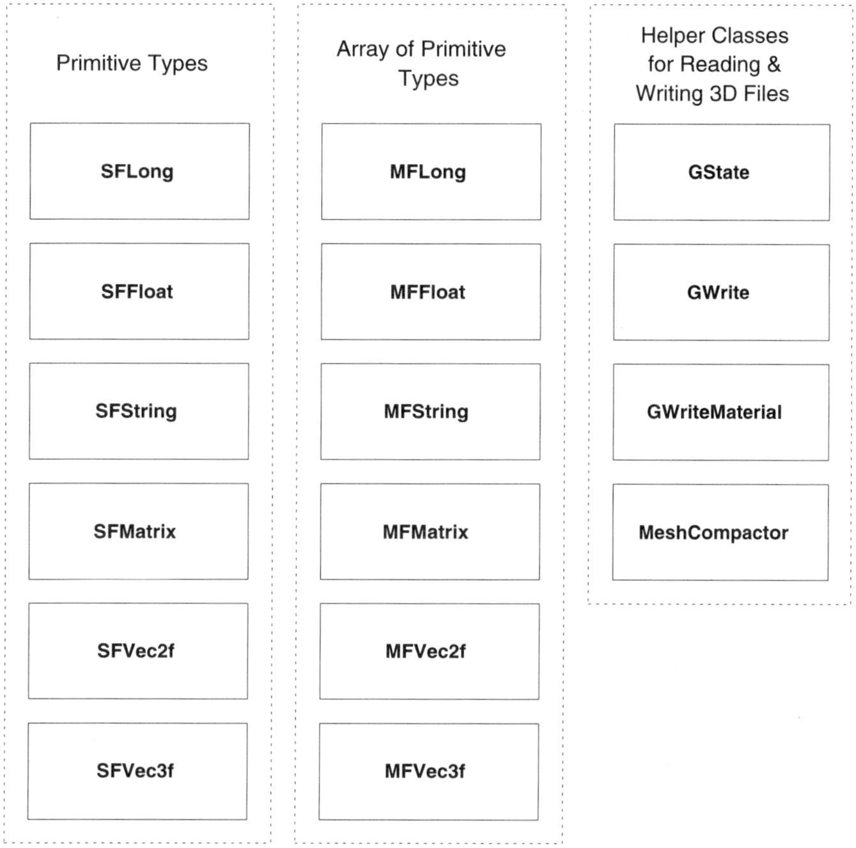

Figure 14.1. Primitive types and classes and helper classes of the internal representation.

SFLong, SFFloat, and SFString Types

The *SFLong*, *SFFloat*, and *SFString* types are simply the following C++ typedefs:

```
typedef long   SFLong;
typedef float  SFFloat;
typedef char*  SFString
```

These types are used for consistency's sake. They allow all of the types used in the internal representation to map directly to the expected VRML type. The type names for VRML language constructs and the internal representation are identical where possible.

SFMatrix Class Definition

The *SFMatrix* class implements a 4 × 4 matrix class. It has a minimal number of member functions, but there are many friend functions to help create an *SFMatrix* instance in many common situations.

Member Variables

There is only one member variable for this class—a 4 × 4 matrix of floating-point values.

```
SFFLoat value[4] [4];
```

Member Functions

```
SFMatrix(void)
```

This member function is the default constructor. It initializes the matrix to the identity matrix.

```
SFMatrix(const SFMatrix&)
```

This member function is the copy constructor. It copies the contents of the passed *SFMatrix* into the newly created *SFMatrix* instance.

```
SFMatrix& operator=(const SFMatrix&)
```

This member function is the assignment operator (=). It copies the matrix value found on the right-hand side of the equals (=) operator into the current matrix instance. A reference to the current *SFMatrix* instance is returned. This process allows multiple assignment operators to be defined in one line.

```
SFFloat* operator[](int)
```

This member function is the index operator ([ ]). It returns a pointer to the float[4] value of the specified row. It allows an *SFMatrix* instance to have its matrix elements be directly referenced or assigned using the index operator. For example,

```
value[0][0] = 1.0;
```

could be used to assign the value 1.0 to the (0, 0) element of the matrix instance.

`SFMatrix operator+(const SFMatrix&)`

This member function is the addition operator (+). It performs an addition of each numeric entry in the current *SFMatrix* instance with the corresponding entry in the *SFMatrix* argument.

`SFMatrix operator-(const SFMatrix&)`

This member function is the subtraction operator (–). It performs a subtraction of each numeric entry in current *SFMatrix* instance with the corresponding entry in the *SFMatrix* argument.

`SFMatrix operator*(const SFMatrix&)`

This member function is the multiplication operator (*). It performs a matrix multiplication of the current *SFMatrix* instance value with the *SFMatrix* argument. The resultant value is returned on the stack.

`int operator==(const SFMatrix&)`

This member function is the equals operator (==). It compares each entry in the *SFMatrix* instance with the corresponding entry in the *SFMatrix* argument. If all the values are equal, `TRUE` (1) is returned; otherwise, `FALSE` (0) is returned.

`int operator!=(const SFMatrix&)`

This member function is the inequality operator ( ). It compares each entry in the *SFMatrix* instance with the corresponding entry in the *SFMatrix* argument. If all the values are equal, `FALSE` (0) is returned; otherwise, `TRUE` (1) is returned.

Friend Functions

`FMatrix operator*(const SFMatrix&, const SFFloat)`

This friend function multiplies each element of a matrix by a floating-point value. The resultant value is returned as an *SFMatrix*.

`SFMatrix operator*(const SFFloat, const SFMatrix&)`

This friend function multiplies each element of a matrix by a floating-point value. The resultant value is returned as an *SFMatrix*.

`SFMatrix Zero(void)`

This friend function returns a matrix of zeros.

`SFMatrix Identity(void)`

This friend function returns a matrix with ones on the diagonal and the rest of the values set to zero. This value is the identity value for the matrix for multiplication.

`SFMatrix Translate(const SFFloat, const SFFloat, const SFFloat)`

This friend function interprets the first argument as the amount to translate in the x-direction, the second argument as the amount to translate in the y-direction, and the third argument as the amount to translate in the z-direction. The transformation matrix returned performs the equivalent translation.

`SFMatrix Translate(const SFVec3f&)`

This friend function returns the transformation matrix that performs the translation specified by the *SFVec3f* argument.

`SFMatrix Scale(const SFFloat, const SFFloat, const SFFloat)`

This friend function interprets the first argument as the x-scale, the second argument as the y-scale, and the third argument as the z-scale. The transformation matrix returned performs the equivalent scale operation.

`SFMatrix Scale(const SFVec3f&)`

This friend function returns the transformation matrix that performs the scale operation specified by the *SFVec3f* argument.

`SFMatrix RotateX(const SFFloat)`

This friend function returns the transformation matrix that performs a rotation around the x-axis. The floating-point argument is the amount of rotation in degrees.

```
SFMatrix RotateY(const SFFloat)
```

This friend function returns the transformation matrix that performs a rotation around the *y*-axis. The floating-point argument is the amount of rotation in degrees.

```
SFMatrix RotateZ(const SFFloat)
```

This friend function returns the transformation matrix that performs a rotation around the *z*-axis. The floating-point argument is the amount of rotation in degrees.

```
SFMatrix Rotate(const SFFloat, const SFFloat, const
SFFloat, const SFFloat)
```

This friend function returns a transformation matrix that performs a rotation around the axis defined by the vector specified by the first three floating-point arguments. The fourth argument is the amount of rotation in degrees.

```
SFMatrix Rotate(const SFFloat, const SFFloat,
const SFFloat)
```

This friend function returns a transformation matrix that rotates the *x*-, *y*-, and *z*-axes by the amounts specified by the arguments. The first argument is the amount of rotation in degrees around the *x*-axis, the second argument is the amount of rotation in degrees around the *y*-axis, and the third argument is the amount of rotation in degrees around the *z*-axis.

```
SFMatrix Rotate(const SFRotation&)
```

This friend function returns the transformation matrix for the specified *SFRotation* value.

SFVec2f Class Definition

The *SFVec2f* class defines a 2D point. It is typically used in the internal representation to define the position of a bitmap texture on a polygon.

Member Variables

This class has two floating-point values as member variables. These variables are private and must be accessed through the corresponding member functions.

```
private: SFFloat m_x, m_y
```

Member Functions

`SFVec2f(void)`

This member function is the default constructor. It sets both internal member variables to 0.0.

`SFVec3f(SFFloat, SFFloat)`

This member function is the constructor. It accepts two arguments. The first sets the member variable *m_x*; the second sets the member variable *m_y*.

`SFVec2f(const SFVec2f&)`

This member function is the copy constructor. It allows other *SFVec2f* instance variables to be used to assign the member values of the currently constructed instance.

`SFFloat& operator[](int)`

This member function is the index operator ([ ]). It allows the member variables to be referenced as if they were members of an array. An index value of 0 returns the *m_x* member variable. A value of 1 returns the *m_y* member variable. Any other value returns the value of *m_y*.

`SFVec2f& operator+= (const SFVec2f&)`

This member function is the operator (+=). It adds the *m_x* value of the argument to the *m_x* value of the current instance and adds the *m_y* value of the argument to the *m_y* value of the current instance. A reference to the current instance is returned.

`SFVec2f& operator-=(const SFVec2f&)`

This member function is the operator (-=). It subtracts the *m_x* value of the argument from the *m_x* value of the current instance and subtracts the *m_y* value of the argument from the *m_y* value of the current instance. A reference to the current instance is returned.

`SFVec2f& operator*=(const SFVec2f&)`

This member function is the operator (*=). It multiplies the *m_x* value of the argument by the *m_x* value of the current instance and multiplies the *m_y* value of the argument by the *m_y* value of the current instance. A reference to the current instance is returned.

```
SFVec2f& operator*=(const SFFloat)
```

This *= operator multiplies the *m_x* value of the current instance by the argument and multiplies the *m_y* of the current instance by the argument. A reference to the current instance is returned.

```
SFVec2f& operator/=(const SFFloat)
```

The /= operator divides the *m_x* value of the current instance by the argument and divides the *m_y* of the current instance by the argument. A reference to the current instance is returned.

```
int operator==(const SFVec2f&)
```

This member function is the equality operator (==). It returns a value of `TRUE` (1) if the member variables of the argument are equal to the member variables of the current instance; otherwise, it returns `FALSE` (0).

```
int operator!=(const SFVec2f&)
```

This member function is the inequality operator (!=). It returns a value of `TRUE` (1) if one or both member variables are different. It returns `FALSE` (0) if the member variables of the argument are equal to the member variables of the current instance.

SFVec3f Class Definition

The *SFVec3f* class defines the 3D vectors used to define points, normals, and colors.

Member Variables

This class defines a 3D point, a 3D vector, a 3D normal, or a color. It is used throughout the internal representation to define 3D polygons, colors, locations, and normals.

```
private: SFFloat m_x, m_y, m_z;
```

Member Functions

```
SFVec3f(SFFloat = 0.0, SFFloat = 0.0, SFFloat = 0.0)
```

This member function is a constructor. It can be used as the default constructor (when no arguments are passed) or as a constructor that sets the newly created instance to the specified values. The first argument sets the *m_x* value, the second sets the *m_y* value, and the third sets the *m_z* value.

```
SFVec3f(SFFloat v[3])
```

This member function is a constructor that allows the newly created instance to be assigned the value of the floating-point array. The value `v[0]` is assigned to *m_x*, `v[1]` to *m_y*, and `v[2]` to `v[3]`.

```
SFVec3f(const SFVec3f&)
```

This member function is the copy constructor. It copies the values of the member variables in the passed *SFVec3f* instance to the members of the newly constructed instance.

```
SFFloat& X(void)
```

This member function returns the value of *m_x*, which is returned as a reference. This means that changes to the returned value cause the underlying member variable to change, too.

```
SFFloat& Y(void)
```

This member function returns the value of *m_y*, which is returned as a reference. This means that changes to the returned value cause the underlying member variable to change, too.

```
SFFloat& Z(void)
```

This member function returns the value of *m_z*, which is returned as a reference. This means that changes to the returned value cause the underlying member variable to change, too.

```
SFFloat& Red(void)
```

This member function returns the value of *m_x*, which is returned as a reference. This means that changes to the returned value cause the underlying member variable to change, too. This member function allows an *SFVec3f* to be used as the representation of an RGB color.

```
SFFloat& Green(void)
```

This member function returns the value of *m_y*, which is returned as a reference. This means that changes to the returned value cause the underlying member variable to change, too. This member function allows an *SFVec3f* to be used as the representation of an RGB color.

`SFFloat& Blue(void)`

This member function returns the value of *m_z*, which is returned as a reference. This means that changes to the returned value cause the underlying member variable to change, too. This member function allows an *SFVec3f* to be used as the representation of an RGB color.

`const SFFloat X(void) const`

This member function returns the value of *m_x*. The const definition specifies that neither the *SFVec3f* instance nor the returned value may be modified.

`const SFFloat Y(void) const`

This member function returns the value of *m_y*. The const definition specifies that neither the *SFVec3f* instance nor the returned value may be modified.

`const SFFloat Z(void) const`

This member function returns the value of *m_z*. The const definition specifies that neither the *SFVec3f* instance nor the returned value may be modified.

`const SFFloat Red(void) const`

This member function returns the value of *m_x*. The const definition specifies that neither the *SFVec3f* instance nor the returned value may be modified. It allows an *SFVec3f* to be used as the representation of an RGB color.

`const SFFloat Green(void) const`

This member function returns the value of *m_y*. The const definition specifies that neither the *SFVec3f* instance nor the returned value may be modified. It allows an *SFVec3f* to be used as the representation of an RGB color.

`const SFFloat Blue(void) const`

This member function returns the value of *m_z*. The const definition specifies that neither the *SFVec3f* instance nor the returned value may be modified. It allows an *SFVec3f* to be used as the representation of an RGB color.

```
void X(SFFloat)
```

This member function sets *m_x* to the value passed.

```
void Y(SFFloat)
```

This member function sets *m_y* to the value passed.

```
void Z(SFFloat)
```

This member function sets *m_z* to the value passed.

```
SFFloat& operator[](int)
```

This member function allows the *m_x*, *m_y*, and *m_z* member variables to be indexed as if they were an *SFFloat* array. An index value of 0 returns the member *m_x*, a value of 1 returns the member *m_y*, and a value of 2 returns the member *m_z*. The return value is an *SFFloat* reference. Hence any subsequent assignment to the reference will change the underlying member variable.

```
SFVec3f& operator+=(const SFVec3f&)
```

This member function adds each member variable of the *SFVec3f* instance that is passed in to each of the corresponding member variables of the current *SFVec3f* instance. A reference to the current *SFVec3f* instance is returned as a reference. Hence any subsequent assignment to the returned value will affect the contents of the current *SFVec3f* instance.

```
SFVec3f& operator-=(const SFVec3f&)
```

This member function subtracts each member variable of the *SFVec3f* instance that is passed in from each of the corresponding member variables of the current *SFVec3f* instance. A reference to the current *SFVec3f* instance is returned as a reference. Hence any subsequent assignment to the returned value will affect the contents of the current *SFVec3f* instance.

```
SFVec3f& operator*=(const SFVec3f&)
```

This member function multiplies each member variable of the *SFVec3f* instance that is passed in by each of the corresponding member variables of the current *SFVec3f* instance. A reference to the current *SFVec3f* instance is returned as a reference. Hence any subsequent assignment to the returned value will affect the contents of the current *SFVec3f* instance.

```
SFVec3f& operator*=(const SFFloat)
```

This member function multiplies each member variable of the current *SFVec3f* instance by the floating-point value passed in the first argument. A reference to the current *SFVec3f* instance is returned as a reference. Hence any subsequent assignment to the returned value will affect the contents of the current *SFVec3f* instance.

```
SFVec3f& operator/=(const SFFloat)
```

This member function divides each member variable of the current *SFVec3f* instance by the floating-point value passed in the first argument. A reference to the current *SFVec3f* instance is returned as a reference. Hence any subsequent assignment to the returned value will affect the contents of the current *SFVec3f* instance.

```
int operator==(const SFVec3f&)
```

This member function compares two *SFVec3f* instances for equality. If all of the member variables of the current *SFVec3f* instance are equal to the corresponding member variables in the *SFVec3f* argument, then `TRUE` (1) is returned; otherwise, `FALSE` (0) is returned.

```
int operator!=(const SFVec3f&)
```

This member function compares two *SFVec3f* instances for inequality. If all of the member variables of the current *SFVec3f* instance are equal to the corresponding member variables in the *SFVec3f* argument, then `FALSE` (0) is returned; otherwise, `TRUE` (1) is returned.

Friend Functions

```
friend SFVec3f Normalize(const SFVec3f&)
```

This friend function divides each of the member variables of the *SFVec3f* argument by the magnitude of the *SFVec3f* argument. If the magnitude is 0.0, then the members are divided by 1.0. The resultant values are returned as a new *SFVec3f* instance.

```
friend SFFloat Magnitude(const SFVec3f&)
```

This friend function returns the magnitude of the *SFVec3f* argument.

```
friend SFFloat Dot(const SFVec3f&, const SFVec3f&)
```

This friend function calculates and returns the dot product of the two *SFVec3f* instances passed in as arguments.

```
friend SFVec3f Cross(const SFVec3f&, const
SFVec3f&)
```

This friend function calculates and returns the cross product of the two *SFVec3f* instances passed in as arguments.

```
friend SFVec3f operator+(const SFVec3f&, const
SFVec3f&)
```

This friend function adds the members *m_x*, *m_y*, and *m_z* of the first *SFVec3f* argument to the corresponding members of the second *SFVec3f* argument. The result is returned in a new *SFVec3f* instance.

```
friend SFVec3f operator-(const SFVec3f&, const
SFVec3f&)
```

This friend function subtracts the members *m_x*, *m_y*, and *m_z* of the second *SFVec3f* argument from the corresponding members of the first *SFVec3f* argument. The result is returned in a new *SFVec3f* instance.

```
friend SFVec3f operator*(const SFVec3f&, const
SFVec3f&)
```

This friend function multiplies the members *m_x*, *m_y*, and *m_z* of the first *SFVec3f* argument by the corresponding members of the second *SFVec3f* argument. The result is returned in a new *SFVec3f* instance.

```
friend SFVec3f operator*(const SFFloat, const
SFVec3f&)
```

This friend function multiplies the members *m_x*, *m_y*, and *m_z* of the second argument by the floating-point value of the first argument. The result is returned in a new *SFVec3f* instance.

```
friend SFVec3f operator*(const SFVec3f&, const
SFFloat)
```

This friend function multiplies the members *m_x*, *m_y*, and *m_z* of the first argument by the floating-point value of the second argument. The result is returned in a new *SFVec3f* instance.

```
friend SFVec3f operator*(const SFMatrix&, const
SFVec3f&)
```

This friend function multiplies the transformation matrix passed in the first argument by the *SFVec3f* passed in the second argument. The result of this transformation is returned in a new *SFVec3f* instance.

```
friend SFVec3f operator/(const SFVec3f&, const
SFVec3f&)
```

This friend function divides the members *m_x*, *m_y*, and *m_z* of the *SFVec3f* passed in the first argument by the corresponding members of the *SFVec3f* passed as the second argument. The result is returned in a *SFVec3f* value.

```
friend SFVec3f operator/(const SFVec3f&, const
SFFloat)
```

This friend function divides the members *m_x*, *m_y*, and *m_z* of the *SFVec3f* in the first argument by the floating-point value passed in the second argument. The result is returned in a *SFVec3f* value.

```
friend int operator==(const SFVec3f&, const
SFVec3f&)
```

This friend function is the equality operator (==). If each member variable of the first *SFVec3f* argument matches the corresponding member of the second *SFVec3f*, then it returns the value `TRUE` (1); otherwise, it returns `FALSE` (0).

```
friend SFVec3f Min(const SFVec3f&, const SFVec3f&)
```

This friend function returns an *SFVec3f* value that is the minimum of each member argument. It is useful when computing the range of an object created from many vertex points.

```
friend SFVec3f Max(const SFVec3f&, const SFVec3f&)
```

This friend function returns an *SFVec3f* value that is the maximum of each member argument. It is useful when computing the range of an object created from many vertex points.

MFArray Class Template

The *MFArray* class is a template definition for a dynamically resizeable array class. It is never used directly. Rather, it is the basis for all of the array primitive types. Any class that begins with the MF prefix is created using the template facilities of this class definition. This class implements a simple array template class.

Creating our own class rather than using MFC's built-in array class makes the resulting code more portable.

Member Variables and Class Definition

The *MFArray* class definition is used to define new *MFArray* expanded classes. Its usage is:

```
MFArray<type> newVariable;
```

or

```
typedef MFArray<type> newType;
```

In the first example, *MFArray* is used to create an instance of *newVariable*, which is an *MFArray* class instance for the specified *<type>*. Subsequent usage of the newly created instance will replace the type `T` with the type specified in the *MFArray* usage.

In the second example, *MFArray* is used to create a new type, with the type `T`'s being replaced with the type passed to the template argument. This is how the types *MFLong*, *MFFloat*, *MFString*, *MFMatrix*, *MFVec2f*, and *MFVec3f* are defined.

```
template <class T> class MFArray {
private:
    T* m_array[MaxArrayBins];
    long  m_size;
    long  m_increment;
    long  m_current;
public:
    MFArray(void);
    ~MFArray(void);
    MFArray(const MFArray&);
    MFArray(const T&);
    MFArray& operator=(const MFArray&);

    void Clear(void);
    void ReSize(long);
    T& operator[](long)
    SFLong LookUp(const T&);
    SFLong NextOccurance(const T&, const SFLong = 0);
```

```
    long Add(const T&, const SFLong = FALSE);
    long Replace(const long, const T&);
    long  Elements(void);
};
```

Member Functions

`MFArray(void)`

This member function is the default constructor. It initializes the newly created *MFArray* instance.

`~MFArray(void)`

This member function is the destructor. It deletes any allocated storage associated with the *MFArray* type.

`MFArray(const MFArray&)`

This member function is the copy constructor. It copies the contents of the passed *MFArray* type to the newly created *MFArray* instance. This is a deep copy.

`MFArray(const T&)`

This member function is a constructor. It initializes the newly created *MFArray* instance and assigns the passed argument to the first element of the array.

`MFArray& operator=(const MFArray&)`

This member function performs a deep copy of the *MFArray* argument to the current *MFArray* instance. The contents of the current *MFArray* instance are destroyed.

`void Clear(void)`

This member function deletes the contents of the *MFArray* instances and reinitializes it to be of zero length.

`void ReSize(long)`

This member function enlarges the current *MFArray* instance. It usually isn't called by the user. Rather, the other members typically use it when the array needs to be dynamically resized.

```
T& operator[](long)
```

This member function returns the value that corresponds to the specified index. The index range is 0 to `Elements()-1`. Passing an index that is out of range will produce unpredictable results.

```
SFLong LookUp(const T&)
```

This member function searches the contents of the *MFArray* instance for any occurrence of the argument. The search starts at element 0 and continues through the end of the array. If a match is found, then the index of that value is returned; otherwise, the value –1 is returned.

```
SFLong NextOccurence(const T&, const SFLong = 0)
```

This member function searches the contents of the *MFArray* instance for the first occurrence of the first argument, starting at the index specified by the second argument. If a match is found, then the index of that value is returned; otherwise, the value –1 is returned. If no second argument is passed, then this function has the same semantics as the `LookUp()` function.

```
long Add(const T&, const SFLong = FALSE)
```

This member function conditionally adds the value passed in the first argument to the end of the array. If the second argument is `FALSE`, then this value is always added. If the second argument is `TRUE`, then the value is added only if it is the first occurrence of that value in the array. This allows to select whether the array contains a single occurrence or multiple occurrences of a value.

```
long Replace(const long, const T&)
```

This member function overwrites an existing value at the index specified by the first argument with the value passed in the second argument. The index written is returned. If the index specified is larger than the current range of the array, the array is automatically resized. If the index is negative, the results are unpredictable.

```
long Elements(void)
```

This member function returns the number of elements currently in the array. The array may be an index value from 0 to `Elements()-1`.

MFLong Class Definition

Functions that begin with MF are arrays of the specified primitive. In this implementation, all MF-derived classes are created by parameterizing the template *MFArray*. The type *MFLong* is created using the following definition:

```
typedef MFArray<SFLong> MFLong;
```

MFFloat Class Definition

Functions that begin with MF are arrays of the specified primitive. In this implementation, all MF-derived classes are created by parameterizing the template *MFArray*. The type *MFFloat* is created using the following definition:

```
typedef MFArray<SFFloat> MFFloat;
```

MFString Class Definition

Functions that begin with MF are arrays of the specified primitive. In this implementation, all MF-derived classes are created by parameterizing the template *MFArray*. The type *MFString* is created using the following definition:

```
typedef MFArray<SFString> MFString;
```

MFVec2f Class Definition

Functions that begin with MF are arrays of the specified primitive. In this implementation, all MF-derived classes are created by parameterizing the template *MFArray*. The type *MFVec2f* is created using the following definition:

```
typedef MFArray<SFVec2f> MFVec2f;
```

MFVec3f Class Definition

Functions that begin with MF are arrays of the specified primitive. In this implementation, all MF-derived classes are created by parameterizing the template *MFArray*. The type *MFVec3f* is created using the following definition:

```
typedef MFArray<SFVec3f> MFVec3f;
```

MFMatrix Class Definition

Functions that begin with MF are arrays of the specified primitive. In this implementation, all MF-derived classes are created by parameterizing the template *MFArray*. The type *MFMatrix* is created using the following definition:

```
typedef MFArray<SFMatrix> MFMatrix;
```

GState Class Definition

The *GState* class is used to push and pop the traversal state. An instance of this class is passed to the following *GNode* class member functions:

```
void GNode::DrawOpenGL(GState&);
void GNode::Write(GState&, GWrite&)
void GNode::Range(GState&, SFVec3f&, SFVec3f&)
void GNode::SetState(GState& state)
void GNode::PushState(GState& state)
void GNode::PopState(GState& state)
```

Each of these functions performs a different task. `DrawOpenGL`, `Write`, and `Range` traverse the current scene, evaluating each object in the scene. The traversal state is preserved in the instance variable passed to each function. `SetState`, `PushState`, and `PopState` set the state and push and pop the current state, respectively. The *GState* helper class is key to the proper evaluation of a scene.

Member Variables

The *GState* class has many member variables, most of which are an array of some type that is used to implement a stack:

```
private:
   GMaterial*      m_material[MaxState];
   SFMatrix        m_transform[MaxState];
   MFVec3f*        m_vertices[MaxState];
   SFLong          m_materialBinding[MaxState];
   MFVec3f*        m_normal[MaxState];
   SFLong          m_normalBinding[MaxState];
   GShapeHints*    m_shapeHints[MaxState];
   long            m_current;
   char*           m_name[MaxState] [255];
   long            m_currentName;
```

The *m_current* variable is used as the stack index for most of the member variables. The *m_currentName* variable is used as the stack index for the *m_name* variable. The *m_name* stack contains the names of the objects in the object hierarchy.

The *m_material* variable holds the stack of *GMaterial* instances. The *m_transform* variable contains a stack of *SFMatrix* instances. These instances hold the transformation matrix that is current for different levels in the scene hierarchy. The *m_vertices* variable holds a stack of *MFVec3f* values. These instances hold the coordinates that will be used by subsequent *GIndexedFaceSet* instances.

The *m_materialBinding* variable contains a stack of *SFLong* values that represent the material binding for the different levels in the scene hierarchy. The *m_normal* variable holds a stack of *MFVec3f* values that contain the surface normals to be used by subsequent scene elements. The *m_normalBinding* variable holds a stack of *SFLong* values that represent the normal binding state for the different levels of hierarchy in the scene.

The *m_shapeHints* variable holds a stack of instances of the *GShapeHints* class. These values are used to specify the automatic smoothing parameters for different levels in the scene hierarchy.

Member Functions

`GState(void)`

This member function is the default constructor for the *GState* class. It clears and initializes the *GState* instance.

`void Push(void)`

This member function pushes the entire state of the *GState* instance. This is accomplished by setting the value of index *m_current+1* to the current state for all of the array member variables (except *m_name*, which is pushed and popped separately).

`void Pop(void)`

This member function pops the entire state of the *GState* instance by decrementing *m_current*.

`void PushName(char* = NULL)`

This member function assigns the passed string to the *m_currentName* index of the *m_name* variable. The *m_currentName* variable is then incremented.

`void PopName(void)`

This member function decrements *m_currentName*.

`void Reset(void)`

This member variable clears all of the member variables and sets *m_current* and *m_currentName* to zero.

`GMaterial* Material(void)`

This member function returns the current *GMaterial* instance.

`void Material(GMaterial*)`

This member function overwrites the current *GMaterial* instance with the value passed in.

`SFMatrix& Transform(void)`

This member function returns the current transformation matrix.

`void Transform(SFMatrix&)`

This member function overwrites the current transformation matrix.

`MFVec3f* Vertices(void)`

This member function returns the current vertices.

`void Vertices(MFVec3f*)`

This member function sets the current vertices using instances of the *GCoordinate3* class.

`SFLong MaterialBinding(void)`

This member function returns the current material binding.

`void MaterialBinding(SFLong)`

This member function sets the current material binding to the value passed in.

`MFVec3f* Normal(void)`

This member function returns the current surface normal array.

```
void Normal(MFVec3f*)
```

This member function sets the current surface normal array to the value passed in.

```
SFLong NormalBinding(void)
```

This member function returns the current normal binding value.

```
void NormalBinding(SFLong)
```

This member function sets the current normal binding value to the value passed in.

```
char* Name(void)
```

This member function returns the name of the current object at this level.

```
void Name(char*)
```

This member function sets the name of the object at this level.

```
void ShapeHints(GShapeHints*)
```

This member function sets the value of the current *ShapeHints* instance to the value passed in.

```
GShapeHints* ShapeHints(void)
```

This member function returns the current *ShapeHints* instance.

```
char* HeirName(void)
```

This member function concatenates the names in the current object hierarchy into one long name. Underscores are sandwiched between the concatenated names to make the individual names distinguishable.

GWrite Class Definition

The *GWrite* class is intended to be the basis for the all 3D file writers. To create support for a new 3D file format writer, you need only create a derived class from the *GWrite* class. This new class will override the member functions necessary to support the file format.

When you use a class derived from *GWrite*, the C++ code that initiates a write looks like this:

```
FILE* fp = fopen(buffer, "wb");
if (fp != NULL) {
   GWriteCOB      write;
   GState         state;

   write.Open(scene, state, buffer);
   scene.Write(state, write);
   write.Close(scene, state);
}
```

Member Variables

The only member variable held by the *GWrite* base class is a file pointer to the file being written. The `GWrite::Open()` member function assigns the opened file pointer to *m_fp*. The `GWrite::Close()` member function closes the `FILE` represented by the *m_fp* variable.

```
FILE* m_fp;
```

Member Functions

`short FileMode(void)`

This member function returns the type of file being opened. The legal return values are `GWriteAsciiFile`, which specifies that the file being written is ASCII, and `GWriteBinaryFile`, which specifies that the file being written is binary. The *GWrite* base class returns `GWriteAsciiFile`. This member needs to be overridden only if the file being written is binary.

`void Prolog(GNode*, GState&)`

This member function is called from the `GWrite::Open()` member function immediately after the file has been opened successfully. It may be overridden if some special initialization is required.

`void Epilog(GNode*, GState&)`

This member function is called from `GWrite::Close()` before the file is closed. It allows some final cleanup to occur prior to the closing of the output file.

`short Close(GNode*, GState&)`

This member function closes the currently open file. If there was an open file to close, it returns the value `TRUE`; otherwise, it returns `FALSE`.

`short Open(GNode*, GState&, char*)`

This member function opens the file specified by the full path name passed in the third argument. The file is opened for ASCII write if the value returned from `GWrite::FileMode()` is `GWriteAsciiFile`. It is opened for binary write if `GWrite::FileMode()` returns `GWriteBinaryFile`.

`GWrite(void)`

This member function is the default constructor. It doesn't have much to do in this class except to set *m_fp* to `NULL`.

`void startPolygons(GState&, char* = NULL)`

This member function is called if the member function `GWrite::PolygonSupported()` returns `TRUE`. It is called every time a group of polygons is encountered. The name of the polygon group is passed in the second argument. It may be overridden if necessary.

`void EndPolygons(GState&)`

This member function is called if the member function `GWrite::PolygonSupported()` returns `TRUE`. It is called when the traversal of the polygons announced by `GWrite::StartPolygon()` has completed. It may be overridden if necessary.

`void Polygon(GState&, long, MFVec3f*, MFVec3f* = NULL, GWriteMaterial* = NULL)`

This member function is called when `GWrite::PolygonSupported()` returns `TRUE` and a shape element that isn't supported directly is encountered. The nonsupported shape is tessellated into a group of equivalent polygons. These polygons are passed with individual calls to this member function.

The polygon is passed in the third argument. The normals for each of the polygon's vertices are passed in the fourth argument. The material for the polygon is passed in the fifth argument.

`short PolygonSupported(void)`

When this member function returns `TRUE`, unsupported shapes will be tessellated and returned as a group of polygons to the `GWrite::Polygon()` member function. When it returns `FALSE`, the `GWrite::StartPolygon()`, `GWrite::EndPolygon()`, and `GWrite::Polygon()` member functions are not called. This member function returns `FALSE` by default. It must be overridden to return `TRUE`.

`void StartSeparator(GState&, char* = NULL)`

When the `GWrite::SeparatorSupported()` member function returns `TRUE` and a *GSeparator* construct is encountered, this member function is called. The first argument is the current state, and the second argument is the name of the *GSeparator* instance.

`void EndSeparator(GState&)`

When the `GWrite::SeparatorSupported()` member function returns `TRUE` and the traversal of the *GSeparator* has been completed, this member function is called.

`short SeparatorSupported(void)`

When this member function returns `TRUE`, it causes *GSeparator* instances to call `GWrite::StartSeparator()` and `GWrite::EndSeparator()` member functions. When it returns `FALSE`, these member functions are not called. This member function returns `FALSE` by default. It must be overridden to return `TRUE`.

`short GroupSupported(void)`

When this member function returns `TRUE`, it causes *GGroup* instances to call the `GWrite::StartGroup()` and `GWrite::EndGroup()` member functions. If it returns `FALSE`, the these member functions are not called. This member function returns `FALSE` by default. It must be overridden to return `TRUE`.

`void StartGroup(GState&, char* = NULL)`

When the `GWrite::GroupSupported()` member function returns `TRUE` and a *GGroup* construct is encountered, this member function is called. The first argument is the current state, and the second argument is the name of the *GGroup* instance.

`void EndGroup(GState)`

When the `GWrite::GroupSupported()` member function returns `TRUE` and the traversal of the *GGroup* has been completed, this member function is called.

`short TransformSeparatorSupported(void)`

When this member function returns `TRUE`, it causes *GTransformSeparator* instances to call the `GWrite::StartTransformSeparator()` and `GWrite::EndTransformSeparator()` member functions. If it returns `FALSE`, the these member functions are not called. This member function returns `FALSE` by default. It must be overridden to return `TRUE`.

`void StartTransformSeparator(GState&, char* = NULL)`

When the `GWrite::TransformSeparatorSupported()` member function returns `TRUE` and a *GTransformSeparator* construct is encountered, this member function is called. The first argument is the current state, and the second argument is the name of the *GTransformSeparator* instance.

`void EndTransformSeparator(GState&)`

When the `GWrite::TransformSeparatorSupported()` member function returns `TRUE` and the traversal of the *GTransformSeparator* has been completed, this member function is called.

`void PointLight(GState&, SFLong, SFFloat, SFVec3f&, SFVec3f&, char* = NULL)`

When the `GWrite::PointLightSupported()` returns `TRUE` and a *GPointLight* instance is encountered, this member function is called. The first argument is the current state. The second is a boolean value that states whether the light source is on. The third defines the intensity of the light; its legal values are 0.0 through 1.0. The fourth is the color of the point light. The fifth is the position of the point light. And the last is the name of the point light instance.

`short PointLightSupported(void)`

When this member function returns `TRUE`, it causes *GPointLight* instances to call the `GWrite::PointLight()` member function. If it returns `FALSE`, `GWrite::PointLight()` is not called. This member function returns `FALSE` by default. It must be overridden to return `TRUE`.

`short SpotLightSupported(void)`

When this member function returns `TRUE`, it causes *GSpotLight* instances to call the `GWrite::SpotLight()` member function. If it returns `FALSE`,

`GWrite::SpotLight()` is not called. This member function returns `FALSE` by default. It must be overridden to return `TRUE`.

```
void SpotLight(GState&, SFLong, SFFloat, SFVec3f&,
SFVec3f&, SFVec3f&, SFFloat, SFFloat, char* = NULL)
```

This member function is called if the `GWrite::SpotLightSupported()` member function returns `TRUE` and a *GSpotLight* instance is encountered. The first argument is the current state. The second is a boolean value that states whether the light source is on. The third defines the intensity of the light; its legal values are 0.0 through 1.0. The fourth is the color of the point light. The fifth is the position of the point light. The sixth is a vector in the direction in which the light is pointing. The seventh is the drop-off rate. The eighth is the cut-off angle. And the last is the name of the spotlight instance.

```
void PerspectiveCamera(GState&, SFVec3f& position,
SFVec3f& lookat, SFVec3f& up, char* = NULL)
```

This member function is invoked whenever the `GWrite::Perspective-CameraSupported()` member function returns `TRUE` and a *GPerspective-Camera* instance is encountered during a `GNode::Write()` call. The first argument is the current state for the *GPerspectiveCamera* instance. The second is the camera's position. The third is the position at which the camera is pointed. The fourth is the up direction vector. And the last is the name of the *GPerspectiveCamera* instance.

```
short PerspectiveCameraSupported(void)
```

When this member function returns `TRUE`, it causes *GPerspectiveCamera* instances to call the `GWrite::PerspectiveCamera()` member function when it is encountered during a `GNode::Write()` call. If it returns `FALSE`, the `GWrite::PerspectiveCamera()` member function is not called. This member function returns `FALSE` by default. It must be overridden to return `TRUE`.

```
short TransformsSupported(void)
```

When this member function returns `TRUE`, it causes *GRotation*, *GTranslation*, *GScale*, and *GMatrixTransformation* instances to call their equivalent transformation *GWrite* member functions when these are encountered during the `GWrite::Write()` invocation. If this member function returns `FALSE`, none of the *GWrite* transformation member functions are called. When it returns `FALSE`, the value of all arguments to the subsequent shape member functions are appropriately transformed. When it returns `TRUE`, the transformations do not occur. This member function returns `FALSE` by default. It must be overridden to return `TRUE`.

`void Rotation(SFRotation&)`

This member function is called when `GWrite::TransformsSupported()` returns `TRUE` and a *GRotation* instance is encountered during the `GWrite::Write()` invocation. Its argument is an *SFRotation* instance that specifies the rotation axis and angle.

`void Translation(SFVec3f&)`

This member function is called when `GWrite::TransformsSupported()` returns `TRUE` and a *GTranslation* instance is encountered during the `GWrite::Write()` invocation. Its argument is an *SFVec3f* instance that specifies the *x*, *y*, and *z* translation amounts.

`void Scale(SFVec3f&)`

This member function is called when `GWrite::TransformsSupported()` returns `TRUE` and a *GScale* instance is encountered during the `GWrite::Write()` invocation. Its argument is an *SFVec3f* instance that specifies the *x*, *y*, and *z* scale factors.

`void MatrixTransform(SFMatrix&)`

This member function is called when `GWrite::TransformsSupported()` returns `TRUE` and a *GMatrixTransform* instance is encountered during the `GWrite::Write()` invocation. Its argument is an *SFMatrix* instance that specifies the transformation matrix.

`short CubeSupported(void)`

When this member function returns `TRUE`, it causes *GCube* instances to call the `GWrite::Cube()` member function when these are encountered during the `GWrite::Write()` invocation. When it returns `FALSE`, the `GWrite::Cube()` member function is not called. This member function returns `FALSE` by default. It must be overridden to return `TRUE`.

`void Cube(GState&, SFFloat, SFFloat, SFFloat)`

This member function is called when `GWrite::CubeSupported()` returns `TRUE` and a *GCube* instance is encountered during the `GWrite::Write()` invocation. The first argument to this member function is the current state.

The second is the width of the cube. The third is the height of the cube. The fourth is the depth of the cube.

```
short SphereSupported(void)
```

When this member function returns `TRUE`, it causes *GSphere* instances to call the `GWrite::Sphere()` member function when these are encountered during the `GWrite::Write()` invocation. When it returns `FALSE`, the `GWrite::Sphere()` member function is not called. This member function returns `FALSE` by default. It must be overridden to return `TRUE`.

```
void Sphere(GState&, SFFloat r)
```

This member function is called when `GWrite::SphereSupported()` returns `TRUE` and a *GSphere* instance is encountered during the `GWrite::Write()` invocation. The first argument to this member function is the current state, and the second argument is the radius of the sphere.

```
short ConeSupported(void)
```

When this member function returns `TRUE`, it causes *GCone* instances to call the `GWrite::Cone()` member function when these are encountered during the `GWrite::Write()` invocation. When it returns `FALSE`, the `GWrite::Cone()` member function is not called. This member function returns `FALSE` by default. It must be overridden to return `TRUE`.

```
void Cone(GState&, SFLong, SFFloat, SFFloat)
```

This member function is called when `GWrite::ConeSupported()` returns `TRUE` and a *GCone* instance is encountered during the `GWrite::Write()` invocation. The first argument to this member function is the current state. The second specifies the visible parts of the cone. A value of 1 means the cone's sides are visible, 2 means the cone's bottom is visible, and 7 means both the sides and bottom are visible. The third argument is the bottom radius. The last is the cone's height.

```
short CylinderSupported(void)
```

When this member function returns `TRUE`, it causes *GCylinder* instances to call the `GWrite::Cylinder()` member function when these are encountered during the `GWrite::Write()` invocation. When it returns `FALSE`, no `GWrite::Cylinder()` member functions are called. This member function returns `FALSE` by default. It must be overridden to return `TRUE`.

`void Cylinder(GState&, SFLong, SFFloat, SFFloat)`

This member function is called when `GWrite::CylinderSupported()` returns `TRUE` and a *GCylinder* instance is encountered during the `GWrite::Write()` invocation. The first argument to this member function is the current state. The second specifies the visible parts of the cylinder. A value of 1 means the cylinder's sides are visible, 2 means the cylinder's bottom is visible, 4 means the cylinder's top is visible, and 7 means both the sides and bottom are visible. The third argument is the cylinder's radius. The last is the cylinder's height.

`short MeshSupported(void)`

When this member function returns `TRUE`, it causes *GIndexedFaceSet* instances to call the `GWrite::VertexList()`, `GWrite::NormalList()`, and `GWrite::FaceList()` member functions when these are encountered during the `GWrite::Write()` invocation. When it returns `FALSE`, no member functions are called. This member function returns `FALSE` by default. It must be overridden to return `TRUE`.

`void VertexList(GState&, MFVec3f*, char* = NULL)`

This member function is called when the `GWrite::MeshSupported()` member function returns `TRUE` and a *GIndexedFaceSet* instance is encountered during the `GWrite::Write()` invocation. The first argument to this member function is the current state. The second specifies the vertices for the mesh. The third specifies the name of the mesh.

`void NormalList(GState&, MFVec3f*, char* = NULL)`

This member function is called when the `GWrite::MeshSupported()` member function returns `TRUE` and a *GIndexedFaceSet* instance is encountered during the `GWrite::Write()` invocation. The first argument to this member function is the current state. The second specifies the surface normals for the mesh. The third specifies the name of the mesh.

`void FaceList(GState&, MFLong*, MFLong* = NULL, MFLong* = NULL, MFLong* = NULL )`

This member function is called when the `GWrite::MeshSupported()` member function returns `TRUE` and a *GIndexedFaceSet* instance is encountered during the `GWrite::Write()` invocation. The first argument to this member function is the current state. The second specifies the face list for the polygons in the mesh. The face list is an array of indexes into the array passed into the `GWrite::VertexList()` member function. The third argument is an array of indexes into the surface normal vertices passed in the `GWrite::NormalList()` member function. The last two arguments are reserved.

GWriteMaterial

The *GWriteMaterial* class defines a single material type. This class is simpler to use than the *GMaterial* class because it represents only one material. The *GWriteMaterial* class also allows the material to be converted into different material models. A *GMaterial* instance can return a *GWriteMaterial* for a specific material and can add a *GWriteMaterial* as an element of the material definition.

Member Functions

`GWriteMaterial(void)`

This member function is the default constructor for the *GWriteMaterial* class. It initializes the material to the default settings.

`void AmbientColor(const SFVec3f&)`

This member function sets the ambient color component for the *GWriteMaterial* instance.

`void DiffuseColor(const SFVec3f&)`

This member function sets the diffuse color component for the *GWriteMaterial* instance.

`void SpecularColor(const SFVec3f&)`

This member function sets the specular color component for the *GWriteMaterial* instance.

`void EmissiveColor(const SFVec3f&)`

This member function sets the emissive color component for the *GWriteMaterial* instance.

`void Shininess(const SFFloat)`

This member function sets the shininess coefficient for the *GWriteMaterial* instance.

```
void Transparency(const SFFloat)
```

This member function sets the transparency coefficient for the *GWriteMaterial* instance.

```
const SFVec3f AmbientColor(void) const
```

This member function returns the current ambient color component for the *GWriteMaterial* instance.

```
const SFVec3f DiffuseColor(void) const
```

This member function returns the current diffuse color component for the *GWriteMaterial* instance.

```
const SFVec3f SpecularColor(void) const
```

This member function returns the current specular color component for the *GWriteMaterial* instance.

```
const SFVec3f EmissiveColor(void) const
```

This member function returns the current emissive color component for the *GWriteMaterial* instance.

```
const SFFloat Shininess(void) const
```

This member function returns the current shininess coefficient for the *GWriteMaterial* instance.

```
const SFFloat Transparency(void) const
```

This member function returns the current transparency coefficient for the *GWriteMaterial* instance.

```
void DefaultColors(void)
```

This member function sets the current *GWriteMaterial* instance to the default value. This is equivalent to the default value defined for the VRML *Material* language construct.

```
SFVec3f Color(void)
```

This member function reduces the current material to a single color value. This value is useful for material models that have a single color definition with ambient and diffuse coefficients.

```
SFFloat AmbientCoefficient(void)
```

This member function tries to reduce the current material into an ambient coefficient. This value is useful for material models that have a single color definition with ambient, diffuse, specular, and hilight coefficients.

```
SFFloat SpecularCoefficient(void)
```

This member function tries to reduce the current material into a specular coefficient. This value is useful for material models that have a single color definition with ambient, diffuse, specular, and hilight coefficients.

```
SFFloat HilightCoefficient(void)
```

This member function tries to reduce the current material into a hilight coefficient. This value is useful for material models that have a single color definition with ambient, diffuse, specular, and hilight coefficients.

Friend Functions

```
friend int operator==(const GWriteMaterial&, const
GWriteMaterial&)
```

This friend function returns `TRUE` if the two *GWriteMaterial* instances are equal; otherwise, it returns `FALSE`.

```
friend int operator!=(const GWriteMaterial&, const
GWriteMaterial&)
```

This friend function returns `TRUE` if the two *GWriteMaterial* instances are not equal; otherwise, it returns `FALSE`.

MeshCompactor Class Definition

The *MeshCompactor* class can simplify the process of reading a 3D file into the internal representation. It also can aid in the conversion of the representation into a new 3D file.

This class allows groups of polygons to be entered as a set of named polygons. The polygons are separated into the coordinates, groups of faces, and materials for future use.

After the polygon mesh has been read, it can be either directly converted into the internal representation using the `MeshCompactor::AddTo(GNode*)` member function or queried for its internal components by other software components. Either way, this class can make reading and writing 3D files much easier.

`MeshCompactor(MFVec3f* = NULL, MFLong* = NULL)`

This member function is the constructor for the *MeshCompactor* instance. If no arguments are passed, then this constructor acts like a default constructor. If a vertex list is passed in the first argument and a face list is passed in the second argument, these values are used as the initial state of the *MeshCompactor* instance.

`~MeshCompactor(void)`

This member function is the destructor for the *MeshCompactor* class. It deletes any storage that is currently held by the *MeshCompactor* instance.

`void Reset(MFVec3f* = NULL, MFLong* = NULL)`

This member function deletes any storage that is currently held by the *MeshCompactor* instance and reinitializes the instance. If a vertex list and a face list are passed, then the instance is initially set to contain those values.

`void BeginPolygon(GWriteMaterial* = NULL)`

This member function is called to start a new polygon. A material may be specified for the polygon by passing a *GWriteMaterial* instance. The polygon is defined by subsequent calls to the `MeshCompactor::AddVertex()` member function. It is closed by a call to the `MeshCompactor::EndPolygon()` member function.

`void EndPolygon(void)`

This member function closes the polygon begun with the `MeshCompactor::BeginPolygon()` member function.

`char* Name(long)`

This member function returns the name for the group of faces specified by the group index passed as an argument. The legal range for the group index is 0 through `MeshCompactor::Groups() -1.`

`void Name(char*)`

This member function specifies the start of a group that has the name specified in the argument. If the name already exists, the current group is set to the named group. If no group with that name exists, a new group with that name is created and is made the current group. All subsequent polygon definitions will have their faces applied to this named group.

```
void AddVertex(SFVec3f)
```

This member function adds the vertex passed in to the current polygon context. The vertex is placed in the vertex list, and a new face index is added to the face list.

```
MFVec3f* Coordinates(void)
```

This member function returns the vertex list for the mesh.

```
MFLong* Faces(long = 0)
```

This member function returns the face list for the group index specified. The legal range for the group index is 0 through `MeshCompactor::Groups() -1`. A face list specifies one or more polygons. The polygons are specified as an index into the vertex list and is terminated with the index value of –1.

```
GMaterial* Material(void)
```

This member function returns the *GMaterial* definition for the entire mesh.

```
SFLong FaceIndex2MaterialIndex(SFLong = 0, SFLong = 0)
```

This member function returns the material index for the face specified in the second argument of the group specified in the first argument.

```
GWriteMaterial FaceIndex2Material(SFLong = 0,
SFLong = 0)
```

This member function returns the material for the face specified in the second argument of the group specified in the first argument.

```
long Groups(void)
```

This member function returns the number of groups defined in the *MeshCompactor* instance.

```
int IsEmpty(void)
```

This member function returns `TRUE` if there are no groups or vertices in the *MeshCompactor* instance.

```
void AddTo(GNode*)
```

This member function converts the current contents of the *MeshCompactor* instance into the internal class representation. The mesh is added as a child to the *GNode* instance specified.

Internal Data Representation Classes

The internal representation of a 3D scene is represented by the instantiation of classes from the Crossroad class library. Figure 14.2 shows the hierarchy of these classes. The base class for all of these data representation classes is the Gnode class. All other classes are derived from this class.

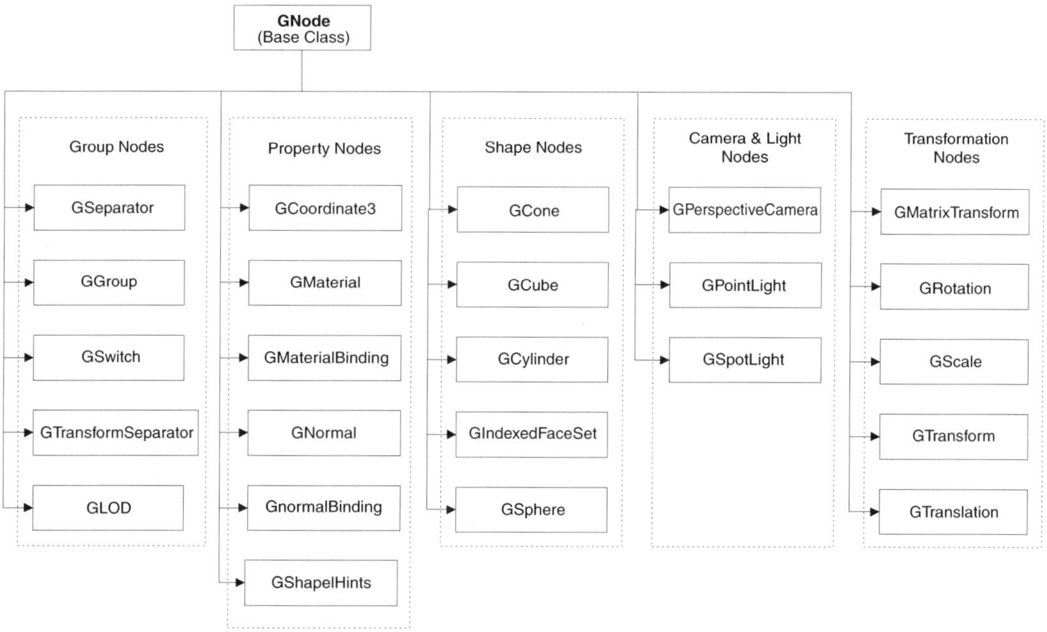

Figure 14.2. Internal data representation classes.

Each of the classes derived from Gnode correspond to a VRML language construct. The subsequent sections defines the GNode class and the classes derived from the GNode class.

GNode Class

The *GNode* class is the base class for all of the derived classes that make up the internal 3D representation. Most capabilities of the derived classes are accessible through the *GNode* class. This means all derived classes can be referred to generically as a *GNode* instance. Since the member functions that need to be customized by subsequent derived classes are defined as virtual functions, the correct member function will be executed even when a *GNode* derived instance is referred to as a *GNode*.

Member Variables

The member variables defined for *GNode* are the minimum necessary to create and maintain the internal representation topology.

```
protected:
    char*    m_name;
    GNode*   m_next;
    GNode*   m_parent;
    GNode*   m_child;
    GNodeType  m_type;
```

The variables include *m_name*, which is optionally defined for all constructs. It maps to VRML's `DEF name` language construct, which allows all *GNode* instances to be referred to by name.

The *m_next* variable allows a list of *GNode* instances to be strung together. This is how the relationship of *GNode* instances at the same hierarchy level is maintained. The *m_parent* variable points to the *GNode* instance that is one up in the hierarchy level. The parent is usually a *GSeparator* or some other grouping construct. The *m_child* variable points to a list of *GNode* instances that are one lower in the hierarchy level. This is how children of grouping constructs are stored. And finally, each instance has a type value, *m_type*, that denotes the *GNode* derived class type of the instance. This information is very useful when searching through the instance hierarchy looking for a specific type construct.

Member Functions

```
GNode(GNodeType = GUnknownType, GNode* = NULL,
GNode = NULL)
```

This member function is the constructor for the *GNode* class. It is not used directly; however, it is called by most derived classes. `GNodeType` is an enumeration that contains a unique value for each class derived from *GNode*. This enumeration is used to identify the class that represents the *GNode* derived instance, thereby allowing the internal representation to be searched at runtime for specific instance types. By default, the `GNodeType` returns `GUnknownType`. A `GNodeType` is always of the format *`type`*`Type`. For example, a *GSeparator* class will have a `GNodeType` of `GSeparatorType` and the *GCone* class will have a `GNodeType` of `GConeType`.

The second argument specifies the *GNode* instance that is defined next at the current hierarchy level. This value sets the *m_next* member variable. The third argument is the *GNode* derived instance that is the child. This argument's value is assigned to the *m_child* member variable.

`virtual ~GNode(void)`

This member function is the virtual destructor for the class. It deletes the storage associated with the *m_name* instance. The deletion of any other storage is handled by the derived class.

`GNode* Next(void)`

This member function returns the value associated with the *m_next* member variable.

`void Next(GNode*)`

This member function sets the value of the *m_next* member variable to the value of the argument.

`GNode* AppendAtLast(GNode*)`

This member function places the passed argument at the end of the current *m_next* list.

`GNode* Parent(void)`

This member function returns the value of *m_parent* for the current *GNode* instance.

`void Parent(GNode*)`

This member function assigns to the member variable *m_parent* the value of the passed argument.

`GNode* Child(void)`

This member function returns the value associated with the member variable *m_child*.

`void Child(GNode*)`

This member function assigns to the member variable *m_child* the value of the passed argument.

`GNode* InsertChild(GNode*)`

This member function places the passed *GNode* derived class instance at the beginning of the child list.

`GNode* AddChild(Gnode*)`

This member function places the passed *GNode* derived class instance at the end of the child list.

`GNode* AddNext(GNode*)`

This member function places the passed *GNode* derived class instance at the end of the next child list.

`GNode* FindTypeByIndex(GState&, GNodeType, long&, long = 0)`

This member function iterates through the current 3D scene. The *GState* value is updated as the iteration progresses. The third argument is a long reference that is used as an iteration counter. It should be set to zero prior to the call to this member function at the beginning of the iteration sequence. The fourth argument is the iteration completion value. This value is incremented every time a *GNode* instance of the type specified in the second argument is encountered. The function returns with the *GNode* instance of the specified occurrence of the requested type. If that occurrence doesn't exist, then the value `NULL` is returned once the iteration of the entire scene is completed. The state of the scene traversal is held in the *GState* variable passed in the first argument in addition to the *GNode* instance associated with the specified occurrence.

`void SetName(char*)`

This member function sets the value of the *m_name* member variable. The value passed is copied into the variable *m_name*.

`char* GetName(void)`

This member function returns the value associated with the *m_name* member variable.

`virtual GNode* Copy(void)`

This member function is a deep copy of this *GNode* instance and its children. All *GNode* derived classes must implement this member function.

`virtual GNodeType Type(void)`

This member function returns the *GNodeType* associated with the current *GNode* instance.

`virtual void StatusMessage(char*, ...)`

This member function allows a status message to be propagated to the user. The root level *GNode* element of any program is a class instance derived from *GSeparator*, which implements this member function. The default implementation is to defer this method to the parent. If there is no parent, then the call is ignored.

`virtual void ErrorMessage(char*, ...)`

This member function allows an error message to be propagated to the user. The root level *GNode* element of any program is a class instance derived from *GSeparator*, which implements this member function. The default implementation is to defer this method to the parent. If there is no parent, then the call is ignored.

`virtual void WarningMessage(char*, ...)`

This member function allows a warning message to be propagated to the user. The root level *GNode* element of any program is a class instance derived from *GSeparator*, which implements this member function. The default implementation is to defer this method to the parent. If there is no parent, then the call is ignored.

`virtual short IsTransform(void)`

This member function returns `TRUE` (1) if the underlying *GNode* derived class represents a transformation; otherwise, returns `FALSE` (0).

```
virtual void SetField(const char*, type)
```

The SetField member functions are defined to make the VRML parser easier to implement. This member function allows any underlying member variable of a *GNode* derived class to be associated with the equivalent VRML field name. In this way, the assignment of the variable can occur by associating the VRML field name string with the currently defined *GNode* instance. Through this technique, the implementation of the VRML reader becomes generic for any *GNode* derived class. The default implementation is to ignore this member function. All *GNode* derived classes must implement the SetField member functions for the fields that are implemented. The second argument may be of type *SFLong*, *SFFloat*, *SFString*, *SFVec2f*, *SFVec3f*, *SFMatrix*, *SFRotation*, *MFLong*, *MFFloat*, *MFString*, *MFVec2f*, or *MFVec3f*.

```
virtual void DrawOpenGL(GState&)
```

This member function iterates through the entire scene and calls the OpenGL functions that are necessary to display the current scene. The *GState* instance passed holds the state for the traversal of the scene.

```
virtual void SetCameraOpenGL(GState&, long, long)
```

This member function is handled only by a *Camera* instance. The first argument is the current state. The second is the width of the display window. The third is the height of the display window. Typically the scene is searched for an appropriate *Camera* instance and then this member function is called.

```
virtual void WriteWRL(FILE*, int = 0)
```

This member function iterates through the scene and writes a VRML file for the scene. The first argument is a pointer to the file being emitted. The second is the current indent level, thereby enabling language elements at different levels in the hierarchy to visually preserve that information with the appropriate indention level. All *GNode* derived classes must implement this member function.

```
virtual void Write(GState&, GWrite&)
```

This member function iterates through the current scene, updating the traversal state passed in the first argument. The second argument is a *GWrite* instance that is called when each language construct is encountered during traversal. Each 3D file format described in this book defines a *GWrite* derived class for emitting its 3D file format. See the *GWrite* class for more information on creating a custom file writer.

```
virtual void Range(GState&, SFVec3f&, SFVec3f&)
```

This member function iterates through the current scene, computing the minimum and maximum range for the objects in the scene. The first argument is the traversal state. This is required in order to perform the transformation required on the underlying representation so as to correctly compute the range. The second argument is an *SFVec3f* reference. After the traversal of the scene is complete, this reference contains the minimum value. The third argument is an *SFVec3f* reference. After the traversal of the scene is complete, this reference contains the maximum value. The minimum and maximum should be initialized to values that are out of range for the minimum and maximum values.

```
virtual void SetState(GState&)
```

This member function calculates the new transform matrix for the *GState* instance. It multiplies the current transformation matrix stored in the *GState* instance by the value returned from the `Transform()` member function for the current *GNode* instance. The result is placed in the transformation matrix for the *GState* instance.

```
virtual void PushState(GState&)
```

This member function saves the current state of the *GState* instance. Subsequent changes will be overwritten with this saved value when the `PopState()` member function is called. This member function is used by *GNode* derived classes such as *GSeparator* to save the current traversal state prior to the function's evaluating its child nodes. After the child nodes have been evaluated, the `PopState()` function is called to restore the state. This member function must be overridden if any state must be saved during scene traversal by an instance of a *GNode* derived class.

```
virtual void PopState(GState&)
```

This member function restores the saved state of the *GState* instance. It is used in conjunction with the `PushState()` member function to save and restore the current traversal state when iterating through the scene. It must be overridden if any state must be restored during scene traversal by an instance of a *GNode* derived class.

GSeparator Class Definition

This class defines a VRML separator construct in the internal representation. The *GSeparator* class defined a *GNode* instance that contains child nodes. It saves the traversal state prior to evaluating its children and restores the traversal state when evaluation is complete.

Member Variables

No member variables are defined for this *GNode* derived class.

Member Functions

`GSeparator(void)`

This member function is the default constructor for the *GSeparator* class. It calls the constructor for *GNode* with `GSeparatorType` as the type argument.

```
GSeparator(void) : GNode(GSeparatorType) {;}
```

`~GSeparator(void)`

This member function is the destructor for the *GSeparator* class. It deletes each item held as a child and then calls the *~GNode* destructor for the instance.

`GNode* Copy(void)`

This member function performs a deep copy on the *GSeparator* instances. All children to this instance are copied and placed in a new *GSeparator* instance, which is returned.

`GNode* FindTypeByIndex(GState&, GNodeType, long&, long)`

This member function checks whether the current instance matches the *GNodeType* passed in the second argument. If it does, the function checks whether the third argument matches the fourth argument. If these arguments match, then the current instance is returned. If they don't, the third argument is incremented and each child node is called with this function. If the function returns a `NULL` value for the child, the iteration continues. If a non-null is returned by the child, then that value is returned. If `NULL` is returned by all of the children, then this function returns a `NULL`.

`void WriteWRL(FILE*, int = 0)`

This member function prints the VRML equivalent construct for the *GSeparator* instance.

`void Write(GState& GWrite&)`

The Write() member function checks whether the *GWrite* instance understands separators. If it does, the appropriate member functions are called in the *GWrite* instance. Each child node has this member function called with the same arguments. After all of the child nodes have been called, the *GWrite* instance is checked to see whether it wants to be notified that the separator iteration has completed. If it does, the appropriate members in the *GWrite* instance are called.

`void PushState(GState&)`

This member function pushes the current traversal state.

`void PopState(GState&)`

This member function pops the current traversal state.

GGroup Class Definition

The *GGroup* class allows *GNode* instances to be grouped as children, but the traversal state is not pushed and popped on entry and exit of the *GGroup* instance.

Member Variables

No member variables are defined.

Member Functions

`GGroup(void)`

This member function is the default constructor for the *GGroup* class. It calls the constructor for *GNode* with `GGroupType` as the type argument.

```
GGroup(void) : GNode(GGroupType) {;}
```

```
~GGroup(void)
```

This member function is the destructor for the GGroup class. It deletes all of the items held as a child and then calls the *~GNode* destructor for the instance.

```
GNode* Copy(void)
```

This member function performs a deep copy on the *GGroup* instances. All of the children to this instance are copied and placed in a new *GGroup* instance, which is returned.

```
void WriteWRL(FILE*, int = 0)
```

This member function prints the VRML equivalent construct for the *GGroup* instance, which is the VRML *Group* construct.

```
void Write(GState&, GWrite&)
```

This member function checks whether the *GWrite* instance understands groups. If it does, the appropriate member functions are called in the *GWrite* instance. Each child node has this member function called with the same arguments. After all of the child nodes have been called, the *GWrite* instance is checked to see whether it wants to be notified that the group iteration has completed. If it does, the appropriate members in the *GWrite* instance are called.

```
void DrawOpenGL(GState&)
```

This member function passes the `DrawOpenGL` message to the children of the *GGroup* instance.

GSwitch Class Definition

The *GSwitch* construct allows *GNode* instances to be grouped as children, but the traversal state is not pushed and popped on entry and exit of the *GGroup* instance.

Member Variables

The member variable for *GSwitch* is a *SFLong* value named *m_switch*.

```
private:
   SFLong   m_switch;
```

This value selects which child will be traversed. A value of –3 means all children are traversed, and a value of –1 means no children are traversed. Any positive value is assumed to be the index of the child to be traversed.

Member Functions

`GSwitch(void)`

This member function is the default constructor for the *GSwitch* class. It calls the constructor for *GNode* with `GSwitchType` as the type argument. A default value of –1 is assigned to the member variable *m_switch*.

```
GSwitch(void) : GNode(GSwitchType), m_switch(-1) {;}
```

`~GSwitch(void)`

This member function is the destructor for the *GSwitch* class. It deletes all of the items held as a child and then calls the *~GNode* destructor for the instance. The C++ implementation for this member function is identical to the destructor for *GSeparator* and is not be repeated here.

`GNode* Copy(void)`

This member function performs a deep copy on the *GSwitch* instances. All of the children to this instance are copied and placed in a new *GSwitch* instance, which is returned.

`GNode* FindTypeByIndex(GState&, GNodeType, long&, long)`

This member function checks whether the current instance matches the `GNodeType` passed in the second argument. If it does, it checks to scc if the third argument matches the fourth argument. If these two match, then the current instance is returned. If they don't, the third argument is incremented and the *m_switch* member is checked to see which children are to be evaluated. If the `FindTypeByIndex()` function returns a `NULL` value for the child, the iteration may continue, depending on the *m_switch* value. If a non-`NULL` is returned by the child, then that value is returned. If `NULL` is returned by all of the evaluated children, then this function returns a `NULL`.

```
void SetField(const char*, SFLong)
```

This member function checks the first argument for the field name that corresponds with a member of the *GSwitch* class. If there is a match, the *SFLong* passed is assigned to the member; otherwise, the value is ignored.

```
void WriteWRL(FILE* fp, int = 0)
```

This member function prints the VRML equivalent construct for the *GSwitch* instance, which is the VRML *Switch* construct.

```
void Write(GState&, GWrite&)
```

This member function checks to see if the *GWrite* instance understands groups. If it does, the appropriate member functions are called in the *GWrite* instance. The member variable *m_switch* is checked to see if none, all, or one of the children are to be evaluated. Each evaluated child calls this member function with the same arguments. After all the child nodes have been called, the *GWrite* instance is checked to see whether it wants to be notified that the group iteration has completed. If it does, the appropriate members in the *GWrite* instance are called.

```
void DrawOpenGL(GState&)
```

This member function passes the `DrawOpenGL` message to the children of the *GSwitch* instance specified by the *m_switch* member variable.

```
void Range(GState&, SFVec3f& min, SFVec3f& max)
```

This member function passes the `Range` message to the children of the *GSwitch* instance specified by the *m_switch* member variable.

GTransformSeparator Class Definition

The *GTransformSeparator* class is nearly identical to the implementation of the *GSeparator* class. It differs mainly in its `PushState()` and `PopState()` member functions. The semantics of the *GTransformSeparator* are identical to the *GSeparator* except that instead of pushing and popping the entire traversal state, only the current transform is pushed and popped. Note that the corresponding VRML command *TransformSeparator* will be dropped from future versions of the specification. You are strongly discouraged from using a language construct, since it will not be portable to future versions of VRML.

Member Variables

No member variables are defined for this class.

Member Functions

The same member functions are defined for this class as are defined for the *GSeparator* class. Only those members functions with a substantially different implementation are discussed here.

```
GTransformSeparator(void)
```

This member function is the default constructor for the *GTransformSeparator* class. It calls the constructor for *GNode* with `GTransformSeparatorType` as the type argument.

```
void PushState(GState& state)
```

This member function's behavior differs from that of the equivalent *GSeparator* member function. It pushes only the current transform, rather than the entire traversal state.

```
void PopState(GState& state)
```

This member function's behavior differs from that of the equivalent *GSeparator* member function. It pushes only the current transform, rather than the entire traversal state.

GLOD Class Definition

The *GLOD* class corresponds to the *LOD* (or level of detail) VRML language constructs. In VRML, this construct is used to allow multiple representations of the same object to be stored. The difference in the object representation is usually just a reduced number of polygons. This allows objects to be rendered with a more detailed model when the camera is close and with a less detailed model when the camera is distant.

Since you are writing a file format translator instead of a VRML browser, you can ignore the less detailed children of this node. Most *LOD* constructs place the most detailed model first in the child list. This is the only child that that will be traversed in this construct.

Member Variables

These members are stored even though they aren't currently used. This value represents the range and center fields of the VRML *LOD* construct.

```
private:
   MMFFloat* m_range;
   SFVec3f   m_center;
```

Member Functions

`GLOD(void)`

This member function is the default constructor for the *GLOD* class. It calls the constructor for *GNode* with `GLODType` as the type argument.

`~GLOD(void)`

This member function is the destructor for the *GLOD* class. It deletes each item held as a child and then calls the *GNode* destructor for the instance. The C++ implementation for this member function is identical to the destructor for *GSeparator* and is not be repeated here.

`GNode* Copy(void)`

This member function performs a deep copy on the *GLOD* instance. A new *GLOD* instance is returned with all of the members and children copied.

`GNode* FindTypeByIndex(GState&, GNodeType, long&, long)`

This member function checks whether the current instance matches the `GNodeType` passed in the second argument. If it does, the function checks to see if the third argument matches the fourth argument. If it does, then the current instance is returned. If it doesn't, then the first child element has its `FindTypeByIndex()` member called with the updated arguments and the return value of that member function is returned. If no child exists, then a `NULL` is returned.

`void SetField(const char*, SFVec3f*)`

This member function is used by the VRML parser to set the member variable the corresponds to the field name passed in the first argument. In this case, there is only one *SFVec3f* member variable for this class, so the value may be set without checking for the name. Note that the storage associated with the argument passed in is deleted.

```
void SetField(const char*, MFFloat*)
```

This member function is used by the VRML parser to set the member variable that corresponds to the field name passed in the first argument. In this case, there is only one *MFFloat* member variable for this class, so the value may be set without checking for the name. Note that the storage associated with the argument passed in is deleted.

```
void WriteWRL(FILE* fp, int = 0)
```

This member function prints the VRML equivalent construct (*LOD*) for the *GLOD* instance.

```
void Write(GState&, GWrite&)
```

This member function checks whether the *GWrite* instance understands groups. If it does, the appropriate member functions are called in the *GWrite* instance. The first child calls this member function with the same arguments. After the child node has been called, the *GWrite* instance is checked to see whether it wants to be notified that the *LOD* iteration has completed. If it does, the appropriate members in the *GWrite* instance are called.

```
void DrawOpenGL(GState&)
```

This member function defers to the first child. If there is no child, then this function returns.

```
void Range(GState&, SFVec3f& min, SFVec3f& max)
```

This member function defers to the first child in the *GLOD* instance. If there is no child, then this function returns.

GCoordinate3 Class Definition

The *GCoordinate3* class corresponds to the VRML *Coordinate3* language construct. This instance of the *GCoordinate3* construct specifies the *MFVec3f* value to be used by subsequent *GIndexedFaceSet* instances.

Member Variables

The *GCoordinate3* class has a single member variable, *m_point*, which corresponds to the field variable point defined in the VRML *Coordinate3* language construct.

```
protected:
   MFVec3f* m_point;
```

Member Functions

```
GCoordinate3(MFVec3f* = NULL)
```

This member function is the default constructor for the *GCoordinate3* class. It calls the constructor for *GNode* with `GCoordinate3Type` as the type argument and sets the member variable *m_point* to the argument passed to the constructor. If no argument is passed, then the value `NULL` is used.

```
GCoordinate3(MFVec3f* point = NULL) :
GNode(GCoordinate3Type), m_point(point) {;}
```

```
~GCoordinate3(void)
```

This member function is the destructor for the *GCoordinate3*. It frees any storage that may be associated with the member variable and then defers to the destructor of its parent class *GNode*.

```
GNode* Copy(void)
```

This member function is a deep copy for the *GCoordinate3* class. It creates a new instance of *GCoordinate3* and then creates a new *MFVec3f*, which it associates with the *m_point* member variable in the new instance. The content of the current instance variable *m_point* is copied into the *m_point* variable for the new instance, and the new instance is returned.

```
void SetField(const char*, MFVec3f*)
```

This member function sets the *m_point* member variable with the value pointer passed in the second argument. Since there are no other member variables, there is no need to verify that the field name corresponds to the member variable.

```
void Point(MFVec3f*)
```

This member function assigns the argument to the *m_point* member variable. It is a more convenient way of assigning the member variable than is using the `SetField()` member function.

`MFVec3f* Point(void)`

This member function returns the value of the *m_point* member variable.

`SFLong Elements(void)`

This member function returns the number of the *SFVec3f* value stored in the *m_point* member variable.

`SFVec3f& Vertice(GState&, long)`

This member function returns the *SFVec3f* value associated with the index value passed in the second argument.

`void WriteWRL(FILE*, int = 0)`

This member function writes the *GCoordinate3* instance as its VRML equivalent language construct.

`void Write(GState&, GWrite&)`

This member function saves the *m_point* member variable in the current traversal state and then checks whether the *GWrite* instance is supporting meshes. If it is, then the *m_point* member variable is passed to it using the `VertexList()` member function.

`void DrawOpenGL(GState&)`

This member function places the *m_point* member variable into the current traversal state so that subsequent *GNode* instances may refer to it.

`void Range(GState&, SFVec3f&, SFVec3f&)`

This member function places the *m_point* member variable into the current traversal state so that subsequent *GNode* instances may refer it.

GMaterial Class Definition

The *GMaterial* class corresponds to the VRML *Material* language construct. A *GMaterial* instance specifies the surface material value for subsequent *GNode* instances.

A *GMaterial* class is created of several arrays that specify multiple surface definitions. The surface in subsequent *GNode* instances is defined as an index into these arrays. However, the arrays do not need to be of the same length. In the case in which the arrays are different lengths, a cycling mechanism is defined (see the member functions `operator[]` and `Elements()` for the implementation of the cycling behavior).

Member Variables

There are member variables for each field defined for the VRML *Material* language construct. Each member variable is an array of *SFVec3f* or an array of *SFFloat*.

```
private:
   MFVec3f*    m_ambientColor;
   MFVec3f*    m_diffuseColor;
   MFVec3f*    m_specularColor;
   MFVec3f*    m_emissiveColor;
   MFFloat*    m_shininess;
   MFFloat*    m_transparency
```

The variables *m_ambientColor*, *m_diffuseColor*, *m_specularColor*, and *m_emissiveColor* define the color for their respective surface material color attribute. The *m_shininess* variable works with the *m_specularColor* variable to define hilighting on the object. The *m_transparency* variable defines the amount of transparency for the surface material. A value of 0 means completely opaque, and the value of 1 means completely clear.

A single material is defined by the value of the member variables for a specific index into their respective arrays. Therefore each material class instance may define more than one material.

`GMaterial(void)`

This member function is the default constructor. It defines a type of *GMaterialType* for the new *GMaterial* instance and then allocates storage for each member variable.

`~GMaterial(void)`

This member function is the destructor for *GMaterial*. It deletes all of the storage associated with the member variables and then calls the destructor for the parent class GNode.

`void DefaultColors(void)`

This member function resets the current material instance to a single material definition, which is the default material definition defined in the VRML specification for the *Material* construct.

```
void AmbientColor(MFVec3f*)
```

This member function deletes the current storage associated with the *m_ambientColor* member variable and then assigns the value passed as an argument.

```
MFVec3f*  AmbientColor(void)
```

This member function returns the *MFVec3f* pointer value associated with the *m_ambientColor* member variable.

```
void DiffuseColor(MFVec3f*)
```

This member function deletes the current storage associated with the *m_diffuseColor* member variable and then assigns the value passed as an argument.

```
MFVec3f* DiffuseColor(void)
```

This member function returns the *MFVec3f* pointer value associated with the *m_diffuseColor* member variable.

```
void SpecularColor(MFVec3f*)
```

This member function deletes the current storage associated with the *m_specularColor* member variable and then assigns the value passed as an argument.

```
MFVec3f* SpecularColor(void)
```

This member function returns the *MFVec3f* pointer value associated with the *m_specularColor* member variable.

```
void EmissiveColor(MFVec3f*)
```

This member function deletes the current storage associated with the *m_emissiveColor* member variable and then assigns the value passed as an argument.

```
MFVec3f* EmissiveColor(void)
```

This member function returns the *MFVec3f* pointer value associated with the *m_emissiveColor* member variable.

```
void Shininess(MFFloat*)
```

This member function deletes the current storage associated with the *m_shininess* member variable and then assigns the value passed as an argument.

```
MFFloat* Shininess(void)
```

This member function returns the *MFFloat* pointer value associated with the *m_shininess* member variable.

```
void Transparency(MFFloat*)
```

This member function deletes the current storage associated with the *m_transparency* member variable and then assigns the value passed as an argument.

```
MFFloat* Transparency(void)
```

This member function returns the *MFFloat* pointer value associated with the *m_transparency* member variable.

```
GNode* Copy(void)
```

This member function performs a deep copy for the *GMaterial* class. It creates a new instance of *GMaterial*, allocates storage for each member variable, and then copies the current member variables to the new instance.

```
void SetField(const char*, MFFloat*)
```

This member function sets the *m_shininess* member variable with the value passed in the second argument, provided the string in the first argument is *shininess*. If the string passed in the first argument is *transparency*, then the *m_transparency* member variable is set to the value passed in the second argument.

```
void SetField(const char*, MFVec3f*)
```

This member function sets the *m_ambientColor* member variable with the value passed in the second argument, provided the string in the first argument is *ambientColor*. If the string passed in the first argument is *diffuseColor*, then the *m_diffuseColor* member variable is set to the value passed in the second argument. If the string passed in the first argument is *specularColor*, then the *m_specularColor* member variable is set to the value passed in the second argument. If the string passed in the first argument is *emissiveColor*, then the *m_emissiveColor* member variable is set to the value passed in the second argument.

```
void DrawOpenGL(GState&)
```

This member function places the current material definition into the current traversal state. This makes the material definition available to subsequent *GNode* instances.

```
void WriteWRL(FILE*, int = 0)
```

This member function writes the *GMaterial* instance as its VRML equivalent language construct.

```
long Lookup(GWriteMaterial*)
```

This member function finds the *GWriteMaterial* with the first matching material in the *GMaterial* instance. If a match is found, the index of the matching material is returned; otherwise, –1 is returned.

```
long Add(GWriteMaterial*)
```

This member function adds a new surface material to the *GMaterial* instance. If the material is already defined in the *GMaterial* instance, then the index to the previously defined entry is returned. If no previous entry is found, then a new entry is created and the new index is returned.

```
long Elements(void)
```

This member function looks at the number of elements in each member variable of the *GMaterial* instance and returns the maximum number of elements.

```
GWriteMaterial operator[](long)
```

This member function returns a *GWriteMaterial* instance (which represents a single surface material definition) for the specified index. This function handles material cycling.

```
void Write(GState&, GWrite&)
```

This member function places the current material into the traversal state so that subsequent *GNode* instances may use it.

GMaterialBinding Class Definition

The *GMaterialBinding* class corresponds to the VRML *MaterialBinding* language construct. It is used to define how the currently specified material is mapped to a shape node. Each shape may interpret each binding differently. Each *GMaterialBinding* instance has a member variable *m_value*. This variable corresponds to the value field for the *MaterialBinding* language construct. The legal values for the *m_value* member variable are `G_DEFAULT`, `G_OVERALL`, `G_PER_PART`, `G_PER_PART_INDEX`, `G_PER_FACE_INDEXED`, `G_PER_VERTEX`, and `G_PER_VERTEX_INDEX`. These values correspond to the VRML constants `DEFAULT`, `OVERALL`, `PER_PART`, `PER_PART_INDEX`, `PER_FACE_INDEXED`, `PER_VERTEX`, and `PER_VERTEX_INDEX`.

Member Variable

```
private: SFLong      m_value;
```

Member Functions

`GMaterialBinding(void)`

This member function is the default constructor. It defines a type of `GMaterialBindingType` for the new *GMaterialBinding* instance.

```
GMaterialBinding(void) : GNode(GMaterialBindingType),
m_value(G_DEFAULT) {;}
```

`GNode* Copy(void)`

This member function creates and returns a new instance of the current *GMaterialBinding*.

`void Value(SFLong)`

This member function assigns its argument to the *m_value* member variable.

`SFLong Value(void)`

This member function returns the value currently stored by the *m_value* member variable.

```
void SetField(const char*, SFLong)
```

This member function assigns the value passed in the second argument to the *m_value* member variable. The field name passed in the first argument is ignored because there is only one member variable.

```
void WriteWRL(FILE*, int = 0)
```

This member function writes this *GMaterialBinding* instance as its VRML equivalent language construct.

```
void DrawOpenGL(GState&)
```

This member function places the current material binding in the traversal state. This instance isn't directly or indirectly visible in the scene, so no OpenGL calls are necessary.

```
void Write(GState&, GWrite&)
```

This member function places the current material binding in the traversal state. The result of a material binding is handled by the shape nodes, so this instance doesn't need to make any calls to the *GWrite* argument.

GNormal Class Definition

The *GNormal* class defines surface normals to be used by subsequent *IndexedFaceSet* nodes. The *GNormal* class corresponds to the VRML *Normal* language construct. The *GNormal* class has a single member variable, *m_vector*. This variable corresponds to the VRML field variable *vector*.

Member Variable

The *GNormal* class has a single member variable, *m_vector*, that holds an array of *SFVec3f* values. These values are used as surface normals to subsequent *GNode* instances.

```
protected:
   MFVec3f* m_vector;
```

```
GNormal(MFVec3f* = NULL)
```

This member function is the default constructor. It defines a type of *GNormalType* for the new *GNormal* instance. The *m_vector* member variable is assigned the value passed. If no value is passed, then `NULL` is assigned to *m_vector*.

```
~GNormal(void)
```

This member function is the destructor for the *GNormal* class. It deletes the storage associated with the *m_vector* member variable and then calls the destructor for the parent class *GNode*.

```
GNode* Copy(void)
```

This member function creates and returns a new instance of the current *GNormal* instance.

```
void SetField(const char*, MFVec3f*)
```

This member function assigns the value passed in the second argument to the *m_vector* member variable. The field name passed in the first argument is ignored because there is only one member variable for this class.

```
SFLong Elements(void)
```

This member function returns the number of elements for the *m_vector* member variable.

```
SFVec3f& Vertice(GState&, long)
```

This member function returns the surface normal for the specified index.

```
void WriteWRL(FILE*, int = 0)
```

This member function writes the *GNormal* instance as its VRML equivalent language construct.

```
void Write(GState&, GWrite&)
```

This member function places the current normal array in the traversal state. Doing this makes the surface normals available to subsequent instances. *GWrite* is queried to see if it supports meshes. If it does, the normal is passed to it through the `GWrite::NormalList()` member function.

```
void DrawOpenGL(GState&)
```

This member function places the current material binding in the traversal state. This instance isn't directly or indirectly visible in the scene, so no OpenGL calls are necessary.

GNormalBinding Class Definition

The *GNormalBinding* class corresponds to the VRML *NormalBinding* language construct. This class is used to define how the currently specified normals are interpreted. Each *GNormalBinding* instance has an *m_value* member variable. This variable corresponds to the *value* field for the *NormalBinding* language construct. The legal values for the *m_value* variable are `G_DEFAULT`, `G_OVERALL`, `G_PER_PART`, `G_PER_PART_INDEX`, `G_PER_FACE_INDEXED`, `G_PER_VERTEX`, and `G_PER_VERTEX_INDEX`. These values correspond to the VRML constants `DEFAULT`, `OVERALL`, `PER_PART`, `PER_PART_INDEX`, `PER_FACE_INDEXED`, `PER_VERTEX`, and `PER_VERTEX_INDEX`.

Member Variable

```
private: SFLong m_value;
```

Member Functions

```
GNormalBinding(void)
```

This member function is the default constructor. It defines a type of `GNormalBindingType` for the new *GNormalBinding* instance.

```
GNormalBinding(void) : GNode(GNormalBindingType),
m_value(G_DEFAULT) {;}
```

```
GNode* Copy(void)
```

This member function creates and returns a new instance of the current *GNormalBinding*.

```
void SetField(const char*, SFLong)
```

This member function assigns the value passed in the second argument to the *m_value* member function. The field name passed in the first argument is ignored because there is only one member variable.

```
void Write(GState&, GWrite&)
```

This member function places the current normal binding in the traversal state. The effects of the normal binding are handled by subsequent shape nodes, so this instance doesn't need to make any calls to the *GWrite* argument.

```
void WriteWRL(FILE*, int = 0)
```

This member function writes the *GNormalBinding* instance as its VRML equivalent language construct.

```
void DrawOpenGL(GState&)
```

This member function places the current material binding in the traversal state. This instance isn't directly or indirectly visible in the scene, so no OpenGL calls are necessary.

GShapeHints Class Definition

The *GShapeHints* class corresponds to the VRML *ShapeHints* language construct. This class is used to inform subsequent shape nodes regarding how to interpret the polygons specified by *GCoordinate3* instances and *GIndexFaceSet* instances.

Member Variables

This class defines four member variables. Each corresponds to a field in the VRML *ShapeHints* language construct.

```
private:
   SFLong        m_vertexOrdering;
   SFLong        m_shapeType;
   SFLong        m_faceType;
   SFFloat       m_creaseAngle;
```

The *m_vertexOrdering* member variable corresponds to the *vertexOrdering* field. This field is used to specify the recommended order in which polygon vertices should be traversed. This information is important when automatically generating surface normals for a polygon. The legal values for *m_vertexOrdering* are G_UNKNOWN_ORDERING, G_CLOCKWISE, and G_COUNTERCLOCKWISE. These values correspond to the field symbolic values UNKNOWN_ORDERING, CLOCKWISE, and COUNTERCLOCKWISE.

The *m_shapeType* member variable defines whether the shape encloses a volume. It corresponds to the *shapeType* field. Its legal values are G_UN-

KNOWN_SHAPE_TYPE and G_SOLID. They correspond to the field symbolic values UNKNOWN_SHAPE_TYPE and SOLID.

The *m_faceType* member variable defines information about the shape. It corresponds to the *faceType* field. Its legal values are G_UNKNOWN_FACE_TYPE and G_CONVEX. They correspond to the field symbolic values UNKNOWN_FACE_TYPE and CONVEX.

The *m_creaseAngle* member variable defines the angle between adjoining polygons that determines whether the surface normal should smooth across the polygons or leave a shape crease. Angles less than the *m_creaseAngle* value are smoothed; those that are greater are not. This member variable corresponds to the *creaseAngle* field in the VRML *ShapeHints* language construct. The default value for the *m_creaseAngle* variable is 0.5.

Member Functions

`GShapeHints(void)`

This member function is the default constructor. It defines a type of GShapeHintsType for the new *GShapeHints* instance and initializes all member variables to their default values.

`GNode* Copy(void)`

This member function creates and returns a new instance of the current *GShapeHints* instance.

`void VertexOrdering(SFLong)`

This member function sets the value of the *m_vertexOrdering* member variable to the value passed.

`SFLong VertexOrdering(void)`

This member function returns the value of the *m_vertexOrdering* member variable.

`void ShapeType(SFLong v)`

This member function sets the value of the *m_shapeType* member variable to the value passed.

`SFLong ShapeType(void)`

This member function returns the value of the *m_shapeType* member variable.

```
void FaceType(SFLong v)
```

This member function sets the value of the *m_faceType* member variable to the value passed.

```
SFLong FaceType(void)
```

This member function returns the value of the *m_faceType* member variable.

```
void CreaseAngle(SFFloat v)
```

This member function sets the value of the *m_creaseAngle* member variable to the value passed.

```
SFFloat CreaseAngle(void)
```

This member function returns the value of the *m_creaseAngle* member variable.

```
void SetField(const char*, SFLong)
```

This member function sets the value of the member variable that corresponds to the field name passed in the first argument to the value passed in the second argument. The field name *vertexOrdering* corresponds to the *m_vertexOrdering* member variable. The field name *shapeType* corresponds to the *m_shapeType* member variable. The field name *faceType* corresponds to the *m_faceType* member variable.

```
void SetField(const char*, SFFloat)
```

Because there is only one member variable with an `SFFloat` type in this class definition, the second argument is directly assigned to the *m_creaseAngle* member variable without the need to check the field name in the first argument.

```
void WriteWRL(FILE*, int = 0)
```

This member function writes the *GShapeHints* instance as its VRML equivalent language construct.

```
void DrawOpenGL(GState&)
```

This member function places the current material binding in the traversal state. This instance isn't directly or indirectly visible in the scene, so no OpenGL calls are necessary.

```
void Write(GState&, GWrite&)
```

This member function places the current shape hints values into the traversal state. The effects of the shape hints values are handled by subsequent shape nodes, so this instance doesn't need to call any *GWrite* member functions.

GCone Class Definition

The *GCone* class defines a Cone solid object. This class definition corresponds to the VRML *Cone* language construct. Instances of this class directly write, tessellate and write, or simply display the underlying Cone object, depending on the member function's call.

Member Variables

A *GCone* instance has three member variables. These correspond to the fields defined for the VRML *Cone* language construct.

```
private:
   SFLong        m_parts;
   SFFloat       m_bottomRadius;
   SFFloat       m_height;
```

The *m_parts* member variable selects which parts of the Cone are defined. Its legal values are `G_SIDES`, `G_BOTTOM`, and `G_ALL` (the default). This member variable corresponds to the VRML field *parts*.

The *m_bottomRadius* member function defines the radius of the bottom of the cone. The default value is 1.0. This member variable corresponds to the VRML field *bottomRadius*.

The *m_height* member variable defines the height of the cone from the center base to the point. The default value is 2.0. This member variable corresponds to the VRML field *height*.

Member Functions

```
GCone(void)
```

This member function is the default constructor. It defines a type of `GConeType` for the new *GCone* instance and initializes all member variables to their default values.

```
GCone(void) : GNode(GConeType), m_parts(G_ALL),
m_bottomRadius(1.0), m_height(2.0) {;}
```

`GNode* Copy(void)`

This member function creates and returns a new instance of the current *GCone* instance.

`SFLong Parts(void)`

This member function returns the value of the *m_parts* member variable.

`void Parts(SFLong)`

This member function sets the value of the *m_parts* member variable to that of the passed argument.

`SFFloat BottomRadius(void)`

This member function returns the value of the *m_bottomRadius* member variable.

`void BottomRadius(SFFloat)`

This member function sets the value of the *m_bottomRadius* member variable to that of the passed argument.

`SFFloat Height(void)`

This member function returns the value of the *m_height* member variable.

`void Height(SFFloat)`

This member function sets the value of the *m_height* member variable to that of the passed argument.

`void SetField(const char*, SFFloat)`

This member function sets the value of the member variable that corresponds to the field name passed in the first argument to the value passed in the second argument. The field name *bottomRadius* corresponds to the *m_bottomRadius* member variable, and the field name *height* corresponds to the *m_height* member variable.

`void SetField(const char*, SFLong)`

There is only one member variable with an `SFLong` type, so the value in the second argument is directly assigned to the *m_parts* member variable without the need to check the field name in the first argument.

```
void DrawOpenGL(GState&)
```

This member function calls the correct OpenGL functions to allow OpenGL to render a cone. The function `GCone::Point()` determines the point on the cone for the specified vertical slice and the uv position on that slice. This function checks to see which parts should be rendered and emits the OpenGL calls only for those parts. It also checks the current *materialBinding* and applies the current materials in the order the *materialBinding* specifies.

```
void WriteWRL(FILE*, int = 0)
```

This member function writes the *GCone* instance as its VRML equivalent language construct.

```
void Write(GState&, GWrite&)
```

This member function calls the appropriate members in the *GWrite* class, depending on the settings of the *GWrite* instance. If the *GWrite* instance indicates that it recognizes the cone, then the cone information is given to it directly. If the *GWrite* instance indicates that it understands polygon meshes instead of cones, then the cone is tessellated and the equivalent polygons are passed to the *GWrite* instance. If neither indication is made, then the code is ignored.

```
void Range(GState&, SFVec3f&, SFVec3f&)
```

This member function computes the minimum and maximum values for the cone. The computed minimum and maximum values are compared with the passed minimum and maximum values, and the passed arguments are updated.

GCube Class Definition

The *GCube* class defines a Cube solid object. This class definition corresponds to the VRML *Cube* language construct. Instances of this class directly write, tessellate and write, or simply render the underlying Cube object, depending on the member function's call.

Member Variables

A *GCube* instance has three member variables. These correspond to the fields defined for the VRML *Cube* language construct.

```
private:
   SFFloat m_width, m_height, m_depth
```

The *m_width* member variable defines the width of the cube. The default value is 2.0. This member variable corresponds to the VRML field *width*. The *m_height* member variable defines the height of the cube. The default value is 2.0. This member variable corresponds to the VRML field *height*. The *m_depth* member variable defines the depth of the cube. The default value is 2.0. This member variable corresponds to the VRML field *depth*.

Member Functions

`GCube(void)`

This member function is the default constructor. It defines a type of `GCubeType` for the new *GCube* instance and initializes all member variables to their default values.

```
GCube(void) : GNode(GCubeType), m_width(2.0), m_height(2.0),
m_depth(2.0) {;}
```

`GNode* Copy(void)`

This member function creates and returns a new instance of the current *GCube* instance.

`SFFloat Width(void)`

This member function returns the value of the *m_width* member variable.

`void Width(SFFloat)`

This member function sets the value of the *m_width* member variable to that of the passed argument

`SFFloat Height(void)`

This member function returns the value of the *m_height* member variable.

`void Height(SFFloat)`

This member function sets the value of the *m_height* member variable to that of the passed argument.

`SFFloat Depth(void)`

This member function returns the value of the *m_depth* member variable.

```
void Depth(SFFloat)
```

This member function sets the value of the *m_depth* member variable to that of the passed argument.

```
void SetField(const char*, SFFloat)
```

This member function sets the value of the member variable that corresponds to the field name passed in the first argument to the value passed in the second argument. The field name *width* corresponds to the *m_width* member variable. The field name *height* corresponds to the *m_height* member variable. The field name *depth* corresponds to the *m_depth* member variable.

```
void DrawOpenGL(GState&)
```

This member function calls the correct OpenGL functions to allow OpenGL to render a cube. Note that the current materials and material bindings effect the rendered output.

```
void Write(GState&, GWrite&)
```

This member function calls the appropriate members in the *GWrite* class, depending on the settings of the *GWrite* instance. If the *GWrite* instance indicates that it recognizes the cube, then the cube information (*width*, *height*, and *depth*) is given to it directly. If the *GWrite* instance indicates that it understands polygon meshes instead of cubes, then the cube is tessellated and the equivalent polygons are passed to the *GWrite* instance. If neither indication is made, then the cube is ignored.

```
void Range(GState&, SFVec3f&, SFVec3f&)
```

This member function computes the minimum and maximum values for the cube. The computed minimum and maximum values are compared with the passed minimum and maximum values, and the passed arguments are updated.

GCylinder Class Definition

The *GCylinder* class defines a Cylinder solid object. This class definition corresponds to the VRML *Cylinder* language construct. Instances of this class directly write, tessellate and write, or simply render the underlying Cylinder object, depending on the member function's call.

Member Variables

A *GCylinder* instance has three member variables. These correspond to the fields defined for the VRML *Cylinder* language construct.

```
private:
   SFLong       m_parts;
   SFFloat      m_radius;
   SFFloat      m_height;
```

The *m_parts* member variable defines the visible portion of the cylinder. Its values are `G_SIDES`, `G_TOP`, `G_BOTTOM`, and `G_ALL` (the default). This member variable corresponds to the VRML field *parts*.

The *m_radius* member variable defines the radius of the cylinder. The default value is 1.0. This member variable corresponds to the VRML field *radius*.

The *m_height* member variable defines the height of the cylinder. The default value is 2.0. This member variable corresponds to the VRML field *height*.

Member Functions

`GCylinder(void)`

This member function is the default constructor. It defines a type of `GCylinderType` for the new *GCylinder* instance and initializes all member variables to their default values.

```
GCylinder(void) : GNode(GCylinderType), m_parts(G_ALL),
m_radius(1.0), m_height(2.0) {;}
```

`GNode*Copy(void)`

This member function creates and returns a new instance of the current *GCylinder* instance.

`SFLong Parts(void)`

This member function returns the value of the *m_parts* member variable.

`void Parts(SFLong)`

This member function sets the value of the *m_parts* member variable to that of the passed argument.

```
SFFloat Radius(void)
```

This member function returns the value of the *m_radius* member variable.

```
void Radius(SFFloat)
```

This member function sets the value of the *m_radius* member variable to that of the passed argument.

```
SFFloat Height(void)
```

This member function returns the value of the *m_height* member variable.

```
void Height(SFFloat)
```

This member function sets the value of the *m_height* member variable to that of the passed argument.

```
void SetField(const char*, SFFloat)
```

This member function sets the value of the member variable that corresponds to the field name passed in the first argument to the value passed in the second argument. The field name *radius* corresponds to the *m_radius* member variable, and the field name *height* corresponds to the *m_height* member variable.

```
void SetField(const char*, SFLong)
```

There is only one member variable with an `SFLong` type, so the value in the second argument is directly assigned to the *m_parts* member variable without the need to check the field name in the first argument.

```
void DrawOpenGL(GState&)
```

This member function calls the correct OpenGL functions to allow OpenGL to render a cylinder. Note that the current materials and material bindings affect the rendered output.

```
void WriteWRL(FILE*, int = 0)
```

This member function writes this *GCylinder* instance as its VRML equivalent language construct.

```
void Write(GState&, GWrite&)
```

This member function calls the appropriate members in the *GWrite* class, depending on the settings of the *GWrite* instance. If the *GWrite* instance indicates that it recognizes the cylinder, then the cylinder information (*parts*, *radius*, and *height*) is given to it directly. If the *GWrite* instance indicates that it understands polygon meshes instead of cylinders, then the cylinder is tessellated and the equivalent polygons are passed to the *GWrite* instance. If neither indication is made, then the cylinder is ignored.

```
void Range(GState& state, SFVec3f& min, SFVec3f&
max)
```

This member function computes the minimum and maximum values for the cylinder. The computed minimum and maximum values are compared with the passed minimum and maximum values, and the passed arguments are updated.

GSphere Class Definition

The *GSphere* class defines a Sphere solid object. This class definition corresponds to the VRML *Sphere* language construct. Instances of this class directly write, tessellate and write, or simply render the underlying Sphere object, depending on the member function's call.

Member Variables

A *GSphere* instance has one member variable. It corresponds to the *radius* field defined for the VRML *Sphere* language construct. The *m_radius* member variable defines the radius for the sphere. The default radius value is 1.0.

```
private:  SFFloat    m_radius;
```

```
GSphere(void)
```

This member function is the default constructor. It defines a type of `GSphereType` for the new *GSphere* instance and initializes all member variables to their default values.

```
GSphere(void) : GNode(GSphereType),  m_radius(1.0) {;}
```

```
GNode* Copy(void)
```

This member function creates and returns a new instance of the current *GSphere* instance.

```
SFFloat Radius(void)
```

This member function returns the value of the *m_radius* member variable.

```
void Radius(SFFloat)
```

This member function sets the value of the *m_radius* member variable to that of the passed argument.

```
void SetField(const char*, SFFloat)
```

This member function sets the value of the member variable that corresponds to the field name passed in the first argument to the value passed in the second argument. The field name *radius* corresponds to the *m_radius* member variable.

```
void DrawOpenGL(GState&)
```

This member function calls the correct OpenGL functions to allow OpenGL to render a sphere.

```
void WriteWRL(FILE*, int = 0)
```

This member function writes this *GSphere* instance as its VRML equivalent language construct.

```
void Write(GState&, GWrite&)
```

This member function calls the appropriate members in the *GWrite* class, depending on the settings of the *GWrite* instance. If the *GWrite* instance indicates that it recognizes the sphere, then the sphere information (*radius*) is given to it directly. If the *GWrite* instance indicates that it understands polygon meshes instead of spheres, then the sphere is tessellated and the equivalent polygons are passed to the *GWrite* instance. If neither indication is made, then the sphere is ignored.

```
void Range(GState& state, SFVec3f& min, SFVec3f&
max)
```

This member function computes the minimum and maximum values for the sphere. The computed minimum and maximum values are compared with the passed minimum and maximum values, and the passed arguments are updated.

GIndexedFaceSet Class Definition

The *GIndexedFaceSet* class uses the current *GCoordinate3* and *GNormal* instances to define an object created out of polygons. This class definition corresponds to the VRML *IndexedFaceSet* language construct.

Member Variables

A *GIndexedFaceSet* instance has four member variables. These correspond to the fields defined for the VRML *GIndexedFaceSet* language construct.

```
protected:
   MFLong*       m_coordIndex;
   MFLong*       m_materialIndex;
   MFLong*       m_normalIndex;
   MFLong*       m_textureCoordIndex;
```

The *m_coordIndex* member variable corresponds to the field *coordIndex*. The *m_materialIndex* member variable corresponds to the field *materialIndex*. The *m_normalIndex* member variable corresponds to the field *normalIndex*. The *m_textureCoordIndex* member variable corresponds to the field *textureCoordIndex*.

Each of these variables is an array of `SFLong` values. These values are indexes into other constructs that are available on the traversal state. Nonnegative values in the *m_coordIndex* array are interpreted as an index into the current *GCoordinate3* instance held in the traversal state. An index of –1 indicates an end of the current polygon definition.

The value of the *m_materialIndex* member variable maps the current material instance to indexes. How the values are mapped to polygons depends on the current *materialBinding* state. See Chapter 3, which describes the VRML specification, for more information on material mapping.

The value of the *m_normalIndex* member variable maps the indexes into the current normal instance that is held in the traversal state to the polygon faces or vertices, depending on the *normalBinding* value held in the current traversal state. See Chapter 3 for more information on how the surface normals are mapped to polygons.

The value of the *m_textureCoordIndex* member variable describes the mapping of bitmap textures onto the polygon faces. The current version of the *Crossroads* class library does not support using bitmap images as textures.

`GIndexedFaceSet(void)`

This member function is the default constructor. It defines a type of `GIndexedFaceSetType` for the new *GIndexedFaceSet* instance and initializes all member variables to their default values.

`GNode* Copy(void)`

This member function creates and returns a new instance of the current *GIndexedFaceSet* instance.

`void CoordIndex(MFLong*)`

This member function sets the value of the *m_coordIndex* member variable to that of the passed argument.

`MFLong* CoordIndex(void)`

This member function returns the value of the *m_coordIndex* member variable.

`void MaterialIndex(MFLong*)`

This member function sets the value of the *m_materialIndex* member variable to that of the passed argument.

`MFLong* MaterialIndex(void)`

This member function returns the value of the *m_materialIndex* member variable.

`void NormalIndex(MFLong*)`

This member function sets the value of the *m_normalIndex* member variable to that of the passed argument.

`MFLong* NormalIndex(void)`

This member function returns the value of the *m_normalIndex* member variable.

`void TextureCoordIndex(MFLong*)`

This member function sets the value of the *m_textureCoordIndex* member variable to that of the passed argument.

```
MFLong*    TextureCoordIndex(void)
```

This member function returns the value of the *m_textureCoordIndex* member variable.

```
void SetField(const char*, MFLong*)
```

This member function sets the value of the member variable that corresponds to the field name passed in the first argument to the value passed in the second argument. The field name *coordIndex* corresponds to the *m_coordIndex* member variable. The field name *materialIndex* corresponds to the *m_materialIndex* member variable. The field name *normalIndex* corresponds to the *m_normalIndex* member variable. The field name *textureCoordIndex* corresponds to the *m_textureCoordIndex* member variable.

```
SFLong Elements(void)
```

This member function returns the number of elements in the *m_coordIndex* member variable.

```
SFVec3f* Vertice(GState&, long)
```

This member function returns the vertex associated with the value passed in the second argument.

```
SFVec3f*  Normal(GState&, long)
```

This member function returns the normal associated with the index passed in the second argument.

```
void DrawOpenGL(GState&)
```

This member function calls the correct OpenGL functions to allow OpenGL to render a Polygon object. It uses the current *material*, *materialBinding*, *normal*, *normalBinding*, and *Coordinate3* to determine how the object should be rendered.

```
void WriteWRL(FILE*, int = 0)
```

This member function writes the *GIndexedFaceSet* instance as its VRML equivalent language construct.

```
void Range(GState&, SFVec3f&, SFVec3f&)
```

This member function computes the minimum and maximum values for the *IndexedFaceSet*. The computed minimum and maximum values are compared with the passed minimum and maximum values, and the passed arguments are updated.

```
void Write(GState&, GWrite&)
```

This member function calls the appropriate members in the *GWrite* class, depending on the settings of the *GWrite* instance. If the *GWrite* instance indicates that it recognizes the polygon, then the *IndexedFaceSet* object is converted into a series of polygons. If the *GWrite* instance indicates that it understands a mesh, then the face list is passed. If neither indication is made, then the *IndexedFaceSet* is ignored.

GPerspectiveCamera Class Definition

The *GPerspectiveCamera* class defines an instance of a perspective camera. It corresponds to the VRML *PerspectiveCamera* language construct.

Member Variables

A *GPerspectiveCamera* instance has four member variables. These correspond to the fields defined for the VRML *PerspectiveCamera* language construct.

```
protected:
   SFVec3f      m_position;
   SFRotation   m_orientation;
   SFFloat      m_focalDistance;
   SFFloat      m_heightAngle;
```

The *m_position* member variable corresponds to the field *position*. The *m_orientation* member variable corresponds to the field *orientation*. The *m_focalDistance* member variable corresponds to the field *focalDistance*. The member *m_height* variable corresponds to the field *height*.

Member Functions

```
GPerspectiveCamera(void)
```

This member function is the default constructor. It defines a type of `GPerspectiveCameraType` for the new *GPerspectiveCamera* instance and initializes all member variables to their default values.

```
void Position(SFVec3f&)
```

This member function sets the value of the *m_position* member variable to that of the passed argument.

```
SFVec3f Position(void)
```

This member function returns the value of the *m_position* member variable.

```
void Orientation(SFRotation&)
```

This member function sets the value of the *m_orientation* member variable to that of the passed argument.

```
SRotation Orientation(void)
```

This member function returns the value of the *m_orientation* member variable.

```
void FocalDistance(SFFloat)
```

This member function sets the value of the *m_focalDistance* member variable to that of the passed argument.

```
SFFloat FocalDistance(void)
```

This member function returns the value of the *m_focalDistance* member variable.

```
void HeightAngle(SFFloat)
```

This member function sets the value of the *m_heightAngle* member variable to that of the passed argument.

```
SFFloat HeightAngle(void)
```

This member function returns the value of the *m_heightAngle* member variable.

```
SFVec3f Position(GState&)
```

This member function returns the value of the *m_position* member variable after it has been transformed by the current transformation matrix passed with the *GState* instance.

`SFVec3f Direction(GState&)`

This member function returns a vector in the direction in which the camera is pointing. This information is useful for converting the VRML camera model into other camera models.

`SFVec3f LookAt(GState& state)`

This member function returns the point at which the camera is pointing. This information is useful for converting the VRML camera model into other camera models.

`SFVec3f Up(GState& state)`

This member function calculates the vector that points in the up direction for the camera. This information is useful for converting the VRML camera model into other camera models.

`void SetField(const char* name, SFVec3f* value)`

This member function sets the value of the member variable that corresponds to the field name passed in the first argument to the value passed in the second argument. The field name *position* corresponds to the *m_position* member variable.

`void SetField(const char*, SFRotation*)`

This member function sets the value of the member variable that corresponds to the field name passed in the first argument to the value passed in the second argument. The field name *orientation* corresponds to the *m_orientation* member variable.

`void SetField(const char*, SFFloat)`

This member function sets the value of the member variable that corresponds to the field name passed in the first argument to the value passed in the second argument. The field name *focalDistance* corresponds to the *m_focalDistance* member variable, and the field name *height* corresponds to the *m_heightAngle* member variable.

`void WriteWRL(FILE*, int = 0)`

This member function writes the *GPerspectiveCamera* instance as its VRML equivalent language construct.

```
void Write(GState&, GWrite&)
```

This member function calls the appropriate members in the *GWrite* class, depending on the settings of the *GWrite* instance. If the *GWrite* instance indicates that it recognizes perspective cameras, then the member function `GWrite::PerspectiveCamera()` is called. If it doesn't recognize perspective cameras, then the construct is ignored.

```
void SetCameraOpenGL(GState&, long, long)
```

This member function sets up the OpenGL camera. It should be called prior to calling the `(DrawOpenGL)` member function call. This means the scene must be searched for the first available *GPerspectiveCamera*. That camera instance is sent this message to get the scene set up for rendering. The *w* and *h* arguments are the width and height, respectively, of the window that is being rendered.

GPointLight Class Definition

The *GPointLight* class defines an instance of a point light. It corresponds to the VRML *PointLight* language construct.

Member Variables

A *GPointLight* instance has four member variables. These correspond to the fields defined for the VRML *PointLight* language construct.

```
private:
   SFLong       m_on;
   SFFloat      m_intensity;
   SFVec3f      m_color;
   SFVec3f      m_location;
```

The *m_on* member variable corresponds to the field *on*. The *m_intensity* member variable corresponds to the field *intensity*. The *m_color* member variable corresponds to the field *color*. The *m_location* member variable corresponds to the field *location*.

Member Functions

```
GPointLight(void)
```

This member function is the default constructor. It defines a type of `GPointLightType` for the new *GPointLight* instance and initializes all member variables to their default values.

```
GNode* Copy(void)
```

This member function creates and returns a new instance of the current *GPointLight* instance.

```
SFLong On(void)
```

This member function sets the value of the *m_on* member variable to that of the passed argument.

```
void On(SFLong)
```

This member function returns the value of the *m_on* member variable.

```
SFFloat Intensity(void)
```

This member function sets the value of the *m_intensity* member variable to that of the passed argument.

```
void Intensity(SFFloat)
```

This member function returns the value of the *m_intensity* member variable.

```
SFVec3f Color(void)
```

This member function returns the value of the *m_color* member variable.

```
void Color(SFVec3f)
```

This member function sets the value of the *m_color* member variable to that of the passed argument.

```
SFVec3f Location(void)
```

This member function returns the value of the *m_location* member variable.

```
void Location(SFVec3f)
```

This member function sets the value of the *m_location* member variable to that of the passed argument.

```
void SetField(const char*, SFLong)
```

This member function sets the value of the member variable that corresponds to the field name passed in the first argument to the value passed in the second argument. The field name *on* corresponds to the *m_on* member variable.

```
void SetField(const char*, SFFloat)
```

This member function sets the value of the member variable that corresponds to the field name passed in the first argument to the value passed in the second argument. The field name *intensity* corresponds to the *m_intensity* member variable.

```
void SetField(const char*, SFVec3f*)
```

This member function sets the value of the member variable that corresponds to the field name passed in the first argument to the value passed in the second argument. The field name *color* corresponds to the *m_color* member variable, and the field name *location* corresponds to the *m_location* member variable.

```
void DrawOpenGL(GState&)
```

This member function calls the OpenGL functions that define a light equivalent to the light specified by the *GPointLight* instance.

```
void WriteWRL(FILE*, int = 0)
```

This member function writes the *GPointLight* instance as its VRML equivalent language construct.

```
void Write(GState&, GWrite&)
```

This member function calls the appropriate members in the *GWrite* class, depending on the settings of the *GWrite* instance. If the *GWrite* instance indicates that it recognizes the point light, then the `GWrite::PointLight()` member function is called with the four member variables as arguments. If it dosen't recognize point lights, then the construct is ignored.

GSpotLight Class Definition

The *GSpotLight* class defines an instance of a spot light. It corresponds to the VRML *SpotLight* language construct.

Member Variables

A *GSpotLight* instance has seven member variables. These correspond to the fields defined for the VRML *SpotLight* language construct.

```
private:
   SFLong        m_on;
   SFFloat       m_intensity;
```

```
SFVec3f      m_color;
SFVec3f      m_location;
SFVec3f      m_direction;
SFFloat      m_dropOffRate;
SFFloat      m_cutOffAngle;
```

The *m_on* member variable corresponds to the field *on*. The *m_intensity* member variable corresponds to the field *intensity*. The *m_color* member variable corresponds to the field *color*. The *m_location* member variable corresponds to the field *location*. The *m_direction* member variable corresponds to the field *direction*. The *m_dropOffRate* member variable corresponds to the field *dropOffRate*. The *m_cutOffAngle* member variable corresponds to the field *cutOffAngle*.

Member Functions

`GSpotLight(void)`

This member function is the default constructor. It defines a type of `GSpotLightType` for the new *GSpotLight* instance and initializes all member variables to their default values.

`GNode* Copy(void)`

This member function creates and returns a new instance of the current *GSpotLight* instance.

`SFLong On(void)`

This member function sets the value of the *m_on* member variable to that of the passed argument.

`void On(SFLong)`

This member function returns the value of the *m_on* member variable.

`SFFloat Intensity(void)`

This member function sets the value of the *m_intensity* member variable to that of the passed argument.

`void Intensity(SFFloat)`

This member function returns the value of the *m_intensity* member variable.

```
SFVec3f Color(void)
```

This member function returns the value of the *m_color* member variable.

```
void Color(SFVec3f)
```

This member function sets the value of the *m_color* member variable to that of the passed argument.

```
SFVec3f Location(void)
```

This member function returns the value of the *m_location* member variable.

```
void Location(SFVec3f)
```

This member function sets the value of the *m_location* member variable to that of the passed argument.

```
SFVec3f Direction(void)
```

This member function returns the value of the *m_direction* member variable.

```
void Direction(SFVec3f)
```

This member function sets the value of the *m_direction* member variable to that of the passed argument.

```
SFFloat DropOffRate(void)
```

This member function returns the value of the *m_dropOffRate* member variable.

```
void DropOffRate(SFFloat)
```

This member function sets the value of the *m_dropOffRate* member variable to that of the passed argument.

```
SFFloat CutOffAngle(void)
```

This member function returns the value of the *m_cutOffAngle* member variable.

```
void CutOffAngle(SFFloat)
```

This member function sets the value of the *m_cutOffAngle* member variable to that of the passed argument.

`void SetField(const char*, SFLong)`

This member function sets the value of the member variable that corresponds to the field name passed in the first argument to the value passed in the second argument. The field name *on* corresponds to the *m_on* member variable.

`void SetField(const char*, SFFloat)`

This member function sets the value of the member variable that corresponds to the field name passed in the first argument to the value passed in the second argument. The field name *intensity* corresponds to the *m_intensity* member variable. The field name *dropOffRate* corresponds to the *m_dropOffRate* member variable. The field name *cutOffAngle* corresponds to the *m_cutOffAngle* member variable.

`void SetField(const char*, SFVec3f*)`

This member function sets the value of the member variable that corresponds to the field name passed in the first argument to the value passed in the second argument. The field name *color* corresponds to the *m_color* member variable. The field name *location* corresponds to the *m_location* member variable. The field name *direction* corresponds to the *m_direction* member variable.

`void DrawOpenGL(GState&)`

This member function calls the OpenGL function define a light equivalent to the light specified by the *GSpotLight* instance.

`void WriteWRL(FILE*, int = 0)`

This member function writes the *GSpotLight* instance as its VRML equivalent language construct.

`void Write(GState&, GWrite&)`

This member function calls the appropriate members in the *GWrite* class, depending on the settings of the *GWrite* instance. If the *GWrite* instance indicates that it recognizes the spot light, then the `GWrite::SpotLight()` member function is called with the seven member variables as arguments. If it doesn't recognize spot lights, then the construct is ignored.

GMatrixTransform Class Definition

The *GMatrixTransform* class defines an instance of a matrix transform. It corresponds to the VRML *MatrixTransform* language construct.

Member Variable

A *GMatrixTransform* instance has a single member variable. This variable corresponds to the *matrix* field defined for the VRML *MatrixTransform* language construct.

```
private:
   SFMatrix      m_matrix;
```

Member Functions

`GMatrixTransform(void)`

This member function is the default constructor. It defines a type of `GMatrixTransformType` for the new *GMatrixTransform* instance and initializes all member variables to their default values.

`GNode* Copy(void)`

This member function creates and returns a new instance of the current *GMatrixTransform* instance.

`void SetField(const char*, SFMatrix*)`

This member function sets the value of the member variable that corresponds to the field name passed in the first argument to the value passed in the second argument. The field name *matrix* corresponds to the *m_matrix* member variable.

`void DrawOpenGL(GState&)`

This member function calls the OpenGL function that applies the transformation matrix *m_matrix* to the current state.

`void WriteWRL(FILE*, int = 0)`

This member function writes the *GMatrixTransform* instance as its VRML equivalent language construct.

```
short IsTransform(void)
```

This member function returns `TRUE`. It is used to inform routines that make calls to *GNode* instances that the underlying instance creates a non-identity transformation matrix.

```
SFMatrix Transform(void)
```

This member function returns the transformation matrix held in the *m_matrix* member variable.

```
void Transform(SFMatrix&)
```

This member function assigns the value passed in the argument to the *m_matrix* member variable.

```
void Write(GState&, GWrite&)
```

This member function calls the appropriate members in the *GWrite* class, depending on the settings of the *GWrite* instance. If the *GWrite* instance indicates that it recognizes the transform, then the `GWrite::MatrixTransform()` member function is called, passing the member variable *m_matrix*. If it doesn't recognize transforms, then the construct is ignored.

GRotation Class Definition

The *GRotation* class defines an instance of a rotation transformation. It corresponds to the VRML *Rotation* language construct.

Member Variable

A *GRotation* instance has a single member variable. This variable corresponds to the *rotation* field defined for the VRML *Rotation* language construct.

```
private:
   SFRotation      m_rotation;
```

Member Functions

```
GRotation(SFRotation = SFRotation(0.0, 0.0, 1.0,
0.0))
```

This member function is the default constructor. It defines a type of `GRotationType` for the new *GRotation* instance and initializes all member variables to their default values.

```
GRotation(SFRotation t = SFRotation((SFFloat) 0.0, (SFFloat)
0.0, (SFFloat) 1.0, (SFFloat) 0.0)) : GNode(GRotationType),
m_rotation(t) {;}
```

```
GNode* Copy(void)
```

This member function creates and returns a new instance of the current *GRotation* instance.

```
void Rotation(SFRotation)
```

This member function sets the value of the *m_rotation* member variable to that of the passed argument.

```
SFRotation Rotation(void)
```

This member function returns the value of the *m_rotation* member variable.

```
void SetField(const char*, SFRotation*)
```

This member function sets the value of the member variable that corresponds to the field name passed in the first argument to the value passed in the second argument. The field name *rotation* corresponds to the *m_rotation* member variable.

```
void DrawOpenGL(GState&)
```

This member function calls the OpenGL function that applies the rotation transformation to the OpenGL current state.

```
void WriteWRL(FILE*, int = 0)
```

This member function writes the *GRotation* instance as its VRML equivalent language construct.

```
short IsTransform(void)
```

This member function returns `TRUE`. It is used to inform routines that make calls to *GNode* instances that the underlying instance creates a non-identity transformation matrix.

```
SFMatrix Transform(void)
```

This member function returns the transformation matrix that is equivalent to the rotation value held by the *m_rotation* member variable.

`void Write(GState&, GWrite&)`

This member function calls the appropriate members in the *GWrite* class, depending on the settings of the *GWrite* instance. If the *GWrite* instance indicates that it recognizes the transform, then the `GWrite:: Rotation()` member function is called, passing the *m_rotation* member variable. If it doesn't recognize transforms, then the construct is ignored.

GScale Class Definition

The *GScale* class defines an instance of a rotation transformation. It corresponds to the VRML *Scale* language construct.

Member Variable

A *GScale* instance has a single member variable. This variable corresponds to the *scaleFactor* field defined for the VRML *Scale* language construct.

```
private:
   SFVec3f m_scaleFactor;
```

Member Functions

`GScale(SFVec3f = SFVec3f(1.0, 1.0, 1.0))`

This member function is the default constructor. It defines a type of `GScaleType` for the new *GScale* instance and initializes all member variables to their default values.

`GNode* Copy(void)`

This member function creates and returns a new instance of the current *GRotation* instance.

`void SetField(const char*, SFVec3f*)`

This member function sets the value of the member variable that corresponds to the field name passed in the first argument to the value passed in the second argument. The field name *scaleFactor* corresponds to the *m_scaleFactor* member variable.

`void ScaleFactor(SFVec3f)`

This member function sets the value of the *m_scaleFactor* member variable to that of the passed argument.

`SFVec3f ScaleFactor(void)`

This member function returns the value of the *m_scaleFactor* member variable.

`void DrawOpenGL(GState&)`

This member function calls the OpenGL function that applies the scale transformation to the OpenGL current state.

`void WriteWRL(FILE*, int = 0)`

This member function writes the *GScale* instance as its VRML equivalent language construct.

`short IsTransform(void)`

This member function returns `TRUE`. It is used to inform routines that make calls to *GNode* instances that the underlying instance creates a non-identity transformation matrix.

`SFMatrix Transform(void)`

This member function returns the transformation matrix that is equivalent to the scale value held by the *m_scaleFactor* member variable.

`void Write(GState&, GWrite&)`

This member function calls the appropriate members in the *GWrite* class, depending on the settings of the *GWrite* instance. If the *GWrite* instance indicates that it recognizes the transform, then the `GWrite:: Scale()` member function is called, passing the *m_scaleFactor* member variable If it doesn't recognize transforms, then the construct is ignored.

```
void GScale::
Write(GState& state, GWrite& write)
{
   SSetState(state);
   if (write.TransformsSupported()) {
      write.Scale(m_scaleFactor);
   }
}
```

GTranslation Class Definition

The *GTranslation* class defines an instance of a rotation transformation. It corresponds to the VRML *Translation* language construct.

Member Variable

A *GTranslation* instance has a single member variable. This variable corresponds to the *translation* field defined for the VRML *Translation* language construct.

```
private:
   SFVec3f  m_translation;
```

Member Variables

```
GTranslation(SFVec3f = SFVec3f(0.0, 0.0, 0.0))
```

This member function is the default constructor. It defines a type of `GTranslationType` for the new *GTranslation* instance and initializes all member variables to their default values.

```
GNode* Copy(void)
```

This member function creates and returns a new instance of the current *GTranslation* instance.

```
void SetField(const char*, SFVec3f*)
```

This member function sets the value of the member variable that corresponds to the field name passed in the first argument to the value passed in the second argument. The field name *translation* corresponds to the *m_translation* member variable.

```
void Translation(SFVec3f)
```

This member function sets the value of the *m_translation* member variable to that of the passed argument.

```
SFVec3f Translation(void)
```

This member function returns the value of the *m_translation* member variable.

```
void DrawOpenGL(GState&)
```

This member function calls the OpenGL function that applies the scale transformation to the OpenGL current state.

```
void WriteWRL(FILE*, int = 0)
```

This member function writes the *GTranslation* instance as its VRML equivalent language construct.

```
short IsTransform(void)
```

This member function returns `TRUE`. It is used to inform routines that make calls to *GNode* instances that the underlying instance creates a non-identity transformation matrix.

```
SFMatrix Transform(void)
```

This member function returns the transformation matrix that is equivalent to the translation value held by the *m_translation* member variable.

```
void      Write(GState& state, GWrite&)
```

This member function calls the appropriate members in the *GWrite* class, depending on the settings of the *GWrite* instance. If the *GWrite* instance indicates that it recognizes the transform, then the `GWrite:: Translation()` member function is called, passing the *m_translation* member variable. If it doesn't recognize transforms, then the construct is ignored.

Index

H

I

Software License